WISC–III
Clinical Use
and
Interpretation

WISC–III
CLINICAL USE
AND
INTERPRETATION

SCIENTIST-PRACTITIONER PERSPECTIVES

EDITED BY

AURELIO PRIFITERA
The Psychological Corporation
San Antonio, Texas

DONALD H. SAKLOFSKE
Department of Educational Psychology
University of Saskatchewan
Saskatoon, Saskatchewan, Canada

ACADEMIC PRESS

San Diego   London   Boston   New York   Sydney   Tokyo   Toronto

Copyright © 1998 by ACADEMIC PRESS

All Rights Reserved.
No part of this publication may be reproduced or transmitted in any form or by any
means, electronic or mechanical, including photocopy, recording, or any information
storage and retrieval system, without permission in writing from the publisher.

Academic Press
A Harcourt Science and Technology Company
525 B Street, Suite 1900, San Diego, California 92101-4495, USA
http://www.apnet.com

Academic Press
Harcourt Place, 32 Jamestown Road, London NW1 7BY, UK
http://www.hbuk.co.uk/ap/

Library of Congress Card Catalog Number: 97-80798

International Standard Book Number: 0-12-564930-4

PRINTED IN THE UNITED STATES OF AMERICA
00 01 02 QW 9 8 7 6 5 4

For their love and support needed to pursue our professional aspirations, this book is dedicated to

My wife Loretta Gertrude, and daughter, Sarah Marie—AP

My sister Bette, brother Brent, and aunt Audrey—DHS

CONTENTS

1

THE WISC-III IN CONTEXT

AURELIO PRIFITERA, LAWRENCE G. WEISS,
AND DONALD H. SAKLOFSKE

2

INTELLIGENCE TEST INTERPRETATION: ACTING IN THE ABSENCE OF EVIDENCE

RANDY W. KAMPHAUS

3

ASSESSMENT OF GIFTED CHILDREN WITH THE WISC-III

SARA S. SPARROW AND SUZANNE T. GURLAND

4

ASSESSMENT OF MENTAL RETARDATION WITH THE WISC-III

JEAN SPRUILL

5

WISC-III ASSESSMENT OF CHILDREN WITH ATTENTION DEFICIT/HYPERACTIVITY DISORDER

VICKI L. SCHWEAN AND DONALD H. SAKLOFSKE

6

ASSESSMENT OF EMOTIONALLY DISTURBED CHILDREN WITH THE WISC-III

PHYLLIS ANNE TEETER AND RICHARD KORDUCKI

7

SIGNIFICANCE OF VERBAL–PERFORMANCE DISCREPANCIES FOR SUBTYPES OF CHILDREN WITH LEARNING DISABILITIES: OPPORTUNITIES FOR THE WISC-III

BYRON P. ROURKE

8

UTILITY OF THE WISC-III FOR CHILDREN WITH LANGUAGE IMPAIRMENTS

LEADELLE PHELPS

9

ASSESSMENT OF HEARING-IMPAIRED
AND DEAF CHILDREN WITH THE WISC-III

JEFFERY P. BRADEN AND JOSEPH M. HANNAH

10

NEUROPSYCHOLOGICAL BASIS
OF INTELLIGENCE AND THE WISC-III

GEORGE W. HYND, MORRIS J. COHEN, CYNTHIA A. RICCIO,
AND JANET M. ARCENEAUX

11

ASSESSMENT OF MINORITY
AND CULTURALLY DIVERSE CHILDREN

ANTONIO E. PUENTE AND GABRIEL D. SALAZAR

12

THE USE OF THE WISC-III WITH ACHIEVEMENT TESTS

BETTY E. GRIDLEY AND GALE H. ROID

13

ASSESSMENT OF TEST BEHAVIORS WITH THE WISC-III

THOMAS OAKLAND AND JOSEPH GLUTTING

CONTRIBUTORS

Numbers in parentheses indicate the pages on which the authors' contributions begin.

Janet M. Arceneaux (203), Department of Professional Studies, University of Alabama, Tuscaloosa, Alabama 35487

Jeffery P. Braden (175), Department of Educational Psychology, University of Wisconsin—Madison, Madison, Wisconsin 53717

Morris J. Cohen (203), Child Neuropsychology, Medical College of Georgia, Augusta, Georgia 30912

Joseph Glutting (289), College of Education, University of Delaware, Newark, Delaware 19716

Betty E. Gridley (249), Department of Educational Psychology, Ball State University, Muncie, Indiana 47306

Suzanne T. Gurland (59), Child Study Center, Yale University, New Haven, Connecticut 06520

Joseph M. Hannah (175), Department of Educational Psychology, University of Wisconsin—Madison, Madison, Wisconsin 53717

George W. Hynd (203), Center for Clinical and Developmental Neuropsychology, The University of Georgia, Athens, Georgia 30602

Randy W. Kamphaus (39), Department of Educational Psychology, The University of Georgia, Athens, Georgia 30602

Edith Kaplan (35), Boston Neuropsychological Foundation, Lexington, Massachusetts 02173

Rick Korducki (119), Department of Educational Psychology, University of Wisconsin—Milwaukee, Milwaukee, Wisconsin 53201

Thomas Oakland (289), Department of Foundations Education, University of Florida, Gainesville, Florida 32611

LeAdelle Phelps (157), Department of Counseling and Educational Psychology, State University of New York at Buffalo, Buffalo, New York 14260

Aurelio Prifitera (1), The Psychological Corporation, San Antonio, Texas 78204

Antonio E. Puente (227), Department of Psychology, University of North Carolina—Wilmington, Wilmington, North Carolina 28403

Cynthia A. Riccio (203), Department of Educational Psychology, College of Education, Texas A & M University, College Station, Texas 77843

Gale Roid (249), Graduate School of Clinical Psychology, George Fox College, Newberg, Oregon 97132

Byron P. Rourke (139), Department of Psychology, University of Windsor, Windsor, Ontario N9B 3P4, and School of Medicine, Yale University, New Haven, Connecticut 06520

Donald H. Saklofske (1, 91), Department of Educational Psychology, University of Saskatchewan, Saskatoon, Saskatchewan, Canada S7N 0X1

Gabriel Salazar (227), Department of Psychology, University of North Carolina—Wilmington, Wilmington, North Carolina 28403

Vicki L. Schwean (91), Department for the Education of Exceptional Children, University of Saskatchewan, Saskatoon, Saskatchewan, Canada S7N 0X1

Sara S. Sparrow (59), Child Study Center, Yale University, New Haven, Connecticut 06520

Jean Spruill (73), Psychology Clinic, University of Alabama, Tuscaloosa, Alabama 35487-0356

Phyllis Anne Teeter (119), Department of Educational Psychology, University of Wisconsin—Milwaukee, Milwaukee, Wisconsin 53201

Lawrence G. Weiss (1), The Psychological Corporation, San Antonio, Texas 78204

PREFACE

The Wechsler Intelligence Scale for Children–Third Edition (WISC-III) continues to be the most widely used measure of cognitive functioning by clinicians and researchers in the United States and around the world. Because of its widespread use and linkage to its predecessors, much is already known about the psychometric properties of the WISC-III and how to interpret the test scores. This book contains new research information and in-depth clinical perspectives that will be of use to researchers and practitioners alike. We believe that the best clinical practices stem from an adherence to the scientist–practitioner model, which is based on a knowledge of research relevant to the use of the WISC-III for the particular groups as well as the sensitive use of test data within the context of a particular person. Tests usually are not in themselves diagnostic. Rather, it is the clinicians using tests as part of their assessment activity who are responsible for diagnostic decisions.

Unlike other books that focus mainly on the interpretation of the Wechsler tests, this book is a collection of perspectives of experts in specific clinical areas rather than the interpretative schema of one author. These multiple perspectives are certainly a strength, but the fact that they may not always be consistent should not be cause for alarm. Out of multiple perspectives can come a broader view of issues that can lead to better practice. The editors asked the chapter authors to review and present the research literature as it relates to the assessment of intelligence for the particular special group that is the topic of their chapter. Most chapters contain case studies that illustrate the authors' treatment of WISC-III data within the context of the chapter's topic.

One of the main themes highlighted in all chapters is that good assessment involves much more than testing and assembling test scores. The emphasis on sound justification for one's interpretation of test results within the context of the individual's personal history is apparent throughout this volume. It is the encouragement of this theme as an integral part of how clinicians approach WISC-III data (and all psychological test data) that we hope will be the impact of this volume on assessment practice. All too often interpretation of test data ignores the context of the scores within an individual's life history and is not grounded in the relevant research supporting or not supporting interpretations. On the other hand, research is often narrowly focused on one aspect of the test and ignores the clinical richness within which test scores are embedded.

The process approach to neuropsychological assessment mentioned in Dr. Kaplan's appendix in Chapter 1 reminds us of the multifactorial nature of all behaviors, including test responses. After all, a standardized test is in many ways a standardized clinical interview in which the sensitive clinician observes behaviors as well as records responses and objectively scores the test. It is the understanding of test scores, the observation of behaviors, and the contextually sensitive integration of this information that make for good professional assessment. Test scores cannot take the place of the clinician or alleviate the clinician of the task of taking a perspective and rendering his or her professional judgment. It is our intent that this volume serves as a reminder that the integration and blending of the research and clinical data are part of what is always done in the practice of responsible assessment. It is also often necessary to rely on one's best professional judgment when the research literature and previous clinical experience cannot help us with a particular case. David Wechsler, the astute clinician, probably would have been less interested in the test score and more interested in how and why the individual arrived at his responses. Good assessment leads to better understanding of the person, and to the extent that this volume aids in such a goal, we consider it successful.

We have sought to present chapters that examine the most frequent childhood disorders and clinical groups for which the WISC-III is used as part of an overall assessment. In addition, several chapters are thematic and deal with general issues of test use and interpretation. These chapters all discuss the importance of placing the WISC-III (or any other test for that matter) within the context of a full assessment and not as an end in itself. Psychological tests are powerful tools that can help the clinician better understand an individual, which in turn can be used to the benefit of the individual being tested. This has to be our first obligation.

We thank the authors who wrote the quality chapters found in the following pages. These outstanding contributors not only shared their research expertise and knowledge but also demonstrated the clinical sensitivity that enhances the utility of the WISC-III in the assessment of children. They both captured and created the scientist–practitioner theme of this book. Nikki Levy of Academic Press has patiently and professionally supported this project from the idea stage to publication. The Psychological Corporation and the University of Saskatchewan provided the scientific and professional environments necessary to ensure the completion of this book. Finally, special thanks to our families for their continuing support of our professional quests.

1

THE WISC-III IN CONTEXT

AURELIO PRIFITERA AND LAWRENCE G. WEISS

The Psychological Corporation
San Antonio, Texas

DONALD H. SAKLOFSKE

Department of Educational Psychology
University of Saskatchewan
Saskatoon, Sakatchewan, Canada

INTRODUCTION AND OVERVIEW
OF THIS CHAPTER

Unlike what one might usually expect in a first chapter in a volume such as this, the intent of this chapter is not to give an extensive overview and description of the Wechsler Intelligence Scale for Children—Third Edition (WISC-III) (Wechsler, 1991). Because of its widespread use by practitioners and researchers, its properties are well known, and full descriptions of the scale can be found in other sources (e.g., Anastasi & Urbina, 1997; Kaufman, 1994; Sattler, 1988, 1992; Wechsler, 1991). The purpose of this chapter is to highlight several critical elements that will be of benefit in the interpretation of the scale and understanding what the scale is best suited for. Therefore, topics addressed will be selective based on what the authors believe are issues that are often not well understood or neglected when using and interpreting the test.

To that end, we will provide a brief description of the scale and rationale for its revision; we will then discuss selected topics that we hope will assist practitioners and researchers with interpreting the results of the scale, including the role of the WISC-III *as part* of a psychological assessment rather than an end in itself, its role in diagnosis, its utility and validity in other countries and with minority groups, and approaches to subtest and scale interpretation. These topic areas were selected either because they are not discussed in detail to date in the available literature (e.g., performance of minority groups on the WISC-III) or to elaborate on the utility of tests in general but IQ tests in particular within the context of an assessment. All too often the assessment is viewed as synonymous with testing and diagnosis is viewed as synonymous with test scores, which we strongly propose are misguided assumptions in both clinical work and research.

DESCRIPTION AND RATIONALE
FOR THE REVISION

The WISC-III, published in 1991, is the latest revision of the scale that has its roots in the Wechsler Bellevue Form II published in 1946 by Wechsler. The predecessor of the WISC-III, the Wechsler Intelligence Scale—Revised (WISC-R) was published in 1974. The WISC-III, like its predecessor the WISC-R, continues to be the most widely used assessment of intellectual functioning of children (Reschly, 1997). As is evident by the chapters in this volume, it is used in a variety of ways and for a variety of purposes in clinical evaluations and for other types of assessments. Its strength has been its robustness and its ability to provide valuable information in a wide variety of assessments including neuropsychological assessments—a field that was in its infancy when Wechsler began developing his scales. (See Appendix A at the end of this chapter for a brief discussion by Dr. Edith Kaplan of an approach using the WISC-III as a neuropsychological instrument).

All tests need revision from time to time and the Wechsler scales are no exception. One of the primary reasons is that scores become inflated over time and norms need to be reestablished. This phenomenon is well documented and has been referred to as the Flynn effect (Flynn, 1984). Therefore, one of the primary reasons for revising the WISC-R was to develop current norms that would give more precise scores for individuals. Changes in test materials and items to make them more contemporary and attractive to examinees was another reason for the revision. Also, items were reviewed for bias and either modified or replaced to make the test fairer. In addition, exploration and attempts to clarify the factor structure of the scale was undertaken. Since the original factor analyses of the Wechsler scales conducted by Cohen (1957, 1959), there has been debate whether the WISC and other Wechsler scales are best described in terms of one, two, or three factors. There has been much controversy about the third factor, which was named "freedom from distractibility" by Cohen. It is now fairly well accepted that this third factor is not a pure measure of distractibility or inattention even though it is often interpreted in that fashion (Kaufman, 1994; Wielkiewicz, 1990). A new subtest, Symbol Search was added to WISC-III with the intent to help better identify what the third factor measures. However, the addition of this subtest resulted in a four-factor solution, with a new factor called "processing speed."

There has been some difference of opinion among both researchers and clinicians over the four-factor solution and the use of the four index scores as an alternative to the traditional Verbal IQ, Performance IQ, and Full Scale IQ scores. Sattler (1992), for example, suggests that a three-factor solution is more appropriate using the criterion of eigenvalues greater than 1 to determine the number of factors to interpret. Reynolds and Ford (1994) concluded that a three-factor solution is most consistent across the age range. Other analyses using both exploratory and confirmatory factor analyses (Roid, Prifitera, & Weiss, 1993; Roid & Worrall, 1996; Wechsler, 1991) have found evidence for the four-factor solution in the original WISC-III standardization sample and have replicated it in other samples as well. Also, Blaha and Wallbrown (1996) found support for the four-factor solution. However, other studies have found a three-factor solution more appropriate for children of Hispanic origin (Logerquist-Hansen & Barona, 1994).

One reason that there continues to be controversy over the factor structure is that there is a difference in using factor analysis as the sole criteria for determining how many factors to interpret in contrast to using factor analysis as a tool to inform how best to interpret relationships among subtests and examine what latent underlying abilities groups of subtests may have in common. Analysis of the WISC-III subtests and factor structure has found that there are differences among clinical groups in their patterns of subtest and factor scores. For example, children with mental retardation show consistent scores across the first three Index scores but have an elevated Processing Speed score on the WISC-III. Children identified as gifted, however, show a relatively lower score on the Processing Speed Index (PSI) compared to scores on the first three factors, which are about equal to each other (Wechsler, 1991). Looking at groups with learning disabilities and attention deficit disorders (ADD), Prifitera and Dersh (1993) found relatively lower scores on the Freedom from Distractibility Index (FDI) and PSI scores compared to the normal population and a high base rate of the ACID Profile. These results for learning disabled (LD) and attention deficit–hyperactivity disorder (ADHD) groups are similar to those reported in other research (Schwean, Saklofske, Yackulic, & Quinn 1993; Thomson, 1991; Wechsler, 1991).

More evidence for the validity of the four-factor structure is reported in a recently published study by Donders (1997) who found that the Perceptual Organization Index (POI) and PSI indexes are depressed in children with traumatic brain injury compared to the other scores. Also, depressed scores on these two indexes are relatively uncommon in the WISC-III standardization sample. Later in this chapter, analysis of minority group data also provides evidence for the use of these scores. The point of citing these studies is to suggest that by not including the four-factor structure, one would miss some very important information about these groups and individuals. So one must look at not only the various factor analytic criteria one uses to determine how many factors make sense but also the psychological meaningfulness of the factors (Snook & Gorsuch, 1989), as well as clinical information.

One must not confuse, however, the fact that a group has relatively lower scores on a test or group of subtests with the fact that any one individual will have low scores in the same areas. Knowledge of scores at the group level is useful in generating hypotheses about the individual case but does not confirm the hypothesis about an individual. Therefore, patterns of performance of groups should inform interpretation by the clinician but should not dictate it. This theme is the central point of this chapter and is discussed in more detail below.

BACK TO GORDON ALLPORT AND HENRY MURRAY: VIEWS ON WISC-III AS A DIAGNOSTIC INSTRUMENT

Allport and Murray were known as personologists. These two grand figures in the history of psychology provided theoretical and clinically rich descriptions of the *person*. As such, they pursued both the nomothetic as well as the idiographic dimensions of personality, although Allport was probably more radical in his viewpoint on the uniqueness of the individual. In the nomothetic approach, one searches for general rules and laws that apply to all individuals. In the idiographic approach strongly advocated by Allport, the best way to understand the person is to view the person as having unique characteristics or personal dispositions. The combinations and interactions of these unique characteristics allow nearly infinite variations of individuals. According to Allport, "each individual is an idiom unto himself, an apparent violation of the syntax of the species" (1955, p. 22). Furthermore, he said "all the animals of the world are psychologically less distinct from one another than one man is from other men." (p. 23). This radical idiographic view underscores the notion in Allport's mind that generalizations are limited in helping us understand the uniqueness of the individual.

Murray, who first used the term *personology* in 1938, maintained that the unit of study should be the individual. However, he was not as radical a believer in the idiographic approach as Allport. Still, both are considered personologists whose primary interest is in the "complexity and *individuality* of human life" (Maddi, 1976, p. 7, italics added).

So what does all of this discussion of personology have to do with WISC-III and intellectual assessment. Everything! Wechsler maintained that intelligence is part of the expression of the whole of personality. This is consistent with personology, which seeks to understand the whole person, which obviously includes his or her intelligence. Also, Wechsler maintained that his tests measure only part of intelligence; the intellective aspects and that the nonintellective aspects were not measured well by his scales. Wechsler at heart was a personologist who was most interested in understanding the person in all his or her complexity. Matarazzo, in his preface to the WISC-III manual states that

> Wechsler was first and foremost a practicing clinician with keenly honed skills and decades of experience in individual assessment. His many years of experience with chil-

dren and adults impressed upon him that intelligence is more than what we are able to measure with tests of psychometric-cognitive performance. Rather, he early discerned that intelligence is a global capacity of the individual and that it is a product of both the individual's genetic makeup, on the one hand, and the individual's socio-educational experiences, drive, motivation, and personality predilections, on the other. Because of the complex interplay of these multiple influences, Wechsler avoided the role of an intelligence-tester or psychometrist-technician. Rather, as did Alfred Binet before him, Wechsler became a practitioner skilled in the art of psychological assessment. Psychological assessment is a clinical activity that employs test scores, but only as one of the sources from which an astute clinician develops a well-integrated and comprehensive psychological portrait of the adult or child examined. (Wechsler, 1991, p. iii).

In his paper entitled "Cognitive, Conative, and Non-Intellective Intelligence," Wechsler (1950) said,

Factors other than intellectual contribute to achievement in areas where, as in the case of learning, intellectual factors have until recently been considered uniquely determinate, and, second, that these other factors have to do with functions and abilities hitherto considered traits of personality. Among those partially identified so far are factors relating primarily to the conative functions like drive, persistence, will and perseveration, or in some instances, to aspects of temperament that pertain to interests and achievement. . . . that personality traits *enter into* the effectiveness of intelligent behavior, and, hence, into any global concept of intelligence itself. (pp. 82–83)

The view that personality (as well as other variables) is related to intelligent behavior persists in practice as well as in the professional literature (Ackerman & Heggestad, 1997; Saklofske & Zeidner, 1995; Teeter & Korducki, chapter 6, this volume).

USE OF THE IQ TEST INFORMATION
AS PART OF ASSESSMENT

So if Wechsler viewed himself as a personologist and clinician first and the test as a tool to understand the person, to what uses is it best to put IQ tests and scores? First, regardless of the referral question, users of IQ tests need to remember that tests yields information that is part of the diagnostic and decision-making process. In both psychology and education, it is rare that one test or score is in and of itself diagnostic of a specific disorder. The approaches to test interpretation and assessment advocated by Kaufman (1994), Kamphaus (1993), Matarazzo (1990), and others speak to the need to view test results as tools used by a clinician in the evaluation process whether for diagnosis, intervention planning, classification, description, etc. Test results need to be viewed in the context of other information and knowledge about the person. Then, based on knowledge of the patient that includes a wide variety of sources (only one of which is test information), the clinician looks at the information to confirm or disconfirm hypotheses of either an a priori or a posteriori nature.

Think of what happens when complaining of headaches, we go to a physician. The physician will take our temperature, blood pressure, medical history, and perform other aspects of a physical exam. Then let's say the result is that we have a high blood pressure reading. Is the diagnosis of hypertension given by the physician based on the results of the scores derived from the sphygmomanometer reading alone? Probably not, because the physician may want to rule out many other factors before simply saying that an abnormally high blood pressure reading is definitive for a diagnosis of essential hypertension. Even then, there are various medical conditions that can produce a short-lived or chronic elevation in blood pressure that will need to be investigated before the final diagnosis is made. In this scenario note that the test instrument yielding a high blood pressure reading was giving an accurate result. Thus it may be highly accurate (or reliable) in describing the high level of blood pressure. But, the high pressure reading may be due to essential hypertension or to numerous other conditions such as heart disease, toxemia, kidney dysfunction, anxiety, and so. Without other corroborative and/or exclusionary evidence, basing a diagnosis on one test score alone can lead to false conclusions. However, the physician does use his or her knowledge base about the relationship of high blood pressure reading and essential hypertension in the diagnostic activity, even though this knowledge does not make the diagnosis in and of itself. Similarly, a relationship between low scores on WISC-III PSI and FDI scores and attentional disorder is not in and of itself diagnostic of ADHD, but the knowledge of this relationship should be included when trying to understand the person who is the object of the assessment.

If one accepts the tenet that tests do not diagnose but clinicians do and that most psychological tests are not in and of themselves conclusive diagnostic indicators (true of tests in medicine as well), then the large number of papers in the literature that criticize tests such as the WISC for failing to properly diagnose a disorder with a high level of accuracy are misguided in their emphasis. Perhaps these studies were needed to point out to practitioners that just looking at profiles of test scores (e.g., McDermott, Fantuzzo, & Glutting, 1990) leads to erroneous diagnostic decisions because subtest patterns in and of themselves are not conclusively diagnostic of a disorder. But the thrust of these papers seems to admonish clinicians for even looking at and comparing scores. Would one want a physician, for example, not to look at patterns of test results just because they in and of themselves do not diagnose a disorder? Would you tell a physician not to take your blood pressure and heart rate and compare them because these two scores in and of themselves do not differentially diagnose kidney disease from heart disease?

The Kavale and Forness article (1984) is often cited as evidence that profile analysis of the Wechsler scores is not useful in the differential diagnosis of learning disorders. The value of this type of research has been helpful to put the brakes on cookbook, simplistic interpretations of test results devoid of the contextualism of the individual's unique life characteristics. However, the criticism of the practice of profile analysis as the sole piece of information used to make diagnostic decision has often become a straw man argument and has been used as justification to eliminate the use of IQ and other psychoeducational tests, which is tantamount to the proverbial throwing out the baby with the bath water. What well-trained clinicians simply rely on test results or patterns as their sole source of information when performing an assessment? If clinicians do not practice in this simplistic way, then to say that a test is not useful because it does not accurately diagnose a disorder is a specious argument because it does not take into account the richness of other sources of information that the clinician is likely to use in arriving at a diagnosis. For example, if a child has a large Verbal IQ–Performance IQ (VIQ–PIQ) discrepancy with a lower VIQ, and based solely on this information one concludes that left hemisphere functioning is impaired, this would most certainly be viewed as naïve and poor practice. Kaufman (1976) demonstrated many years ago, for example, that discrepancies between VIQ and PIQ are not uncommon in the normal population. However, there is a sufficient body of research supporting the notion that injuries to the left hemisphere result in lower VIQs compared to PIQs. Well, if we have additional information that our client recently suffered a head injury, that perhaps other areas of functioning related to verbal abilities are impaired, and that previous functioning in relevant cognitive areas was higher, then the test results are certainly strong evidence that help corroborate a hypothesis of left hemisphere impairment that has resulted in cognitive impairments of certain types. It would appear that studies looking at the validity of test scores and profiles in the assessment process need to also look at the other variables that clinicians use in their assessment and not just at test results. Also, studies that conclude that test results are not helpful in such assessments ignore the value of the descriptive nature of tests (e.g., this person has these types of strengths and weaknesses).

One of the papers in this volume by Rourke (chapter 7) on WISC VIQ–PIQ discrepancies in children with learning disabilities illustrates the utility and value of looking at score discrepancies in the assessment of children with learning disabilities. Rather than postulate that a large VIQ–PIQ discrepancy is indicative of a LD, his research shows that VIQ–PIQ discrepancies are related to different patterns of cognitive strengths and weaknesses within different types of learning disabilities. For example, Rourke's research has shown that LD children with VIQ > PIQ show a pattern of learning problems that are quite different than those children with a PIQ > VIQ. Furthermore, such differences in VIQ–PIQ also appear in conjunction with different types of emotional and behavioral problems in groups of children with learning disabilities. To ignore such findings in trying to understand a child just because VIQ–PIQ discrepancies in and of themselves do not diagnose LD is as misguided as trying to diagnose LD solely on the basis of this discrepancy.

In most other chapters in this volume the message clearly is that good assessment involves looking at multiple sources of information in interpreting WISC scores. It should also be remembered that good practice in using other tests should also include looking at test results in the context of multiple sources of information, which include the WISC scores. The importance of taking into account test session behaviors on the WISC advocated by Oakland and Glutting (chapter 13) and others in this volume when interpreting scores also speaks to the fact that one cannot look at scores on any one test in isolation. Test session behaviors enable us to more accurately describe and evaluate a child's strengths and weakness. If we accept this type of notion as a necessary condition of sound clinical practice, then the idea of simply looking at patterns of test scores in isolation from other pieces of information whether in clinical assessment or research is limited and probably wrong in most cases. Truly multivariate thinking is needed, which is what the good clinician does.

USE OF THE WISC-III IN OTHER COUNTRIES AND WITH MINORITY POPULATIONS

The Wechsler scales are the most often used, individually administered, standardized tests for assessing the intelligence of children in the United States and have been frequently translated into other languages and been used in other countries. This raises important questions: Is intelligence as defined and measured by the Wechsler scales a universal trait? How well do intelligence tests like the WISC-III "travel" across national, cultural, and linguistic boundaries?

There is general agreement about the universality of 'g,' or general intelligence, despite the debate regarding the various kinds of factors that are hypothesized to comprise general mental ability or the extent of the item content required to provide an adequate sampling of 'g.' The robustness of 'g' is also generally accepted in both theoretical and empirical descriptions of intelligence. Its clinical utility is evident in the widespread use of the Wechsler scales for assessing preschool, school-age, and adult intelligence.

However, the appropriateness or fairness of the item content in intelligence tests in general continues to be a focus of debate. This argument goes one step further to include the appropriateness of test norms for individuals and groups not represented in the standardization studies. It has been observed that particular groups of children may score differently on the same test for reasons varying from the item content issue to "real" differences that may exist outside of the test itself (i.e., motivation, test-taking behaviors, gender differences, etc.). Although the WISC-III was carefully standardized and normed on a representative sample of American children, the question most often asked is, How well the test will "perform" when applied to culturally or linguistically different children, or children from different countries? The test should demonstrate its robustness across national and cultural boundaries both in terms of its content as well as in the norms used to represent varying levels of performance.

A plethora of psychological literature exists on test bias (e.g., Reynolds, 1995), much of which has spilled over into the political and legal domains. There may be good reason to suspect that a particular test or some specific items may "work" less well with some children who are different from those on which the test was normed. For example, a child may not answer correctly an item only because he has never been exposed to that specific task or item content. In contrast, another child will perform poorly on an intelligence test because of low ability. In comparison to chronometric measures of intelligence (e.g., reaction time), the WISC-

III and other similar tests are intended to yield estimates primarily of crystallized ability, although fluid ability may also be tapped along with processing speed and working memory. We are reminded of Vernon's (1950) intelligence A, B, and C. Intelligence C is what the tests that we create actually measure in contrast to the more pure descriptions of intelligence A (genotypic intelligence) and intelligence B (phenotypic intelligence). Thus if the WISC-III is an example of Intelligence C and reflects crystallized ability in the main, then it is also more open to concerns about item and score bias.

These issues have been raised in Canada and other countries that employ the WISC-III for the assessment of children's intelligence. Considerable controversy was heard about the item content of the WISC-R, especially in relation to the Information subtest (see Beal, 1988). Some research also reported differences in scores earned by Canadian children, suggesting that the American norms were not applicable in the Canadian setting (e.g., Holmes, 1981). Studies comparing changes over time in the ability scores across different countries further indicated that American WISC-III norms may not accurately reflect the current ability distribution in other countries (see Flynn, 1984, 1987). Although such major tests as the WISC-III are likely to be "imported" by other countries, the concerns that might result from this practice were summarized by Saklofske and Janzen (1990, p. 9):

> This situation can sometimes present rather major problems in the assessment process especially when norm-referenced tests are employed or the product being measured is tied to specific and unique experiences. . . . It is not always such a straight-forward matter of simply using well-constructed American tests in Canada. . . . Some American instruments that are brought into Canada may be renormed or modified following the accumulation of data from research and clinical use.

THE WISC-III IN OTHER COUNTRIES

The WISC-R has now been translated into 13 different languages, and there are currently 11 translations of the WISC-III either in progress or completed, ranging from Japanese and Chinese to Greek and French. Following from the above debates about intelligence in general, and intelligence tests more specifically, there have been standardization studies of the WISC-III carried out in several English-speaking countries including Australia, the United Kingdom, and Canada.

The U.K. version of the WISC-III was published in 1992 (Wechsler, 1992) and included a standardization sample of 824 children. As stated in the manual, "the majority of items in the final U.S. selection work throughout Europe" (pp. 24–25). Some artwork changes were required as were some minor scoring changes to reflect the specific U.K. setting. The Australian WISC-III study was based on samples of students from five age groupings ($N = 468$). The manual (Wechsler, 1995) states:

> The results indicated that the presentation order of some items should be modified in each of the Picture Completion, Information, Similarities, Picture Arrangement, Vocabulary, and Comprehension subtests. There was insufficient evidence to suggest the need to develop a full set of Australian norms. (p. 3)

The WISC-III Canadian Study (Wechsler, 1996) evolved from a smaller study of the test performance of a representative sample of English-speaking Canadian children. When differences that were larger than could be accounted for by measurement error were found, a comprehensive standardization study was initiated that resulted in the publication of Canadian norms. The results showed that Canadian children scored 3.34 IQ points above the U.S. normative sample, with differences ranging from 1.03 points for FD to 4.96 points for PIQ in favor of Canadian children. Furthermore, significantly higher scores were earned by Canadian children on every subtest except Information and Arithmetic. Distribution differences were observed following adjustments for mean score differences and reported in the manual:

> The distributions of Full Scale IQ, Verbal Comprehension Index, and Processing Speed Index differed significantly and among the scaled scores the Coding, Digit Span, and Mazes subtests showed the most discrepancies ($p <.005$). The results across scales generally found the Canadians with more low-average IQs and scaled scores and with somewhat higher percentages in the high-average (100–119) and high categories (120–129) than in the U.S. sample. (p. 29)

The reliability and factor structure for the Canadian WISC-III data replicated the American results. Although no changes were made to any of the test items, guidelines were presented for scoring several of the items from each of the verbal subtests, with the exception of Similarities.

These three examples of WISC-III validity and standardization studies conducted outside of the United States suggest that although the psychometric properties of the test are remarkably sound in their consistency and replicability, there are score differences that need to be taken into account in the measurement and assessment of intelligence when moving across national and cultural boundaries.

WISC-III AND MINORITY POPULATIONS IN THE UNITED STATES

Perhaps more relevant in the United States has been the literature on the performance of minority groups on intelligence tests. The use of IQ tests with minority students has been controversial because of concerns of test bias. Despite many concerns over test bias, the vast majority of studies investigating ethnic bias in IQ tests in general and in the Wechsler series have not produced evidence of test bias (Reynolds & Kaiser, 1990). Still, studies have consistently found that African Americans score on average 15 points lower than Whites, and Hispanics score somewhere between these two groups on IQ tests (Neisser et al., 1996). It is therefore natural to ask, Does the WISC-III show evidence of test bias towards minorities?

In studies of prediction bias (Weiss, Prifitera, & Roid, 1993; Weiss & Prifitera, 1995), the WISC-III predicted achievement scores equally well for African-American, Hispanic, and White children. The results of these studies are similar to other studies using the WISC-R (Reynolds & Kaiser 1990). Such results are interpreted as evidence that the scales are not biased against minorities. In addition, item selection for the WISC-III was done in conjunction with item bias analyses and content bias reviewers (Wechsler, 1991). Results of the Canadian, British, and Canadian studies mentioned above also demonstrated that the WISC-III was valid for these samples.

Wechsler was fully aware of the controversies regarding IQ testing with minority children. Wechsler, however, viewed the differences in mean scores not as indicators of lower intelligence among certain groups but as indicators of differences in our society and how variations in social, economic, political, and medical opportunities have an impact on intellectual abilities. Wechsler (1971) discussed the fact that individuals with lower socioeconomic status (SES) tended to score lower on IQ tests. He viewed this fact as evidence for a call to change the social conditions that cause these differences rather than as an indictment of the IQ test. In discussing differences in IQs among socioeconomic groups, Wechsler stated, "The cause is elsewhere, and the remedy not in denigrating or banishing the IQ but in attacking and removing the social causes that impair it" (Wechsler, 1971).

If differences in IQ among groups are attributable primarily to social and economic factors, then what implications do these have for the interpretation of IQ? First, it is important to view the IQ score not as a fixed entity but a reflection of an individual's current level of cognitive functioning. All too often in psychological reports one sees a phrase that states directly or strongly implies that the IQ reflects the individual's potential or inherited ability. But there are many factors including the socioeconomic, medical, temporary and transitory states of the organism, motivation, inherent test unreliability, and so on, that all may impact the person's score. It is well accepted by the professional community that IQ is not a measure of genetic endowment (Neisser et al., 1996), even though there is substantial evidence for the role of genetic factors in intelligence. In our clinical practice, we need to make sure that we do not confuse or infuse a person's IQ score with genetic explanations. IQs scores are reflections of current level of functioning and expressed abilities, not an immutable number.

There is clear evidence from the WISC-III standardization sample as well as data from other IQ tests of a substantial correlation between IQ and SES. One of the reasons that test developers stratify their samples by SES variables is to control for this effect. In the WISC-III, the standardization sample was stratified by parental level of education because this variable is related to SES and considered a good measure of SES. Results show that children from homes whose parents have the highest level of education (college level or above) score considerably higher than all the other four levels of education groups (i.e., <8th grade, 8–11 years of education, high school graduate, some postsecondary education, or technical school). The mean Full Scale IQ (FSIQ) scores for the entire WISC III standardization sample for the five educational levels from highest to lowest are 110.7, 103.0, 97.9, 90.6, and 87.7, respectively. The impact of SES on IQ scores is another "truth" generally accepted among the professional community.

As mentioned above, African-American groups on average tend to score 15 points lower than White samples on IQ tests. However, just looking at groups at this level conceals many issues and often leads to the erroneous conclusion that the intelligence of minority groups is lower than that of whites. This is erroneous, because these overall group differences do not take into account other relevant variables such as SES. One issue that affects this outcome is that when developing IQ tests, developers stratify SES within racial and ethnic groups in order to obtain a representative sample of the U.S. population. The effect of this is that a larger percentage of minority group samples have lower SES, which reflects the population characteristics. Therefore, a simple comparison of means between minority groups and Whites will yield scores that do not take into account the impact of socioeconomic and other demographic variables that might affect scores. Also, focusing on the overall IQ score alone misses other aspects of an individual's functioning. Remember what the IQ score represents: it tells us the score or standing of an individual relative to a reference group. Thus the individual's score must be interpreted in light of the reference group characteristics.

Group Differences

In order to investigate differences among different racial/ethnic groups, we examined the WISC-III IQ and Index scores of African Americans, Hispanics, and Whites in the WISC-III standardization sample (see Table 1.1). In addition, rather than just looking at overall means, we compared samples that were matched on SES (level of education). Through matching we also controlled for sex, age (in years), region of the country (Northeast, South, Midwest, and West), and number of parents living at home. Tables 1.2 and 1.3 present data for these matched samples.

When looking at this data, several important points should be considered. First in Table 1.1, the mean FSIQ difference between the White and African-American sample is one standard deviation, which is consistent with previous research on IQ tests (Neisser et al., 1996) and on the WISC-R (Kaufman & Doppelt, 1976). The difference between the White and Hispanic sample is smaller (approximately 9 points.)

TABLE 1.1   Mean IQ and Index Scores by Race or Ethnicity for the WISC-III Standardization Sample[a]

IQ or index score[b]	African American	Hispanic	White
FSIQ	88.6	94.1	103.5
VIQ	90.8	92.1	103.6
PIQ	88.5	97.7	102.9
VCI	90.8	92.2	103.7
POI	87.5	97.5	103.4
FDI	95.7	95.4	103.1
PSI	95.8	100.2	101.9

[a]Total $N = 2200$; African-American group, $n = 338$; Hispanic group, $n = 242$. Data and Table Copyright © 1997 by The Psychological Corporation. All rights reserved.
[b]FSIQ, Full Scale Intelligence Quotient; VIQ, Verbal IQ; PIQ, Performance IQ: VCI, Verbal Comprehension Index; POI, Perceptual Organization Index; FDI, Freedom from Distraction Index; PSI, Processing Speed Index.

The second point, however, is that there is considerable variation in the differences among African Americans, Hispanics, and Whites among the other IQ and Index scores. For example, African Americans score only 6.1 and 7.4 points, respectively, below Whites on PSI and FDI scores. Hispanics continue to show a relatively higher PIQ and POI score compared to their VIQ and Verbal Comprehension Index (VCI) scores, which is consistent with the previous literature. The difference in the PIQ between Hispanics and Whites is only 5.2 points. In addition, the Hispanic group's PSI score is virtually identical to that of Whites, and there is only a 7.7-point difference between the groups on the FDI score. These results strongly suggest that simply looking at the FSIQ differences ignores relative strengths in the various domains of cognitive functioning among minority groups. It also strongly supports the practice of using the Index scores even though factor analyses do not always clearly support the four-factor structure for minority groups (e.g., Logerquist-Hansen & Barona, 1994).

SES and Group Differences

To further investigate the relationship of SES variables with IQ scores, we looked at matched samples of African Americans, Hispanics, and Whites. Subjects were matched on age, region, sex, parental education level, and number of parents living in the household. Analyses of the WISC-III standardization data found that children who live in a one-parent household have on average a FSIQ score that is approximately 6 points lower than children living in a two-parent household. Therefore, we matched on this variable as well. Results are provided below in Tables 1.2 and 1.3. The score differences between African Americans and Whites are significantly reduced when one takes into account these gross SES and demographic variables. Also of interest is that contrary to what is often assumed, African Americans do in fact do somewhat better on the verbal compared to the

TABLE 1.2   WISC-III Scores of African Americans and Whites Based on a Sample Matched on Age, Parental Level of Education, Region, Sex, Number of Parents Living in the Household[a]

IQ or index score[b]	African American (N = 252)	White (N = 252)[c]
FSIQ	89.9	100.9
VIQ	91.9	100.8
PIQ	89.8	101.2
VCI	91.9	100.7
POI	88.8	101.6
FDI	97.0	102.5
PSI	96.9	100.9

[a]Data and Table Copyright © 1997 by The Psychological Corporation. All rights reserved.

[b]FSIQ, Full Scale Intelligence Quotient; VIQ, Verbal IQ; PIQ, Performance IQ; VCI, Verbal Comprehension Index; POI, Perceptual Organization Index; FDI, Freedom from Distraction Index; PSI, Processing Speed Index.

[c]All differences between groups significant; $p < .05$.

TABLE 1.3   WISC-III Scores of Hispanics and Whites Based on a
Sample Matched on Age, Parental Level of Education, Region, Sex, Number
of Parents Living in the Household[a]

IQ or index score[b]	Hispanic (n = 151)	White (n = 151)
FSIQ	96.8	99.6*
VIQ	95.0	98.6*
PIQ	99.7	100.9
VCI	95.2	98.2*
POI	99.5	101.8
FDI	97.2	101.5*
PSI	101.1	99.6

[a]Data and Table Copyright © 1997 by The Psychological Corporation. All
rights reserved.
[b]FSIQ, Full Scale Intelligence Quotient, VIQ, Verbal IQ; PIQ, Performance
IQ; VCI, Verbal Comprehension Index; POI, Perceptual Organization Index;
FDI, Freedom from Distraction Index; PSI, Processing Speed Index.
    *$p < .05$.

nonverbal, performance tasks. This is contrary to the usual assumption that African Americans perform more poorly on the verbal tasks because it is commonly assumed that verbal items are more culturally loaded and biased than nonverbal tasks. Also, the relatively lower score on performance measures cannot be attributed to the likelihood that African Americans are disadvantaged on speeded tests because the smallest discrepancy (4 points) is found on the PSI. What these data do suggest is that socioeconomic and demographic factors do have a strong impact on scores, and again that there are considerable variations in scores among the cognitive components measured in the WISC-III. This again underscores the value of using both the Index scores and IQ scores or else these patterns of relative strengths would be overlooked.

The score differences between Hispanics and Whites are also significantly reduced when samples are matched on these demographic variables (see Table 1.3). All differences are less than four points, and several scores show no statistical significance. The higher score on the PSI by the Hispanic group (although not statistically significant) is of particular interest because it is sometimes assumed that Hispanics score lower than Whites on the WISC-III because of the speeded nature of some of the tasks. The reasoning behind this is that speed and time is valued differently in Hispanic cultures so on tasks requiring quick performance, Hispanics are likely to score lower. However, on the PSI which is highly speeded, the Hispanic group did not differ significantly (and actually scored higher) than the White sample.

Finally, we also looked for age trends in score differences between African Americans and Whites. Table 1.4 presents the difference scores between groups by age bands. This is the same matched sample as in Table 1.2, broken up into two

TABLE 1.4 Difference Scores between Whites and African Americans by Age Group on WISC-III IQ and Index Scores for a Matched Sample[a]

IQ or index score[b]	6–11-year-old group (n = 143)	12–16-year-old group (n = 109)
FSIQ	8.6	14.1
VIQ	6.6	11.9
PIQ	9.4	14.0
VCI	6.9	11.4
POI	10.8	15.4
FDI	3.1	8.6
PSI	2.3*	6.3

[a]Data and Table Copyright © 1997 by The Psychological Corporation. All rights reserved.

[b]FSIQ, Full Scale Intelligence Quotient, VIQ, Verbal IQ; PIQ, Performance IQ; VCI, Verbal Comprehension Index; POI, Perceptual Organization Index; FDI, Freedom from Distraction Index; PSI, Processing Speed Index.

*$p. > 05$; all other differences are significant, $p < .05$.

age bands: 6–11-year-olds and 12–16-year-olds. The patterns in this table clearly illustrate that the difference between groups are even smaller for the younger age group. The reasons for this age difference are unknown. However, it does have implications for how we view scores and how and when we intervene. The impact of earlier intervention on outcomes of children when score difference are smaller should obviously be further investigated.

These data also strongly suggest that research needs to look at more refined SES, cultural, linguistic, home environment, medical, and other variables that affect opportunity to learn and the development of cognitive abilities. Such age trends were not found for the matched Hispanic sample.

The view that minorities have lower abilities is clearly wrong. IQ score differences between younger African-American and White children and Hispanic and White samples with only gross matches on SES are much less than a standard deviation, and the index scores are even smaller. What would the difference be if even more refined variables had been controlled for, such as household income, home environment (e.g., parental time spent with children), per-pupil school spending, medical and nutritional history, and exposure to toxins. This finding also strongly supports not interpreting IQ scores as indicators of some inherent or genetic endowment.

Some may argue that the smaller differences between African-American and Whites discussed above do not support the notion of small IQ differences among groups because the FDI and PSI scores are less related to g. However, there is sufficient evidence that processing speed is in fact related to g (Matthews & Dorn, 1995). Moreover, the subtests (Arithmetic and Digit Span) that comprise the FDI are both good measures of working memory (Sternberg, 1993). Recent research in working memory suggests that working memory and reasoning (or general ability) are highly similar constructs that are highly correlated (Kyllonen & Christal, 1990).

It is hoped that the above discussion has underscored the point to the reader that test scores in and of themselves are not sufficient for a proper psychological assessment. Scores should be interpreted in the context of other relevant information, all of which may not be clear and objective but rely in part on the integrative skills and professional expertise of the evaluator. This is one of the main themes in Matarazzo's (1990) APA presidential address, in which he describes psychological assessment as an activity that

> is not, even today, a totally objective, completely science-based activity. Rather, in common with much of medical diagnosis . . . the assessment of intelligence, personality, or type or level of impairment is a highly complex operation that involves extracting diagnostic meaning from an individual's personal history and objectively recorded test scores. Rather than being totally objective, assessment involves a subjective component. Specifically, it is the activity of a licensed professional, an artisan familiar with the accumulated findings of his or her young science, who in each instance uses tests, techniques, and a strategy, that, whereas also identifying possible deficits, maximizes the chances of discovering each client's full ability and true potential. (p.1000)

APPROACHES TO WISC-III SCORE INTERPRETATIONS

INTERPRETATIVE STRATEGIES

It is common knowledge and practice that reports of intellectual functioning should begin with a discussion of the most global score and proceed in successive levels to less global, more specific scores. However, is it best to begin a prereport investigation of a profile at the Full Scale level and proceed with an analysis of the scores in the same top-down manner? In order to determine if the global scores are valid, or which global scores to focus interpretation upon, it is necessary to begin the investigation at a more detailed level and build up to the global interpretations. Once the investigation is accomplished in this detailed, bottom-up manner, an integrated report is then written in the traditional top-down manner, focusing on the most appropriate global scores.

Investigation of the scores should be conducted in ecological context. Interpretations of score patterns may vary depending on the sociocultural background, family educational values, pattern of academic strengths and weaknesses, test session compliance, motivation, and psychiatric and medical history. Another common mistake is to offer stock interpretations of score patterns that do not vary as a function of such mediating influences on the expression of intelligent behavior. Not only will interpretations differ with the examinees personal context and history, but the examiner's expectations of the likeliness of finding certain patterns will be influenced by the referral information and ecological context. A pattern of strengths and weaknesses anticipated based on such factors and subsequently observed in the test data leads to a stronger interpretation than the same identified through a "buckshot" approach of comparing all possible test scores. This section discusses interpretive strategies that take these issues into account.

INTERPRETING IQ VERSUS INDEX SCORES

It is first necessary to determine which scores, IQ or Index scores, will be the main focus of interpretation. This can vary depending on the overall context. The initial goal is to determine if the VIQ is a valid and appropriate indicator of verbal reasoning ability, or if interpretation should focus upon the VCI. Typically, the VIQ score is the best indicator of verbal reasoning ability. In some cases, however, the VCI may be a better estimate of the student's verbal ability. This may occur if the Arithmetic subtest score is significantly different from the other verbal subtest scores.

As you know, the VIQ and VCI differ only because the Arithmetic subtest scaled score enters the calculation of the VIQ score but not the VCI score. Therefore, if the Arithmetic subtest score reflects a significant weakness among the child's scores on the five Verbal subtests, then his or her VIQ score will be less than the VCI score. This is more often the case with students in special education than in regular education programs. This is because the Arithmetic subtest taps the student's problems with attention, concentration, and working memory—thus lowering the IQ score because of his or her disability. Furthermore, the Arithmetic subtest is not as highly correlated with verbal intelligence as are the other Verbal subtests, and Arithmetic loads on another factor, which is summarized by a separate index score (e.g., FDI). The VCI is, in essence, a *purer* measure of verbal reasoning than VIQ. In these cases the VCI is a fairer way to represent the child's overall verbal reasoning ability since it is less effected by the disability.

Therefore, if the Arithmetic subtest scaled score is significantly different from the child's mean of the five Verbal subtest scores, then the VCI score can be considered a better estimate of verbal reasoning than the VIQ score. Table B.3 in the WISC-III Manual provides the needed data for making this comparison (Wechsler, 1991). This applies regardless of whether the Arithmetic subtest score is significantly lower or *higher* than the mean of the five Verbal subtests. Thus, students who happen to possess an isolated strength with numbers, for example, in the context of generally average or even lower than average overall ability will not have their IQ score pushed upward by this one task, perhaps resulting in them being saddled with unrealistically high expectations.

Other highly regarded strategies for interpreting WISC-III profiles recommend that the VCI score be utilized when there is a large amount of *scatter* among the five subtests entering the VIQ (Kaufman, 1994). Verbal scatter is determined by subtracting the highest from the lowest Verbal subtest scaled scores. If the scatter is large among the five subtests entering the VIQ, then the VCI would be emphasized in favor of the VIQ. However, if the scatter is the result of, say, a very high score on the Comprehension subtest and a very low score on the Information subtest then the VCI will not provide a better estimate of verbal reasoning than the VIQ. This is because the culprits (Comprehension and Information in this example) are both included in the VCI as well as in the VIQ. In fact, this would be true if the large scatter were caused by any subtest other than Arithmetic. This is why we prefer that the decision to switch to VCI hinge on the discovery of a significant difference between Arithmetic and the mean of the five regular Verbal subtests. Alternatively, large Verbal scatter (eight or more points) that *is* caused by an aberrant Arithmetic score would also be an appropriate trigger for selecting the VCI over the VIQ.

On the performance side, the PIQ and POI scores differ only because the Coding subtest scaled score enters the calculation of the PIQ score but not the POI score. If the Coding subtest scaled score reflects a significant weakness among the child's scores on the five Performance subtests, then his or her PIQ score will be less than the POI score. Again, this is more often the case with students in special education than in regular education programs. The Coding subtest taps the student's problems with speed of information processing—thus penalizing the child with a lower IQ score because of his or her disability. Also, the Coding subtest is not as highly correlated with nonverbal intelligence as are the other Performance subtests, and Coding loads on another factor, which is summarized by a separate index score (i.e., Processing Speed Index).

In such profiles, the POI may be a fairer way to represent the child's overall nonverbal reasoning ability since it is less effected by the disability. The POI is a *purer* measure of nonverbal reasoning than the PIQ. So, if the Coding subtest score is significantly different from the other Performance subtest scores, then the POI may be a better indicator of overall nonverbal reasoning ability, and interpretation should focus upon the POI. Again, this strategy applies regardless of whether the Coding subtest scaled score is significantly lower *or higher* than the mean of the five Performance subtests. Table B.3 of the WISC-III Manual (Weschler, 1991) also gives the necessary data to determine if Coding is a significant difference in the child's performance profile.

DETERMINING THE BEST WAY TO SUMMARIZE
OVERALL INTELLECTUAL ABILITY

Historically, the Full Scale IQ score has been the only method available within the Wechsler scales for summarizing general cognitive ability. In any given profile, if VIQ and PIQ are each unitary constructs and are not especially different from each other, then the best estimate of overall ability is indeed the traditional Full Scale IQ score.

The traditional FSIQ is not necessarily the best way to summarize overall ability, however, when the VCI is a better estimate of verbal reasoning or the POI is a better estimate of nonverbal reasoning than the traditional VIQ and PIQ, respectively. In fact, when a child's verbal reasoning ability is not fully represented by the VIQ, it may not make a good deal of sense to summarize his or her intelligence with a composite score that includes the same subtests that compose the

VIQ! It may be equally difficult to defend using the traditional FSIQ when non-verbal reasoning is underrepresented by the PIQ. To date, practitioners have not had an option in this regard because the WISC-III manual does not provide any alternative to the traditional Full Scale IQ.

In this chapter, we provide an alternative composite score, which is derived from the four subtests that enter the VCI and the four subtests that enter the POI. As noted above, the VCI is a purer measure of verbal reasoning ability than the VIQ, and the POI is a purer measure of nonverbal reasoning ability than the PIQ. We refer to this composite as the *General Ability Index* (GAI) in order to distinguish it from the traditional ten subtest Full Scale IQ, which includes two subtests (i.e., Arithmetic and Coding) that are not as highly correlated with verbal and non-verbal intelligence as are the other Verbal and Performance Subtests, and which load on independent factors in four-factors solutions of the WISC-III. The GAI score is an eight-subtest composite that *excludes* Arithmetic and Coding—which load on the FDI and PSI, respectively.

We recommend that the GAI be reported under any of the following conditions:

1. When interpretation of verbal abilities focus on the VCI rather than the VIQ. In other words, when Arithmetic is significantly different that the mean of the student's five Verbal subtest scaled scores.
2. When POI is interpreted over the PIQ. That is, when Coding is significantly different than the mean of the student's five Performance subtests.
3. When both VIQ and PIQ are abandoned in favor of interpreting VCI and POI.

The norms table for the GAI is provided in Table 5. This norms table was derived using the WISC-III standardization sample of 2,200 children ages 6–16 representative of the U.S. population by racial or ethnic group, parent education level, and region of the country. To use this table, first calculate the General Ability Sum of Scaled Scores (GASSS) by adding the scaled scores for the following eight subtests: Picture Completion, Information, Similarities, Picture Arrangement, Block Design, Vocabulary, Object Assembly, Comprehension. Find the resulting General Ability SSS in the column labeled Sum of Scaled Scores in Table 1.5 and read across the row to determine the GAI score, associated percentile rank, and confidence interval.

Estimates of overall intelligence calculated in this way should *always* be clearly identified as GAI scores in psychological and educational reports. Yet, when a decision is made to report the GAI in lieu of the FSIQ, it is better to avoid viewing it only as a novelty item—some type of supplemental or alternative score with real-life decisions still being made based on the traditional FSIQ. When the GAI is selected based on the above decision steps, it may represent the best summary of the student's overall intelligence and, when clinically appropriate, could be given primary consideration in most relevant psychological, educational, and vocational decisions. We recommend that when appropriate, the GAI be used to determine eligibility for services and placement decisions in the same manner as

A. PRIFITERA, L. G. WEISS, AND D. H. SAKLOFSKE

TABLE 1.5 General Ability Index Equivalents of Sums of Scaled Scores[a]

Sum of scaled scores	GAI	Percentile rank	Confidence interval 90%	95%	Sum of scaled scores	GAI	Percentile rank	Confidence interval 90%	95%
8	50	<.1	47–58	46–59	51	78	7	74–84	73–85
9	50	<.1	47–58	46–59	52	79	8	75–85	74–86
10	50	<.1	47–58	46–59	53	79	8	75–85	74–86
11	50	<.1	47–58	46–59	54	80	9	76–86	75–87
12	50	<.1	47–58	46–59	55	81	10	77–87	76–88
13	50	<.1	47–58	46–59	56	81	10	77–87	76–88
14	50	<.1	47–58	46–59	57	82	12	78–88	77–89
15	50	<.1	47–58	46–59	58	83	13	79–89	78–90
16	50	<.1	47–58	46–59	59	84	14	80–90	79–91
17	51	0.1	48–59	47–60	60	84	14	80–90	79–91
18	52	0.1	49–60	48–61	61	85	16	80–91	80–92
19	53	0.1	50–61	49–62	62	86	18	81–92	80–93
20	54	0.1	51–62	50–63	63	87	19	82–93	81–94
21	55	0.1	52–63	51–63	64	88	21	83–94	82–95
22	56	0.2	53–63	52–64	65	88	21	83–94	82–95
23	57	0.2	54–64	53–65	66	89	23	84–95	83–96
24	58	0.3	55–65	54–66	67	90	25	85–96	84–97
25	58	0.3	55–65	54–66	68	91	27	86–97	85–98
26	59	0.3	56–66	55–67	69	91	27	86–97	85–98
27	60	0.4	57–67	56–68	70	92	30	87–98	86–99
28	61	0.5	58–68	57–69	71	93	32	88–99	87–100
29	62	1	59–69	58–70	72	94	34	89–100	88–101
30	63	1	60–70	59–71	73	94	34	89–100	88–101
31	63	1	60–70	59–71	74	95	37	90–101	89–101
32	64	1	61–71	60–72	75	96	39	91–101	90–102
33	64	1	61–71	60–72	76	97	42	92–102	91–103
34	65	1	61–72	61–73	77	98	45	93–103	92–104
35	66	1	62–73	61–74	78	98	45	93–103	92–104
36	67	1	63–74	62–75	79	99	47	94–104	93–105
37	67	1	63–74	62–75	80	100	50	95–105	94–106
38	68	2	64–75	63–76	81	101	53	96–106	95–107
39	69	2	65–76	64–77	82	102	55	97–107	96–108
40	70	2	66–77	65–78	83	103	58	98–108	97–109
41	70	2	66–77	65–78	84	103	58	98–108	97–109
42	71	3	67–78	66–79	85	104	61	99–109	98–110
43	72	3	68–79	67–80	86	105	63	99–110	99–111
44	73	4	69–80	68–81	87	106	66	100–111	99–112
45	74	4	70–81	69–82	88	107	68	101–112	100–113
46	75	5	71–82	70–82	89	107	68	101–112	100–113
47	75	5	71–82	70–82	90	108	70	102–113	101–114
48	76	5	72–82	71–83	91	109	73	103–114	102–115
49	77	6	73–83	72–84	92	109	73	103–114	102–115
50	77	6	73–83	72–84	93	110	75	104–115	103–116

(continued)

TABLE 1.5   (*continued*)

Sum of scaled scores	GAI	Percentile rank	Confidence interval 90%	Confidence interval 95%	Sum of scaled scores	GAI	Percentile rank	Confidence interval 90%	Confidence interval 95%
94	111	77	105–116	104–117	124	138	99	131–141	130–142
95	112	79	106–117	105–118	125	139	99.5	132–142	131–143
96	112	79	106–117	105–118	126	140	99.6	133–143	132–144
97	113	81	107–118	106–119	127	141	99.7	134–144	133–145
98	114	82	108–119	107–120	128	142	99.7	135–145	134–146
99	115	84	109–120	108–120	129	143	99.8	136–146	135–147
100	116	86	110–120	109–121	130	143	99.8	136–146	135–147
101	117	87	111–121	110–122	131	144	99.8	137–147	136–148
102	118	88	112–122	111–123	132	145	99.9	137–148	137–149
103	119	90	113–123	112–124	133	146	99.9	138–149	137–150
104	119	90	113–123	112–124	134	147	99.9	139–150	138–151
105	120	91	114–124	113–125	135	148	99.9	140–151	139–152
106	121	92	115–125	114–126	136	149	99.9	141–152	140–153
107	122	93	116–126	115–127	137	150	>99.9	142–153	141–154
108	122	93	116–126	115–127	138	150	>99.9	142–153	141–154
109	123	94	117–127	116–128	139	150	>99.9	142–153	141–154
110	124	95	118–128	117–129	140	150	>99.9	142–153	141–154
111	125	95	118–129	118–130	141	150	>99.9	142–153	141–154
112	126	96	119–130	118–131	142	150	>99.9	142–153	141–154
113	127	96	120–131	119–132	143	150	>99.9	142–153	141–154
114	128	97	121–132	120–133	144	150	>99.9	142–153	141–154
115	129	97	122–133	121–134	145	150	>99.9	142–153	141–154
116	130	98	123–134	122–135	146	150	>99.9	142–153	141–154
117	131	98	124–135	123–136	147	150	>99.9	142–153	141–154
118	132	98	125–136	124–137	148	150	>99.9	142–153	141–154
119	133	99	126–137	125–138	149	150	>99.9	142–153	141–154
120	134	99	127–138	126–139	150	150	>99.9	142–153	141–154
121	135	99	128–139	127–139	151	150	>99.9	142–153	141–154
122	136	99	129–139	128–140	152	150	>99.9	142–153	141–154
123	137	99	130–140	129–141					

the traditional FSIQ is used when that score is appropriate (e.g., when Arithmetic and Coding are not significantly divergent from the respective composites).

What are the likely consequences of using the GAI in educational decisions? In many special education cases, the GAI will result in a higher estimate of overall intellectual ability than the traditional FSIQ. This will occur when Arithmetic and/or Coding are significantly below their respective scale means and thus drag down the traditional FSIQ score. In determining eligibility to receive services for learning disabilities, this will likely increase the discrepancy between achievement and ability as estimated by the GAI, thus improving the chances of receiving special assistance for some students. In placement decisions for entrance into gifted and talented programs, high functioning LD students will also have a better chance of being determined eligible based on the GAI score than the traditional FSIQ score. Because there is also some evidence that children identified as gifted tend to score lower on Coding (and Symbol Search) (Wechsler, 1991, p. 210), the GAI score may also boost some children over their school districts "magical" cut-off score for entrance into gifted and talented programs. Of course, the situation can be different for any given student, especially those whose Arithmetic and/or Coding Subtests scaled scores are significantly higher than their respective composite means.

On the low end of the distribution, the situation is more unclear. Although the GAI score may tend to be higher than the traditional FSIQ among certain special education populations, there is also some evidence that very low functioning children tend to score higher on Coding (and Symbol Search) than on other subtests (Wechsler, 1991, p. 210). This may be because these tasks are similar to the matching and copying drills used in many classrooms for children with mental retardation, and are highly practiced skills. Thus, for some children in the intellectually deficient range (FSIQ < 70), the GAI score may tend to be lower than the traditional FSIQ score. But, placement decisions for children with mental retardation should also be based on measures of adaptive functioning.

One final comment about the GAI: We have described this eight-subtest composite as a purer measure of general cognitive ability than the traditional Full Scale IQ. However, this is in no way meant to imply that we think GAI is a measure of true, innate ability! Like the Full Scale IQ, the GAI is a summary measure of *expressed* abilities that are known to be effected by education, environment, and various conative factors that can moderate the expression of intelligent behavior, as described earlier in this chapter. Our discussion of GAI as a purer measure of intelligence is meant to imply a *psychometric* pureness relative to the traditional Full Scale IQ, which can be unduly influenced by certain working memory and speed-of-information-processing subtests.

DETERMINING WHEN NOT TO SUMMARIZE OVERALL INTELLECTUAL ABILITY

Before rushing to interpret overall intellectual ability, either FSIQ or GAI, there is another important question to consider: Do these summary measures represent unitary constructs for the student at hand? For each profile, are the verbal and performance scale scores sufficiently similar so that the full scale score is clinically meaningful? If the student scores very differently on the Verbal and Performance subtests, than the Full Scale score is simply the average of two widely divergent sets of abilities and therefore not very meaningful as summary of overall intelligence. For example, if a child's score is 83 on Verbal and 120 on Performance then the Full Scale score of 100, although a numerically accurate summary, is very misleading from any clinical or practical perspective. Of course, the problem is the same whether one is interpreting the traditional FSIQ or the new GAI.

When the verbal–performance (V-P) discrepancy is large, the Full Scale score should either not be reported or reported with appropriate cautions. In these situations it is best to state in the report that, for example, "Johnny's nonverbal reasoning abilities are much better developed than his verbal reasoning abilities, and this unique set of thinking and reasoning skills make his overall intellectual functioning difficult to summarize by a single score." Then go on to describe his performance on the appropriate verbal (VIQ or VCI) and performance (PIQ or POI) composites separately.

What size V-P discrepancy invalidates the Full Scale score? Although a 12-point discrepancy is statistically significant at the $p < .05$ level for both VIQ–PIQ and VCI–POI discrepancies, differences of this size are not uncommon. In fact, more than one-third of the children in the WISC-III standardization sample obtained V-P splits of 12 points or greater (Wechsler, 1991, p. 262). This occurs because the formula for statistical significance takes into account the size of the sample, and the same size V-P discrepancy will be more statistically significant in larger samples. With 2,200 children in the WISC-III standardization sample, a V-P difference of only 12 points is significant. Interestingly, in the military, where tens of thousands of recruits are tested annually, a difference of only 2 or 3 points between IQ scores may be statistically significant, but probably not clinically meaningful. This is why many researchers are moving away from a rigid reliance on traditional criteria of statistical significance when evaluating data. With large samples, we can determine the clinical relevance of a difference by the frequency with which differences of that size occur in the sample. Often we say that if it occurs in 10% of cases or less, than it is considered rare and therefore likely to be clinically meaningful. But, this 10% criterion is rather arbitrary.

As a general rule of thumb, we think that a 20-point V-P discrepancy should raise large red flags in the examiner's mind. A 20-point or greater VIQ–PIQ discrepancy was obtained by approximately 12% of the WISC-III standardization sample. A 20-point or greater VCI–POI discrepancy was obtained by about 14% of the sample. Less than 10% of the sample obtained 22-point or greater discrepancies on either of these measures (Wechsler, 1991, p. 262).

The situation becomes more complicated, however, when we take into account sociocultural factors such as the racial and ethnic group of the student, the educational level of the student's parents, and the direction of the difference (e.g., V < P or V > P) (Weiss, Prifitera, & Dersh, 1995). Table 6 presents cumulative percentages of VIQ–PIQ and VCI–POI discrepancies by direction for all Hispanic children in the WISC-III standardization sample ($n = 242$). Table 1.7 presents the same information for all African-American children in the standardization sample ($n = 338$). Note that these data are especially compelling because these samples are very closely representative of the U.S. population percentages of Hispanics and African Americans in terms of region of the country and parent education level, and contain equal numbers of subjects at each year of age between 6 and 16. These data are reproduced here in order to encourage culturally sensitive assessment decisions.

TABLE 1.6 Cumulative Percentages of WISC-III Verbal IQ–Performance IQ (VIQ–PIQ) and Verbal Comprehension Index–Perceptual Organization Index (VCI–POI) Discrepancies in Hispanic Children[a]

Amount of discrepancy	IQ discrepancies[b]		Index discrepancies[c]	
	VIQ > PIQ	PIQ > VIQ	VCI > POI	POI > VCI
36	0.0	0.0	0.0	0.8
35	0.0	0.0	0.0	1.2
34	0.0	0.4	0.0	1.2
33	0.0	0.4	0.0	1.2
32	0.4	0.4	0.0	1.7
31	0.4	1.2	0.4	2.5
30	0.4	1.7	0.4	2.9
29	0.4	2.1	0.4	3.3
28	0.4	2.1	1.2	3.3
27	0.4	2.1	1.2	3.7
26	1.7	3.3	1.2	3.7
25	1.7	4.1	1.2	4.5
24	1.7	6.2	1.7	5.0
23	1.7	8.3	1.7	5.8
22	2.5	9.9	1.7	7.0
21	2.5	11.6	2.5	9.9
20	2.5	13.6	2.9	12.0
19	2.9	14.9	3.3	12.8
18	3.3	15.7	4.1	14.5
17	3.3	17.4	4.1	16.1
16	3.3	18.6	4.5	18.6
15	4.1	20.2	4.5	21.1
14	4.5	22.3	5.0	22.3
13	5.8	25.6	5.8	22.7
12	5.8	28.9	7.0	26.9
11	7.0	33.1	8.3	30.6
10	7.9	34.7	9.1	35.1
9	8.3	37.2	9.9	38.0
8	9.9	39.7	12.0	39.3
7	11.6	41.7	14.5	42.6
6	14.0	46.7	16.5	45.9
5	15.3	52.5	18.6	50.4
4	18.2	56.2	20.7	56.6
3	20.7	61.2	22.3	60.7
2	24.0	64.5	23.1	65.7
1	26.4	69.0	26.4	70.2

[a]$N = 242$. Data and Table Copyright © 1994 by The Psychological Corporation. All rights reserved.
[b]Verbal IQ = Performance IQ (VIQ = PIQ) for 4.6% of the sample.
[c]Verbal Comprehension Index = Perceptual Organization Index (VCI = POI) for 3.4% of the sample.

TABLE 1.7   Cumulative Percentages of WISC-III Verbal IQ–Performance IQ and Verbal Comprehension Index–Perceptual Organization Index Discrepancies in African-American Children[a]

Amount of discrepancy	IQ discrepancies[b]		Index discrepancies[c]	
	VIQ > PIQ	PIQ > VIQ	VCI > POI	POI > VCI
31	0.0	0.3	0.0	0.0
30	0.0	0.3	0.3	0.0
29	0.3	0.3	1.2	0.0
28	0.3	0.6	1.5	0.0
27	1.5	0.6	2.1	0.0
26	1.8	0.6	2.7	0.3
25	3.0	0.9	4.4	0.6
24	3.8	1.5	4.7	0.6
23	5.0	2.1	5.9	0.6
22	5.6	2.7	6.8	2.7
21	6.5	3.3	8.0	3.6
20	7.7	4.4	8.9	4.1
19	9.8	4.4	10.4	4.4
18	10.9	5.6	10.7	4.7
17	12.1	6.8	12.4	5.6
16	13.3	7.4	15.1	6.5
15	14.5	8.6	16.3	8.3
14	16.6	10.7	19.2	9.5
13	18.3	11.2	21.9	11.8
12	19.5	13.0	23.7	13.3
11	22.8	13.9	28.4	13.6
10	25.4	14.8	30.5	16.0
9	27.8	16.3	35.2	16.6
8	32.8	18.6	37.6	18.0
7	36.1	21.9	39.1	20.1
6	39.9	24.3	42.6	22.5
5	42.6	28.4	45.0	23.1
4	47.0	30.2	49.4	26.6
3	50.9	32.0	53.8	29.3
2	53.6	36.7	58.3	32.0
1	57.1	40.5	61.8	34.9

[a]N = 338. Data and Table Copyright © 1994 by The Psychological Corporation. All rights reserved.
[b]Verbal IQ = Performance IQ (VIQ = PIQ) for 2.4% of the sample.
[c]Verbal Comprehension Index − Perceptual Organization Index (VCI = POI) for 3.3% of the sample.

Most experienced examiners are aware that Hispanic children tend to score higher on the Performance than the Verbal subtests. As shown in Table 1.6, 69% of the Hispanic sample obtained higher PIQ than VIQ scores. On average, Hispanic children scored approximately 5 points higher on PIQ than VIQ, and 5½ points higher on POI than VCI. A 20-point PIQ > VIQ difference was obtained by 13.6% of the Hispanic sample, and a 20-point POI > VCI difference was obtained by 12%

TABLE 1.8   Means and Standard Deviations for WISC-III Verbal IQ–Performance IQ and Verbal Comprehension Index–Perceptual-Organization Index Discrepancies in Hispanic and African-American Samples by Parent Education Level and Overall[a]

| Parent education level | Sample[b,c] | | | |
| | Hispanic | | African American | |
	VIQ–PIQ	VCI–POI	VIQ–PIQ	VCI–POI
< 9	−8.6 (10.9) n = 73	−8.7 (11.4) n = 73	4.7 (11.6) n = 23	5.5 (11.9) n = 23
9–11	−5.7 (9.4) n = 57	−5.3 (9.8) n = 57	1.4 (10.8) n = 78	2.5 (11.4) n = 78
12	−4.7 (13.7) n = 65	−4.3 (13.7) n = 65	2.6 (11.9) n = 142	3.4 (11.7) n = 142
13–15	−2.6 (8.9) n = 35	−1.5 (8.8) n = 35	1.8 (12.7) n = 65	3.5 (12.5) n = 65
> 15	0.2 (11.8) n = 12	0.2 (13.4) n = 12	1.8 (11.1) n = 30	2.6 (11.8) n = 30
Overall	−5.6 (11.4) n = 242	−5.2 (11.7) n = 242	2.2 (11.7) n = 338	3.3 (11.8) n = 338

[a]Data and Table Copyright © 1994 by The Psychological Corporation. All rights reserved.
[b]Negative signs indicate Verbal < Performance (V < P).
[c]VIQ-PIQ, Verbal IQ–Performance IQ; VCI–POI, Verbal Comprehension Index–Perceptual Organization Index.

of this sample. Less than 10% of the Hispanic sample obtained PIQ > VIQ discrepancies of 22 points or more, and POI > VCI discrepancies of 21 points or more.

Table 1.8 shows the mean discrepancy scores by parent education level for the Hispanic and African-American samples. A clear trend is evident in the Hispanic sample: The lower the level of parent education, the larger the mean P > V discrepancy. Thus, examiners should expect larger P > V discrepancies to occur more frequently among Hispanic children whose parents have little education. On the other hand, even moderate P > V discrepancies may be viewed with suspicion in Hispanic children whose parents have graduated college.

Even very large P > V discrepancies, however, can be given psychoeducational meaning only within the context of the full clinical picture. Hispanic children who have been speaking English as a second language for 4–5 years, for example, may appear bilingual in normal conversation but continue to experience difficulty with tasks that require abstract verbal reasoning in English (e.g., the Similarities and

Comprehension subtests). Practitioners must use appropriate clinical sensitivity when interpreting individual V-P discrepancies, taking into account the level of acculturation as suggested by the age at which English was first taught, value placed on English language development in the home, parent education level, and so on, in order to help differentiate between language loss, arrested language development, and other possible interpretations.

Only 26% of the Hispanic sample obtained a verbal score higher than the performance score. Less than 10% of the Hispanic sample obtained VIQ > PIQ discrepancies of 8 points or more, and VCI > POI discrepancies of 9 points or more. For an Hispanic child, therefore, a VIQ of 100 and PIQ of 92 is rare and may indicate a clinically meaningful discrepancy between the children's verbal and nonverbal reasoning abilities. This is true even though an 8- or 9-point difference is not statistically significant. Relying purely on the criteria of statistical significance would cause examiners to miss these cases.

As shown in Table 7, there was a general tendency for African-American children to score higher on verbal than performance subtests. Fifty-seven percent of the African-American children obtained higher VIQ than PIQ scores, and approximately 62% obtained higher VCI than POI scores. On average, African-American children scored approximately 2 points higher on VIQ than PIQ, and 3 points higher on VCI than POI. Less than 10% of the African-American sample obtained VIQ > PIQ splits of 19 points or greater, and VCI > POI splits of 20 points or more. Thus, when an examiner identifies discrepancies of this magnitude in an African-American child, he or she may consider any full-scale score to be an inappropriate summary of overall intelligence, and proceed with exploring the possible meaning of this discrepancy for the child's psychoeducational functioning.

Performance > Verbal discrepancies do occur among African-American children. PIQ > VIQ differences of 15 points or greater, and POI > VCI splits of 14 points or more were obtained by less than 10% of the African-American sample. Again, practitioners should be careful not to ignore moderate P > V discrepancies in African-American children, as they occur infrequently.

Finally, these critical values should not be applied in a rigid fashion. There is nothing magical about identifying a 22-point discrepancy, for example, that makes a child noticeably different from a child with a 19- or 20-point discrepancy. As always, test results must be interpreted in the context of a full sensitivity toward the child's culture combined with an understanding of his or her medical and educational history, parental and environmental factors, and premorbid level of functioning.

STRATEGIES FOR INTERPRETING THE FREEDOM FROM DISTRACTIBILITY INDEX

The most crucial element in the proper interpretation of the FDI score is the examiner's knowledge that this index does not really measure distractibility. This composite was originally named Freedom from Distractibility in the interest of simplicity (Cohen, 1959), and the name was retained in the WISC-III for reasons of historical continuity. But, Freedom from Distractibility is a misleading name for this construct because it encourages naive interpretations on the part of lay readers of WISC-III reports such as teachers, parents, principals, and even pediatricians, as well as some inexperienced or poorly trained examiners! This composite of Arithmetic and Digit Span is better conceptualized as a Working Memory Index (WMI). Working memory is the ability to hold information in mind temporarily while performing some operation or manipulation with that information, or engaging in an interfering task, and then accurately reproducing the information or correctly acting on it. Working memory can be thought of as mental control involving reasonably higher order tasks (rather than rote tasks), and it presumes attention and concentration. Thus, this index measures the ability to sustain attention, concentrate, and exert mental control. In the new WAIS-III (Wechsler, 1997), a composite of the Arithmetic, Digit Span, and Letter-Number Sequencing subtests was named the WMI.

Digit Span backwards is an excellent example of a task designed to tap working memory because the student must hold in mind a string of numbers while reversing their sequence and then correctly reproduce the numbers in the new order. The Arithmetic subtest is a more ecologically valid working memory task because we are frequently called upon to calculate arithmetic problems mentally in real-life situations; such as when checking our change at the grocery store, estimating driving time at a certain rate of speed, halving a cake recipe, remembering a telephone number to call while entering the security code on your front door, or even figuring out what combination of touchdowns and field goals a losing football team needs to score in order to win the game.

But, working memory does not involve only numbers. Other examples include writing the main points of a teacher's lecture in a notebook while continuing to attend to the lecture, or keeping a three-part homework assignment in mind while recording the first two parts in an assignment pad, or keeping in mind the next points you want to make while explaining your first point. Clearly, a serious deficit in working memory can have major implications in the academic life of a student, and create difficulties in daily life functioning as well as in many vocational settings.

Children with learning or attentional disorders are more likely to experience problems with working memory as suggested by significantly lower scores on this index (Wechsler, 1991). Children with serious deficits in working memory are academically challenged, but not necessarily because of lower intelligence. A weakness in working memory may make the processing of complex information more time consuming and drain the student's mental energies more quickly as compared to other children of the same age, perhaps contributing to more frequent errors on a variety of learning tasks.

At home, these children can appear oppositional when they fail to "remember" that they were supposed to clean their room after watching a TV show, or "forget" a second instruction while performing the first task or chore assigned. When this index is low, practitioners should inquire with teachers and parents about these behaviors and help them reframe the problem. Viewing these children as distractible oversimplifies the problem and leads to treatment strategies designed to reduce extraneous stimulation, which will largely be ineffective. Even worse, viewing these children as oppositional leads to inappropriate treatment recommendations designed to shape behavioral compliance. Even when these behavioral strategies are based on principles of positive reinforcement (not always likely in the home), the child's self-esteem can suffer when they continue to "forget" despite putting forth their best effort. Some of these children are dismayed by the way ideas seem to fly out of their minds, while others willingly accept the role of the class clown (or worse) cast upon them by others.

To evaluate the FDI as a possible strength or weakness in the profile, the FDI score can be compared to the VCI and POI scores. If the FDI score is significantly greater or less than either the VCI or POI scores, then FDI is considered a relative strength or weakness respectively. Table B.1 in the WISC-III Manual (Wechsler, 1991, p. 261) shows the differences between factor-based index scores required for statistical significance, and Table B.2 (p. 262) shows the base rate of occurrence of differences of various magnitudes. If a good portable rule of thumb is needed for hypothesis generation, 15 points (or one standard deviation) difference makes a good deal of sense. A difference of this magnitude or greater between FDI and VCI is significant and was obtained by 27% of the standardization sample, and a 15 or more point difference between FDI and POI was obtained by approximately 32% of the sample. As also shown in Table B.1, however, the critical differences for significance at the $p < .05$ level show considerable variation by age. For example, a difference between FDI and VCI of 15 points would be needed at age 7, whereas a difference of only 11 points is significant at age 15. Thus, the careful examiner will refer to the appropriate tables.

Of course, interpretation of the FDI presumes that the index is valid. If the Arithmetic and Digit Span (DS) subtest scaled scores are very different from each other, then the FDI score can only represent the average of two widely divergent sets of abilities and would therefore have little intrinsic meaning. These two subtests load on the same factor in factor analyses of the WISC-III, yet correlate only moderately ($r = .43$ across ages). So, divergent scores are certainly possible.

How large a difference is required before abandoning the FDI as an interpretable score? Table 9 shows percentages of the WISC-III standardization sample obtaining various Arithmetic–DS discrepancies. As shown in the table, approximately 17.5% of the sample obtained a 5-point difference or greater. Furthermore, it would appear clinically inappropriate to us to report that a child obtained an average score on the FDI when the Arithmetic and DS subtest scaled scores are 7 and 12 respectively, a difference of 5 points. (Other examiners may consult this table and choose different guidelines depending on the personal context within which the profile is being interpreted.) When the Arithmetic and DS subtest scaled scores are 5 or more points apart, then these subtests should be interpreted independently. Both of these subtests measure attention, concentration, and mental control, but the Arithmetic subtest also measures specific skills in numerical operations and mathematics reasoning. Table B.3 of the WISC-III Manual can be consulted to determine if either subtest constitutes a significant strength or weakness in the child's profile.

Let's take the case when DS is a weakness and Arithmetic is not. A direct assessment of short-term auditory memory, performance on the DS subtest requires attention, concentration, and mental control, and can be influenced by the ability to correctly sequence information. If performance on DS Span Backward is also impaired, then the working memory interpretation is further supported. However, the interpretation varies depending on the absolute elevation of these subtests. If Arithmetic is in the average range and DS is below average, then the working memory interpretation is primary. If, however, Arithmetic is in the above range and DS is significantly lower but still within the average range, this may suggest better developed skills in numerical calculation or mathematics reasoning rather than a deficit in working memory.

As noted above, DS (DS) Backwards is an excellent example of a working memory task. The requirement to manipulate (e.g., reverse) the digits in DS Backwards makes this a more difficult working memory task than DS Forward, in which numbers are simply repeated in sequence. DS Backward is a purer measure of mental control than DS Forward. Both tasks tap short-term auditory memory, numerical sequencing ability, attention, and concentration, but DS Backwards demands more working memory to complete successfully. For this reason it is often helpful to examine the student's performance on DS Backward and DS Forward separately. Even when FDI is not a specific deficiency in the profile, a DS Backward scaled score that is much less than the DS Forward scale score raises the question of a relative weakness in working memory. Tables B.6 and B.7 in the WISC-III manual (Wechsler, 1991) provide the needed information to assess discrepancies between DS Forward and Backward.

On the other hand, if Arithmetic is a weakness and Digit Span is not, then there is less evidence of a deficit in working memory. This is especially true if performance on Digit Span Backward is not impaired. In this case, you may suspect poorly developed skills in numerical calculation or mathematics reasoning and perhaps even a specific learning disability in math. This warrants further study, perhaps with an achievement test that has broader coverage of the domain of arithmetic.

STRATEGIES FOR INTERPRETING
THE PROCESSING SPEED INDEX

On the surface, the Coding and Symbol Search subtests are simple visual scanning and tracking tasks. A direct test of speed and accuracy, the Coding subtest assesses ability in quickly and correctly scanning and sequencing simple visual information. Performance on this subtest also may be influenced by short-term visual memory, attention, or visual-motor coordination. On the Symbol Search subtest the student is required to inspect several sets of symbols and indicate if special target symbols appeared in each set. Also a direct test of speed and accuracy, this subtest assesses scanning speed and sequential tracking of simple visual information. Performance on this subtest may be influenced by visual discrimination and visual-motor coordination.

Yet, it could be a mistake to think of the PSI as a measure of simple clerical functions that are not especially related to intelligence. Performance on this index is an indication of the rapidity with which a student can process simple or routine information without making errors. Because learning often involves a combination of routine information processing (such as reading) and complex information processing (such as reasoning), a weakness in the speed of processing routine information may make the task of comprehending novel information more time-consuming and difficult. A weakness in simple visual scanning and tracking may leave a child less time and mental energy for the complex task of understanding new material. This is the way in which these lower order processing abilities are related to higher order cognitive functioning.

The pattern of processing speed abilities lower than reasoning abilities is more common among students who are experiencing academic difficulties in the classroom than among those who are not (Wechsler, 1991, p. 213). Although little research exists on this topic, it is possible to hypothesize that children with processing speed deficits may learn less material in the same amount of time, or take longer to learn the same amount of material as compared to those without processing speed deficits. We think that these children may also mentally tire more easily because of the additional cognitive effort required to perform routine tasks, and that this could lead to more frequent errors and possible expressions of frustration. Conversely, a strength in processing speed may facilitate the acquisition of new information.

The PSI score can be compared to the VCI and POI scores in order to evaluate it as a possible strength or weakness in the profile. If the PSI score is significantly greater or less than either the VCI or POI scores, then PSI is considered a relative strength or weakness respectively. Tables B.1 and B.2 of the WISC-III Manual provide the necessary data for evaluating comparisons between these index scores. As a rule of thumb, a 15 or more point difference may be sufficient to generate a hypothesis of a relative weakness in processing speed functions. Differences of this magnitude or greater are statistically significant at the $p < .05$ level and were obtained by slightly more than one-third of the standardization sample. Larger differences, of course, generate more serious concerns about a deficit in this area. PSI–POI or PSI–VCI discrepancies of 20 or more points occur in approximately 21% and 24% of cases, respectively, while discrepancies of 25 points are observed in about 12% and 13% of cases, respectively.

If the Coding and Symbol Search subtest scaled scores are very different from each other, however, then the PSI composite will have little intrinsic meaning, and should not be interpreted as a unitary construct. Table 1.9 shows percentages of the WISC-III standardization sample obtaining various Coding–Symbol Search discrepancies. We recommend that a difference of 5 or more points between Coding and Symbol Search raise strong concerns about interpreting the POI index as

TABLE 1.9   Cumulative Percentages of
the WISC-III Standardization Sample Obtaining
Various Coding-Symbol Search Discrepancies and
Various Arithmetic-Digit Span Discrepancies[a]

Difference[b]	CD-SS[c]	AR-DS[d]
11	0.5	0.2
10	1.2	0.8
9	2.6	1.7
8	4.0	3.6
7	6.9	6.2
6	11.0	10.1
5	17.5	17.5
4	27.8	29.4
3	43.2	43.7
2	63.7	66.4
1	88.2	89.3
0	100.00	100.0

[a]Data and Table Copyright © 1997 by The
Psychological Corporation. All rights reserved.
[b]Absolute value of the difference.
[c]CD-SS, Coding-Symbol Search Discrepancies.
[d]AR-DS, Arithmetic-Digit Span Discrepancies.

a unitary construct. Actually, a difference between these two subtests of only 4 points is significant at the $p < .05$ level (see Table B.4 of the WISC-III Manual), but a difference of this size or greater was obtained by more than 1 out of every 4 children (27.7%) in the standardization sample. Only 17% of the sample obtained a 5-point difference or greater. If the difference between Coding and Symbol Search is 5 points or greater, then PSI may not be considered valid, and these two subtests are best interpreted separately.

When considering possible reasons for a disparity in performance on these two subtests, note that both measure skills in quickly scanning and correctly sequencing simple visual information, and each can be influenced by attention, psychomotor speed, and visual-motor coordination. They differ, however, in the content of the stimulus material.

The coding subtest includes symbolic content, while the content of the Symbol Search subtest is purely figural. The symbolic content of the Coding B subtest, for example, allows the child to form paired associations between the numbers and shapes. To the extent that a student adopts this approach to the Coding subtest, it is sensitive to the student's ability to learn these associations, and performance can be influenced by a weakness in short-term visual memory of the learned associations.

The Symbol Search subtest is not effected by associative learning, and may be a purer measure of psychomotor speed than the Coding subtest. The Symbol Search subtest also does not require fine motor skills (e.g., drawing) as does Coding. Because the Symbol Search symbols are complex and similar in appearance, however, the Symbol Search subtest may be more readily influenced by the student's visual discrimination skills than the Coding subtest.

Only careful observation of the student's approach to these tasks can shed further light on these alternative hypotheses for explaining the differential performance observed on these two subtests. For example, did the child form the relevant associations in the Coding task? Did he remember them? Did she refer to the key throughout the Coding task? Did he have difficulty manipulating the pencil? Did she make discrimination errors in the Symbol Search subtest? Did he make no errors on Symbol Search, but work too slowly and fail to complete a sufficient number of items? Answers to these questions, based not on the test scores but on astute observations of the child's behavior during testing, are clues to unearth the explanation for large observed differences between the Coding and Symbol Search subtests. This strategy is referred to as the "process approach" (Kaplan, Fein, Morris, & Delis, 1991) in that it emphasizes the process by which the student approaches the solution to the task rather than the score he or she obtains (see Appendix A for a fuller description of this approach).

PUTTING IT ALL TOGETHER

When evaluating a child's intelligence, it is important for the examiner to separate the investigative process of profile interpretation from the structure of the interpretive report. As professionals, our detailed investigative strategies lead us to conclusions that we present to the lay public in our interpretive report. An archeologist examining an ancient bone, for example, may go through an analytical process involving complex statistical analyses of shape, structure, function, and carbon dating results leading to the conclusion that the bone is from the hind leg of a prairie dog between 12,000 and 15,000 years old. Too often the investigative process is confused with the interpretation, leading to reports that are technically correct but lack meaning and relevance to the nontechnical reader. This problem is easily recognizable in reports that spew statistical findings without conclusions such as, "The twenty point difference between the VIQ and PIQ scores is statistically significant at the .05 level, and a difference of this magnitude or greater was obtained by 12.3% of the standardization sample." Reports written in this fashion represent correct restatements of the examiner's analytical processes, but do not provide the reader with an appropriate professional interpretation of the data. There is an important distinction between "data" and "information." Information is data with meaning, and the interpretive process involves taking data and turning it into information. A meaningful interpretation of these data would be, "The child's nonverbal reasoning abilities are much better developed than his verbal reasoning abilities." Thus, the examiner explains the meaning of the statistical data for the reader, rather than simply restating the analytical process in narrative form.

One of the major themes of this chapter is that meaningful interpretation of WISC-III scores also includes consideration of the personal and sociocultural context within which the scores are observed and any conative factors related to each child's unique pattern of abilities. The above example interpretation might continue, and this is evidenced by his interest in art classes." Thus, the investigative process is separate and distinct from the report writing process. The investigative process is bottom up and contextual. The report writing process is top down and contextual.

Perhaps the most ecologically meaningful correlate of high scores on intelligence tests is the ability to learn new information and to apply that information appropriately in an adaptive manner. There are many different strategies for acquiring new information. Learning acquisition strategies are a class of variables that can effect the expression of intelligent behavior in the real world beyond the testing paradigm. Good working memory and speed of information processing may make these learning strategies more efficient, increasing one's store of knowledge and thereby his or her ability to evaluate, classify, and assimilate still new levels information. The interplay between intelligence, working memory, speed of information processing, and learning acquisition strategies is ripe for future exploration.

CHAPTER SUMMARY

In this chapter we have discussed the value and role of the WISC-III as part of an evaluation. The proper interpretation of the WISC-III or any other psychological tests must be made within the context an individual's life history. We have maintained that clinical assessment is much more than a collection of test scores. Rather, it is an activity conducted by a professional that is informed by test scores, observations, personal history, and a familiarity with the scientific and research literature that is relevant to the tests and disorders being assessed.

We have presented data on different ethnic and socioeconomic groups that illustrate the importance of looking at scores within the context of the individual's personal history. We have also discussed an approach to the investigation and interpretation of test scores that takes into account these factors. The multivariate nature of assessment requires that the clinician integrate a great deal of information. It is often not clear which elements or factors are relevant or not in any particular case. We advocate that future research on tests go beyond the approach that is often taken, which analyzes test scores of various groups in isolation from other clinical data. While such research does provide some useful information, it is only a starting point because it ignores the many other individual variables that scientist–practitioners take into account when performing an assessment. If clinical assessment requires multiple sources of information, then, both in our research and clinical practice, we need to look at scores as one of the sources of information for investigation, not the sole source.

APPENDIX:
THE WISC-III AS A NEUROPSYCHOLOGICAL
INSTRUMENT[1]

The WISC-III is an instrument that is widely used by psychologists to evaluate the intellectual abilities of school-age children.[2] Because this test surveys a broad range of cognitive functions, it is therefore frequently used as the initial part an evaluation to help target specific areas that may be problematic for a given child. The traditional approach to WISC-III interpretation relies primarily on test scores and "achievement" in the sense of how many items did the child respond to properly. However, looking at errors made by the child on the WISC-III can yield additional information. An examination of the nature of the errors and the particular stimulus parameters of the items that are failed reveals the multifactorial nature of most of the subtests. A process-oriented approach to the WISC-III is intended to parse the component factors that may be contributing to a child's less than adequate performance.

In the development of this approach, each WISC-III subtest was analyzed at the content level, the particular task requirements, the modality of input and output, and the stimulus features. For example, the Information subtest has at least five different content areas: number facts, directions, geography, science, and names. A child may demonstrate selective content problems that may be referable to, for example, the presence of a developmental Gerstmann Syndrome. Note that lumping all these areas into one total score may hide differential performance across these content areas.

In addition to sampling the child's knowledge store, linguistic competency can also be assessed on the Information subtest because the questions must be understood and a verbal response made. For those children who have difficulty articulating a response, or for minimal responders, the provision of a multiple choice format (the foils having been drawn from error notes in the original standardization sample and the clinical validity groups) on the one hand permits a better assessment of the information that child has, and on the other hand the error choices have diagnostic value. Multiple choice formats for the Vocabulary subtest were developed in the same way and similarly permit error analyses that are helpful diagnostically and prescriptively.

Whenever possible, a given function is tested in another modality: we developed the Spatial Span test as a visual analog to the Digit Span test; a Sentence Arrangement test as an analog of Picture Arrangement. A Picture Vocabulary was introduced to add a receptive component to the analysis of verbal competence, thus making it possible to evaluate both expressive and receptive language for the same vocabulary words.

---

[1]The author of this appendix, Edith Kaplan, is currently at Boston University School of Medicine, Department of Neurology and Psychiatry, 85 E. Newton Street, Boston, MA 02118.

[2]Currently we are developing a set of tasks and procedures to enhance WISC-III interpretation using a process-oriented approach entitled the *WISC-III as a Neuropsychological Instrument* (Kaplan, Fein, Kramer, Morris, & Delis, in press). This approach is similar to that found in the *WAIS-R as a Neuropsychological Instrument* (Kaplan, Fein, Morris, & Delis, 1991).

WISC-III performance subtests have also been modified with regard to administration and scoring (e.g., the contribution of the distinctive components of incidental learning and motor speed to performance on the Coding subtest can be analyzed). Two new Block Design procedures have been introduced. One provides a scoring system that is sensitive to hemispheric laterality issues as well as a systematic way of testing clinical limits. The other is a motor-free Block Design subtest that can evaluate the perceptual component without motor contamination. Finally, an adaptation of the Elithorn Mazes was introduced because of their sensitivity to identify problems such as impulsivity, poor planning ability, and deficits in working memory.

In sum, the process approach to the investigation of WISC-III scores and performance provides an analysis of the various component processes that contribute to performance on selected critical subtests. Close observation and recording of the child's responses (i.e., a process-oriented approach) permits an analysis of the strategies that a child uses and the errors that are made en route to the final solution for an item. Such as approach permits the identification of profiles to identify spared and impaired cognitive functions. Because of its focus on the specific bases of success and failure, this method lends itself directly to the development of individualized interventions.

REFERENCES

Ackerman, P. L., & Heggestad, E. D. (1997). Intelligence, personality, and interests: Evidence for overlapping traits. *Psychological Bulletin, 121,* 219–245.

Allport, G. W. (1955). *Becoming: Basic considerations for a psychology of personality.* New Haven: Yale University Press.

Anastasi, A. & Urbina, S. (1997). *Psychological testing* (7th ed.). Upper Saddle River, NJ: Prentice Hall.

Beal, A. L. (1988). Canadian content in the WISC-R: Bias or jingoism. *Canadian Journal of Behavioral Science, 20,* 154–166.

Blaha J. & Wallbrown, F. H. (1996). Hierarchical factor structure of the Wechsler Intelligence Scale for Children-III. *Psychological Assessment, 8,* 214–218.

Cohen, J. (1957). The factorial structure of the WAIS between early adulthood and old age. *Journal of Consulting Psychology, 21,* 283–290.

Cohen, J. (1959).The factorial structure of the WISC at ages 7–6, 10–6, and 13–16. *Journal of Consulting Psychology, 23,* 285–299.

Donders, J. (1997). Sensitivity of the WISC-III to head injury with children with traumatic brain injury. *Assessment, 4,* 107–109.

Flynn, J. R. (1984). The mean IQ of Americans: Massive gains 1932–1978. *Psychological Bulletin, 95,* 29–51.

Flynn, J. R. (1987). Massive gains in 14 nations: What IQ tests really measure: *Psychological Bulletin, 101,* 171–191.

Holmes, B. J. (1981). Individually administered intelligence tests: An application of anchor test norming and equating procedures in British Columbia. *Education Research Institute of British Columbia; Report No. 81:11,* Vancouver, B.C.

Kamphaus, R. W. (1993). *Clinical assessment of children's intelligence.* Needham Heights, MA: Allyn & Bacon.

Kaplan, E., Fein, D., Morris, R., Delis, D. (1991). *Manual for WAIS-R as a Neuropsychological Instrument*. San Antonio, TX: The Psychological Corporation.

Kaplan, E., Fein, D., Kramer, J., Morris, R., Delis, D. (in press). *Manual for WISC-III as a Neuropsychological Instrument*. San Antonio, TX: The Psychological Corporation.

Kaufman, A. S. (1976). Verbal-Performance IQ discrepancies on the WISC-R. *Journal of Consulting and Clinical Psychology, 44*, 739–744.

Kaufman, A. S. (1994). *Intelligent testing with the WISC-III*. New York: Wiley.

Kaufman, A. S., & Doppelt, J. E. (1976). Analysis of WISC-R standardization data in terms of stratification variables. *Child Development, 47*, 165–171.

Kavale, K. A., & Forness, S. R. (1984). A meta-analysis of the validity of Wechsler scale profiles and recategorizations: Patterns or parodies? *Learning Disability Quarterly, 7*, 136–156.

Kyllonen, P. C., & Christal, R. E. (1990). Reasoning ability is (little more than) working memory capacity?! *Intelligence, 14*, 389–433.

Logerquist-Hansen, S., & Barona, A. (1994, August). *Factor structure of the Wechsler Intelligence Scale for Children-III for Hispanic and Non-Hispanic white children with learning disabilities*. Paper presented at the annual meeting of the American Psychological Association, Los Angeles.

Maddi, S. (1976). *Personality theories: A comparative analysis* (3rd ed.). Homewood, IL: The Dorsey Press.

Matarazzo, J. D. (1990). Psychological assessment versus psychological testing: Validation from Binet to the school, clinic, and courtroom. *American Psychologist, 45*, 999–1017.

Matthews, G., & Dorn, L. (1995). Cognitive and attentional processes in intelligence. In D. H. Saklofske & M. Zeidner (Eds.), *International handbook of personality and intelligence* (pp. 367–396). New York: Plenum Press.

McDermott, P. A., Fantuzzo, J. W., & Glutting, J. J. (1990). Just say no to subtest analysis: A critique on Wechsler theory and practice. *Journal of Psychoeducational Assessment, 8*, 290–302.

Neisser, U., Boodoo, G., Bouchard, T. J., Boykin, A. W., Brody, N., Ceci, S. J., Halpern, D. F., Loehlin, J. C., Perloff, R., Sternberg, R. J., & Urbina, S. (1996). Intelligence: Knowns and unknowns. *American Psychologist, 51*, 77–101.

Prifitera, A., & Dersh, J. (1993). Base rates of WISC-III diagnostic subtest patterns among normal, learning-disabled, and ADHD samples. *Journal of Psychoeducational Assessment monograph series, Advances in psychological assessment: Wechsler Intelligence Scale for Children—Third Edition, 43*–55.

Reschly, D. J. (1997). Diagnostic and treatment utility of intelligence tests. In D. P. Flanagan, J. L. Genshaft, & P. L. Harrison (Eds.), *Contemporary intellectual assessment: Theories, tests, and issues* (pp. 437–456). New York: Guilford.

Reynolds, C. R. (1995). Test bias and the assessment of personality and intelligence. In D. H. Saklofske & M. Zeidner (Eds.), *International handbook of personality and intelligence* (545–573). New York: Plenum Press.

Reynolds, C. R., & Kaiser, S. M. (1990). Test bias in psychological assessment. In T. B. Gutkin & C. R. Reynolds (Eds.), *The handbook of school psychology* (2nd ed., pp. 487–525). New York: Wiley.

Reynolds, C. R., & Ford, L. (1994). Comparative three-factor solutions of the WISC-III and WISC-R at 11 age levels between 6½ and 16½ years. *Archives of Clinical Neuropsychology, 9*, 553–570.

Roid, G. H., & Worrall, W. (1996, August). *Equivalence of factor structure in the U.S. and Canada editions of the WISC-III*. Paper presented at the annual meeting of the American Psychological Association, Toronto.

Saklofske, D. H. & Janzen, H. L. (1990). School-based assessment research in Canada. McGill Journal of Education, *25*, 1, 5–23.

Saklofske, D. H., & Zeider, M. (Eds.) (1995). *International handbook of personality and intelligence*. New York: Plenum Press.

Sattler, J. M. (1988). *Assessment of children* (3rd ed.). San Diego: Author.

Sattler, J. M. (1992). *Assessment of children* (revised and updated, 3rd ed.). San Diego: Author.

Schwean, V. L., Saklofske, D. H., Yackulic, R. A., & Quinn, D. (1993). WISC-III performance of ADHD children. Journal of Psychoeducational Assessment monograph series. *Advances in psychological assessment: Wechsler Intelligence Scale for Children—Third Edition,* 56–70.

Snook, S. C., & Gorsuch, R. L. (1989). Component analysis versus common factor analysis: A Monte Carlo study. *Psychological Bulletin, 106,* 148–154.

Sternberg, R. J. (1993). Rocky's back again: A review of the WISC-III. *Journal of Psychoeducational Assessment* monograph series, *Advances in psychological assessment: Wechsler Intelligence Scale for Children—Third Edition* (pp. 161–164).

Thomson, B. (1991). *Comparison of the WISC-R and WISC-III.* Unpublished Masters Thesis. Trinity University, San Antonio, TX.

Vernon, P. E. (1950). *The structure of human abilities.* New York: Wiley.

Wechsler, D. (1950). Cognitive, conative, and non-intellective intelligence. *American Psychologist, 5,* 78–83.

Wechsler, D. (1971). Intelligence: Definition, theory, and the IQ. In R. Cancro (Ed.), *Intelligence: Genetic and environmental influences* (pp. 50–55). New York: Gruene and Stratton.

Wechlsler, D. (1974). *Manual for the Wechsler Intelligence Scale for Children-Revised.* San Antonio: The Psychological Corporation.

Wechsler, D. (1991). *Manual for the Wechsler Intelligence Scale for Children—Third Edition.* San Antonio: The Psychological Corporation.

Wechsler, D. (1992). *Manual for the Wechsler Intelligence Scale for Children—Third Edition U.K. Edition.* Sidcup, Kent: The Psychological Corporation.

Wechsler, D. (1995). *Manual Australian Supplement to the Wechsler Intelligence Scale for Children— Third Edition.* Sydney: The Psychological Corporation.

Wechsler, D. (1996). *Manual: Canadian Supplement to the Wechsler Intelligence Scale—Third Edition.* Toronto: The Psychological Corporation.

Wechsler, D. (1997). *Manual for the Wechsler Adult Intelligence Scale—Third Edition.* San Antonio: The Psychological Corporation.

Weiss, L. G., Prifitera, A. (1995). An evaluation of differential prediction of WIAT Achievement scores from WISC-III FSIQ across ethnic and gender groups. *Journal of School Psychology, 33,* 297–304.

Weiss, L.G., Prifitera, A., & Dersh, J. (1995). *Base rates of WISC-III verbal-performance discrepancies in Hispanic and African American children.* Unpublished manuscript.

Weiss, L. G. Prifitera, A., & Roid, G. H. (1993). The WISC-III and fairness of predicting achievement across ethnic and gender groups. *Journal of Psychoeducational Assessment,* monograph series, *Advances in psychological assessment: Wechsler Intelligence Scale for Children—Third Edition* (pp. 35–42).

Wielkiewicz, R. Z. (1990). Interpreting low scores on the WISC-R third factor: It's more than distractibility. *Psychological Assessment: A Journal of Consulting and Clinical Psychology, 2,* 91–97.

2

INTELLIGENCE TEST INTERPRETATION: ACTING IN THE ABSENCE OF EVIDENCE

RANDY W. KAMPHAUS

Department of Educational Psychology
The University of Georgia
Athens, Georgia

> *It is a good morning exercise for a research scientist to discard*
> *a pet hypothesis every day before breakfast.*
> —*Konrad Lorenz (1903–1989)* On Aggression

An early chapter[1] in an edited volume should prepare the reader for the remaining treatises. Of course, there are many routes that one may take to meet such an objective. This chapter is based on the overriding assumption that intelligence testing can be enhanced if psychologists function as scientifically based practitioners. The identification of science as the basis for WISC-III interpretation provides one framework for readers in subsequent chapters.

This chapter is based on four additional premises (or biases) that influence clinical interpretation of the WISC-III:

1. WISC-III interpretation should be based on scientific findings.
2. Many of the interpretations made by the practicing psychologist are not grounded in scientific research.
3. Many popular WISC-III interpretations lack scientific support.

[1]The title of this article is inspired by a quote from the book written by Louise Russell (p. 86, 1994). I also wish to express my appreciation to Ellen W. Rowe for her invaluable assistance with the literature review and, to A. Shayne Abelkop, Carolyn Imperato-McCammon, Martha Petoskey, Ellen W. Rowe, and Cheryl Hendry for their editorial feedback.

4. Strenuous and novel efforts must take place in order to ensure a closer relationship of science to practice.

SCIENCE AS FOUNDATION

Calls for a scientific approach to psychology practice, or at least a greater integration of practice and science are emanating from all quarters. Scientists are interested in developing standards of practice that reflect the best scientific knowledge available (Dawes, 1995). Clinicians are suggesting that clinical psychology has strayed too far from the Boulder model of the "scientist–practitioner" (Bush, 1997). The magnitude of the consensus may be such that practice standards (guidelines) for some areas of psychology practice are imminent (Clinton, McCormick, & Besteman, 1994). If these trends continue it may eventually be concluded that it took at least 50 years to implement the Boulder model.

The initial implementation of the scientist–practitioner model in clinical psychology training was uneven. Many of the large land grant universities tilted their curriculum toward an emphasis on scientific training to the exclusion of training for practice (Stricker, 1997). This trend proved unsatisfactory to many would-be practitioners, and some trainers, leading to the development of independent schools of psychology (Stricker, 1997). It is then predictable that these training programs would often emphasize practice to the exclusion of scientific training. Now an increasing number of articles are making attempts to reconcile these two approaches to training (Beutler & Davison, 1995). One of the forces leading the way toward reconciliation is the attempt by scientists to increase the likelihood that practice is based on empirical research (Dawes, 1995). There are, in addition, clinicians that are sympathetic to this movement. The scientist–practitioner model may be one important way of distinguishing the value of applied psychology from other health-care professions (Stricker, 1997). Stricker (1997) even supports the development of practice guidelines by saying, "The development of treatment guidelines is an ideal potential intersection between the contributions of science and the exigencies of clinical care" (p. 447).

There are many reasons to argue for some variant of the scientist–practitioner model as the ideal for intelligence test interpretation. Quality of care, the need to practice "defensive medicine," accountability for outcomes, and the desire to preserve the guild are a few reasons to ensure that intelligence test interpretation is grounded in rigor. These rationales are also interrelated. The logic is frequently offered, for example, that quality of care can only be provided by skilled providers necessitating preservation and enhancement of the guild.

One guild issue that has only recently received attention is the public perception of the profession. It could very well be that an improved public perception of psychology may be one way to further enhance a profession that can deliver high-quality care. One point of view is that psychologists have failed to educate the public about the state of scientific knowledge in psychology (Follette & Naugle, 1995). The lack of such communication from scientific psychology has left a void for others to fill. The psychologist impostors of all types have filled the bookstores with nonscientific treatises on human behavior (Follette & Naugle, 1995). Moreover, individual psychologists can affect the perception of the public by practicing in a colloquial versus scientific manner. Dawes (1995) apparently developed a very negative view of the profession due to the experiences of friends and colleagues who learned that their child custody decisions were based in part on Thematic Apperception Test (TAT) and Rorschach results. There appears to be an emerging consensus that much of current psychology practice is not based on the best available scientific findings.

PROTOTYPICAL PRACTICE

Practitioners who use the WISC-III have essentially three interpretive options: (a) to act in the absence of scientific evidence, (b) to act in opposition to scientific evidence, or (c) to act in accordance with the scientific evidence. Psychologists probably behave in a manner similar to medical and other professionals in that they often resort to their original training and interpret the WISC-III using approaches a and b.

Current intellectual assessment practice relies primarily on the theories and experiences of the practicum and internship supervisors and professors who train each new generation of practitioners. Unfortunately, some of the rules handed down to the new generation of professionals are questionable. In the case of diagnostic practice, Dawes (1995) concludes that

> we often make diagnoses consistent only with the numerator in the likelihood form of Bayes' theorem—thereby making what is technically termed a pseudo-diagnostic judgment as a result of evaluating only the degree to which evidence supports a particular hypothesis, rather than comparing that support to the degree to which the evidence supports alternative hypotheses as well. (p. 38)

ANALOGOUS PROBLEMS IN MEDICINE

Psychologists, however, should not single themselves out for punishment or self-recrimination for testing practices that are not clearly supported by science. Medical tests and testing practices are sometimes used in the absence of scientific support. In fact, some of our most publicized and prized medical screening procedures are plagued by ineffective tests that lead to dubious interventions (Russell, 1994).

One analysis of three popular medical screening practices concluded that while screening for cervical cancer results in significant savings in lives and suffering, prostate and cholesterol screening may have value for only a small number of individuals. Russell (1994) elucidates the problem of using prostate screening tests in order to trigger the delivery of preventive interventions (i.e., radical prostatectomy) with a research study involving 58 men in the United States and 58 in Sweden whose screening test results identified cancer. She noted at 10-year follow-up the morbidity rate of the two samples is virtually identical, in spite of dramatic differences in treatment approaches between the two countries. Consequently, the utility of prostate screening, which often triggers expensive and invasive surgery in the U.S., is questionable (Russell, 1994).

It is beyond the scope of this chapter to detail the flaws endemic to many of the most popular tests and screening regimens associated with medical testing. This example is merely offered to demonstrate that testing often occurs on the basis of common practice and good intentions rather than because of strong scientific evidence. Psychologists probably acquire their assessment knowledge in the same manner as other professionals, which may hinder the integration of science and practice. Professional psychologists likely depend heavily on the recommendations of "experts" such as their professors, valued colleagues, practicum, and internship supervisors. Their assessment practices are then altered, "correctly or incorrectly" (Russell, 1994), by subsequent clinical experiences.

Given this scenario it is a difficult task indeed for the "typical" psychologist to integrate science with the use of the WISC-III. Science-based practice is made more unlikely given that the state of WISC-III research may be unclear to trainers and practitioners alike. Specifically, the perceived scientific basis for some popular WISC-III interpretations may be at odds with empirical research findings.

WISC-III SCIENCE

There is a Milky Way of potential WISC-III interpretations; far too many to be considered in a single chapter. A chapter of this nature could focus on the Full Scale score, the Verbal and Performance scores, the four Index Scores, interpretations of profiles, or individual subtest interpretations, for example. In the interest of practicality, this chapter focuses exclusively on a few subtests and the third factor.

It is important to consider interpretations of the Wechsler subtests since they remain a popular unit of interpretation. It seems as if psychologists continue to presume that Wechsler subtests assess "specific capacities" (Lipsitz, Dworkin, & Erlenmeyer-Kimling, 1993). Only the Picture Arrangement subtest will be considered in some detail because of space limitations. Some validity evidence for the Picture Arrangement, Similarities, and Coding subtests, and the third factor is presented in Table 2.1.

The evaluation of scientific evidence presented in Table 2.1 must be interpreted with numerous cautions. For example, the data are evaluated against my assumptions, which may not be supported by other researchers. Moreover, the research accumulated may or may not be exhaustive, and some studies undoubtedly have been overlooked. A truly thorough review of the literature would require considerable time and expense. The conclusions drawn in Table 2.1 are merely intended as a starting point for a standard setting dialogue.

TABLE 2.1   Abilities Posited and Scientific Evidence Related to WISC-III Subtest and Third Factor Interpretation[a]

Subtest	Hypothesized abilities	Research evidence[b]
Similarities	Perception of simple verbal stimuli	None
	Verbal comprehension	Cohen (1959) (+), Kaufman (1975) (+), Carroll (1994) (+ or –) (Language Development), Blaha & Wallbrown (1996) (+ or –) (Verbal: Educational)
	Crystallized intelligence	Carroll (1994) (+)
	Fluid intelligence	Carroll (1994) ( )
	Cognition of semantic stimuli	None
	Verbal conceptualization	None
	Degree of abstract thinking	None
	Distinguishing essential from nonessential details	None
	Verbal reasoning	Carroll (1994) (–)
	Verbal concept formation	None
	Verbal expression	None
Picture Arrangement	Perceptual organization	Cohen (1959) (+), Kaufman (1975) (+), Carroll (1994) (+ or –) (Visualization), Blaha & Wallbrown (1996) (+ or –) (Spatial: Mechanical)
	Crystallized intelligence	Carroll (1994) (–)
	Fluid intelligence	Carroll (1994) (–)
	Integrated brain functioning	None
	Convergent production and evaluation of semantic stimuli	None
	Simultaneous processing	Kaufman & McLean (1987) (+)
	Planning	None
	Common sense	None
	Distinguishing essential from nonessential details	None
	Reasoning	Carroll (1994) (–)
	Social judgment	Lipsitz et al. (1993) (–)
	Speed of mental processing	Carroll (1994) (–)
	Synthesis	None
	Visual organization without essential motor activity	Carroll (1994) (+ or –) (Visualization)
Coding	Visual perception of abstract stimuli	None
	Auditory perception of complex verbal stimuli	None
	Perceptual organization	Cohen (1959) (+), Kaufman (1975) (+), Wechsler (1991) (–), Carroll (1994) (–), Blaha & Wallbrown (1996) (+ or –) (Spatial: Mechanical)
	Coding A – Convergent production and evaluation of figural stimuli	None
	Convergent production and evaluation of symbolic stimuli	None

(continues)

TABLE 2.1 (*continued*)

Subtest	Hypothesized abilities	Research evidence[b]
	Integrated brain functioning	None
	Sequential	Kaufman & McLean (1987) (−)
	Sequential processing	Kaufman & McLean (1987) (−)
	Encoding information for further cognitive processing	None
	Coding B—Facility with numbers	None
	Learning ability	None
	Reproduction of models	None
Third factor	Short-term acquisition and retrieval	None
	Number ability	Carroll (1994) (+)
	Sequential processing	Kaufman & McLean (1987) (−)
	Distractibility/attention span	Cohen (1959) (+), Kaufman (1975) (+), Wechsler (1991) (+), Carroll (1994) (−), Kamphaus et al. (1994) (−), Blaha & Wallbrown (1996) (+)

[a]The abilities posited for the WISC-III are adapted from the comprehensive treatise by Kaufman, 1994.

[b]Favorable (+) or unfavorable (−).

SUBTEST INTERPRETATION

Picture Arrangement

The Picture Arrangement (PA) subtest is unusual in that some research has been devoted to identifying the latent trait that is unique to PA. The preponderance of evidence suggests that performance on PA is determined by a single cognitive ability (see Table 2.1). The difficult issue is reaching consensus regarding a label for this ability. Several researchers have suggested that the PA subtest measures a construct requiring some type of visuospatial ability (Carroll, 1994; Cohen, 1959). The popular labels for this ability include perceptual organization, visualization, spatial:mechanical, and simultaneous processing. Furthermore, Carroll's (1994) reanalysis of some WISC-R data sets suggest that this subtest measures the same ability as a broad visualization factor. He goes on to say that PA cannot easily be categorized as either fluid or crystallized ability.

There has also been some research that identifies the abilities that are not assessed by PA. In particular, the theory that PA measures social judgment of some variety has been tested in at least four studies. The apparently robust finding is that this subtest does not measure social judgment.

In a detailed study of the relationship of the PA subtest to criterion measures of social adjustment, Lipsitz et al. (1993) drew the following conclusion:

> The absence of a positive association between performance on the Picture Arrangement subtest and either social adjustment measure is consistent with earlier negative findings in both clinical (Johnson, 1969) and normal (Krippner, 1964; Simon & Evans, 1980) samples.

Moreover, in this investigation, comparisons using Picture Arrangement scatter scores suggest that normal adolescents for whom the Picture subtest was a relative strength (positive Picture Arrangement scatter) in fact had greater deficits in social adjustment. Brannigan (1975) has observed that even if Picture Arrangement performance does reflect sensitivity in the social environment, this is not synonymous with positive social adjustment or competence. (p. 435)

There remain many untested hypotheses regarding the central ability assessed by PA (see Table 2.1). Some of these hypotheses include integrated brain functioning, convergent production and evaluation of semantic stimuli, planning, common sense, distinguishing essential from nonessential details, and synthesis. Some of these hypotheses could be subsumed under the general PA ability of visualization (e.g., synthesis, distinguishing essential from nonessential details). Until proven otherwise, the semantic aspects of this task are secondary or of minimal importance in the determination of PA factor loadings. Moreover, tasks of the PA variety are not identified as markers of reasoning ability or speed of mental processing in the numerous factor studies conducted by Carroll (1993).

The difficult task remains to describe the central ability that is measured by PA and, perhaps, the Perceptual Organization Index (POI) score. One definition that may be of value to the practitioner was offered by Carroll (1993). He observed that

in all these tests having salient loadings on factor VZ, it seems that the subject's task is to apprehend a spatial form, shape, or scene in order to match it with another spatial form, shape or scene, often with the necessity of rotating it in two or three dimensions one or more times. (p. 324).

This description of the ability that is primarily responsible for determining PA scores is presented with one caution: PA is not one of the strongest measures of the perceptual organization factor (Kamphaus, 1993).

The current body of PA evidence could be used to draw two implications for WISC-III scientist–practitioners: (a) interpretation of a PA score as a measure of some variation of visualization and spatial ability constitutes a case of interpretation that is supported by some scientific evidence, whereas (b) making an inference regarding social adjustment and judgment based on PA scores is contraindicated by research. A similar approach to the evaluation of WISC-III interpretive research could be conducted for the full range of potential interpretations, with the overriding goal of providing the practitioner with a usable summary of the research evidence.

Other Tests and Factors

The current review of the research cited in Table 2.1 leads to the conclusion that the Wechsler tests may measure fewer constructs than are typically suggested in most textbooks that are used to train practitioners. An essential conclusion to make, however, is that most of the presumed abilities that are offered for WISC-III interpretation are just that: Presumptions that are not supported by a preponderance of scientific evidence. The number of untested hypothesized abilities is far larger than the list of tested ones. The parsimonious conclusion to draw from a review of studies of subtest abilities is that the scientific evidence for WISC-III interpretation rests solely on factory analytic evidence, thus increasing the probability that making subtest interpretations constitutes a case of acting *in the absence of evidence.*

Some Wechsler subtests, however, are more frequently studied. There are a few studies, for example, of the information processing components of the Block Design task (e.g., Royer, 1984; Schorr, Bower, & Kiernan, 1982). This series of studies, however, has not led to agreement regarding the central processes that are assessed by the Block Design task, but to the development of new stimuli that better isolate cognitive processes (Royer, 1984).

The Digit Span subtest has also generated much research. The results of this research, however, have not clarified the nature of the underlying ability being assessed. A central impediment to the understanding of Digit Span performance is the finding that the forward and backward spans measure different traits (Reynolds, in press).

Some research is not included in Table 2.1 because it does not purport to identify the latent trait assessed by a subtest, although its findings could have implications for understanding the trait. A study of Similarities subtest errors by Hall and LaDriere (1969) is such an example. These researchers rescored Similarities errors according to several criteria. For example, they scored errors in categories such as "inadequate conceptual," and "narrative and descriptive." They found that children identified as "emotionally disturbed" were significantly more likely to obtain inadequate conceptual errors than children diagnosed as "organic" (Hall & LaDriere, 1969). An unknown amount of research of this type is not summarized by major WISC-III textbook authors, as a result, it is less likely to be used by modern psychologists.

Another example of a study not included in Table 1 was conducted by Whitehouse (1983). This study concludes that low Coding subtest scores are likely not due to memory but, rather, processing speed problems. Again, it is noteworthy that we are appealing to factor analytic results (which led to the construction of the Processing Speed Index score) to explain the central ability assessed by a subtest.

A review of Table 2.1 leaves the reader with the impression that many interpretations of the WISC are either untested by science or unsupported by scientific findings. This state of affairs is inconsistent with a scientist–practitioner approach to psychology practice. Moreover, practice that is not congruent with science may place our clients in unnecessary peril or, at the very least, expose them to substandard practices.

MODERN INTERPRETIVE PRACTICE

There are identifiable trends in test interpretation practice (Kamphaus, Petoskey, & Morgan, 1997). During the early part of the 1900s psychologists emphasized quantification of a general intellectual level. After World War II and the publication of the first of the Wechsler scales, interpretive practice became dominated by profile analysis. In addition, specific profiles and subtest results were linked to diagnosis. A relative strength on the Object Assembly test, for example, was specifically linked to the diagnosis of "simple schizophrenia" (Kamphaus et al., 1997). Profile analysis changed in the 1970s due to the ready availability of factor analysis. Many factor analyses yielded the familiar WISC-R three factors, which served as alternatives to interpreting clinically derived subtest profiles or the overall IQ's. This psychometric approach to intelligence test interpretation was accompanied by an emphasis on using numerous calculations to identify significant profiles and factors.

The current wave of intelligence test interpretation identifies theory as central to interpretation. The works of John Carroll (three stratum theory) and John Horn (g fluid/g crystallized theory) are noteworthy examples of an emphasis on theoretical approaches to deriving score meaning.

I have attempted to develop an interpretive approach that incorporates both theory and research findings (Kamphaus, 1993). The essential elements of this method are a priori and a posteriori hypothesis generation and testing. Psychologists are advised to begin the interpretation of scores in the early stages of the assessment process. Theory and research-based hypotheses may be stated at any time prior to the calculation of scores. A priori hypotheses of this nature are likely to be based on theory and research since the child's results are not yet available. The psychologist then systematically tests each a priori hypothesis against the data much in the same way that confirmatory factor analysis is conducted.

A posteriori hypotheses are offered upon review of the obtained scores and a search is made for supportive evidence. Therefore, a posteriori hypotheses are an analog to exploratory factor analysis that is less dependent on explicit prediction of outcomes based on theory.

This interpretive method has some apparent value in that it does try to force a link between research, theory, and test interpretation. The technique, however, still does not satisfy Dawes's (1995) criticism that psychologists often do not consider plausible competing hypotheses. Clearly, much progress on interpretive methods needs to be made. One impediment to such progress is the lack of availability of a systematic summary of WISC scientific findings.

PRACTICE STANDARDS

Although mounds of intelligence test validation research exists, there are few, if any, publications devoted to a thorough examination of the relationship between science and test interpretation practice. Numerous individual studies assess some aspect of test validity, but a comprehensive compendium of the relationship of these findings to practice is not yet available. Although most of the popular texts

(Kamphaus, 1993; Kaufman, 1994) and others, summarize considerable validity evidence, they do not devote adequate attention to tabulating the scientific support for individual WISC-III interpretations. All of these texts, for example, suggest numerous potential interpretations for Wechsler subtests and factors. Some of these interpretations appear to be either untested or unsupported by available scientific evidence when that evidence is critically evaluated from a practice standards framework. Specifically, most texts have suggested that the WISC-III third factor could be interpreted as a measure of distractibility or inattentiveness if such behaviors are observed during the test session. Although this conclusion seems eminently reasonable at first consideration, it is not overwhelmingly supported by the research and, in fact, there is considerable evidence that contraindicates such a conclusion (see Table 2.1).

There are potential solutions to the problem of the lack of match between science and practice. The recent movement toward the development of practice standards suggests the possibility of a framework for evaluating the adequacy of intelligence test interpretive evidence. A practice standards approach to guiding WISC-III interpretation differs from the "expert" model that depends on the wisdom of a single textbook author or author team. Practice standards are typically based on the collective wisdom of practitioners, scientists, and consumers alike. These individuals bring a variety of viewpoints, biases, and expertise to the standard setting process. This process, however, is arduous and expensive; both of these issues have probably inhibited the development of standards to date.

Practice standards can be defined in several ways. Dawes (1995), for example, identifies two types: Hortatory and minatory. A hortatory standard states a standard in the positive direction. That is, psychologists must or should follow the prescriptions outlined in the ethics code of the American Psychological Association. Minatory standards, on the other hand, proscribe or prohibit inferior practices. Dawes (1995) suggests that the Ten Commandments may serve as an example of minatory standards. Some of the *Standards for Educational and Psychological Testing* (APA, 1985) are primarily hortatory standards. Standard 5.1, for example, states that, "a technical manual should be made available to prospective users at the time a test is published or released for operational use" (p. 35). Regardless of the type of standards employed, all those suggested for psychology practice assert that standards should be based in science (Beutler & Davison, 1995).

PRECURSORS TO PRACTICE STANDARDS

Perhaps the work of Oscar Buros represents the earliest significant approximation of the development of practice standards for testing. His efforts to systematically evaluate the psychometric properties of newly published tests were ground breaking. As a result of his work, Buros clearly recognized that scientific research was typically not the determinant of test selection. In 1961, he lamented:

> When we initiated critical test reviewing (1938) we had no idea how difficult it would be to discourage the use of poorly constructed tests of unknown validity. . . . Counselors, per-

sonnel directors, psychologists, and school administrators seem to have an unshakable will to believe the exaggerated claims of test authors and publishers. (Buros, 1961, p. xxix)

In this partial quote, Buros reveals some of the rationale for the development of his Mental Measurements Yearbooks. He was attempting to interject psychometric science as a consideration in test selection and use.

The *Standards for Educational and Psychological Testing* (APA, 1985) represent another attempt to imbue assessment practice with science. The Test Standards (which, at the time of this writing, are currently nearing the final stages of revision) provide guidelines, primarily for test authors and publishers, for manual preparation and procedures for conducting prepublication research. Specifically, one of the Test Standards asserts that, "evidence of validity should be presented for the major types of interpretations for which a test is recommenced" (p. 13).

One could argue, however, that WISC-III interpretation is not an appropriate topic to discuss in the context of practice standards. The WISC-III is by most "standards" one of the most well-researched psychological tests. The counterargument is that the quantity of research on a test is not necessarily highly correlated with the extent of its validity evidence. For example, drawing techniques have benefited from almost a century of research. They have been shown to be clearly inferior screening measures of intelligence, yet they are still widely used (Kamphaus & Pleiss, 1991; Saklofske & Braun, 1992).

MODERN PRACTICE STANDARDS

The creation of scientifically based practice guidelines in the United States began with the establishment of the Agency for Health Care Policy and Research (AHCPR) in 1989 (Clinton, McCormick, & Besteman, 1994). In the mental health arena, the guidelines for the treatment of depression in primary care have received the most attention. Practice guidelines were developed due primarily to the finding that there were wide variations in medical patient care. Specifically, "When faced with contradictory reports in the health care literature, clinicians generally rely on their own professional judgment or the judgment of their peers when making practice decisions" (Clinton et al., 1994, p. 30). Similarly, it is reasonable to conclude that there are many variations in psychologists' use of the WISC-III.

The AHCPR has established an effective process for developing practice guidelines. These guidelines could be emulated by the field of psychology. The attributes of the guidelines may be summarized as follows (adapted and paraphrased from Clinton et al., 1994). The *Validity* criterion is met if the guidelines, when followed correctly, lead to better outcomes. Evidence of validity considers the quality of scientific support, the method of evaluation of the evidence, and the congruence of the evidence and practice guidelines. The validity criterion may depend on considerable consensus building because numerous professional groups, including consumers, participate in the deliberations. *Reliability–reproducibility* refers to two principles: (a) the guidelines are applied and interpreted consistently by practitioners who are faced with similar clinical circumstances, and (b) a second group of professionals would develop similar guidelines if provided with the same procedures for developing guidelines and the same scientific evidence. *Clinical applicability* refers to the premise that practice guidelines should review all evidence available for clinical populations and clearly identify the populations to whom the guidelines are applicable. The principle of *Clinical flexibility* requires that guidelines identify the exceptions to the use of the recommended treatment guidelines. Practice guidelines must also be characterized by *Clarity* in that they must be presented in a manner that can be easily followed by practitioners. A variety of provider groups are represented in the guideline development process by making recommendations, reviewing guideline drafts, and providing evidence resulting in a *Multidisciplinary process*. An ongoing committee is designed to periodically review new research and practice trends in order to conduct a *Scheduled review* of existing guidelines. This review may result in a revision of practice guidelines being released every 18 to 36 months. The *documentation* of the guideline development process must be comprehensive and detailed, including descriptions of procedures, premises, rationales, and participants, among other issues.

The efforts to develop standards for psychological practice are still in their early stages (e.g., The APA Task Force on Promotion and Dissemination of Psychological Procedures of 1993, as cited in Beutler & Davison, 1995). According to the APA report, an effective treatment is one that is supported by at least two studies of groups of individuals, by different researchers, that demonstrate the effectiveness of the intervention (The APA Task Force on Promotion and Dissemination of Psychological Procedures of 1993, as cited in Beutler & Davison, 1995).

The standards-setting process, however, is fraught with problems. Even a standard such as replicability is likely to be difficult to apply to the evaluation of assessment procedures. As Beutler and Davison (1995) note, there are many details regarding the acceptance of this standard that require elucidation and consensus building on the part of a standard setting group. Psychologists would have to operationally define a successful replication and determine an adequate balance of positive and negative findings. In the case of the WISC-III Distractibility Factor, for example, the relationship of studies that find significant group differences for ADHD samples and those that do not would have to be identified. Would the distractibility factor be validated for use in ADHD diagnosis if six studies were supportive and four studies produced negative findings?

Similarly, Beutler and Davison (1995) point out that it may be difficult to define the sufficient number of replications necessary for a test to meet standards. The field would have to determine if 2, 3, or 12 supportive studies were needed to determine that the Distractibility Factor was valid for use as part of the ADHD diagnostic process. If, however, the criterion of replicability was adopted by a standards-setting group, then certain tests and interpretations are more likely to be accepted than others because their replicability is more easily assessed (Beutler & Davison, 1995). In other words, "This approach to validity favors approaches based on the simplest models, applied to the least complex problems, and that embody the most concrete outcomes" (Beutler & Davison, 1995).

Any attempt to compare the WISC-III and its associated interpretations to practice standards will generate as many questions as answers. The effort to critically evaluate the WISC-III interpretation research, however, must be made regardless of the shortcomings of the process. The construction of Table 1 represented an initial minimal step in the direction of producing practice standards.

METHODOLOGICAL CONSIDERATIONS

Any method to tabulate and evaluate WISC research evidence will have to consider numerous methodological issues. These issues likely do not benefit from consensual support at the time of this writing. Even without consensus the issues need to be elucidated for public scrutiny and debate by practitioners and scientists alike.

Study Selection

Any standards-setting approach to WISC-III interpretation must consider criteria for inclusion of research studies. The majority of studies aimed at identifying the latent traits underlying WISC-III scores and profiles are typically factor analytic. Therefore, criteria for identifying technically adequate factor analyses should be addressed. Some of the initial questions to consider in evaluating factor analytic studies are as follows:

1. *Sample size.* Should a minimally adequate sample include 100, 200, 500, or 1000 cases per group? Relatedly, what is the minimal sample size for an individual age group? I chose primarily large, national standardization samples in the partial review of evidence cited earlier.

2. *Sample composition.* Are exceptional samples alone appropriate or should a nationally representative sample be preferred?

3. *Differing interpretations of the same results.* How should such interpretations be reconciled? In his landmark factor analytic study, Carroll (1994) finds that Vocabulary, Information, Comprehension, and Similarities load on the same factor. Rather than the traditional label of verbal comprehension (Cohen, 1959), however, he places the WISC-III in the larger context of the study of human abilities and refers to this factor as language development (LD).

4. *Differing results given the same interpretations.* On the one hand, Cohen (1959) labels the third WISC factor as Freedom from Distractibility; he characterizes it so, "primarily due to the loadings of subtests which clearly do not involve memory (Mazes, Picture Arrangement, Object Assembly), but which it seems reasonable to suppose are quite vulnerable to the effects of distractibility" (p. 288). On the other hand, Blaha and Wallbrown (1996) assign the same label as Cohen to the third factor with significant loadings only for the Arithmetic and Digit Span subtests.

5. *Types of evidence.* There is not a clear consensus on the issue of weighting evidence differentially. Although it may seem that factor analytic studies have been reified to a special status in the evaluation of intelligence test validity, other

forms of validity may be equally if not more important depending on the issue under study. If, for example, the research question deals with the issue of using an intelligence test for differential diagnosis then research on various diagnostic groups would be weighted heavily.

6. *The preponderance of evidence.* There are numerous factor analytic studies that support the label of the third factor as Freedom from Distractibility. Yet, the opinions of a factor analyst, such as John Carroll (1993), who has produced one of the most impressive summaries of factor analytic studies of intelligence, may be difficult to dismiss. For example, Carroll (1994) asserts that "the WISC-III was not designed for factor analysis because the various factors that it may measure—at least beyond the Verbal and Performance factors—are not represented adequately by the multiple measures of those factors" (p. 138). Clearly, numerous questions emerge and remain with this type of discussion. For example, how should the factor labels assigned by various researchers be weighted in the decision-making process used to evaluate validity evidence? Also, what is an acceptable ratio of positive to negative findings?

7. *Exploratory versus confirmatory methods.* Generally speaking, confirmatory factor analytic methods have gained considerable popularity over exploratory methods in modern factor analysis. Confirmatory methods may also result in stricter tests of the WISC-III factor structure (Kamphaus, Benson, Hutchinson, & Platt, 1994). Should such methods be preferred over traditional factor analysis or devalued?

8. *Myopic research evidence.* Can WISC-III interpretations really be understood by reading only the WISC research literature? Are factor analyses of the WISC-III inherently likely to produce noncontributory results because of the nature of the scale (Carroll, 1994)? A standards-setting committee should undoubtedly review research on the broadly defined construct of intelligence, and other relevant topics in order to evaluate the adequacy of WISC-III interpretations. How do we define the universe of relevant research?

9. *Lack of evidence.* What should standards conclude when empirical evidence is not present? It is conceivable that some of the interpretations could be found valid if they are researched. If unresearched interpretations are deemed inappropriate by practice standards, then research regarding these interpretations could be stifled. Clearly, psychology is no different from medicine and other professions where professionals have to take action or make nonscientifically based interpretations in unusual cases and circumstances. The standards-setting process should not be allowed to limit experimentation. Standards perhaps also could be developed for using untested interpretations.

10. *Theoretical evidence.* Some WISC-III interpretations may be untested, and yet they may be based on a theory that has some empirical support. There is, for example, some research to support the sequential–simultaneous model of the Kaufman Assessment Battery for Children (K-ABC) (Kaufman & McClean, 1987). This model has not been used to test the validity of some WISC-III interpretations, although it has been utilized on a limited basis to investigate the rela-

tionship of WISC-R subtests to the model (Kaufman & McClean, 1987). Is a theoretically based interpretation of the WISC-III adequate to support use?

11. *Incorporating new evidence.* Obviously, any standards-setting process will be outdated on its date of publication. Some mechanism for ongoing review of evidence and updating of the standards is central to their proper use. How does one disseminate test interpretation standards when psychology does not have an official body, to oversee this function such as the U.S. Food and Drug Administration?

12. *Applicability of research from previous editions.* Should WISC-R research be utilized to support WISC-III interpretation? The addition of the Symbol Search subtest may make factor analytic evidence for the WISC R irrelevant to the WISC-III.

13. *Definition of terms.* Much of the WISC research is characterized by similar-sounding terms that are offered without operational definitions. For instance, are the terms Spatial: Mechanical, Visualization, Perceptual Organization, and Spatial Organization without Essential Motor Activity, interchangeable? What is the definition of *integrated brain functioning* and implications for interpretation? Such terms make interpretation of intelligence test results unduly confusing for many psychologists, particularly those in training. At the same time, psychologists usually have agreed upon informal definitions for interpreting scales of anxiety, reading, social skills, short-term memory, and other constructs. It could be that intelligence test subtests and scales measure more than one latent trait. In turn, this finding could be interpreted to mean that the tests are poorly constructed.

CONCLUSIONS AND RECOMMENDATIONS

The scientific support for individual subtest interpretation is not well documented (Kamphaus, 1993). In fact, it appears that the secrets of understanding the latent traits that are measured by the subtests reside in the four factors of the WISC-III. The scientific evidence associated with the four factors is voluminous and often supportive, making the lack of evidence for individual subtest interpretations even more disturbing. Although it is our duty to ensure that interpretation is individualized, we must also keep in mind that making subtest interpretations can constitute a case of *acting in the absence of or in opposition to evidence.*

Although it is permissible and necessary to sometimes act in the absence of evidence, or in opposition to it, we must know when we are doing so. Many of our consumers are sophisticated, and they can understand our approach to interpretation. We need merely to inform them of the interpretive option that we have selected. By doing so, we are at least recognizing the role of science in our practice and guiding our clients honestly. In the process, we are also engaging in a cognitive problem-solving effort. This exercise will invariably compel us to return to the search for evidence to support or refute our interpretations. In addition, the search for scientific support can and should be enhanced by organized psychology's efforts to review and disseminate the state of the scientific evidence on a regular basis.

This chapter represents only a minimal effort to tabulate the scientific evidence for a few of the myriad WISC-III interpretations. A systematic effort is needed in order ensure a fair appraisal of WISC-III research. The field of psychology needs an organizational body that is willing to take on the next step of setting standards for WISC-III interpretation. This group can use an approach such as the one outlined by AHCPR, and it must satisfactorily address the methodological questions offered earlier. Such a task is daunting but necessary for aligning practice with science.

The group that would be charged with reviewing the scientific evidence and setting the practice standards should be diverse. Clinicians from various subspecialties, applied and basic researchers, consumers, graduate students, governmental representatives, and others should be represented. A diverse group with broad-based expertise will ensure that all views are represented. Furthermore, the diverse representation will enhance the applicability of the resulting standards.

A standards-setting process of this type may or may not be realistic. The American Psychological Association has developed guidelines and standards before as exemplified by the case of the Test Standards and other panels. An entity or set of groups, such as a single psychological association or federation of groups, needs to be convinced to take the next step beyond the revision of the Test Standards.

It seems that any standards for intelligence test interpretation would have to be test specific. If I were charged with developing a WISC-III test interpretation standard for the PA subtest I would suggest the following as a starting point:

> A Picture Arrangement subtest score should not be interpreted
> as a measure of social judgment.

This conclusion is based on several studies that have not supported a particular PA interpretation. Obviously, this is a minatory standard. This example suggests that standard setting for the WISC-III would constitute an ambitious project. This example also highlights the fact that practice standards are ultimately strictures on WISC-III interpretive practice. Although the development of practice guidelines has been met with resistance (Stricker, 1997) the effort must continue. We may welcome such strictures provided that they approximate the goal of helping to ensure that we do not poorly serve our consumers.

It may be also said that psychological science is not yet adequate to guide the process of developing standards. One response to this criticism is offered by Dawes (1995) who observed the following:

> Yes. It is true that standards do not yield knowledge of exactly what to do—any more than principles of physics and aerodynamics yield knowledge of exactly how to construct airplanes for specific purposes. But aeronautical engineers do not construct airplanes following the common intuition that their wings should flap; they don't construct airplanes in ways that are inconsistent with principles of physics and aerodynamics. (p. 31).

Follette and Naugle (1995) suggest that it would be helpful to at least explicate the conflicting scientific findings for the public. If some WISC-III research findings are inconsistent, or a standards-setting panel cannot reach consensus, the opposing findings or positions can be summarized so that clinicians and consumers are at least aware of the extent to which science is valuable, or lacks value, for guiding their care.

There is probably a cascade of efforts that could be used to link research and practice. Some of the options may include the following:

1. Joint symposia by practitioners and measurement scientists at professional meetings that are aimed at defining the relationship of science to practice standards.

2. Intelligence testing textbooks that do a better job of documenting the scientific findings that support or refute WISC-III interpretations.

3. Comprehensive review articles or books that summarize the research associated with a set of WISC-III interpretations. In the case of competing findings the opposing points of view could be published simultaneously.

4. A task force summary of research that is sponsored by a single association.

5. Developing formal practice standards for intelligence test interpretation using committee guidelines that are commonly associated with medical practice standards. This most ambitious effort would require financial support from multiple organizations.

In the event that none of these suggested options come to pass I have one recommendation for psychology practitioners. I suggest incorporating the wisdom of Lorenz into everyday assessment practice. The practitioner psychologist can at least aspire to scientifically based practice by considering it a good morning exercise to discard a pet WISC-III test interpretation every day before breakfast.

REFERENCES

American Psychological Association (1985). *Standards for educational and psychological testing.* Washington, D.C.: Author.

Beutler, L. E., & Davison, E. H. (1995). What standards should we use? In S. C. Hayes, V. M. Follette, R. M. Dawes, & K. E. Grady (Eds.), *Scientific standards of psychological practice: Issues and recommendations* (pp. 11–24). Reno, NV: Context Press.

Beutler, L. E., Williams, R. E., Wakefield, P. J., & Entwistle, S. R. (1995). Bridging scientist and practitioner perspectives in clinical psychology. *American Psychologist, 50,* 984–994.

Blaha, J., & Wallbrown, F. H. (1996). Hierarchical factor structure of the Wechsler Intelligence Scale for Children—III. *Psychological Assessment, 8,* 214–218.

Buros, O. K. (1961). *Tests in print: A comprehensive bibliography of tests for use in education, psychology, and industry.* Highland Park, NJ: Gryphon Press.

Brannigan, G. G. (1975). Wechsler Picture Arrangement and Comprehension scores as measures of social maturity. *Journal of Psychology, 89,* 133–135.

Bush, J. W. (1997). It's time we stuck up for the Boulder model. *American Psychologist, 52,* 181.

Carroll, J. B. (1994). What abilities are measured by the WISC-III? *Journal of Psychoeducational Assessment, Monograph,* 134–143.

Carroll, J. B. (1993). *Human cognitive abilities: A survey of factor analytic studies.* New York: Cambridge University Press.

Clinton, J. J., McCormick, K., & Besteman, J. (1994). Enhancing clinical practice: The role of practice guidelines. *American Psychologist, 49,* 30–33.

Cohen, J. (1959). The factorial structure of the WISC at ages 7–6, 10–6, and 13–6. *Journal of Consulting Psychology, 23,* 285–299.

Dawes, R. M. (1995). Standards of practice. In S. C. Hayes, V. M. Follette, R. M. Dawes, & K. E. Grady (Eds.), *Scientific standards of psychological practice: Issues and recommendations* (pp. 31–43). Reno, NV: Context Press.

Follette, V. M., & Naugle, A. E. (1995). Discussion of Beutler and Davidson: Psychology's failure to educate. In S. C. Hayes, V. M. Follette, R. M. Dawes, & K. E. Grady (Eds.), *Scientific standards of psychological practice: Issues and recommendations* (pp. 25–30). Reno, NV: Context Press.

Hall, L. P., & LaDriere, L. (1969). Patterns of performance on WISC Similarities in emotionally disturbed and brain-damaged children. *Journal of Consulting and Clinical Psychology, 33,* 357–364.

Herrnstein, R. J., & Murray, C. (1994). *The bell curve: Intelligence and class structure in American life.* New York: Free Press.

Johnson, D. T. (1969). Introversion, extroversion, and social intelligence: A replication. *Journal of Clinical Psychology, 25,* 181–183.

Kamphaus, *Clinical assessment of children's intelligence.* Needham Heights, MA: Allyn & Bacon.

Kamphaus, R. W. (1993). *Clinical assessment of children's intelligence.* Needham Heights, MA: Allyn & Bacon.

Kamphaus, R. W., Benson, J., Hutchinson, S., & Platt, L. O. (1994). Identification of factor models for the WISC-III. *Educational and Psychological Measurement, 54,* 174–186.

Kamphaus, R. W., Petoskey, M. D., & Morgan, A. W. (1997). A history of intelligence test interpretation. In D. P. Flanagan, J. L. Genshaft, and P. L. Harrison (Eds.), *Contemporary intelligence assessment: Theories, tests, and issues* (pp. 32–47). New York: The Guilford Press.

Kamphaus, R. W., & Pleiss, K. (1991). Draw-a-person techniques: Tests in search of a construct. *Journal of School Psychology, 29,* 395–401.

Kaufman, A. S. (1994). *Intelligent testing with the WISC-III.* New York: Wiley.

Kaufman, A. S. (1975). Factor analysis of the WISC-R at 11 age levels between 6½ and 16½ years. *Journal of Consulting and Clinical Psychology, 43,* 135–147.

Kaufman, A. S., & McLean, J. E. (1987). Joint factor analysis of the K-ABC and WISC-R with normal children. *Journal of School Psychology, 25,* 105–118.

Keith, T. Z. (1994). Intelligence is important, intelligence is complex. *School Psychology Quarterly, 9,* 209–221.

Krippner, S. (1964). WISC Comprehension and Picture Arrangement subtests as measures of social competence. *Journal of Clinical Psychology, 20,* 366–367.

Lipsitz, J. D., Dworkin, R. H., & Erlenmeyer-Kimling, L. (1993). Wechsler Comprehension and Picture Arrangement subtests and social adjustment. *Psychological Assessment, 5,* 430–437.

Reynolds, C. R. (in press). Forward and backward memory span should not be combined for clinical analysis. *Archives of Clinical Neuropsychology, 12.*

Royer, F. L. (1984). Stimulus variables in the Block Design task: A commentary on Schorr, Bower, and Kiernan. *Journal of Consulting and Clinical Psychology, 52,* 700–704.

Russell, L. B. (1994). *Educated guesses: Making policy about medical screening tests.* Berkeley, CA: University of California Press.

Saklofske, D. H., & Braun, S. M. (1992). A psychometric study of the Draw-A-Person: A Quantitative Scoring System. *Canadian Journal of School Psychology, 8,* 111–115.

Schorr, D., Bower, G. H., & Kiernan, R. (1982). Stimulus variables in the Block Design task. *Journal of Consulting and Clinical Psychology, 50,* 479–487.

Simon, J. M., & Evans, J. R. (1980). WISC-R Picture Arrangement and peer acceptance/rejection. *Perceptual and Motor Skills, 51,* 588.

Stricker, G. (1997). Are science and practice commensurable? *American Psychologist, 52,* 442–448.

Wechsler, D. (1991). *Manual, WISC-III: Wechsler Intelligence Scale for Children—Third Edition.* San Antonio, TX: The Psychological Corporation.

Whitehouse, C. C. (1983). Analysis of WISC-R Coding performance of normal and dyslexic readers. *Perceptual and Motor Skills, 57,* 951–960.

3

ASSESSMENT OF GIFTED CHILDREN WITH THE WISC-III

SARA S. SPARROW AND SUZANNE T. GURLAND

Child Study Center
Yale University
New Haven, Connecticut

INTRODUCTION

Ever since Terman published his seminal work on gifted children in 1925 (Terman, 1925), educators and parents have sought to better understand, provide for, and identify gifted children. Such identification has been undertaken in the interest of providing for the educational needs of these special children and adolescents.

This chapter addresses the assessment of gifted children using the WISC-III. The WISC-III is probably the most widely used instrument for this purpose, in part because it is the most widely used intelligence test in schools in the United States today, and because most school systems usually view the gifted child or adolescent as gifted either intellectually, academically, or both. While other intelligence tests, such as the Stanford Binet Intelligence Scale LM, and later the Stanford Binet—IV, have frequently been used in the past, Klausmeier, Mishra, and Maker (1987) conducted a national survey of assessment practices among school psychologists, and found that the Wechsler scales had become the overwhelming first choice for the assessment of gifted children.

DEFINITION OF GIFTEDNESS

Gifted children represent a special subset of the population of children at large, and as such, require attention to their particular social, emotional, and educational needs. However, as with any special subset of the population, the first challenge is to define the membership of the group. What do we mean by "gifted children"? Clearly, to say that a child is a gifted musician means he has extraordinary natural ability in music. A child who is a gifted athlete has superb natural ability in sports. And to say that particular children are gifted mathematicians means they have superior mathematical reasoning skills. First, how competent does a child have to be in athletics, math, or art to be classified as gifted? What are the criteria? Second, to say simply that a child "is gifted," begs the question, "Gifted at what?"

According to the U.S. Office of Education, under Public Law 91-230, section 806 (Marland, 1972), gifted and talented children are those who have high-performance capability in one or more of the following areas: (a) Intellectual Ability, (b) Creative and Productive Thinking, (c) Leadership Ability, (d) Visual and Performing Arts, (e) Specific Ability Areas, (f) Psychomotor Ability. Later, Public Law 95-561 removed Psychomotor Ability as one of the areas of giftedness, retaining the original five areas (Marland, 1972). Although federal law defines giftedness, special educational services for gifted children are not federally mandated. Furthermore, individual states are not bound to the federal definition, but rather are free to develop their own mandates and definitions regarding gifted children. Despite the variability from state to state in definitions of giftedness, the challenge to psychologists and educators in every state is to identify those children who satisfy the local criteria for giftedness.

Accurately identifying gifted children, however, is easier said than done. Of the five federally identified areas of giftedness, intellectual ability alone has a long-standing history of assessment by psychometrically sound measures. The remaining four areas simply have not been as rigorously explored. For example, while Sternberg and Lubart (1996) advocate the importance of further study of creativity, they concede that "the definition and criteria for creativity are a matter of ongoing debate" (p. 681), and note that the measures that have been developed to assess creativity are brief paper-and-pencil tests that have been "criticized . . . as trivial, inadequate measures of creativity" (p. 681). But does our current lack of psychometrically sound instruments for measuring children's artistic, musical, creative, and other talents mean that we cannot reliably identify gifted children?

The identification and assessment of gifted children is done largely in the interest of providing them with appropriate educational placement and planning, and our educational institutions are charged primarily with developing children's academic achievement and development, not their artistic, musical, or creative development. Therefore, for the practical purposes of educational placement and planning, giftedness is best regarded as academic giftedness, which, within certain limitations, we can measure reliably. Furthermore, intelligence tests are currently the best predictor of academic achievement. In thinking about gifted children, then, we may theoretically conceptualize giftedness broadly so as to include children with a variety of intellectual, creative, and artistic gifts and talents. However, for the remainder of this chapter, with an eye toward the practical purposes of educational planning and placement, "giftedness" will refer to intellectual giftedness as measured by such instruments as the WISC-III. It is our view that intellectual giftedness is a necessary component for the classification of gifted individuals in schools.

REVIEW OF THE LITERATURE

Paralleling the ongoing debate regarding the definition of giftedness, the literature evidences an analogous debate over the use of intelligence tests to identify gifted children. Tyerman (1986) argues that the cultural bias of intelligence tests unfairly places gifted children of "deprived or immigrant background[s]" at a disadvantage, even when conventional methods for reducing cultural bias are employed. He advocates instead the use of ability tests such as Raven's Progressive Matrices and Kohs' Block Design Test.

Others do not oppose the use of intelligence tests for the identification of gifted children, but caution against the misapplication or misinterpretation of IQ scores. Harrington (1982), for example, cites a host of dangers in intelligence testing with gifted children. He points out that gifted children's IQ scores can be depressed by ceiling effects, the use of a recently revised test, or cultural bias. In addition, the use of arbitrary "cutoff scores" and the instability of IQ scores among preschool children can lead to misidentification of gifted children. Furthermore, intelligence tests can penalize gifted children by rewarding convergent-type responses, but granting no credit for divergent-type responses.

Like Harrington, Sternberg (1982) identifies widely used, but not necessarily sound practices in intelligence testing. Namely, he questions the premise that speed is an indication of intelligence; the claim that intelligence tests measure only intelligence, and not achievement; the practice of administering intelligence tests in anxiety-provoking or stressful environments; and, the tendency to treat a precise score as a necessarily valid score.

Still other psychologists and educators acknowledge the limitations of intelligence tests, but stress their value, when used properly, as a clinical tool for evaluating a child's intellectual abilities and as a predictor of future educational achievement. Robinson and Chamrad (1986), for example, take note of the valuable information yielded by intelligence tests, such as a child's scores, mental age estimates, predictions regarding the child's future academic achievement, and clinical observations made during the testing session. At the same time, they acknowledge that intelligence tests are not perfect and will not result in 100% accurate identification of gifted children, and that intelligence tests measure only intelligence, and not other worthwhile characteristics of a child, such as creativity and musical or artistic talents.

Kaufman and Harrison (1986), too, acknowledge the limitations of intelligence tests, but argue convincingly in favor of their use for identifying gifted children.

Intelligence tests, they argue, are very good predictors of academic achievement and academic success, and they have the most solid psychometric properties of all other kinds of tests used with gifted individuals. In addition, they point out that intelligence tests can identify as gifted, children who might otherwise go undetected because of behavior problems, learning disabilities, physical handicaps, or other attention-demanding characteristics that might cause educators or other professionals to overlook the child's intellectual abilities.

Kaufman and Harrison (1986) also caution psychologists and educators to use intelligence tests responsibly. In particular, they cite the importance of using multiple criteria, not a single intelligence test score, in determining eligibility for gifted programs, and they stress that standard errors of measurement should always be taken into account. Further, they caution against making placement decisions in the absence of educational planning. That is, a child who is identified as gifted may be placed in a gifted program, but this placement should be made in the context of longer term educational planning for that child.

Despite the numerous cautions against misuse of, or overreliance on, intelligence tests for identification of gifted children, Kaufman and Harrison's (1986) point is well taken that there currently exists no method that has been demonstrated to be superior to intelligence tests for this purpose. Within the realm of intelligence tests, however, are some instruments better than others for identifying gifted children? How useful is the WISC-III for gifted children?

Sevier, Bain, and Hildman (1994) investigated the relationship between the WISC-R and the WISC-III with gifted children by administering the WISC-III to 35 elementary school students in a gifted program who had previously been administered the WISC-R. They found the WISC-III global scores to be significantly lower than the WISC-R scores, such that 14 children (or 40%) in their sample would not have been placed in the local gifted program if the WISC-III had been used to determine eligibility. Sabatino, Spangler, and Vance (1995) conducted a similar investigation, but did it more robustly by using a counterbalanced design. They administered both tests, in a counterbalanced design, to 51 gifted children. They found very high agreement between the two tests, such that all 51 of their subjects who were found eligible for a gifted program with one test, also would have been found eligible had the other test been used.

Without comparing it to other tests, Kaufman (1992) evaluated the psychometric strength of the WISC-III for gifted children. He found that the WISC-III places unduly high emphasis on the speed of a child's performance, and that low subtest stability can complicate an educator's or psychologist's efforts to interpret children's profiles. Overall, however, he states that the WISC-III is quite useful for gifted children in that it is a "carefully constructed, technically superior instrument[], with attractive materials, sensitive items (by gender and ethnicity), exceptional standardization[s], strong construct validity, reliable and stable IQ scores, and intelligently written manuals that facilitate test interpretation" (p. 158). Furthermore, he points out that the majority of subtests have ceilings ranging "from adequate to exceptional" (p. 158).

Even on the strength of the many arguments in favor of the use of intelligence tests to identify gifted children, and with all of the appropriate cautions taken into consideration, there are additional issues to consider in assessing potentially gifted children. Most often, intelligence testing is conducted with gifted children or children suspected of intellectual giftedness for purposes of educational planning and placement. The psychologist is charged with determining whether a given child is indeed academically gifted, and with making recommendations about educational programs that would best suit the child's needs. In many schools, psychologists will administer the WISC-III to a group of children and then classify them as "gifted" or "not gifted," solely on the basis of an arbitrary Full Scale IQ cutoff score, and without regard to important issues regarding the interpretation of the score. Although this approach is dictated by mandated regulations, the resulting placement decisions can relegate a child to an inappropriate educational setting indefinitely.

ISSUES

In the interest of preventing inappropriate placements and providing the best possible educational program for each child, psychologists and educators should take into full account the following issues surrounding intelligence testing of gifted children with the WISC-III: nontypical gifted children, ceiling effects, cultural bias, and timed subtests.

NONTYPICAL GIFTED CHILDREN

A commonly seen profile among gifted children includes unusually high verbal and performance abilities (e.g., Verbal IQ [VIQ], Performance IQ [PIQ], and Full Scale IQ [FSIQ] above 125), and an impressive record of school achievement. However, psychologists and educators encounter a great variety of less common profiles among gifted children, as well. For example, consider a child with a VIQ of 131 and a PIQ of 95 (VIQ–PIQ difference = 36). This child is intellectually gifted, based on the VIQ, but may also have some problems to be addressed, based on the remarkable discrepancy between the VIQ and PIQ. The FSIQ for this child will be 115, and in a state where guidelines specify the FSIQ as the only criterion for giftedness, this child will be identified as "not gifted." This example is somewhat extreme, given the unusually big difference between the verbal and performance IQs. However, significant VIQ–PIQ discrepancies were found among gifted children in the WISC-III standardization sample with more frequency than one might expect. Of the 2,200 children in the standardization sample, 118 children had an FSIQ ≥ 125. Of those 118 children, 54 (or 45.8%) had VIQ–PIQ discrepancies (ignoring the direction of difference) ≥ 11 points. An 11-point difference is significant at the .05 level. Even at the .01 level, corresponding to a 16-point difference, 32 children (or 27.1%) of the 118 were statistically significant (Psychological Corporation, personal communication, January 1997).

With significant VIQ–PIQ discrepancies being so common among gifted children, it is easy to see how narrowly defined or strictly FSIQ-based guidelines can fail to address a child's giftedness, and in some cases other issues, possibly leading to less-than-ideal educational planning and placement recommendations. The application of narrowly defined guidelines is likely to have the same negative outcomes, regardless of the particular intelligence test used to assess children. However, these negative outcomes are often avoidable, particularly with the WISC-III, since the WISC-III provides additional interpretive procedures to aid psychologists and educators in understanding and interpreting a child's performance (see the case study of George later in the chapter).

CEILING EFFECTS

Each subtest of an intelligence test should include enough difficult items to make attainment of the maximum score a genuinely rare event. If too many children are able to respond correctly to all items, then all of those children will earn the same score and will appear to have equal intelligence. In fact, however, some of the children may be more academically able than others, but the test simply did not allow them to demonstrate the full extent of their abilities. When children's scores are depressed due to an inadequate number of difficult items on the test, the test is said to have not enough "top" and to cause a "ceiling effect." According to Kaufman (1992), the WISC-III subtests

> have excellent top for distinguishing among gifted children between the ages of 6 and 14 years. Picture Completion begins to falter at age 14; Information begins to evidence problems at age 15; and a number of other tasks are less than ideal for gifted 16-year-olds. (p. 156)

CULTURAL BIAS

Historically, minority children have been underrepresented in gifted programs (Frasier, Garcia, & Passow, 1995). Although a variety of explanations for this underrepresentation have been ventured, according to Frasier et al. (1995), bias in standardized testing is the most frequently offered explanation. For example, certain test items might be easier or more difficult for different groups of children, based on their family history, cultural background, or life experiences. Responsible developers of intelligence tests attempt to avoid such biases by employing careful standardization sampling procedures. According to Kaufman (1993), "the standardization of the WISC-III is immaculate. The 2,200 children . . . are stratified exceptionally well on race/ethnicity, geographic region, and parental education" (p. 351). Psychometrically, the developers of the WISC-III have taken all of the appropriate steps to minimize cultural bias in the test. Despite such efforts, however, Frasier et al. (1995) would argue that a culture-free test simply does not exist. Even when using a carefully standardized test like the WISC-III, therefore,

TABLE 3.1   Maximum Possible Scaled Score on Four WISC-III Subtests for Children Who Solve Each Item Perfectly, but Earn No Bonus Points for Speed[a,b]

Subtest	Maximum scaled score at age				
	8	10	12	14	16
Arithmetic	19	18	16	13	12
Picture Arrangement	14	10	8	7	6
Block Design	16	12	9	8	7
Object Assembly	14	11	9	8	7

[a]The number of raw score points earned for correctly solving all items on each subtest are as follows (the number of bonus points that one can earn for speed are shown in parentheses): Arithmetic, 24 (6); Picture Arrangement, 28 (36); Block Design, 42 (27); Object Assembly, 30 (14).

[b]Reprinted from *Journal of School Psychology,* Volume 31, Alan S. Kaufman, King WISC the Third assumes the throne, Pages 345–354, Copyright (1993), with kind permission from Elsevier Science Ltd, The Boulevard, Langford Lane, Kidlington 0X5 1GB, UK.

psychologists and educators should be alert to circumstances of a child's background, race, or ethnicity that might affect the child's performance.

TIMED SUBTESTS

The WISC-III places significant emphasis on the speed of a child's responses. Some subtests are timed, such as Coding and Symbol Search. Other subtests award bonus points for speed, such as Object Assembly, Arithmetic, and Picture Arrangement. Children who are thoughtful and reflective are bound to be "punished" by such subtests (see the case study of Jane later in the chapter), since a slow-to-respond child will earn less than a perfect score even if every item has been answered correctly. Table 3.1, borrowed from Kaufman (1993), shows how severely a child's score can be limited if the child is not quick to respond.

According to Kaufman (1993), "Gifted children may score well below the cutoff needed to qualify for an enrichment program when the WISC-III is administered if they tend to be reflective or have even a mild coordination problem" (p. 350). Being aware that speed of processing and motor coordination are significant features in the WISC-III is essential for those involved in classification of the gifted. Fortunately, a psychologist may have information available to suggest administration of a different psychometrically sound intelligence test that places less emphasis on speed. Therefore, a psychologist or educator can take appropriate steps if he or she feels a child's scores have been depressed by lack of speed. For example, the child might be given a different intelligence test that places less emphasis on speed, or perhaps a test of motor coordination to demonstrate why the WISC-III performance was depressed. Substitution of symbol search for coding can also lessen the effects of poor motor coordination on a child's scores.

PROTOTYPICAL CASES

The following two prototypical cases demonstrate how it is possible, using the WISC-III, to find students who might well be quite appropriate for identification as gifted but because of some specific aspect of the WISC-III and/or some aspect of individual differences, he or she would not meet criteria for such a classification. In both cases, alternate classification criteria, plus some flexibility in the interpretation of scores, would find these students appropriate for classification as students who are gifted.

GEORGE: AGE 13 YEARS, 11 MONTHS

The following case demonstrates how alternative interpretive procedures might change whether or not a child will be classified as gifted. George, an almost fourteen-year-old boy, has a history of special interests in science and space exploration. George is also an adolescent who tends to be a perfectionist and is highly invested in accuracy. He has always been somewhat awkward motorically in both fine and gross motor skills and has illegible handwriting. Mathematics has been difficult for him and he finds math tests or, in fact, any tasks involving numbers, very anxiety provoking. Reviewing George's overall scores, index scores, and individual subtest scores as presented in Tables 3.2, 3.3, and 3.4 respectively, it is indeed quite possible that his VIQ, PIQ, and FSIQ would just miss a common traditional cutoff score of 125 to meet the eligibility requirements for a gifted program. (Of course, given the caveats addressed earlier, more than one criterion should always be used in the identification of children for any special programs.) However, George's WISC-III profile exhibits highly significant scatter. In fact, the difference between his highest and lowest Verbal subtest scores is 13 points, far exceeding Kaufman's (1994) suggested threshold of 6 points or less in order to treat the VIQ as a unitary construct. Similarly, the scatter among his Performance subtests exceeds the 7-point threshold suggested by Kaufman. Thus, neither George's VIQ nor his PIQ represents a unitary construct and thus, both have limited interpretability. The Index scores Verbal Comprehension (VC) and Perceptual Organization (PO), however, provide a far more interpretable set of scores. Only the Freedom from Distractibility (FD) factor is not interpretable (due to scatter in excess of 3 points). None of the other three factors (VC, PO, and Processing Speed [PS]) reveal significant differences between their highest and lowest scores. The

TABLE 3.2   George's Overall Scores on the WISC-III

Scale	IQ	90% Confidence interval	Percentile rank	Classification
Verbal Score	121	115–125	92	Superior
Performance Score	123	114–128	94	Superior
Full Scale Score	123	117–127	94	Superior

TABLE 3.3   George's Index Scores on the WISC-III

Index name	Index	90% Confidence interval	Percentile ranking
Verbal Comprehension	131	123–135	98
Perceptual Organization	132	122–136	98
Freedom from Distractibility	87	81–96	19
Processing Speed	80	75–91	9

TABLE 3.4   George's Individual Subtest Scores on the WISC-III

Subtest	Scaled score	Percentile rank	Strength (S)/ weakness (W)
Verbal			
Information	16	98	S
Similarities	18	>99	S
Arithmetic	5	5	W
Vocabulary	15	95	
Comprehension	13	84	
(Digit Span)	10	50	
Performance			
Picture Completion	15	95	
Coding	6	9	W
Picture Arrangement	17	99	S
Block Design	15	95	
Object Assembly	14	91	
(Symbol Search)	6	9	W

VC and PO indices reveal scores clearly in the gifted range (in the 98th percentile), while the PS index reveals scores in the 9th percentile. The question is, does the PS index score negate his classification as gifted? To our mind, the most compelling index scores for the classification of "giftedness" are those that represent the most robust clusters and the strongest "g" loadings. Also, FD is the weakest of the indices psychometrically and, on PS, speed is a major factor. As we discussed previously, speed of processing is not necessarily a hallmark of high intelligence. Thus, we would suggest that flexibility and professional judgment be taken into account in the classification of George and others with similar profiles as gifted.

JANE: AGE 16 YEARS, 5 MONTHS

To illustrate the way in which the WISC-III can put reflective gifted children at a disadvantage, suppose that Jane, who was observed during testing to be quite thoughtful and slow to respond, gets almost every item of every subtest correct, but earns very few bonus points for speed. Her overall scores, index scores, and individual subtest scores are presented in Tables 5, 6, and 7 below.

TABLE 3.5   Jane's Overall Scores on the WISC-III

Scale	IQ	90% Confidence Interval	Percentile rank	Classification
Verbal Score	132	125–136	98	Very superior
Performance Score	91	85–99	27	Average
Full Scale Score	113	108–117	81	High average

TABLE 3.6   Jane's Index Scores on the WISC-III

Index name	Index	90% Confidence interval	Percentile ranking
Verbal Comprehension	136	128–140	99
Perceptual Organization	94	88–102	34
Freedom from Distractibility	118	108–123	88
Processing Speed	86	80–96	18

TABLE 3.7   Jane's Individual Subtest Scores on the WISC-III

Subtest	Scaled score	Percentile rank	Strength (S)/ weakness (W)
Verbal			
Information	16	98	
Similarities	16	98	
Arithmetic	12	75	
Vocabulary	17	99	
Comprehension	16	98	
(Digit Span)	14	91	
Performance			
Picture Completion	13	84	S
Coding	7	16	
Picture Arrangement	7	16	
Block Design	9	37	
Object Assembly	7	16	
(Symbol Search)	7	16	

Is Jane gifted? Her full-scale IQ, taken alone, would indicate that she is currently functioning in the High Average range, and would fall short of the vast majority of cutoff points established for admission to gifted programs. Jane's high Verbal IQ (in the Very Superior range) might suggest giftedness, but the remarkable difference between her Verbal IQ and her Performance IQ (VIQ – PIQ = 41) would be enough for some schools to deny her placement in a gifted program, or to suspect that she has a learning disability.

Given that she has correctly responded to almost every item on the test, the WISC-III's emphasis on speed has clearly depressed Jane's scores because of her tendency toward reflection and thoughtfulness. The psychologist is placed in a difficult position. Should Jane be recommended for placement in a gifted program? On what basis could the psychologist make the argument to place her there?

To estimate the magnitude of the effect of Jane's slowness on her scores, suppose now that Jane had responded only slightly more quickly, earning one additional bonus point per item on those subtests that award bonus points, and performing 10 sec faster on those subtests that are timed but do not award bonus points. Table 3.8 indicates the dramatic effect we would see in Jane's scores.

Notice that differences appear primarily in Performance subtests, because five of the six timed subtests are Performance subtests. Arithmetic is the only timed test of the Verbal subtests. This explains why Jane's lack of speed depressed her PIQ much more remarkably than her VIQ, contributing to the originally observed 41-point discrepancy between her PIQ and VIQ. When Jane's new hypothetical scaled scores are converted into VIQ, PIQ, and FSIQ, the scores presented below

TABLE 3.8   Jane's Actual Individual Subtest Scores Compared to Her Estimated Scores if She Had Performed Faster

Subtest	Actual scaled score	Scaled score with one additional bonus point earned (or 10 sec faster)[a]	Difference
Verbal			
Information	16	16	0
Similarities	16	16	0
Arithmetic	12	18	6
Vocabulary	17	17	0
Comprehension	16	16	0
(Digit Span)	14	14	0
Performance			
Picture Completion	13	13	0
Coding	7	9	2
Picture Arrangement	7	10	3
Block Design	9	11	2
Object Assembly	7	9	2
(Symbol Search)	7	8	1

[a]Coding and Symbol Search are the only two subtests that are timed, but do not award bonus points. To estimate Jane's score on each of these two subtests if she had been 10 sec faster, we calculated her average number of responses per 10 sec interval, and then added it to her raw score. For example, her original raw score on Coding was 60. Jane responded to 60 items in 120 seconds, which is an average of 5 items per 10 seconds. Therefore, we estimate that, if Jane had been ten seconds faster, she would have responded to 5 more items, giving her a raw score of 65.

TABLE 3.9   Jane's Actual Overall Scores Compared to Her Estimated
Scores If She Had Performed Faster

	Original IQ	IQ with one additional bonus point (or 10 sec faster)
Verbal Score	132	139
Performance Score	91	100
Full Scale Score	113	123

in Table 3.9 would result. Notice that a marked difference still exists between Jane's VIQ and PIQ, but they have jumped up by 7 and 9 points respectively, and suddenly her FSIQ is on the cusp of commonly used cutoffs for entrance into gifted programs.

Jane's case illustrates a number of important points with regard to testing gifted children with the WISC-III. First, the psychologist must look beyond the scores, and take into account valuable behavioral observations, such as reflection and thoughtfulness, in interpreting a child's profile. Second, a single test must never be used in isolation to assess a gifted child or to make recommendations regarding a child's school placement. Further testing with Jane, using instruments that do not award bonus points for speed, is likely to yield very different results from the WISC-III results presented above. Third, Jane's case points out the need to challenge the assumption, implicit in the WISC-III, that "fast = smart," or in Jane's case, that "slow = not smart." Fourth, the psychologist must attend closely to the referral question and be aware of assessment issues particular to gifted children. If the goal is to determine *whether* Jane is gifted, the WISC-III will probably yield adequate information to make the determination. However, if the goal is to determine *how* gifted Jane is, the psychologist can expect to encounter ceiling effects that will prevent Jane's intelligence from being assessed with any precision. At 16 years old, Jane is at the upper limit of the WISC-III age range, and furthermore, she has responded to almost every item correctly. According to Kaufman (1992), the WISC-III subtests

> have excellent top for distinguishing among gifted children between the ages of 6 and 14 years. Picture Completion begins to falter at age 14; Information joins in at age 15; and a number of other tasks are less than ideal for gifted 16-year-olds. (p. 156).

Therefore, Jane's VIQ in particular, although it is currently assessed in the Very Superior range, is nonetheless likely to be an underestimate of her actual ability.

DISCUSSION

When deciding which tools to use in the identification of gifted students for gifted programs, many variables must be considered. The use of intelligence testing is a core tool, and justifiably so. In terms of reliability and validity, standardized intelligence tests are usually the most psychometrically sound instruments available. In addition, there is probably more consistency (reliability) among the many psychologists who administer these tests than any other tests developed for school-aged children and adolescents. Because the goal of our public schools is mainly to provide for the academic education of our youth, it is understandable that a test most predictive of an individual's academic achievement would be the most appropriate selection for use in identifying those children and adolescents who are best equipped to perform at the highest levels.

The WISC-III, for many reasons, is one of the most appropriate IQ tests to be used for this purpose. For example, it is used even more widely than the Stanford-Binet IV (Klausmeier et al., 1987), is well standardized with a culturally diverse sample of gifted children (Kaufman, 1992), and has adequate top for most gifted children and adolescents through age 14 (Kaufman, 1992). In addition, the WISC-III is a recent revision, and therefore has up-to-date items and test materials.

Despite the strengths of the WISC-III, psychologists and educators must take note of important issues relevant to gifted or potentially gifted students. For example, not all gifted children fit the traditional profile of a gifted child. For a child like George (see case study later in the chapter), a nontypical profile could lead to a less-than-ideal educational setting unless the psychologist recognizes the value of the WISC-III's alternative interpretive procedures. In addition, although the WISC-III has more than ample top for most children and adolescent through age 14, gifted students who are 15 and 16 years old are likely to have depressed scores due to ceiling effects. A number of subtests on the WISC-III have time limits or award bonus points for fast performance. Such subtests can penalize a gifted child who is motorically compromised in any way, or who tends toward thoughtfulness and reflection in a test-taking situation (see the case study of Jane later in the chapter). Therefore, although the WISC-III is a good choice for assessing potentially gifted children, psychologists and educators should take into account those issues that are relevant to the academically gifted, and should support their assessments and recommendations with data from additional tests. No one test alone should be used for classification.

Although this chapter has focused on the identification and assessment of *academically* gifted children with the WISC-III, the debate over what "giftedness" really means rages on. As noted above, there are a wide variety of opinions and suggestions regarding the appropriate use of the term "gifted." The difficulty in defining "gifted" is due, in part, to the fact that the term gifted does not represent a unitary construct. Experts disagree about the meaning of gifted because of the multiple factors inherent in the term. It is important to understand a psychologist evaluating children for any reason should be "an intelligent tester" or in other words, an experienced professional psychologist who uses strict clinical procedures, yet reasoned and appropriate clinical judgment to aid in the classification of children and adolescents.

ACKNOWLEDGMENTS

The authors would like to thank Cindi Kreiman for providing prompt and thorough responses to requests for WISC-III standardization data and statistics.

REFERENCES

Frasier, M. M., Garcia, J. H., & Passow, A. H. (1995). *A review of assessment issues in gifted education and their implications for identifying gifted minority students.* February, #RM95204 of catalogued manuscripts in Roeper collection.

Harrington, R. G. (1982). Caution: Standardized testing may be hazardous to the educational programs of intellectually gifted children. *Education, 103,* 112–117.

Kaufman, A. S. (1992). Evaluation of the WISC-III and WPPSI-R for gifted children. *Roeper Review, 14,* 154–158.

Kaufman, A. S. (1993). King WISC the Third assumes the throne. *Journal of School Psychology, 31,* 345–354.

Kaufman, A. S. (1994). *Intelligent testing with the WISC-III.* New York: Wiley & Sons.

Kaufman, A. S. & Harrison, P. L. (1986). Intelligence tests and gifted assessment: What are the positives? Special issue: The IQ controversy. *Roeper Review, 8,* 154–159.

Klausmeier, K. L., Mishra, S. P., & Maker, C. J. (1987). Identification of gifted learners: A national survey of assessment practices and training needs of school psychologists. *Gifted Child Quarterly, 31,* 135–137.

Marland, S. P. (Submitter) (1972). *Education of the gifted and talented.* Washington, D.C.: U.S. Office of Education.

Robinson, N. M., & Chamrad, D. L. (1986). Appropriate uses of intelligence tests with gifted children. Special issue: The IQ controversy. *Roeper Review, 8,* 160–163.

Sabatino, D. A., Spangler, R. S., & Vance, H. B. (1995). The relationship between the Wechsler Intelligence Scale for Children—Revised and the Wechsler Intelligence Scale for Children—III scales and subtests with gifted children. *Psychology in the Schools, 32,* 18–23.

Sevier, R. C., Bain, S. K., & Hildman, L. K. (1994). Comparison of the WISC—R and WISC-III for gifted students. *Roeper Review, 17,* 39–42.

Sternberg, R. J. (1982). Lies we live by: Misapplication of tests in identifying the gifted. *Gifted Child Quarterly, 26,* 157–161.

Sternberg, R. J., & Lubart, T. I. (1996). Investing in creativity. *American Psychologist, 51,* 677–688.

Terman, L. M. (1925). *Mental and physical traits of a thousand gifted children.* Stanford, CA: Stanford University Press.

Tyerman, M. J. (1986). Gifted children and their identification: Learning ability not intelligence. *Gifted Education International, 4,* 81–84.

4

ASSESSMENT OF MENTAL RETARDATION WITH THE WISC-III

JEAN SPRUILL

Psychology Clinic
University of Alabama
Tuscaloosa, Alabama

Adequate assessment of mental retardation (MR) involves more than just the administration and interpretation of a standardized test of intelligence. In order to accurately diagnose MR and make recommendations for interventions, the clinician must know the definition of MR, something about the etiology of MR, and the behavioral concomitants of MR. This chapter provides a brief overview of the definition, etiology, and behavioral aspects of mental retardation, then focuses on the use of the WISC-III as an assessment instrument in the comprehensive evaluation of an individual with MR.

DEFINITION OF MENTAL RETARDATION

A number of definitions and classifications have been used to describe the individual with MR with respect to behavior, degree of impairment, and etiology. Tests of intelligence were originally designed to diagnose MR; and for many years, an individual's score on an intelligence evaluation was the primary criteria for a diagnosis of MR. However, in the 1960s the American Association on Mental Deficiency (AAMD) defined MR as follows: "Mental retardation refers to significantly subaverage general intellectual functioning existing concurrently with deficits in adaptive behavior and manifested during the developmental period" (Grossman, 1983, p. 1). *The Diagnostic and Statistical Manual of Mental Disorders: Fourth Edition* (*DSM-IV*, American Psychiatric Association, 1994) has essentially the same definition.

The most recent definition of MR by the Editorial Board of Division 33 (Mental Retardation) of the American Psychological Association is as follows: "Mental Retardation refers to (a) significant limitations in general intellectual functioning; (b) significant limitations in adaptive functioning, which exist concurrently; and (c) onset of intellectual and adaptive limitations before the age of 22 years" (Jacobson & Mulick, 1996, p. 13). The increase in age of onset from 18 to 22 years is the only change from earlier definitions of MR.

LEVELS OF MENTAL RETARDATION

The criterion for significant limitation of intellectual functioning generally is considered to be an IQ score 2 or more standard deviations (SD) below the population mean, usually an IQ score below 70. MR is further divided into four classifications (mild, moderate, severe, and profound) based on the severity of the intellectual deficit. The descriptions below represent a compilation of information from several sources (Weiss & Weisz, 1986; Sattler, 1988; Kamphaus, 1993). Whereas the IQ scores given are those specified by the deviations below the population mean, the DSM-IV specifies that the standard error of the mean be considered in a diagnosis of retardation. Thus a range of scores at either end of the classifications is most appropriate. The cutoff scores for each category may vary among various state and federal agencies, school systems, etc., and the clinician must be aware of the criteria required by the various agencies or states in which he or she works. Adaptive functioning consistent with the level of MR also is important in the classification of the individual. When discrepancies between the IQ score and degree of adaptive deficits exist, the clinician may need to administer alternative measures of intelligence and/or adaptive functioning to clarify the ability levels of the individual.

1. *Mild mental retardation.* (IQ scores of 55–69 for the WISC-III, or between 2 and 3 (SDs below the population mean). Although these individuals may have been noted to be somewhat slow in developing, typically their intellectual deficits are not identified until they enter school. Individuals classified as having mild MR can learn to read and write, most to about the sixth grade level by late adolescence; are capable of gainful employment; may become self-supporting; and may marry and raise a family. Those individuals at the high end of the mild MR range often are labeled MR only with respect to academic endeavors. Once out of school, they blend into the population at large, requiring extra assistance only in periods of severe personal or economic stress.

2. *Moderate mental retardation.* (IQ scores of 40–54, or between 3 and 4 SD below the mean). These individuals usually are identified as having MR during infancy or early childhood. They often have physical abnormalities and are slow learning to walk and talk. Their social skills usually show marked deficits. With special education services, they can learn academic skills between a first and fourth grade level by late adolescence. These individuals require assistance and/or

supervision in all aspects of daily living. With proper training, some may work at unskilled or semiskilled jobs.

3. *Severe mental retardation.* (IQ scores of 25–39, or between 4 and 5 SD below the mean). These individuals are identified in infancy because of their significant delays in motor and speech skills. They frequently have physical abnormalities. They can learn many self-help skills but are not capable of functioning independently. These individuals will require close supervision their entire life.

4. *Profound Mental Retardation.* (IQ scores below 25, or below 5 SD below the mean). Individuals in this group require constant supervision and life-long custodial care. When communication skills exist, they are extremely limited. Often physical abnormalities preclude their being able to walk, talk, or care for any of their own needs.

ETIOLOGY OF MENTAL RETARDATION

There are many known causes of MR, and numerous factors (social, environmental, nutritional, etc.) have been associated with MR. Generally speaking MR falls into two broad groupings—familial and organic. Although there is some overlap, these two distinct groups of individuals seem to be represented by IQs above and below 50. The etiology of the MR in most individuals with IQ scores above 50 (approximately 75–80% of the individuals with MR) is believed to represent simple genetic variation (Grossman, 1983) and is of the familial type. Neurological problems in these individuals, if they exist, are difficult to detect. These individuals typically are from low socioeconomic groups, seldom have obvious physical deformities, and most often are diagnosed as MR during their elementary school years. The other group, represented by IQs below 50 (about 20–25% of the individuals with MR) often have known organic causes for their MR, usually are diagnosed in infancy or early childhood with MR, and frequently have physical abnormalities (Grossman, 1983). Organic causes of MR are varied; approximately 200 syndromes associated with MR have been identified (Terdal, 1981). For a more complete discussion of factors associated with MR, the reader is referred to works by Grossman (1983) and Jacobson and Mulick (1996).

ADAPTIVE FUNCTIONING

To be diagnosed as having MR, individuals also must display significant deficits in adaptive behavior during the developmental period. In general, adaptive behavior refers to the ability of an individual to meet the standards of personal behavior and independence expected for individuals within their culture and of their chronological age. Measures of adaptive behavior are usually ratings of typical performance, or how the individual typically behaves, rather than ability to perform some task. Obviously, motivation to perform the task enters into the assessment of various skills. Unfortunately, the criteria for deficits in adaptive behavior are not as agreed upon, or as reliably measured, as are intellectual deficits. The domains typically measured include daily living, or self-help, skills (e.g., feeding, dressing); communication skills (e.g., articulation, expression); socialization (e.g., interactions with others during play and leisure activities); and, for younger children, some assessment of fine- and gross-motor skills. It is important to note that there may be considerable variation in individuals' adaptive skills and that individuals with MR may not show significant deficits in all areas of functioning.

There are several standardized measures of adaptive behavior available. Some of the more commonly used ones are the Vineland Adaptive Behavior Scales (Sparrow, Balla, & Cicchetti, 1984), the Adaptive Behavior Inventory for Children (Mercer & Lewis, 1978), and the Scales of Independent Behavior (Bruininks, Woodcock, Weatherman, & Hill, 1985).

A combination of standardized measures and clinical judgment is the most commonly used method of assessing adaptive behavior (Kamphaus, 1993; Sattler, 1988). Adaptive behavior and its components have been studied extensively; however, the construct "remains debated and relatively elusive in the field of MR" (Simeonsson & Short, 1996, p. 146). Nevertheless, adaptive behavior must be assessed in any evaluation of individuals known or suspected to be retarded. Some of the controversies about the use of intelligence tests and misclassifications of individuals have come about because of the failure of psychologists in schools and clinics to consider the adaptive functioning of the referred individuals before classifying them as having MR.

ASSESSING MENTAL RETARDATION USING THE WISC-III

Measures of intelligence play a crucial role in the assessment of individuals with MR. The WISC-III is considered to be a reliable and valid instrument for assessing mild and, to a lesser extent, moderate levels of mental retardation.

FACTOR STRUCTURE OF THE WISC-III

The WISC-III manual (Wechsler, 1991) reported both exploratory and confirmatory factor analyses that found two major factors, Verbal Comprehension (VC) and Perceptual Organization (PO), and two minor factors, Freedom from Distractibility (FD) and Processing Speed (PS). There has been considerable debate with regard to the factor structure of the various editions of the WISC. For a review of literature on this debate, see Allen and Thorndike (1995). It is important to ascertain if the factor structure of the WISC-III for individuals with various exceptionalities such as MR or learning disabilities (LDs) is the same as the factor structure for the standardization group.

According to Sattler (1988), the factor structure of the WISC-R in various exceptional populations is generally similar to that found for the standardization group. There is some evidence that, like the WISC-R, the factor structure of the WISC-III holds for exceptional as well as nonexceptional populations. The WISC-III manual reports results of a factor analysis for three groups of subjects (a clinical group, a high-ability group, and a low-ability group). Subjects in the low-ability group were subjects in the standardization group with Full Scale IQ (FSIQ) scores of 75 or less. For all three groups, the best fitting model was the four-factor model. To date, only one independent study delineating the factor structure of the WISC-III for an exceptional group has been published. Using a group of students in a special school for individuals who were gifted and/or learning disabled, Hishinuma and Yamakawa (1993) obtained results that were supportive of the four-factor structure of the WISC-III, although PS and FD were not delineated as clearly as were VC and PO. Further research is needed to provide the clinician with clear guidelines for the WISC-III interpretation and to determine if the same factor structure is found in individuals with exceptionalities such as MR.

WISC-III VERSUS WISC-R

In line with previous research with updated norms, the WISC-III manual reports average lower scores than the WISC-R of 2, 7, and 5 points for the Verbal IQs (VIQ), Performance IQ (PIQ), and FSIQ scores, respectively, and high correlations between WISC-R and WISC-III VIQs (.90), PIQs (.81), and FSIQs (.89). As one might expect, in general, the patterns of subtest composite reliabilities and subtest specificities are very similar for the WISC-III and WISC-R (Bracken, McCallum, & Crain, 1993; Kamphaus & Platt, 1992).

WISC-III VERSUS WISC-R: CHANGES IN IQ SCORES FOR SUBJECTS WITH MENTAL RETARDATION

There is little published research comparing WISC-R and WISC-III for individuals with MR. The results of a study reported in the WISC-III manual (Wechsler, 1991) showed WISC-III IQ scores lower than their respective WISC-R IQ Scores of 9, 7, and 8 points for the VIQ, PIQ, and FSIQs, respectively. Several researchers, using special education students (a combination of subjects with MR and/or LD), have found differences ranging from 2 to 9 points between WISC-R and WISC-III IQ scores, with the WISC-III being the lower score in all cases. Table 4.1 summarizes these studies. It appears that studies using only MR subjects and those using a combination of MR and LD subjects are very similar in the amount of discrepancy between the respective IQ scores for the WISC-R and WISC-III. In general, the average discrepancies between the WISC-R and WISC-III for the MR and LD/MR groups are about the same as the standardization group for the PIQ and FSIQ scores and slightly greater than the standardization group

TABLE 4.1   Summary of Studies Comparing the WISC-R and WISC-III Using Mental
Retardation and Learning Disabled Populations: Differences between WISC-R and WISC-III[a]

Authors	Subjects[b]	Verbal IQ	Performance IQ	Full scale IQ
Wechsler (1991)	28 MR	9	7	9
Nagel and Daley (1994)[c]	93 MR	Reported lower WISC-III IQs ranging from 5 to 8 points.		
Spruill (1996a)	26 MR	2	2	4
Slate and Jones (1995)	31 LD/MR	3	4	4
Post (1992)[d]	68 LD/MR	6	7	7
Smith et al. (1994)[a]	LD/MR	Reported lower WISC-III IQs ranging from 1 to 6 points		
Slate (1995)	53 LD/MR	5	7	8

[a]In all cases, the WISC-III IQ scores were lower than the WISC-R IQ scores.
[b]MR, mentally retarded; LD, learning disabled.
[c]Cited in Lyon (1995).
[d]Cited in Post and Mitchell (1993).

for the VIQ score. Because scores on the WISC-III are typically lower than scores
on the WISC-R, children originally diagnosed as having MR using the WISC-R
also are likely to be diagnosed with MR using the WISC-III.

VERBAL–PERFORMANCE DIFFERENCES
FOR SUBJECTS WITH MENTAL RETARDATION

The average Verbal–Performance (V-P) difference has been found to be 10.0 for
the WISC-III standardization group (Wechsler, 1991) versus 9.7 for the WISC-R
standardization group (Wechsler, 1974). To date few researchers have focused on
differences between WISC-III VIQ and PIQ scores for individuals with MR. In
one study, reported in the WISC-III manual (Wechsler, 1991), the researchers
found equal VIQ (59.2) and PIQ (59.2) scores for a group of 43 children identified with mild MR. Spruill (1996a) has found a difference of 1 point between
WISC-III VIQ (64.6) and PIQ (65.5) scores for a group of 26 children with MR.
Slate (1995) investigated the WISC-III VIQ–PIQ discrepancy for 476 students divided into three groups (202 with LD, 115 with MR, and 159 Not Classified).
There were significant differences among the three groups. The LD group had the
largest discrepancy (average of 4.8 points), followed by the MR group (average of
3.8 points), and then the Not Classified group (average difference of 1.5 points).
In all cases, the PIQ score was higher than the VIQ score. In Slate's study, the
VIQ–PIQ differences for the MR group ranged from 0 to 27 points: 60% had differences of less than 10 points; 26% had differences between 10 and 19 points;
and 4% had differences greater than 19 points. Although there does seem to be a
mild trend for subjects with MR to have PIQ scores greater than VIQ scores, differences cannot be used to differentiate among different diagnostic categories.

COMPARISONS WITH OTHER TESTS
OF INTELLIGENCE

STANFORD-BINET INTELLIGENCE SCALE:
FOURTH EDITION (BINET IV)

Lukens and Hurrell (1996) compared WISC-III and Binet IV (Thorndike, Hagen, & Sattler, 1986) in a group of 31 children with mild MR. The Binet IV was higher than the WISC-III for 29 of the 31 children; the differences ranged from 1 to 20 points, with an average difference of 7.7 points. Prewett and Matavitch (1994) obtained significant correlations between Binet IV and WISC-III with a group of 73 children referred for academic difficulties. They found a correlation of .81 between the WISC-III FSIQ score (Mean = 74.55) and the Binet IV Composite Standard Age Score (SAS) (Mean = 83.99, adjusted to same scale). The high correlation indicates the two tests are measuring a similar general ability. However, of concern to Prewett and Matavich (1994), and to other researchers finding similar results, is that the average discrepancy of 9.4 points in their study suggests that, depending upon which test is used, differences in classification could result. It is possible that some of the differences between the WISC-III and the Binet IV may be due to differences in standardization dates, 1986 for the Binet IV versus 1991 for the WISC-III.

The age range of the Binet IV completely overlaps that of the WISC-III, and either test may be appropriate for children of all ages and ability levels. Although the floor of the Binet SAS scores is 36 versus 46 for the WISC-III, the Binet IV is not necessarily the better test for very low-functioning individuals (Spruill, 1996b). The magnitude of the difference between the scores on the Binet IV and WISC-III found by Prewett and Matavich (1994) and Lukens and Hurrell (1996) indicates that both tests cannot be giving equally accurate estimates of the intellectual abilities of the individuals. This is an example in which other information (e.g., adaptive functioning, grades, background information) may be very important in making diagnostic decisions.

KAUFMAN ASSESSMENT BATTERY FOR CHILDREN

No studies were located that compared the Kaufman Assessment Battery for Children (K-ABC) (Kaufman & Kaufman, 1983) and WISC-III using individuals with MR. When comparing the K-ABC and WISC-R in groups with MR, researchers have found correlations in the .70s between the WISC-R FSIQ and the K-ABC Mental Processing Composite; and the WISC-R FSIQ averaged 5 points below the K-ABC Mental Processing Composite. Given the high correspondence between the WISC-R and WISC-III, similar correctional results can be expected for the WISC-III and K-ABC. Because WISC-III scores tend to be lower than WISC-R scores, I expect the difference between WISC-III scores and K-ABC scores will be greater than the difference between WISC-R scores and K-ABC scores.

There is considerable overlap in ages between the WISC-III and K-ABC, and either instrument may be appropriate for children with Average ability levels. When researchers have compared the K-ABC and WISC-R in MR populations, they generally have found high correlations between the scores for the two tests, indicating that the rank order of children on the two tests was similar. However, the average score for children with MR was higher on the K-ABC (standardized in 1983) than on the WISC-R (standardized in 1974), a finding contrary to the usual score decrease found in the more recently standardized test. A significant problem in using the K-ABC for diagnosing MR is an inadequate floor for all of the cognitive subtests. The K-ABC lacks many easy items for young, developmentally delayed children, a problem that may not exist for older children with mild MR. However, at all age levels, the K-ABC lacks sufficient floor for individuals with moderate to severe MR. Research comparing the WISC-III and K-ABC for subjects of various exceptionalities, including MR, is needed to determine the relationship between the two tests. Until research results show otherwise, it is my opinion that the WISC-III is the better test for children referred for assessment of possible MR.

RELATIONSHIP OF WISC-III SCORES WITH OTHER TESTS

ADAPTIVE BEHAVIOR

Most research indicates that correlation between measures of intelligence in which parents serve as the informant, such as the WISC-R and K-ABC and the Vineland Adaptive Behavior Scales, are low, generally in the .20 to .60 range (Kamphaus, 1993). As you might expect, the correlation between the two measures is somewhat higher when the individuals have MR than when they are of normal intelligence. This finding has not been replicated for the WISC-III, but there is no reason to expect that measures of adaptive behavior would be more or less highly correlated with the WISC-III than with the WISC-R. It seems clear that the domain of adaptive behavior measures different types of information, information that is central to the diagnosis of MR and to the treatment plans for the child. Measures of adaptive functioning may be the most importance in differentiating among individuals in the moderate or below levels of intelligence.

ACHIEVEMENT

Median correlations between the WISC-III and measures of achievement and school grades range from the upper .30s to the low .70s (Wechsler, 1991). In general, correlations between WISC-III IQ scores and measures of achievement are similar to those found between the WISC-R and measures of achievement. Slate (1994) used 115 subjects with MR and found average correlations of .68, .73, and .48 between the subtests of the Wechsler Individual Achievement Test (WIAT,

Wechsler, 1992) and the FSIQ, VIQ, and PIQ scores, respectively. In this study, Slate also had two other groups of subjects, an LD group and a group with academic problems but not classified as LD or MR. For his MR and LD groups, Slate generally found significantly higher correlations between the WISC-III and WIAT than those reported in the WIAT manual, whereas the correlations for the remaining group were similar to those in the WIAT manual. Thus, for MR and LD subjects, it appears that the correlation between intelligence and achievement may be somewhat higher than for the population at large.

One advantage in comparing the WISC-III and WIAT scores is the fact that the two tests were normed at approximately the same time and had a substantial overlap in standardization groups. As studies that compare the WISC-III with other tests of achievement are published, the reader needs to keep in mind that differences in scores may be a function of differences in standardization dates. This is particularly true when investigating achievement–intelligence discrepancies. Great care needs to be taken in interpreting discrepancies between the WISC-III and outdated measures of academic achievement.

WHICH TEST TO USE?

Diagnoses of MR and LD depend heavily upon the IQ score, and the choice of which test to use in deciding special education eligibility is generally not specified. When retesting children for eligibility for special education services, differences in scores from one test to another or changes in IQ scores resulting from changes in the standardization date of the same test (e.g., WISC-R versus WISC-III) may result in changes in the child's eligibility for services. In choosing tests for assessment, the examiner needs to be aware of the relationship among the various tests as well as the changes expected from the restandardization of an existing test.

WISC-III

In general, the WISC-III is the preferred instrument for assessing the intellectual ability of individuals suspected of having MR. However, the WISC-III may not be useful in diagnosing 6-year-olds with MR, especially if the child is low functioning. In developing the WISC-III, the researchers made extensive efforts to improve the floor and ceiling of the subtests. The bottoms of Similarities, Arithmetic, Picture Arrangement, and Block Design were improved by adding a few easier items to each subtest. The extra counting items on Arithmetic improved its bottom substantially, but Similarities, Block Design, and Picture Arrangement still have inadequate bottoms on the WISC-III for 6-year-olds, as does Information. For example, a raw score of 1 on Similarities, Information, Picture Arrangement, or Block Design earns a 6-year-old a scaled score of 4; a raw score of 2 yields a scaled score of 5. Raw scores of 0 on every subtest yields scaled scores of 1. Thus, a child can receive at least 10 scaled-score points for giving no correct answers. This translates into a VIQ score of 46, a PIQ score of 46, and a FSIQ score of 40. When a child obtains a raw score of 0 on one or two subtests of a scale, I recommend that the IQ score be interpreted cautiously. If a child obtains a raw score of 0 on more than two subtests of a scale, I recommend that the examiner not compute an IQ score for that scale and that a FSIQ not be computed. There is no research to support this recommendation; rather, it seems to be "common sense." If a child is not getting at least some answers correct on most subtests, the test is not an appropriate measure of his or her ability.

THE WISC-III VERSUS WPPSI-R/WAIS-R

The WISC-III overlaps with the Wechsler Primary and Preschool Scale of Intelligence-Revised (WPPSI-R, Wechsler, 1989) at ages 6–0 to 7–3 and with the Wechsler Adult Intelligence Scale-Revised (WAIS-R, Wechsler, 1981) at ages 16 years 0 months to 16 years 11 months. For children aged between 6 years 0 months and 6 years 11 months, Sattler (1992) recommends using the WPPSI-R instead of the WISC-III if they have Below Average ability, either test if they have Average Ability, and the WISC-III if they have Above Average ability. For other ages, in which the WISC-III overlaps with the WPPSI-R or the WAIS-R, Sattler recommends using the WISC-III. The primary reason for this recommendation is the number of items sampled by the different tests. For example, to obtain a scaled score of 5 on Information, a child aged 6 years 0 months must get a raw score of 2 on the WISC-III, but he or she must get a raw score of 16 on the WPPSI-R; thus, you are sampling more content when using the WPPSI-R. Similarly, to obtain a scaled score of 5 when using the WAIS-R, a child aged 16 years 11 months needs a raw score of 6 on the WAIS-R Information but a raw score of 14 on the WISC-III, again sampling more content. I agree with Sattler's recommendations above, except I suggest the WISC-III be used for 6-year-old children with Average Ability instead of the WPPSI-R because of the later standardization of the WISC-III.

DIAGNOSTIC AND CLINICAL ISSUES

VERBAL AND PERFORMANCE IQ SCORES DIFFER: WHICH SCORE DO YOU USE?

What happens when V-P score differences exist and one of the scores is outside the range of MR? Which IQ score (Verbal, Performance, or Full Scale) should you use? If the VIQ-PIQ difference is significant, and *unusual* (that is, such a difference occurs infrequently in the population), I agree with Kaufman (1990, 1993) and Kamphaus (1993) that the FSIQ score may not be meaningful and that the focus of interpretation should be on the VIQs and PIQs rather than the FSIQ score. The definition of "unusual" is determined by the base-rate of differences occurring in the standardization sample (Table B.2, Wechsler, 1991, p. 262). As a rule of thumb, I use a base-rate of 10% or less (22 points) as my definition of un-usual. This is a personal preference. Kamphaus suggests that "a discrepancy of 25 points that occurs in 5% or less of the standardization sample is rare" (Kamphaus, 1993, p. 171) and consequently renders the overall composite standard score (FSIQ Score) relatively useless as an overall estimate of intelligence.

Research indicates that the base-rate of V-P differences probably is not the same for children with MR as that of the standardization group. One researcher has investigated the incidence of V-P differences in children with MR. Slate (1995), using a sample of 115 children with MR, found that differences of 20 points or more occurred in 3.6% of his sample versus 12.3% of the standardization group, and that differences of 15 points or more occurred in 13.3% of the MR sample in contrast to 24.3% of the standardization group. Thus, for children with MR, unusual differences between VIQ and PIQ scores may be slightly lower than unusual differences for normal children.

To some extent, the decision as to which score to use depends upon the size of the discrepancy and the classification of the VIQ–PIQ scores. A VIQ score at the lower end of the MR distribution and a PIQ score in the Borderline range proba-bly would result in a diagnosis of MR, whereas a VIQ score towards the upper end of the MR range and a PIQ score in the Average range might result in a different decision. In general, the consensus among professionals is that the VIQ probably is a more accurate predictor of a child's academic success than the PIQ (Post & Mitchell, 1993). However, for minority and culturally disadvantaged children, Post and Mitchell have found that the PIQ of the WISC-III often is a more reliable estimate of students' abilities. Thus, when you have a minority child with a V-P discrepancy, the VIQ may not be the best choice for decisions about academic placement.

Fortunately, other information usually is available to assist in the decision-making progress. Background information, such as developmental history, other test scores, academic functioning, and adaptive behavior, are factors that influence the diagnostic decision. In particular, deficits in adaptive functioning are required for a diagnosis of MR. Quite different diagnostic decisions may be made based on the same set of IQ scores, depending upon the other information available to the examiner. Clinicians must not be restricted to rigid cutoff scores or diagnostic for-mulas. When a recommendation for placement is made using an IQ score other than the traditional FSIQ score, it is important for the clinician to explain why the particular diagnostic decision was made. Explaining the decision should not be a problem. If the examiner cannot adequately explain the decision, it probably is not the correct decision!

TEST–RETEST SCORES DIFFER: WHICH SCORE DO YOU USE?

Suppose you have tested a child and found that the WISC-III FSIQ score is 10 points lower (or higher) when retested than his or her previous score. Is this score significantly different from the previous score? How do you decide? If two tests, which presumably measure the same (or highly related) construct, produce scores that are different by 1 SD or more, Sattler (1988) has suggested that the difference is significant. This is very reasonable criterion, particularly for tests that are highly reliable and that have small standard errors of measurement, as is generally true for tests of intelligence or achievement. A well-established finding is that newer tests tend to have lower scores than tests standardized at an earlier date (Flynn, 1987) and that the longer the interval between publication dates, the larger the score differences between the two tests (Bracken, 1988). The normative difference between IQ scores for tests that are restandarized usually is less than 15 points (1 SD for most IQ, Achievement tests). For example, for the sample of children tested on the WISC-III and the WISC-R, the average FSIQ difference was 5 points (Wechsler, 1991). Some studies (see Table 1) report slightly higher differences for exceptional groups such as those with MR. However, the differences are still less than 15 points and thus probably would not be considered "significantly different."

Unfortunately, the laws or guidelines that govern placement decisions for most regulatory agencies, such as state departments of education, do not always take into consideration changes in tests scores resulting from restandardization or use of different instruments in the determination of a person's eligibility for services. Laws or regulations do not change as easily as do test scores! Therefore, it is incumbent upon the psychologist or examiner to fully explain the reasons for his or her diagnostic decision. The decision as to which score may more accurately reflect a child's ability level (the first or second test score) can be supported by other test data. If the child's IQ score has changed, and this change is accompanied by corresponding changes in adaptive functioning, achievement test scores, grades, and so on, then the "newer" test score may be the most accurate. If other scores have not changed, then the "old" test score may be the most accurate.

There are many reasons for significant differences among the scores on tests that purport to measure the same construct. Some of the reasons for these differences are a result of personal variables (e.g., motivation, rapport, health, distractions, etc.); other reasons are psychometric. Bracken (1988) provides an excellent discussion of the ten most common psychometric reasons for discrepancies between test scores. One of the most common psychometric reasons is the differences in standardization or publication dates (discussed previously); another is the phenomenon known as regression to the mean (discussed next).

REGRESSION EFFECTS

Another issue to consider in the diagnosis of MR is the effect of regression to the mean on test scores. Over time, group mean scores for subjects with MR can be expected to move toward the normative mean (regression to the mean). For example, Spitz (1983) found the mean WISC-R FSIQ for a group of subjects with MR to be 55 at age 13 and 58 at age 15. Thus, when you are evaluating a child using the WISC-III and find a current score somewhat higher (and outside the usual MR range) than his or her previous WISC-III score, is the child still classified as MR? Suppose the current FSIQ score is 75 and the previous FSIQ score was 68. At present, except for the test–retest study reported in the WISC-III manual, there are no studies comparing changes in WISC-III IQs over time. The manual reports an increase of approximately 2, 11, and 7 points, respectively, for VIQ, PIQ, and FSIQ scores. However, the median test–retest interval for this study was 23 days, hardly equivalent to the typical 3 years between retesting for eligibility for special education services. The results of numerous studies have indicated that WISC-R IQ scores are relatively stable over time and that changes in IQ scores are clinically insignificant (e.g., Naglieri & Pfeiffer, 1983). It seems reasonable to expect that practice effects of the WISC-III also will diminish with time. It is impossible to say how much of the difference between the FSIQ scores of 75 and 68 in the example above is due to random, expected changes over time and how much is due to regression effects. Even knowledge of group or average changes expected over time would not be of much help, as knowledge of group differences is not very meaningful for individualized test interpretation.

PROFILE INTERPRETATION

To date there are no studies reporting on typical WISC-III profiles for children with MR. Researchers have used the WISC-R to explore typical subtest profiles for individuals with MR. As reported earlier, there does seem to be a slight tendency for PIQ scores to be a little higher than VIQ scores for this group. Harrison (1990) reported average difficulty level of WISC-R subtests for subjects with MR. She summarized the results of 10 studies and found that, on average, the four most difficult subtests are Vocabulary, followed by Information. Similarities and Arithmetic were tied for third most difficult. The four easiest subtests for subjects with MR were Picture Completion, Object Assembly, Comprehension, and Picture Arrangement, in that order. Whether the same pattern of scores will be found for the WISC-III remains to be seen. Even if the same pattern exists in the WISC-III, the reader should be cautioned that characteristic profiles should not be used for differential diagnosis of MR or discrimination of MR from other handicaps.

CONCLUSIONS

Mental retardation is a disability about which we are still learning. MR may exist concurrently with other developmental disabilities, mental and/or neurological disorders. A diagnosis of MR can be made only after careful interpretation of the entire clinical data set: background information, history, intellectual and adaptive behavior measures, behavioral observations, academic achievement, and various other factors relevant to a particular individual.

CASE EXAMPLES

This information is to be used in each of the three case examples given below.

Name: Eric Schmidt   Age: 7 years 6 months

WISC-III

Verbal scaled scores		*Performance scaled scores*	
Information	1	Picture Completion	5
Similarities	5	Coding	8
Arithmetic	2	Picture Arrangement	6
Vocabulary	2	Block Design	6
Comprehension	1	Object Assembly	9
Digit Span	4	Symbol Search	8

Summary: Score	*Percentile rank*	*Classification*
VIQ = 56 ± 7	0.2	Intellectually Deficient
PIQ = 80 ± 9	9.0	Low Average
FSIQ = 65*		

*The V-P IQ split is significant (.01 level, Table B.1, Wechsler, 1991). A difference of 24 points or more occurred in 6.4% of the standardization sample (Table B.2, Wechsler, 1991). I would not report the FSIQ in the psychological evaluation, and instead, I would focus on the interpretation of the VIQ and PIQ scores.

Vineland Domains	*Score**	*Standard percentile Rank*	*Classification*
Communication	65	1	Low
Daily Living skills	70	2	Moderately low
Socialization	72	3	Moderately low
Adaptive Behavior Composite	64	1	Low

*Note: There were no significant differences among the various Domain Standard Scores.

EXAMPLE 1

Eric has been referred by his first-grade teacher because of academic problems in the classroom. He had difficulty passing kindergarten and is repeating the first grade. His parents have tutored him extensively throughout his schooling. He gets along well with the other children, but he prefers to play with children slightly younger. According to his mother, Eric's achievement of development milestones were within normal limits, but perhaps at the lower end of the normal range. He seemed to be a bit slower in learning to sit, crawl, walk, talk, and so on than his older siblings.

Given this information and the test data above, it seems relatively clear that Eric is unable to perform in a regular classroom setting and probably would benefit from special education services. A recommendation for placement in resource or special education classes, with mainstreaming in nonacademic subjects, would be the most appropriate recommendation. To obtain these services for Eric may require a diagnosis of MR. Admittedly, this diagnosis is more a function of his VIQ than his PIQ. Research has shown that academic skills are more closely related to VIQ than to PIQ.

EXAMPLE 2

Eric has been referred by his second-grade teacher for an evaluation. She cites a record of academic and behavioral problems and difficulty in getting along with his peers. Except for speech, his development was reported to be normal. He has an articulation disorder and, at times, he is very difficult to understand. Eric's living situation is chaotic; he has been removed from his family and has lived in three different foster homes during the past year. His current foster mother describes his behavior as erratic. At times, he will refuse to do chores, fight with the other children in the home, talk back to them, and at other times, he is described as "a little angel." Eric's teacher says his grades are variable. Sometimes he makes As, other times Fs. His behavior in the classroom also is erratic. He fights with peers, throws things in class, and he makes comments such as "No one loves me. I hate you. I'm going to kill you." At other times, his teacher describes him as "a sweet child."

During the test, the examiner noted that on almost all of the subtests, Eric failed easy items and passed more difficult items. This was particularly true during the verbal subtests. He would miss two or three items in a row, followed by one or two correct items, then again miss one or two items that were subsequently followed by correct items. The examiner estimated that if Eric's "early incorrect responses had been correct," his IQ scores would have been in the low average to average range. The examiner also noted that, in general, she understood most of Eric's speech; however, when his answers were queried, Eric tended to say "I don't know," rather than elaborate. Thus, his reluctance to clarify his answers may have lowered his scores.

Based on the above information, a diagnosis of mental retardation is less likely than in Case A. Emotional factors and possible reluctance to speak (i.e., clarify questionable answers) may have lowered his score, particularly his VIQ score. His adaptive functioning is low, probably because of his chaotic living situation and lack of consistent training in self-help skills. Behavioral problems (e.g., refusal to do tasks of which he is capable) also interfere with his daily functioning. Although Eric might benefit from special education, it is classes for the emotionally conflicted rather than MR that may be more appropriate.

EXAMPLE 3

Eric Schmidt has lived in the United States for approximately 11 months. He moved from Germany with his parents, and German is his native language. He began learning English when he arrived in the United States. At home, his family speaks German because his mother has not learned English. His parents requested the evaluation because he is having some difficulty in school, particularly in language-related subjects, and they want to know whether it is "language-related difficulties that might be expected to dissipate with time, or whether there are cognitive problems interfering with his learning."

Eric is an only child, whom his parents say they have "spoiled." He lives in a household with several servants, most of whom speak limited English, and he is not expected to do chores, choose his clothes, prepare snacks or simple meals, and so on. Thus, his low score on the Daily Living Skills Domain of the Vineland probably reflects his upbringing and the lack of expectation and/or opportunity to do many of the tasks assessed in this Domain. His low scores in Communication and Socialization probably reflect language and cultural differences rather than deficits per se.

Given this information, a diagnosis of MR is highly unlikely. Eric's scores are minimal estimates of his ability and would be expected to improve as he learns English and becomes acculturated.

REFERENCES

Allen, S. R., & Thorndike, R. L. (1995). Stability of the WPPSI-R and WISC-III factor structure using cross-validation of covariance structural models. *Journal of Psychoeducational Assessment, 13* (1), 3–20.

American Psychiatric Association (1994). *Diagnostic and statistical manual of mental disorders* (4th ed.). Washington, DC: Author.

Bracken, B. (1988). Ten psychometric reasons why similar tests produce dissimilar results. *Journal of School Psychology, 26,* 155–166.

Bracken, B. A., McCallum, R. S., & Crain, R. M. (1993). WISC-III subtest composite reliabilities and specificities: Interpretative aids. *Journal of Psychoeducational Assessment, Monograph Series: Advances in Psychoeducational Assessment, WISC-III,* 22–34.

Bruininks, R. H., Woodcock, R. W., Weatherman, R. F., & Hill, B. K. (1984). *Scales of Independent Behavior: Woodcock-Johnson Psycho-Educational Battery: Part IV,* Allen, TX: DLM Teaching Resources.

Flynn, J. R. (1987). Massive IQ gains in 14 nations: What IQ tests really measure. *Psychological Bulletin, 101,* 171–191.

Grossman, H. J. (1983). *Classification in mental retardation.* Washington, DC: American Association on Mental Deficiency.

Harrison, P. L. (1990). Mental retardation: Adaptive behavior assessment, and giftedness. In A. S. Kaufman (Ed.), *Assessing adolescent and adult intelligence* (pp. 533–585). Needham, MA: Allyn and Bacon.

Hishinuma, E. S., & Yamakawa, R. (1993). Construct and criterion related validity of the WISC-III for exceptional students and those who are "at risk." *Journal of Psychoeducational Assessment, Monograph Series: Advances in Psychoeducational Assessment, WISC-III,* 94–104.

Jacobson, J. W., & Mulick, J. A. (1996). *Manual of diagnosis and professional practice in mental retardation.* Washington, DC: American Psychological Association.

Kamphaus, R. W. (1993). *Clinical assessment of children's intelligence.* Boston: Allyn and Bacon.

Kamphaus, R. W., & Platt, L. O. (1992). Subtest specificities for the WISC-III. *Psychological Reports, 70,* 899–902.

Kaufman, A. S. (1990). *Assessing adolescent and adult intelligence.* Needham, MA: Allyn and Bacon.

Kaufman, A. S., & Kaufman, N. L. (1983). *K-ABC: Kaufman Assessment Battery for Children: Administration and scoring manual.* Circle Pines, MN: American Guidance Service.

Kaufman, A. S. (1993). King WISC the third assumes the throne. *Journal of School Psychology, 31,* 345–354.

Lukens, J. & Hurrell, R. M. (1996). A comparison of the Stanford-Binet IV and the WISC-III with mildly retarded children. *Psychology in the Schools, 33,* 24–27.

Lyon, M. A. (1995). A comparison between WISC-III and WISC-R scores for learning disabilities reevaluations. *Journal of Learning Disabilities, 28(4),* 253–255.

Mercer, J. R., & Lewis, J. E. (1978). *Adaptive behavior inventory for children.* New York: The Psychological Corporation.

Naglieri, J. A., & Pfeiffer, S. I. (1983). Reliability and stability of the WISC-R for children with below average IQs. *Educational and Psychological Research, 3,* 203–208.

Post, K. R., & Mitchell, H. R. (1993). The WISC-III: A reality check. *Journal of School Psychology, 31,* 541–545.

Prewett, P. N., & Matavich, M. A. (1994). A comparison of referred students' performance on the WISC-III and the Stanford-Binet Intelligence Scale: Fourth Edition. *Journal of Psychoeducational Assessment, 12,* 42–48.

Sattler, J. M. (1988). *Assessment of children (3rd ed.).* San Diego, CA: Author.

Sattler, J. M. (1992). *Assessment of children: WISC-III and WPPSI-R Supplement.* San Diego, CA: Author.

Simeonsson, R. J., & Short, R. J. (1996). Adaptive development, survival roles, and quality of life. In J. W. Jacobson & J. A. Mulick (Eds.,) *Manual of diagnosis and professional practice in mental retardation* (pp. 137–146). Washington, DC: American Psychological Association.

Slate, J. R. (1994). WISC-III correlations with the WIAT. *Psychology in the Schools, 31,* 278–285.

Slate, J. R. (1995). Discrepancies between IQ and index scores for a clinical sample of students: Useful diagnostic indicators? *Psychology in the Schools, 32,* 103–108.

Slate, J. R., & Jones, C. H. (1995). Preliminary evidence of the validity of the WISC-III for African American students undergoing special education evaluation. *Educational and Psychological Measurement, 55(6),* 1039–1046.

Sparrow, S. S., Balla, D. A., & Cicchetti, D. V. (1984). *Vineland adaptive behavior scales.* Circle Pines, MN: America Guidance Service.

Spitz, H. (1983). Intratest and intertest reliability and stability of the WISC, WISC-R and WAIS full scale IQs in a mentally retarded population. *Journal of Special Education, 17,* 69–80.

Spruill, J. (1996a). [A comparison of WISC-R and WISC-III in subjects with mental retardation]. Unpublished raw data.

Spruill, J. (1996b). The composite SAS of the Stanford Binet Intelligence Scale, Fourth Edition: Is it determined by only one area SAS? *Psychological Assessment, 8,* 328–330.

Terdal, L. G. (1981). Mental retardation. In J. E. Lindemann, *Psychological and behavioral aspects of physical disability* (pp. 179–216). New York: Plenum.

Thorndike, R. L., Hagen, E. P., & Sattler, J. M. (1986). *Guide for administering and scoring the Stanford-Binet Intelligence Scale: Fourth Edition.* Chicago, IL: Riverside.

Wechsler, D. (1974). *Manual for Wechsler Intelligence Scale for Children-Revised.* San Antonio, TX: The Psychological Corporation.

Wechsler, D. (1981). *Manual for Wechsler Adult Intelligence Scale—Revised.* San Antonio, TX. The Psychological Corporation.

Wechsler, D. (1989). *Manual for Wechsler Preschool and Primary Scale of Intelligence—Revised.* San Antonio, TX: The Psychological Corporation.

Wechsler, D. (1991). *WISC-III manual.* San Antonio, TX: The Psychological Corporation.

Wechsler, D. (1992). *Wechsler Individual Achievement Test: Manual.* San Antonio, TX: The Psychological Corporation.

Weiss, B., & Weisz, J. R. (1986). General cognitive deficits: Mental retardation. In R. T. Brown & C. R. Reynolds (Eds.), *Psychological perspectives on childhood exceptionality* (pp. 344–390). New York: Wiley.

5

WISC-III Assessment of Children with Attention Deficit/Hyperactivity Disorder

Vicki L. Schwean* and Donald H. Saklofske[†]

*Department for the Education of Exceptional Children
[†]Department of Educational Psychology
University of Saskatchewan
Saskatoon, Saskatchewan, Canada

The debate over whether the Wechsler Intelligence Scales for Children (WISC) have clinical utility for describing the cognitive and intellectual characteristics associated with various childhood exceptionalities has occupied psychologists and educators since the publication of the first test. The controversy has been particularly active among researchers and practitioners who study attention-deficit/ hyperactivity disorder (ADHD) and has largely centered around whether patterns of test scores on these measures are descriptive and reliably diagnostic of the condition. The recent refinement and elaboration of the Wechsler scales has once again fueled this debate, and studies evaluating the scales' psychometric properties and clinical utility relative to this population of children occupy the pages of many developmental journals. Although the merits of this explorative work for informing clinical measurement practice are unquestioned, contemporary efforts at developing unifying accounts of the various cognitive deficits associated with ADHD give measures like the Wechsler Scales a "new" role to play in theory construction. This chapter aims to review critical issues with respect to the role of the Wechsler Intelligence Scale for Children—Third Edition (WISC-III; Wechsler, 1991) in the description and diagnosis of ADHD and to briefly visit potential contributions of WISC-III subtests in substantiating theoretical models of ADHD.

DIAGNOSTIC CLASSIFICATION OF ADHD:
DSM-IV CRITERIA

ADHD is a relatively common neurobehavioral disorder, affecting approximately 9% of school-age boys and 3% of girls (Szatmari, 1992). Although this population of children was recognized as early as 1902, with Still's reference to children exhibiting "defects in moral control," clinical nosology for the disorder was first introduced in the *Diagnostic and Statistical Manual of Mental Disorder* (*DSM-II;* American Psychiatric Association [APA], 1968) under the label of Hyperkinetic Reaction of Childhood. As the label implies, defining criteria emphasized the observable disruptive behavioral excesses characteristic of the disorder. Reflecting scientific advances in the field of ADHD, each subsequent edition of the *DSM* included a substantial revision in both nomenclature and nosology.

Empirical findings have demonstrated that subtle cognitive deficits in response inhibition and attention are more prominent and reliable diagnostic indicators in children with ADHD than are motor excesses (Douglas, 1983). This research proved to be the impetus for a change in nomenclature to attention deficit disorder (ADD) in the 1980 revision of the *DSM* (*DSM-III,* APA, 1980) and for the distinction between ADD with and without hyperactivity, with subtypes differentiated only in the presence or absence of hyperactivity. In the 1987 edition (*DSM-III-R,* APA, 1987), however, subtype differentiation was abandoned because of lack of empirical support and a new generic category was created, ADHD, characterized by developmentally inappropriate degrees of inattention, impulsiveness, and hyperactivity.

Keeping with factor analytic studies supporting the two-factor solution of inattention and hyperactive–impulsive factors together with studies documenting the external validity of subgroups differentiated on these factors (see Lahey et al., 1994), the *DSM-IV* (APA, 1994) recognizes three subtypes of ADHD: ADHD, Combined Type (ADHD/COM); ADHD, Predominantly Inattentive Type (ADHD/I); and, ADHD, Predominantly Hyperactive–Impulsive Type (ADHD/HI). The predominantly inattentive type is analogous to ADD without hyperactivity and the combined subtype to ADD with hyperactivity. The category of predominantly hyperactive-impulsive has no precedent in the *DSM* classification system (McBurnett et al., 1993).

The *DSM-IV* criteria outline two clusters of symptoms, inattention and hyperactivity–impulsivity, each of which consist of nine behaviors (see Table 5.1). A child must present with six (or more) of the symptoms in either the inattentive or hyperactivity–impulsivity clusters or both to meet the diagnostic criteria for ADHD/I, ADHD/HI, or ADHD/COM, respectively. The criteria specify that the symptoms must be developmentally inappropriate, have been present before the age of 7 years, cause impairment in at least two settings, and result in a clinically significant impairment in social, academic, or occupational functioning.

In addition to the criterion deficits specified by the *DSM-IV,* research studies have unveiled a myriad of other associated features of ADHD thought to have cognitive substates. These include, among others, response perseveration (McBurnett

TABLE 5.1   Behavioral Symptoms for Diagnosis of Attention-Deficit Hyperactivity Disorder in *DSM-IV*

Inattention

    often fails to give close attention to details or makes careless mistakes

    often has difficulty sustaining attention in tasks or play activities

    often does not seem to listen when spoken to directly

    often does not follow through on instructions and fails to finish tasks

    often has difficulty organizing tasks and activities

    often avoids, dislikes, or is reluctant to engage in tasks requiring sustained mental effort

    often loses things necessary to tasks and activities

    is often easily distracted by extraneous stimuli

    is often forgetful in daily activities

Hyperactivity

    often fidgets with hands or feet or squirms in seat

    often leaves seat in classroom or in other situations in which remaining seated is expected

    often runs about or climbs excessively in situations in which it is inappropriate

    often has difficulty playing or engaging in leisure activities quietly

    is often "on the go" or often acts as if "driven by a motor"

    often talks excessively

Impulsivity

    often blurts out answers before questions have been completed

    often has difficulty awaiting turn

    often interrupts or intrudes on others

et al., 1993); impaired working memory (Ackerman, Anhalt, & Dykman, 1986; Zentall & Smith, 1993; Barkley, Murphy, & Kwasnik, 1996); greater variability in autonomic arousal patterns (Douglas, 1983, 1988; Rothenberger, 1995); idiosyncratic responses to reinforcement (Douglas & Parry, 1994; Campbell, Pierce, March, Ewing, & Szomowski, 1994; Rapport, Tucker, DuPaul, Merlo, & Stoner, 1986); greater emotional reactivity (Douglas, 1983, 1988); less adequate skills in problem solving and organization (Adams & Curtin, 1992; Garber, Garber, & Spizman, 1996; Hamlett, Pellegrini, & Conners, 1987); and motor control deficits (Guevremont, DuPaul, & Barkely, 1990; Grodzinsky & Diamond, 1992).

RESEARCH ON INTELLIGENCE
WITH ADHD CHILDREN: A CAUTIONARY NOTE

Within the past 20 years, ADHD has clearly become the most-researched and best-known childhood behavior disorder (Weiss & Hechtman, 1993). As in any burgeoning field of study, ADHD research studies are marked by numerous methodological problems that ultimately lead to substantial variability amongst research findings and limited generalizability. Notable methodological criticisms include inconsistent subject selection criteria (e.g., different cutoff criteria, varied diagnostic criteria, selection biases, failure to control for ADHD subtypes and comorbid conditions, information variation); small sample sizes; failure to operationally define and label constructs according to the measurement scale or technique used; measurement techniques that fail to capture the complex cognitive processes operative in ADHD; failure to elucidate on operational criteria utilized with respect to exclusion; inattention to medication status; and, failure to take into account gender and developmental considerations (Barkley, 1997; Shaywitz & Shaywitz, 1988). The reader is advised to remain cognizant of these methodological weaknesses as they may prove explanatory when faced with inconsistent results.

WISC-III: PSYCHOMETRIC PROPERTIES IN ADHD SAMPLES

To use a test with any degree of confidence requires that it be reproducible, stable (reliable), and meaningful (valid) (Sattler, 1992). The reliability and validity of a test may be sensitive to an exceptional condition like ADHD and, therefore, its use with this population rests on data attesting to its psychometric soundness. We will review several studies that have recently examined the psychometric properties of the WISC-III with reference to children with ADHD.

RELIABILITY STUDIES

The standardization studies of the WISC-III in the United States but also in Canada, Australia, and the United Kingdom, provide impressive reliability data for large, heterogeneous samples of children. To date, there have not been any studies that explore the internal consistency reliability of the WISC-III for children with ADHD. Although further research is necessary to examine this issue, the authors of this chapter have recently completed a study of the stability of WISC-III scores with ADHD children.

It is generally expected that scores from intelligence tests like the WISC-III will become quite stable by the time a child enters school. The WISC-III manual reports test–retest correlations ranging from .87 to .94 for the IQ scores over a 12- to 63-day period for a sample of 353 children. As expected, the correlations are generally slightly lower for the subtests and factor scores. However, relatively brief intervals between testing times generally result in score improvements, more so on the Performance than on the Verbal subtests of the WISC-III. Further score variability in test scores may result from changes in motivation, varied educational opportunities, test-taking behaviors, as well as factors in the test itself (see Saklofske & Schwean-Kowalchuk, 1992). Although conditions that impair cognitive and intellectual functioning are also expected to result in less score stability on intelligence tests over time, previous studies with the WISC-R (Wechsler, 1974) over a 3-year period with learning disabled (LD; Juliano, Haddad, & Carroll, 1988) and cognitively disabled children (Webster, 1988) show relatively stable, albeit small score increases.

Children diagnosed with ADHD are known to exhibit particular cognitive deficits as described in the introduction to this chapter. Furthermore, they are

TABLE 5.2   WISC-III Means and Standard Deviations at Time 1 and Time 2 and Retest Correlations ($N = 37$)

Scales	Time 1		Time 2		Retest correlations[a]
	X	SD	X	SD	
VIQ	95.45	13.66	97.00	12.49	.86
PIQ	101.30	13.63	105.11	12.86	.74
FSIQ	97.95	13.40	100.68	12.15	.84
VC	97.05	14.18	98.46	12.00	.87
PO	105.00	13.88	107.16	12.69	.74
FD	93.27	13.49	94.19	16.05	.74
PS	91.87	14.73	100.19	14.61	.58

[a]All correlations are significant at $p < .01$.

[b]VIQ, Verbal IQ; PIQ, Performance IQ; FSIQ, Full Scale IQ; VC, Verbal Comprehension; PO, Perceptual Organization; FD, Freedom from Distractibility; PS, Processing Speed.

likely to be the recipients of individual educational programs and pharmacological treatments. If the condition of ADHD and the somewhat unique treatments results in score instability, this will certainly impact on how we use and interpret the WISC-III results. It is, therefore, of clinical importance to determine the test–retest reliability of the WISC-III for children with ADHD.

In a recently completed and unpublished study, Saklofske and Schwean readministered the WISC-III to 37 clinically referred ADHD children who had participated in an earlier study. At the time of the first testing, the children ranged in age from 8 to 12 years of age. Approximately 30 months later, subjects were readministered the WISC-III. Table 5.2 compares the means and standard deviations for the two testings, along with the retest correlations.

Of note is that although the period between testing was approximately 30 months, all test–retest correlations were quite high and statistically significant. An examination of the mean scores also confirms the stability of WISC-III scores over this rather lengthy time period. The Processing Speed (PS) factor demonstrated the lowest, although significant, correlation between testings due to the overall increase of almost 9 points. Although all scores increased slightly, PS was the most sensitive to change over time. This is reassuring because PS is the one factor score that is most likely to be lower in ADHD children as a group. Thus, although the WISC-III scores of individual children with ADHD might be expected to vary, this study offers preliminary evidence that WISC-III scores remain relatively stable over longer time intervals for these children as a group.

VALIDITY STUDIES

Although the WISC-III is the most often used test for assessing children's intelligence, it may be necessary to reexamine a child's ability span to confirm the first test results or to ensure an accurate diagnosis. As well, children may be reassessed to evaluate the effects of cognitive or other interventions following a brief time interval. Although the WISC-III may be administered more than once to a child, it is often advisable to employ a different test if the time interval between testing is fairly brief. Though this may reduce practice effects, it is necessary to "equate" the two tests to determine if they yield equivalent scores and information. If score differences occur, it is necessary to determine how much of this difference is due to 'real' change and how much is due to the imperfect correlations between different tests.

The Stanford-Binet Intelligence Scale—Fourth Edition (SB:FE; Thorndike, Hagen, & Sattler, 1986) is another of the more often used tests of intelligence. The SB:FE reflects a three-level hierarchical model of cognitive abilities with general reasoning at the top. This is followed by three broad factors (i.e., crystallized ability, fluid-analytic ability, and short-term memory) and then by three more specific factors (verbal reasoning, quantitative reasoning, and abstract-visual reasoning). Psychologists are well aware that scores are not interchangeable across tests and that two intelligence tests do not necessarily measure the same composition of abilities, including "g." This highlights the importance of knowing the correlations between different intelligence tests and also the degree of similarity between tests scores.

ADHD children are likely to be reassessed on measures of intelligence, achievement, and behavior to determine changes resulting from prescribed programs (e.g., methylphenidate trials, cognitive training). Since the WISC-III and SB:FE are so often used to assess children's intelligence, the comparison of scores from these two tests with a sample of 45 ADHD children was conducted by Saklofske, Schwean, Yackulic, and Quinn (1994). The six subtest short form of the SB:FE was administered to these children at the intake session following referral. This abbreviated form provides "a reasonably accurate estimate of overall cognitive level and pattern of cognitive abilities" (Thorndike et al., 1986; p. 35) and is suggested for the assessment of children with school learning problems. Four to six weeks later, children were reassessed with all 13 subtests of the WISC-III. Although half of the children were receiving methylphenidate at the time of the WISC-III testing, this stimulant medication does not seem to have a significant effect on the WISC-III performance of children with ADHD (Schwean et al., 1993).

Table 5.3 presents the WISC-III and SB:FE mean and standard deviations. Examination of the results reveals that the mean WISC-III Full Scale IQ (FSIQ) was slightly lower than that obtained for the SB:FE Partial Composite. Of interest is that the FSIQ and Partial Composite scores varied from 1 to 29 points and that 33 of the 45 children obtained a lower score on the WISC-III. Other scores are shown in Table 3, with the greatest difference between similarly related score groupings observed on the WISC-III Verbal Comprehension (VC) factor and the SB:FE Verbal Reasoning Area Score. Although all mean scores fell in the average range, the highest scores were observed for the Perceptual Organization (PO) and Abstract Visual Reasoning, whereas the Freedom from Distractibility (FD) and Short Term Memory scores from the two tests are relatively lower.

The correlation patterns between the IQ, Index, and Area Scores indicated that there is a fair amount of variance shared by the two tests. A correlation of .73 was

TABLE 5.3   WISC-III and Stanford-Binet, Fourth Edition Means and
Standard Deviations[a]

Measure	Mean	Standard deviation
WISC-III		
Verbal Comprehension	97.04	13.31
Perceptual Organization	105.07	13.97
Freedom from Distractibility	93.00	12.96
Processing Speed	92.60	14.25
Verbal IQ	95.51	13.00
Performance IQ	101.36	13.89
Full Scale IQ	97.96	12.58
Stanford-Binet, Fourth Edition		
Verbal Reasoning	105.73	12.24
Abstract Visual Reasoning	106.87	13.25
Quantitative Reasoning	95.96	10.23
Short Term Memory	97.84	13.83
Partial Composite	102.00	11.33

[a]Adapted from Saklofske et al. (1994).

found between the WISC-III FSIQ and SB:FE Partial Composite. Further, VC and
Verbal Reasoning correlated .76, PO and Abstract Visual Reasoning correlated
.55, and FD and Short Term Memory correlated .52. Lower correlations were observed between other Index–Area composites supporting in part the convergent–
discriminant validity of these scales. Thus, it would appear that both tests may be
employed in the assessment of general intellectual functioning in children with
ADHD provided that examiners are aware that identical scores are not to be expected and will likely be slightly lower on the WISC-III.

Another aspect of test validity is reflected in the pattern of correlations between the parts of complex tests like the WISC-III. As a measure of g, it is expected that all subtests are positively correlated, but in such a pattern as to also
support the measurement of verbal and performance IQs, four factors, and the
meaningfulness of the various subtests themselves.

A sample of 45 clinically referred 8- to 11-year-old children with ADHD was
employed in a convergent–discriminant validity study of the WISC-III reported
by Schwean, Saklofske, Yackulic, and Quinn (1993). Intercorrelations between
subtests, index scores, and IQs were examined. Findings revealed that the patterns
of correlations for the ADHD sample were similar to those reported in the WISC-
III manual for the standardization sample across parallel age groupings. Subtests
within the Verbal Scale tended to cluster together, as did those within the Performance Scale. Lower correlations were noted between the subtests from the two
scales. Relative to the standardization data, only small differences were observed
in the subtest correlation patterns (e.g., Digit Span and Coding were much more
variable in their correlations with other subtests). Correlations of the subtests with
Index scores were in keeping with a four-factor description. Intercorrelations

among the factor scores, Verbal IQ (VIQ), Performance IQ (PIQ), and FSIQ were also consistent with trends reported for the standardization sample. The authors concluded that these findings suggest that the WISC-III is a highly robust measure that retains its psychometric characteristics when employed in an examination of children with ADHD.

FREEDOM FROM DISTRACTIBILITY FACTOR:
A VALID MEASURE OF ATTENTION?

Factor analytic studies of the WISC-R have identified three factors: VC, PO, and a third factor, comprised of the Arithmetic, Digit Span, and Coding subtests, labeled FD factor (but see O'Grady, 1989, where support for a three-factor solution was not found). Its label implies that the primary construct tapped by this factor is that of attention, and consequently, it has received considerable interest as a potential marker variable in the identification of ADHD. Research findings, however, are often at variance with the assumption that this factor singularly taps attention; indeed, a particularly thorny issue has been identifying just what are the central construct or constructs that underlie this factor. Although a number of studies have yielded significant correlations between the WISC-R third factor with measures of attention (e.g., McLarty & Das, 1993; Ozawa & Michael, 1983), others have not (e.g., Cohen, Becker, & Campbell, 1990). Still others refute the notion that the third factor represents any unitary variable (Ownby & Mathew's, 1985; Stewart & Moely, 1983). Kaufman (1994), in summarizing the literature on possible third-factor explanations, references a multiplicity of cognitive processes including attention or concentration, sequencing ability or sequential processing, memory, number ability, automatic processing, and executive processing or planning ability and concludes that the extant research underscores the cognitive complexity of the tests comprising the third factor. Factor analysis of the WISC-III has also yielded a FD component; however, unlike its predecessor, the third factor on the WISC-III excludes the Coding subtest. It, together with the Symbol Search subtest, comprises a fourth factor, PS.

Support for the construct validity of the FD factor of the WISC-III was obtained in a study reported by Anastopoulos, Spisto, and Maher (1994). A sample of 40 clinic-referred children with ADHD were administered the WISC-III and scores from the FD factor were correlated with parent and teacher ratings on the ADHD Rating Scale (DuPaul, 1991), the Child Attention Problem Rating Scale (CAPRS; Edelbrock, 1991), and the Child Behavior Checklist (CBCL: Achenbach, 1991). None of the correlations between FD and the mothers' ratings of inattention reached significance; however, significant correlations between FD and teacher ratings on the Inattention Factors and Total Scores of the ADHD Rating Scale and the CAPRS were attained.

Results of another validity study, however, led the authors to caution against using the FD scores as a measurement of attention. In this two-part study, Lowman, Schwanz, and Kamphaus (1996) asked undergraduate students in an introductory educational psychology class to label the factor represented by items like those on the Arithmetic and Digit Span subtests. In addition, a sample of 76 clinic-referred children on whom the Behavior Assessment System for Children–Teacher Rating Scale (BASC-TRS; Reynolds & Kamphaus, 1992) had been completed were administered the WISC-III. Correlations were then computed between the WISC-III FD index scores and the Hyperactivity, Attention Problems, and Learning Problems of the BASC-TRS. Results revealed that participants unfamiliar with the content of the FD subtests did not choose labels that corresponded with attention; rather, they corresponded with terminology associated with problem solving, memory, and quantitative skills. Moreover, findings from the correlational analyses showed a significant relationship between FD and teacher ratings of learning problems but not attention and hyperactivity.

Despite the many research investigations designed to clarify the nature of the constructs that are being tapped by the FD factor, the issue remains unresolved. One conclusion, however, remains incontrovertible; use of the FD factor as a unitary measure of attention is fraught with problems and oversimplifies the complex processes underlying performance on this factor (Kamphaus, 1993; Kaufman, 1994).

DIAGNOSTIC UTILITY OF THE WISC-III FOR ADHD

Douglas (1983) argued that the intellectual development of children with ADHD would be limited by the immediate and long-term impact of the defective mechanisms operative in ADHD. Evidence to support this hypothesis stems from a number of studies that have used earlier versions of the Wechsler scales to assess the intellectual competencies of heterogeneous groups of children with ADHD and have generally found poor performance relative to normal controls (Barkley, DuPaul, & McMurray, 1990; Goldstein, 1987a, 1987b; Loney, 1974; McGee, Williams, Moffitt, & Anderson, 1989; Palkes & Stewart, 1972; Schaughency, Lahey, Stone, Piacentini, & Frick, 1989) and more subtest variability (Douglas, 1972). Studies that have controlled for the presence of comorbid disorders continue to point to lower intelligence scores in ADHD versus normal subjects (Barkley et al., 1990; Goldstein, 1987a, 1987b; McGee, Williams, & Silva, 1984a, 1984b). Lower intelligence is certainly not diagnostic of ADHD; aside from children with mental retardation, other groups of children with exceptionalities (e.g., learning disabled [LD.]) also attain lower mean IQ scores relative to normally developing children (Newby, Recht, Caldwell, & Schaefer, 1993; Teeter & Smith, 1993).

Several studies have examined the WISC-III profiles of children with ADHD. Prifitera and Dersh (1993) report WISC-III results for 65 children with ADHD, ages 7 to 16 years, obtained as part of the development and validation of the test. Data are also available from the Schwean et al. (1993) and Anastopoulos et al. (1994) studies cited earlier. Table 5.4 compares the results for the three studies.

TABLE 5.4   Means for IQ, Factor Index, and Subtests for Prifitera & Dersh (1983), Schwean
et al. (1993), and Anastopoulos et al. (1994) Samples

	Sample		
	Prifitera (N = 65)	Schwean (N = 45)	Anastopoulos (N = 40)
IQ			
Verbal IQ	99.5	95.5	101.9
Performance IQ	102.9	101.4	102.9
Full Scale IQ	101.0	98.0	102.4
Factor Index			
Verbal Comprehension Index	102.3	97.0	103.9
Perceptual Organization Index	106.8	105.1	103.3
Freedom from Distractibility Index	94.6	93.0	96.0
Processing Speed Index	93.2	92.6	—
Subtest Scaled			
Picture Completion	12.0	11.9	10.7
Information	9.8	8.7	10.4
Coding	7.8	7.9	10.0
Similarities	9.5	9.8	10.2
Picture Arrangement	9.6	8.9	10.2
Arithmetic	9.3	8.3	9.3
Block Design	11.1	11.4	10.6
Vocabulary	10.6	9.3	10.9
Object Assembly	11.3	10.6	10.0
Comprehension	10.2	9.8	10.4
Symbol Search	9.1	8.8	—
Digit Span	8.4	8.9	9.0
Mazes	10.1	11.0	—

Inspection of Table 5.4 reveals that in all three studies, children with ADHD demonstrated their lowest performance on the FD and, where administered, the PS factors (Anastopoulos et al. did not administer the Symbol Search subtest and thus the PS Index could not be computed). One notes that in the Prifitera and Dersh and Schwean et al. studies, the FD and PS factors are within two points of each other, suggesting possible impairments in the abilities measured by both of these factors (Kaufman, 1994). Again in the Prifitera and Dersh and Schwean et al. studies, children with ADHD showed their strongest performance on tasks cojointly measuring PO, whereas VC skills were only slightly less developed. Kaufman (1994) notes that a similar PC > VC pattern has been found in numerous samples of exceptional children and reasons that it is related to the vulnerability of verbal tasks to children's learning difficulties. It is his recommendation that in many exceptional populations, the PO factor provides the best estimate of cognitive potential. Relative to their PO scores, the Prifitera and Dersh and Schwean et al. subjects attained scores on the FD and PS factors that were almost a standard deviation lower. In examining subtest scores across the three studies, it is apparent that subtests with the lowest mean scores are generally those that compose the FD and PS factors (i.e., Coding, Arithmetic, Symbol Search, Digit Span). Both the Prifitera and Dersh and Schwean et al. studies report the lowest mean subtest score for their ADHD subjects was on the Coding subtest. In the Anastopoulos et al. study, the Digit Span subtest was the lowest mean score.

FREEDOM FROM DISTRACTIBILITY FACTOR

Because of its title as the "distractibility factor" and some research suggesting that performance on the third factor is affected by behavioral distractibility (note earlier discussion), the FD factor has been considered as potentially useful in the clinical identification of attentional disorders (Kamphaus, 1993). However, evidence for the discriminative validity of the FD factor in earlier editions of the Wechsler scales has been conflicting. A number of studies have yielded few differences among subgroups of ADHD, LD, behaviorally disordered, and normal controls and further argue for caution in interpreting the scale as a single cognitive construct (Ownby & Mathews, 1985; Stewart & Moely, 1983; Wielkiewicz, 1990). For example, Barkley et al. (1990) found that the FD factor was unable to distinguish ADHD from LD and normal children. Halperin, Gittelman, Klein, and Rudel (1984) found that hyperactive children differed from hyperactive/reading-disabled children only on the Object Assembly subtest. Semrud-Clikeman and Lorys-Vernon (1988) reported that the WISC-R FD factor failed to discriminate their ADHD group from conduct disordered and normal control groups. Traver and Hallahan (1974), on the other hand, claim that the FD factor differentiated among groups of LD, ADD-LD, and normals. Lufi, Cohen, and Parish-Plass (1990) found that the Arithmetic subtest had the greatest weight in differentiating among their ADHD, emotionally disturbed, and control groups. Worland, North-Jones, and Stern (1973) reported that the Coding subtest was the most sensitive. Massman, Nussbaum, and Bigler (1988) suggest that the factor structure of the WISC-R in samples of children with ADHD may depend on the age of the children studied. They found that although there was no significant correlation between hyperactivity, attentional problems, and poor performance on the FD factor for children aged 6 to 8 years, for children 9 to 12 years, there was a significant association for these problems and poor testing performance.

The diagnostic utility of the WISC-III factor was examined in the Prifitera and Dersh study. Although this factor differentiated both ADHD and LD groups from the standardization sample, the performance of the clinical groups was similar on this factor. Anastopoulos et al. report that their ADHD sample scored significantly lower on the FD factor than on either the VC or PO factors, with more children exhibiting significant PO–FD differences than VC–FD differences. When these data were analyzed at an individual level, however, a significant percentage of children did not show any significant VC–FD or PO–FD differences. Other variables such as gender, the presence of comorbid disorders, age, socioeconomic status, or behavioral ratings were found to have little bearing on whether children displayed significant VC–FD or PO–FD factor score differences. Anastopoulos et al.'s findings led them to conclude that the FD factor has limited utility in the diagnosis of ADHD. The results also support the assertion that no matter how homogeneously a sample is defined, group data do not immediately transfer to each individual in that group: "Variability in test performance is axiomatic, and the need to treat each referral as a separate individual is the crux of intelligence testing" (Kaufman, 1994; p. 213).

THE ACID PROFILE

The ACID profile, a pattern of low scores on the Arithmetic, Coding, Information, and Digit Span, has similarly been advanced as a means of differentiating children with ADHD (Prifitera & Dersh, 1993). Although Dykman, Ackerman, and Oglesby (1980) reported a lower mean score on the ACID subtests of the WISC-R for their sample of children with ADHD, a similar pattern has been found in other exceptional populations (e.g., LD and reading-disabled groups; see Joschko & Rourke, 1985; Petrauskas & Rourke, 1979). Using the WISC-III standardization data, Prifitera and Dersh (1993) compared the percentage of children in the standardization sample with ACID profiles to percentages in an LD and an ADHD group. Their calculations indicated that although the full ACID pattern was quite rare in the standardization sample (1.1%), it was much more common in the LD (5.1%) and ADHD (12.3%) samples. Similar findings were reported when the clinical groups were compared to the standardization sample on the Bannatyne profile (Spatial > Verbal Conceptualization > Sequential). Keeping with FD findings on the WISC-III, the results suggest that while the ACID and Bannatyne profiles may contribute to the identification of an exceptionality, they have limited utility for the differential diagnosis of ADHD.

THE SCAD PROFILE

In analyzing the above ACID results, Kaufman (1994) points out that the contribution of the Information subtest is minimal; differences between clinical and nonclinical groups are largely attributable to the subtests comprising the FD and PS factors. His suggestion is to abandon use of the ACID profile and to focus instead on the SCAD profile (Symbol Search-Coding-Arithmetic-Digit Span). Although Kaufman acknowledges that the SCAD has no greater utility than the ACID profile for differentially diagnosing ADHD, he reasons that the SCAD profile, being composed of subtests that largely measure process, is not as vulnerable to contamination of content as is the ACID profile, which includes the product-oriented Information subtest, best thought of as a measure of school learning. He further argues that in analyzing profile patterns, a discrepancy between the SCAD and PO subtests versus the SCAD and VC subtests is more meaningful given that performance on the VC subtests is likely to be degraded by learning or language impairments. Data are presented to show that groups of LD and ADHD children differ significantly from normal children in the magnitude of the discrepancy between PO and SCAD subtests and that large PO–SCAD differences are more likely to occur for abnormal than normal samples. Kaufman provides empirical tables for computing SCAD/PO and SCAD/VC differences, as well as a SCAD Index score, and presents numerous interpretive guidelines. The reader is encouraged to consult Kaufman (1994) for further elaboration.

THE DETERIORATION INDEX

Finally, Bowers et al. (1992) suggest that the Wechsler's Deterioration Index (WDI), an index of cognitive deterioration that comprises the "hold" (Vocabulary, Information, Object Assembly, and Picture Completion) versus "don't hold" (Digit Span, Similarities, Coding, and Block Design) subtests, and is computed using the formula

$$WDI = \frac{hold - don't\ hold}{hold}$$

may serve as a useful screening index of ADHD or support behavioral and observational indications of ADHD. On the basis of WISC-R results, Bower et al. compared the WDI of LD, ADHD, and behaviorally disordered (but not ADHD) groups to nondisabled children. Although WDI did not predict LD status or severity, the WDI scores did significantly distinguish children with ADHD from non-ADHD samples. Rather than implying cortical impairment in ADHD children, the authors argue that elevated WDI scores may suggest a lag in the development of some types of intellectual functions associated with attention, concentration, and abstract thinking. At this juncture, future research is clearly needed to clarify the conceptual and diagnostic utility of the WDI in evaluating children with ADHD.

SUBTYPING AND WISC-III PROFILES

No disorder in the history of childhood psychopatholgy has been subject to as many reconceptualizations, redefinitions, and renamings as ADD (Lahey et al., 1988). At the heart of this activity is the simple fact that the disorder is characterized by considerable heterogeneity. Research findings underscore the diversity among children with attention disorders in etiology, cognitive, academic, psychological, and family correlates, clinical courses, outcomes, and intervention responses. This diversity in presentation has led to calls for and efforts towards delineating more homogeneous, clinically meaningful subgroups (Barkely, 1990; Shaywitz, Fletcher, & Shaywitz, 1994). Particular controversy has centered around whether ADDH and ADD without hyperactivity (ADD/WO) represent two subtypes of a single disorder or comprise two distinct, separate disorders (Cantwell & Baker, 1992; Lahey, Schaughency, Strauss, & Frame, 1984).

Although internal validation studies would appear to support the hypothesis that ADHD and ADD/WO are distinct syndromes (Bauermeister, Alegria, Bird, Rubio-Stipec, & Canino, 1992; Lahey et al., 1988; Lahey & Carlson, 1992), external validation studies have yielded more contradictory results. This has been the case with respect to intellectual differences. Although a number of studies suggest that ADD/WO and ADHD children have similar intellectual profiles on assessment devices such as the WISC-R (Ackerman, Anhalt, & Dykman, 1986; Barkley, 1990; Berry, Shaywitz, & Shaywitz, 1985; Frank & Ben-Nun, 1988; Hynd et al., 1991; Zagar, Arbit, Hughes, Busell, & Busch, 1989), others have found varying results. For example, whereas Barkley, DuPaul, and McMurray (1991) reported that ADD/WO children in their study demonstrated lower IQs compared to ADHD counterparts, Carlson, Lahey, and Neeper (1986) found just the opposite (i.e., lower WISC-R FSIQ and VIQ scores in ADHD children compared to ADD/WO children). In another study, Barkley et al. (1990) found that the performance of ADD/WO children on the Coding subtest of the WISC-R was significantly poorer than that of the ADHD children.

In a taxonomic validation study, Burt, Schwean, and Saklofske (1997) examined the predictive relationships between teacher- and mother-related ADHD symptomatology (i.e., hyperactivity/impulsivity and inattention) and varied cognitive, intellectual, academic, and behavioral competencies in a sample of 51 heterogeneously defined ADHD children ages 7 to 12 years. Intellectual proficiencies were measured by the WISC-III. Results indicated that although mother-rated symptomatology did not predict intellectual functioning on the factor scores of the WISC-III, teacher-rated symptoms of hyperactivity–impulsivity were predictive of lower scores on the PS factor. Although the PS factor is purported to be a measure of mental and psychomotor speed, Kaufman (1994) presents data to show that it also measures planning ability and successive processing. If this is the case, Burt et al.'s findings are in line with those reported by Naglieri, Das, and Jarman (1990). These author's observed that ADHD children have average simultaneous processing ability, but are less well developed on tasks that measure attention, planning, and successive processes. The findings also support arguments made by Barkley (1997) that hyperactive children evidence impairments in working memory and its subfunctions, which may be evident on tasks dependent on planning ability and visual short-term memory, among others. Finally, Burt et al.'s findings underscore the importance of informant source (e.g., parent, teacher) in determining correlate patterns between the symptoms of ADHD and intelligence.

Considerable research has shown that aggression and ADHD overlap to a marked degree. Several positions have been advanced to explain this high co-occurrence, including the hypothesis that the two disorders represent distinct subtypes within a heterogeneous disorder (see Biederman, Newcorn, & Sprich, 1991). Schwean, Saklofske, Yackulic, and Quinn (1995) investigated this hypothesis by comparing the performance of 20 mother-rated aggressive and 24 nonaggressive boys with ADHD on measures of attention, planning, intelligence, and behavior. Although results demonstrated significant behavioral differences, performance on the Attention and Planning tasks of the Cognitive Assessment System (CAS; Das, Naglieri, & Kirby, 1994) and the four WISC-III index scores did not differentiate the groups.

COMORBIDITY AND WISC-III PERFORMANCE

Much research has documented high comorbidity of ADHD with conduct and oppositional disorders, anxiety, depression, and language/learning impairments (Biederman et al., 1991; McGee et al., 1989). The presence of comorbid disorders in cognitive studies of children with ADHD may serve to compound the interpretation of results; intellectual deficits associated with the comorbid disorder may erroneously be attributed to the ADHD symptoms (Caron & Rutter, 1991).

Several studies that have attempted to clarify the neuropsychological correlates of various childhood disorders have reported intellectual impairments specific to ADHD (Frick et al., 1991; Frost, Moffitt, & McGee, 1989). However, other studies remind us that these research findings are tentative. For example, Faraone et al. (1993) administered the Vocabulary, Block Design, Arithmetic, Digit span, and Coding subtests of the WISC-R to 140 children with ADHD and 120 normal controls. Results revealed that compared with controls, ADHD subjects had lower scores on all subtests and on estimated FS and FD IQs. When linear regression models using the presence of comorbid conduct disorder, major depression, and anxiety disorders were employed to predict WISC-R scores for the ADHD subjects, findings revealed a significant effect for the Block Design and FSIQ. Interestingly, post hoc analyses indicated that for both scores, ADHD with depression predicted higher scores than ADHD alone, whereas conduct and anxiety disorders predicted lower scores. Although the findings indicating that intellectual impairments were exacerbated by the presence of conduct and anxiety disorders, results demonstrating that depression predicted higher test scores were seen as enigmatic and suggest the need for further research.

EFFECTS OF MEDICATION
ON WISC-III PERFORMANCE

The research literature attests to the benefits of methylphenidate (Ritalin) in temporarily redressing the core symptoms of ADHD and on secondary social and behavioral problems (e.g., Barkley et al., 1991; Douglas, Barr, Amin, O'Neill, & Britton, 1986). Concerns that psychostimulants failed to produce improvements in learning have also been dispelled by recent research showing direct short-term beneficial effects on various aspects of learning and memory (Barkley et al., 1991; Douglas et al., 1988; Lahey et al., 1987; Whalen & Henker, 1991).

Although methylphenidate's locus of action within the central nervous system remains a matter of some debate (see Hynd et al., 1991), growing evidence indicates that specific cognitive operations are enhanced by stimulant therapy. Saklofske and Schwean (1993) evaluated the efficacy of a standard 10-mg dose of methylphenidate on the cognitive processes of planning, attention, simultaneous, and successive processing (i.e., PASS) in 29 clinically referred ADHD children. Subjects were randomly assigned to either a methylphenidate or placebo condition and were administered various tests tapping components of the PASS Model elaborated by Das et al. (1994). Results revealed that methylphenidate enhanced both efficiency and accuracy of performance on the two planning tasks dependent on the organization of selective attention and coding at the perceptual level. Also sensitive to methylphenidate was an attentional task conjointly dependent on focused and divided attention and two simultaneous processing subtests. Analysis of the responses to the latter measures suggested that improvements appeared to be related to an enhanced ability to inhibit particular behaviors (e.g., inhibition of being misled by salient but less informative cues). No improvements were noted on any of the three successive processing tasks as a function of medication condition.

Two studies have examined the short-term effects of methylphenidate on the WISC-III. A preliminary investigation of the impact of a 10-mg dose of methylphenidate on the WISC-III performance of an undifferentiated sample of children with attentional problems was reported by Saklofske and Schwean (1991). Results did not reveal significant methylphenidate treatment effects on IQ scores. In another study, Schwean et al. (1993) compared the performance of 45 clinically referred ADHD children randomly assigned to either a 10-mg dose of methylphenidate or placebo drug condition on the WISC-III. Analysis conducted to ascertain whether methylphenidate exercised any short-term effects on WISC-III scores did not reveal any statistically significant treatment effects for the subtest and factor scores. Similarly, no significant differences were found between the two treatment groups on FSIQ, VIQ, and PIQ. Although the results indicate that methylphenidate had no immediate intellectual benefits, the authors argued that studies showing that there is a complex interplay between methylphenidate dosage and the complexity of the cognitive processes tapped suggest that it may be premature to conclude that psychostimulants do not enhance intellectual performance. Future studies will need to examine the intellectual effects of varying doses of methylphenidate.

RECENT CONCEPTUALIZATIONS OF ADHD AND THEIR RELATIONSHIP TO THE WISC-III

How best to conceptualize the underlying mechanisms of ADHD has been the subject of much debate over the years. The earliest attempts focused on excessive motor activity theoretically arising from minimal brain damage or dysfunction

(Strauss & Lehtinen, 1947; Wender, 1971). A major conceptual shift occurred in the 1970s when Douglas and colleagues argued for the primacy of constitutional impairments in attention, inhibitory control, arousal, and responses to reinforcement in ADHD (Douglas, 1972, 1976; 1980, 1983; Douglas & Peters, 1979). Based on her review of the research literature on the cognitive weaknesses and pharmacological treatment responses of ADHD children, Douglas (1988) later concluded that abnormalities observed in ADHD pointed to an underlying defect in self-regulation. In several articles, Douglas postulated that the impairments operative in ADHD exert a secondary and spiralling effect on the development of metacognitive abilities, effectance motivation, and cognitive schemata (Douglas, 1980; Douglas & Peters, 1979). Studies cited earlier showing lower IQ scores in ADHD children relative to controls provides some support for this assertion. Douglas (1983) also asserts that over time, the cognitive impairments in ADHD children will become more pronounced. Although she offers data to support this contention (Douglas, 1980; Douglas & Peters, 1979), the Saklofske and Schwean reliability study described earlier shows small positive changes in intellectual functioning over a 30-month period.

Most recently, Barkley (1997) has attempted to provide a unifying account of the various cognitive deficits associated with ADHD. Barkley's model presumes that the essential impairment in ADHD is a deficit involving response inhibition. He argues that this deficit leads to secondary impairments in four neuropsychological abilities (i.e., working memory, the internalizing of speech, self-regulation of affect-motivation-arousal, and reconstitution) that are partially dependent on inhibition for their effective execution. Barkley asserts that in turn, these secondary impairments lead to decreased control of motor behavior by internally represented information and self-directed action. The motor control-fluency-syntax component emphasizes not only the features of control or management of the motor system that these executive functions afford but also the synthetic capacity for generating a diversity of novel, complex responses and their sequences in a goal-directed manner.

Although it is beyond the scope of this chapter to fully discuss this comprehensive model, germane to the present chapter is the role of intelligence tests in refuting or supporting Barkley's hypotheses. Aspects of working memory, as operationalized by Barkley, are captured by subtests like the Digit Span (Digits Backward) and Arithmetic in the Wechsler scales and as noted earlier, performance on these tasks may be impaired in children with ADHD. That factors such as deficient arithmetic knowledge may account for ADHD children's lowered abilities on the latter task have been ruled out and give greater weight to the explanatory hypothesis that working memory is deficient in these children (Zentall & Smith, 1993). Subtests in other measures of intelligence that may have utility in evaluating Barkley's model include the Hand Movements Test from the Kaufman Assessment Battery for Children (K-ABC, Kaufman & Kaufman, 1983), purported by Barkley to evaluate motor control-fluency-syntax and the Selective Attention subtest on the CAS (Das et al., 1994), a measure of interference control.

Finally, one should briefly note that measures of intelligence may also have a contribution to play in evaluating the genetic components of ADHD. Faraone et al. (1993) contend that if ADHD has a genetic component that influences neuropsychological functioning, then the siblings of ADHD probands should show more signs of intellectual impairment than the siblings of controls. To evaluate this hypothesis, Faraone et al. conducted intellectual assessments of 140 children with ADHD, 120 normal controls, and their 303 siblings. Results confirmed that relative to the siblings of controls, the siblings of ADHD children obtained lower, but nonsignificant, scores on the FD factor and FSIQ. Similar results were obtained when siblings with ADHD were excluded from the analyses. The authors suggest that methodological factors may have accounted for the weak effects and call for independent replication studies.

GUIDELINES FOR USE OF THE WISC-III WITH ADHD CHILDREN

Our summary of the psychometric properties of the WISC-III with ADHD children informs us that the test provides a good measure of intellectual performance in children with ADHD. At an individual level, the test yields a measure of the child's cognitive strengths and weaknesses, useful in the development of individualized intervention, and has utility in contributing to a diagnosis of a possible abnormality (Kaufman, 1994). The test *is not,* however, *diagnostic of ADHD, nor should we expect it to be.* We concur with Greene and Barkley (1995) that there is no single definitive assessment strategy or instrument for diagnosing ADHD and that the information-gathering processing should rely on a multimethod assessment strategy. An essential component of such broad-based assessment is intelligence tests, as they provide a description of intellectual abilities and also serve as vehicle for ruling out other disorders that may share features or coexist with ADHD (e.g., retardation, learning disabilities).

In utilizing intelligence tests like the WISC-III in clinical and school settings, practitioners need to be particularly aware that the behavior of children with ADHD is highly sensitive to contextual conditions. Zentall and Javorsky (1995) argue that for students with ADHD, behavior difficulties often arise or increase when (a) the task is too difficult, unclear, or ambiguous; (b) the task or activity is too repetitive, nonengaging, or tedious; (c) there is little situational predictability or control; (d) there is little flexibility for movement or choice; (e) there is little educator supervision or proximity; (f) there are few opportunities for active responding or social interaction; (g) there is an extended period of seatwork; (h) there are transition periods with little structure; and (i) there are frequent or long wait or delay times (for review see Zentall, 1995). Knowledge of the most enabling conditions to enhance the test-taking behaviors, a high degree of clinical skill, and the implementation of best assessment practices are essential when evaluating the intelligence of ADHD children. Although the clinician must ensure that

departures from standard testing procedures do not preclude the use of standardized norms (Sattler, 1992), a wide range of modifications appear permissible.
After many rewarding years of providing psychoeducational services to children
and adults with ADHD, the authors have identified a number of testing adaptations that allow the ADHD client to demonstrate his or her intellectual capabilities. Although not exhaustive, the following suggestions may enhance testing
outcomes for children with ADHD.

- Administering a test like the WISC-III to a child who is extremely hyperactive and impulsive may tax the capabilities of even the most competent examiner. To ensure that the child stays on task, remains motivated, and
  exhibits behaviors that are conducive to test taking necessitates the full attention of the examiner. As such, the examiner must be able to administer
  the test with relative automaticity so that he or she can remain vigilant to
  the child's behaviors. The first author recalls a testing session in which a
  graduate student was attempting to administer the WISC-III to 7-year-old
  Kayla, who presented with ADHD, predominantly hyperactive–impulsive.
  After briefly meeting with Kayla and the graduate student, the first author
  returned to her office just down the hall from where Kayla was being assessed. Within 10 minutes, shrieks of laughter, followed by a musical ren-
  dition of grade one songs, and the sounds of an office being rearranged
  emanated from the walls of the testing room. The author hurriedly returned
  to the source of the commotion to observe a very harried examiner strug-
  gling to control his test materials in the midst of one little, but most active,
  girl who clearly had control of the room!
- It is also important that the examiner be fully prepared for the child by having all the test materials arranged prior to testing and out of the child's view.
  We have had more than one stopwatch dismantled by impulsive little hands.
- In most testing situations, the examiner elects to sit across from the child.
  We have found it helpful to situate ourselves next to the ADHD child.
  Being in close proximity to the child allows the examiner to more easily
  manage the child's behavior and to keep him or her on task. A simple act
  such as gently placing one's hand on the child's shoulder, for example,
  serves as an external reminder to the child to redirect his or her attention.
- Best assessment practices dictate that it is essential to establish rapport with
  the testee prior to testing. Our experience with ADHD children tells us that
  the nature of the tester–testeee relationship must be a working one. Many
  children with ADHD experience significant difficulty with altering behavior
  to meet situational demands. If the examiner initially relates to the child in
  a "therapeutic" manner, it may be problematic for the child to adapt his behavior when performance demands change. To establish a working relationship, we ensure that before testing, we explain in developmentally sensitive
  language the purpose of our activity and what our behavioral expectations
  are. We clearly indicate to the child what he or she can do to enhance his or

her performance (e.g., remain in the chair, feet on the ground). This is particularly important for younger children who are not sophisticated regarding appropriate test-taking behavior.

- Strategies that we have found helpful in keeping children with ADHD on task include (a) verbally cuing the child that you are about to introduce an activity (e.g., "Ready"); (b) ensuring we have eye contact with the child before presenting a stimulus; (c) being particularly sensitive to the changes in the child's behavior and attention by legitimizing movement (e.g., requesting the child to retrieve an object inconspicuously placed in the room) or through short breaks; and, (d) removing all distractions from the testing room and keeping test materials out of the child's sight.

- Because of ADHD children's idiosyncratic responses to reinforcement, we have found it best to use social reinforcers on a continuous basis when administering IQ tests. It is our experience that when activity or tangible reinforcers are used on an intermittent basis, ADHD children tend to become more focused on the reinforcer than on what they have to do to earn the reinforcer and hence performance is degraded.

- Subtyping research has shown that cognitive speed may be a differentiating variable between ADHD—predominantly hyperactive–impulsive and ADHD—predominantly inattentive, with the latter demonstrating a slower speed of processing. It is important for the examiner to recognize these differences and alter both the tempo of the delivery of instructions and where appropriate, the time allowed for responses.

- Children with ADHD experience difficulties with transitions. An ADHD child who has been overstimulated prior to testing (or during a testing break) will experience difficulty adapting his behavior to fit new contextual demands. The examiner should take the child's preceding activities into account when scheduling IQ testing.

- Cognitive impulsivity may interfere with test performance. The examiner must remain alert to the child's cognitive style and provide cues to encourage the child to slow down (e.g., "take your time and think it through").

- Many ADHD children have low frustration tolerance, which is readily exhibited when tasks become more cognitively complex. We have found it helpful to encourage the child through statements such as, "This is getting tough—but give it a try anyway." If the frustration gets out of hand and is debilitating performance, the sensitive examiner should recognize it's time for a break.

- Although studies have not found group effects for psychostimulant medications on the intellectual performance of children with ADHD, there may be a great deal of variability among individuals. Virtually every clinician who has experience in the assessment of children with ADHD will relate instances where medication (or lack of) significantly altered the intellectual performance of a child with ADHD. Clinicians must remain aware of the potential confound of medication on test scores and ideally reassess the child to determine the positive or negative effects of pharmacological treatments. At minimum, the drug condition should be taken into account when interpreting the findings. The first author vividly recalls the first administration of an IQ test to Dylan, an 8-year-old unmedicated child with severe symptoms of ADHD. After exhausting every management strategy in her repertoire, she recommended that testing be rescheduled at a time when Dylan was receiving his Ritalin. Although it would be a gross exaggeration to suggest that Dylan's behavior at the second testing was normalized, it was possible to complete the test and obtain a reasonably accurate estimate of aptitude.

JENNA: A CASE STUDY

Jenna, age 12 years, was referred by her teacher for assessment because of aggressiveness, poor impulse control, inability to concentrate, poor task completion, and developmentally immature social skills. According to the teacher, Jenna was frequently irritable and argumentative and was often reprimanded for annoying other children. Academic difficulties were also evident; although Jenna was in a grade four placement, she was unable to cope with the regular curriculum in mathematics and reading. Jenna's parents indicated during a structured diagnostic interview that Jenna was also irritable and defiant at home, often expressed resentment towards her siblings for perceived indiscretions, was perseverative in her demands, required constant reminders to complete tasks, and was easily frustrated.

Jenna's birth and medical history was unremarkable except for a musculoskeletal abnormality that was treated through physiotherapy. With the exception of walking, which was delayed due to the musculoskeletal condition, all other developmental milestones were met in a normal temporal sequence. Temperamentally, Jenna was described by her parents as easily overstimulated in play, impulsive, emotionally volatile, and lacking in self-control. The parents indicated that Jenna's interactions with other children were almost always strained as a result of her aggressive and uncompromising stance. Jenna's parents also revealed that their past family life had been extremely stressful as a result of alcoholism in the father and an anxiety disorder in the mother. Although the father had been in remission for the previous two years and the family environment had normalized, Jenna continued to exhibit hostility towards her father.

A multimodal, multisource assessment was undertaken with Jenna to provide a comprehensive profile of her strengths and weaknesses. Direct assessment involved measurement of her intelligence using the WISC-III, an academic evaluation, and administration of tasks designed to tap varied aspects of impulsivity and inattention (e.g., Hand Movements subtest of the Kaufman Assessment Battery for Children). Jenna also completed a self-rating of personality (Behavior Assessment System for Children—Self-report of Personality) and a measure of self-perception.

An observation of her on-task behavior was undertaken by the school counselor and parent and teacher ratings of behavior were also obtained.

Intelligence testing revealed a VIQ of 95, a PIQ of 90, and a FSIQ of 92 on the WISC-III. Analysis of subtest patterns within the Verbal scale revealed a significantly lower score on the Digit Span subtest while within the Performance scale, no significant differences among scores were noted, suggesting uniform development. Comparison of the factor scores revealed that the FD and PS scores were almost one standard deviation lower than the VC factor and approximately 10 points lower than the PO factor. Analysis of composites indicated that Jenna demonstrated her strongest performance on tasks conjointly dependent on abstract thought, remote memory, simultaneous processing, discrimination of essential versus nonessential detail, and trial-and-error learning. Weakest performance was evident on tasks comprising the WISC-III FD, ACID profile, ACIDS profile, and sequential processing. Testing on other direct measures of attention and cognitive impulsivity provided confirmatory evidence of deficits in attention and response inhibition. Achievement evaluation revealed that Jenna had the most difficulty with arithmetic, and it is only in this one area that a significant discrepancy between predicted and actual performance was apparent. This findings suggested the presence of a specific learning disability in mathematics. Classroom observation, conducted over a 30-minute teacher-directed lesson, guided note taking, and student-directed group work, demonstrated that Jenna was on task 54% of the time. Qualitative notes indicated that Jenna gave no evidence of any active participation even when she was directly called upon by her teachers and peers.

Ratings on the teacher and parent ratings scales were relatively congruent and suggested a cluster of behaviors characteristic of ADHD—combined type co-occurring with oppositional problems. Ratings of the severity of problem behaviors in a variety of situations by both the parents and teacher indicated a moderate and pervasive disorder. Self-ratings suggested that although Jenna did exhibit a depressed confidence, as evidenced by a perception of being unsuccessful in academic and social pursuits together with a discomfort with school, there was no evidence of clinical anxiety or depression.

In concert, the assessment results suggested the presence of ADHD-combined type comorbid with oppositional disorder. Recommendations were based on the premise that although the ADHD symptoms were neurological in nature and therefore not under Jenna's volitional control, the oppositional behaviors were likely rooted in both temperament and environmental experiences (i.e., family discord). Thus, a comprehensive and multifaceted intervention program that included the following elements was suggested for Jenna: (a) a behavior modification and management program for home and school; (b) parent training and family-based counselling; (c) direct instruction in anger management, social skills, coping techniques, problem-solving strategies, and stress management; (d) pharmacological intervention; and (e) parent, teacher, and child education on ADHD.

SUMMARY

The WISC-III will continue to be an important assessment tool for the measurement of intelligence in children with ADHD, as with all children. Our review of the literature provides preliminary evidence that the psychometric properties of the WISC-III hold for this clinical group, thereby reassuring practitioners that this test can be used with reasonable confidence. On the other hand, there is little support for the use of the WISC-III as a reliable diagnostic indicator of ADHD, nor is it clinically useful in discriminating between various subtypes of this population. In relation to pharmacological treatment with stimulant medications, the more cognitively complex nature of the WISC-III tasks renders them less sensitive to drug conditions than is observed on more precise and narrow cognitive measures.

Assessing the intelligence of children with ADHD presents some unique challenges. To ensure the optimal performance of these children requires considerable clinical sensitivity and flexibility while still adhering to the standardized nature of the test. In the hands of a skilled examiner, data resulting from measures like the WISC-III will be important in the multisource, multimodal assessment of ADHD.

REFERENCES

Achenback, T. M. (1991). *Manual for the Child Behavior Checklist and Revised Child Behavior Profile.* Burlington, VT: Author.

Ackerman, P. T., Anhalt, J. M., & Dykman, R. A. (1986). Arithmetic automatization failure in children with attention and reading disorders: Associations and sequela. *Journal of Learning Disabilities, 19,* 222–232.

Adams, P., & Curtin, C. (1992). The proactive teacher and the student with an attention deficit: A partnership for success. *Challenge, 6,* 1–5.

American Psychiatric Association (1968). *Diagnostic and statistical manual of mental disorders* (2nd ed.). Washington, DC: Author.

American Psychiatric Association (1980). *Diagnostic and statistical manual of mental disorders* (3rd ed.). Washington, DC: Author.

American Psychiatric Association (1987). *Diagnostic and statistical manual of mental disorders* (3rd ed., rev.). Washington, DC: Author.

American Psychiatric Association (1994). *Diagnostic and statistical manual of mental disorders* (4th ed.). Washington, DC: Author.

Anastopoulos, A. D., Spisto, M. A., Maher, M. C. (1994).The WISC-III freedom from distractibility factor: Its utility in identifying children with attention deficit hyperactivity disorder. *Psychological Assessment, 6,* 368–371.

Barkley, R. A. (1990). *Attention deficit hyperactivity disorder: A handbook for diagnosis and treatment.* New York: Guilford Press

Barkley, R. A. (1997). Behavioral inhibition, sustained attention, and executive functions: Constructing a unifying theory of ADHD. *Psychological Bulletin 121* (01), 65–94.

Barkley, R. A., DuPaul, G. J., & McMurray, M. B. (1990). Comprehensive evaluation of attention deficit disorder with and without hyperactivity as defined by research criteria. *Journal of Consulting and Clinical Psychology, 58,* 775–798.

Barkley, R. A., DuPaul, G. J., & McMurray, M. B. (1991). Attention deficit disorder with and without hyperactivity: Clinical response to three dose levels of methylphenidate. *Pediatrics, 87,* 519–531.

Barkley, R. A., Murphy, K. R. & Kwasnik, D. (1996). Psychological adjustment and adaptive impairments in young adults with ADHD. *Journal of Attention Disorders, 1,* 41–54.

Bauermeister, J. J., Alegria, M., Bird, H. R., Rubio-Stipec, M., & Canino, G. (1992). Are attentional–hyperactivity deficits unidimensional or multidimensional syndromes? Empirical findings from a community survey. *Journal of the American Academy of Child and Adolescent Psychiatry, 31,* 423–431.

Berry, C. A., Shaywitz, S. E., & Shaywitz, B. A. (1985). Girls with attention deficit disorder: A silent minority? A report on behavioral and cognitive characteristics. *Pediatrics, 76,* 801–809.

Biederman, J., Newcorn, J., & Sprich, S. E. (1991). Comorbidity of attention deficit hyperactivity disorder with conduct, depressive, anxiety, and other disorders. *American Journal of Psychiatry, 148,* 564–577.

Bowers, T. G., Risser, M. G., Suchanec, J. F., Tinker, D. E., Ramer, J. C., & Domoto, M. (1992). A developmental index using the Wechsler Intelligence Scale for Children: Implications for the diagnosis and nature of ADHD. *Journal of Learning Disabilities, 25,* 179–185.

Burt, K., Schwean, V. L., & Saklofske, D. H. (1997). *Cognitive, academic, behavioral, and developmental characteristics of AD/HD symptomatology.* Manuscript in preparation.

Campbell, S. B., Pierce, E. W., March, C. L., Ewing, L. J., & Szomowski, E. K. (1994). Hard-to-manage preschoolers: Symptomatic behavior across contexts and time. *Child Development, 65,* 836–851.

Cantwell, D. P., & Baker, L. (1992). Association between attention deficit-hyperactivity disorder and learning disorders. In S. E. Shaywitz & B. A. Shaywitz (Eds.), *Attention deficit disorder comes of age: Toward the twenty-first century* (pp. 145–164). Austin, TX: Pro-Ed.

Carlson, C. L., Lahey, B. B., & Neeper, R. (1986). Direct assessment of attention deficit disorders with and without hyperactivity. *Journal of Psychopathology and Behavioral Assessment, 8,* 69–86.

Caron, C., & Rutter, M. (1991). Comorbidity in child psychopathology: Concepts, issues and research strategies. *Journal of Child Psychology and Psychiatry, 32,* 1063–1080.

Cohen, M., Becker, M. G., & Campbell, R. (1990). Relationships among four methods of assessment of children with Attention Deficit Hyperactivity Disorder. *Journal of School Psychology, 28,* 189–202.

Das, J. P., Naglieri, J. A., & Kirby, J. R. (1994). *Assessment of cognitive processes: The PASS theory of intelligence.* Chicago, IL: Riverside.

Douglas, V. I. (1972). Stop, look and listen: The problem of sustained attention and impulse control in hyperactive and normal children. *Canadian Journal of Behavioural Science, 4,* 259–282.

Douglas, V. I. (1976). Perceptual and cognitive factors as determinants of learning disabilities: A review chapter with special emphasis on attentional factors. In R. M. Knights & D. J. Bakker (Eds.), *The neuropsychology of learning disorders: Theoretical approaches* (pp. 413–421). Baltimore: University Park Press.

Douglas, V. I. (1980). Higher mental processes in hyperactive children: Implications for training. In R. M. Knights & D. J. Bakker (Eds.), *Rehabilitation, treatment, and management of learning disorders* (pp. 65–92). Baltimore: University Park Press.

Douglas, V. I. (1983). Attentional and cognitive problems. In M. Rutter (Ed.), *Developmental neuropsychiatry* (pp. 280—329). New York: The Guilford Press.

Douglas, V. I. (1988). Cognitive deficits in children with attention deficit disorder with hyperactivity. In L. M. Bloomingdale & J. A. Sergeant (Eds.), *Attention deficit disorder: Criteria, cognition, intervention* (pp. 65–82). London: Pergamon.

Douglas, V. I., Barr. R. G., Amin, K., O'Neill, M. E., & Britton, B. G. (1988). Dosage effects and individual responsivity to methylphenidate in attention deficit disorder. *Journal of Child Psychology and Psychiatry, 29,* 453–475.

Douglas, V. I., & Parry, P. A. (1994). Effects of reward and non-reward on attention and frustration in attention deficit disorder. *Journal of Abnormal Child Psychology, 22,* 281–302.

Douglas, V. I., & Peters, K. G. (1979). Toward a clearer definition of the attentional deficit of hyperactive children. In G. A. Hale & M. Lewis (Eds.), *Attention and the development of cognitive skills* (pp. 173–247). New York: Plenum Press.

DuPaul, G. J. (1991). Parent and educator ratings and ADHD symptoms: Psychometric properties in a community-based sample. *Journal of Clinical Child Psychology, 20,* 245–253.

Dykman, R. A., Ackerman, M. A., & Oglesby, B. A. (1980). Correlates of problem solving in hyperactive, learning disabled and control boys. *Journal of Learning Disabilities, 13,* 23–32.

Edelbrock, C. (1991). Child Attention Problem Rating Scale. In R. A. Barkley, *Attention deficit hyperactivity disorder: A clinical workbook* (pp. 49–51). New York: Guilford Press.

Faraone, S. V., Biederman, J., Lehman, B. K., Spencer, T., Norman, D., Seidman, L. J., Kraus, I., Perrin, J., Chen, W. J., & Tsuang, M. T. (1993). Intellectual performance and school failure in children with attention deficit hyperactivity disorder and in their siblings. *Journal of Abnormal Psychology, 102(4),* 616–623.

Frank, Y., & Ben-Nun, Y. (1988). Toward a clinical subgrouping of hyperactive and nonhyperactive attention deficit disorder. *American Journal of Diseases of Children, 142,* 153–155.

Frick, P. J., Lahey, B. B., Kamphaus, R. W., Loeber, R., Christ, M. A. G., Hart, E. L., & Tannenbaum, L. E. (1991). Academic underachievement and the disruptive behavior disorders. *Journal of Consulting and Clinical Psychology, 59,* 289–294.

Frost, L. A., Moffitt, T. E., & McGee, R. (1989). Neuropsychological correlates of psychopathology in an unselected cohort of young adolescents. *Journal of Abnormal Psychology, 98,* 307–313.

Garber, S. W., Garber, M. D., & Spizman, F. (1996). *Beyond Ritalin: Facts about medication and other strategies for helping children, adolescents, and adults with attention deficit disorders.* New York: Random House.

Goldstein, H. S. (1987a). Cognitive development in low attentive, hyperactive, and aggressive 6-through 11-year-old children. *Journal of the American Academy of Child and Adolescent Psychiatry, 26,* 214–218.

Goldstein, H. S. (1987b). Cognitive development in inattentive, hyperactive, and aggressive children: Two to five-year follow-up. *Journal of the American Academy of Child and Adolescent Psychiatry, 26,* 219–221.

Greene, R. W., & Barkley, R. A. (1995). Clinic-based assessment of attention-deficit/hyperactivity disorder. *Journal of Psychoeducational Assessment, ADHD Monograph Series,* 42–60.

Grodzinsky, G. M., & Diamond, R. (1992). Frontal lobe functioning in boys with attention-deficit hyperactivity disorder. *Developmental Neuropsychology, 8,* 427–445.

Guevremont, D. C., DuPaul, G. J., & Barkely, R. A. (1990). Diagnosis and assessment of attention deficit-hyperactivity disorder in children. *Journal of School Psychology, 28,* 51–78.

Halperin, J. M., Gittelman, R., Klein, D. F., & Rudel, R. G. (1984). Reading-disabled hyperactive children: A distinct subgroup of attention deficit disorder with hyperactivity? *Journal of Abnormal Child Psychology, 12,* 1–14.

Hamlett, K. W., Pellegrini, D. S., & Conners, C. K. (1987). An investigation of executive processes in the problem-solving of attention deficit disorder-hyperactive children. *Journal of Pediatric Psychology, 12,* 227–240.

Hynd, G. W., Lorys, A. R., Semrud-Clikeman, M., Nieves, N., Huettner, M., & Lahey, B. B. (1991). Attention deficit disorder with and without hyperactivity: A distinct behavioral and neurocognitive syndrome. *Journal of Child Neurology, 6*(Supp.), S37–S43.

Joschko, M., & Rourke, B. P. (1985). Neuropsychological subtypes of learning-disabled children who exhibit the ACID pattern on the WISC. In B. P. Rourke (Ed.), *Neuropsychology of learning disabilities: Essentials of subtype analysis* (pp. 65–88). New York: Guilford Press.

Juliano, J. D., Haddad, F. A., & Carroll, J. L. (1988). Three year stability of WISC-R factor scores for black and white, female and male children classified as learning disabled. *Journal of School Psychology, 26,* 317–325.

Kamphaus, R. W. (1993). *Clinical assessment of children's intelligence.* Boston, MA: Allyn and Bacon.

Kaufman, A. S. (1994). *Intelligent testing with the WISC-III.* New York: John Wiley & Sons, Inc.

Kaufman, A. S., & Kaufman, N. L. (1983). *Kaufman Assessment Battery for Children (K-ABC): Administration and scoring manual.* Circle Pines, MN: American Guidance Services.

Lahey, B. B., Applegate, B., McBurnett, K., Biederman, J., Greenhill, L., Hynd, G. W., Barkley, R. A., Newcorn, J., Jensen, P., Richters, J., Garfinkel, B., Kerdyk, L., Frick, P. J., Ollendick, T., Perez, D., Hart, E. L., Waldman, I., & Shaffer, D. (1994). DSM-IV field trials for attention deficit/hyperactivity disorder in children and adolescents. *American Journal of Psychiatry, 151,* 1673–1685.

Lahey, B. B., & Carlson, C. L. (1992). Validity of the diagnostic category of attention deficit disorder without hyperactivity: A review of the literature. In S. E. Shaywitz & B. Shaywitz (Eds.), *Attention deficit disorder comes of age: Toward the twenty-first century* (pp. 119–144). Austin, TX: Pro-Ed.

Lahey, B. B., Pelham, W. E., Schaughency, E. A., Atkins, M. S., Murphy, H. A., Hynd, G., Russo, M., Hartdagen, S., & Lorys-Vernon, A. (1988). Dimensions and types of attention deficit disorder. *Journal of the American Academy of Child and Adolescent Psychiatry, 27,* 330–335.

Lahey, B. B. Schaughency, E. A., Hynd, G. W., Carlson, C. L., & Nieves, N. (1987). Attention deficit disorder with and without hyperactivity: Comparison of behavioral characteristics of clinic-referred children. *Journal of the American Academy of Child & Adolescent Psychiatry, 26,* 718–723.

Lahey, B. B., Schaughency, E. A., Strauss, C. C., & Frame, C. L. (1984). Are attention deficit disorders with and without hyperactivity similar or dissimilar disorders? *Journal of the American Academy of Child and Adolescent Psychiatry, 23,* 302–309.

Loney, J. (1974). The intellectual functioning of hyperactive elementary school boys: A cross-sectional investigation. *American Journal of Orthopsychiatry, 44,* 754–762.

Lowman, M. G., Schwanz, K. A., & Kamphaus, R. W. (1996). WISC-III third factor: Critical measurement issues. *Canadian Journal of School Psychology, 12,* 15–22.

Lufi, D., Cohen, A., & Parish-Plass, J. (1990). Identifying ADHD with the WISC-R and the Stroop Color and Word Test. *Psychology in the Schools, 27,* 28–34.

Massman, P. J., Nussbaum, N. L., & Bigler, E. D. (1988). The mediating effect of age on the relationship between Child Behavior Checklist hyperactivity scores and neuropsychological test performance. *Journal of Abnormal Child Psychology, 16,* 89–95.

McBurnett, K., Harris, S. M., Swanson, J. M., Pfiffner, L. J., Tamm, L., & Freeland, D. (1993). Neuropsychological and psychophysiological differentiation of inattention/overactivity and aggression/defiance symptom groups. *Journal of Clinical Child Psychology, 22,* 165–171.

McGee, R., Williams, S., Moffitt, T., & Anderson, J. (1989). A comparison of 13-year-old boys with attention deficit and/or reading disorder on neuropsychological measures. *Journal of Abnormal Child Psychology, 17,* 37–53.

McGee, R., Williams, S., & Silva, P. A. (1984). Behavioral and developmental characteristics of aggressive, hyperactive and hyperactive-aggressive boys. *Journal of the American Academy of Child Psychiatry, 23,* 270–290.

McLarty, M. L., & Das, J. P. (1993). Correlations between objective tests of attention and third factor in WISC-R. *Canadian Journal of School Psychology, 9,* 86–94.

Naglieri, J. A., Das, J. P., & Jarman, R. F. (1990). Planning, attention, simultaneous, and successive cognitive processes as a model for assessment. *School Psychology Review, 19,* 423–442.

Newby, R. F., Recht, D. R., Caldwell, J., & Schaefer, J. (1993). Comparison of WISC-III and WISC-R IQ changes over a 2-year time span in a sample of children with dyslexia. In B. A. Bracken & R. S. McCallum (Eds.), *Journal of Psychoeducational Assessment, WISC-III Monograph,* pp. 87–93.

O'Grady, K. (1989). Factor structure of the WISC-R. *Multivariate Behavioral Research, 24,* 177–193.

Ownby, R. L, & Mathews, C. G. (1985). On the meaning of the WISC-R Third Factor: Relations to selected neuropsychological measures. *Journal of Consulting and Clinical Psychology, 53,* 531–534.

Ozawa, J. P., & Michael, W. B. (1983). The concurrent validity of a behavioral rating scale for assessing attention deficit disorder. *Educational and Psychological Measurement, 43,* 623–632.

Palkes, H., & Stewart, M. A. (1972). Intellectual ability and performance of hyperactive children. *American Journal of Orthopsychiatry, 42,* 35–39.

Petrauskas, R. J., & Rourke, B. P. (1979). Identification of subtypes of retarded readers: A neuropsychological, multivariate approach. *Journal of Clinical Neuropsychology, 1,* 17–37.

Prifitera, A., & Dersh, J. (1993). Base rates of WISC-III diagnostic subtest patterns among normal, learning-disabled, and ADHD samples. *Journal of Psychoeducational Assessment, WISC-III Monograph Series,* 43–55.

Rapport, M. D., Tucker, S. B., DuPaul, G. J., Merlo, M., & Stoner, G. (1986). Hyperactivity and frustration: The influence of control over and size of rewards in delaying gratification. *Journal of Abnormal Child Psychology, 14,* 181–204.

Reynolds, C. R., & Kamphaus, R. W. (1992). *Behavior Assessment System for Children.* Circle Pines, MN: American Guidance Service.

Rothenberger, A. (1995). Electrical brain activity in children with hyperkinetic syndrome: Evidence of a frontal cortical dysfunction. In J. A. Sergeant (Ed.), *Eunethydis: European approaches to hyperkinetic disorder* (pp. 255–270). Amsterdam: Editor.

Saklofske, D. H., & Schwean, V. L. (1993). Standardized procedures for measuring the correlates of ADHD in children: A research program. *Canadian Journal of School Psychology, 9,* 28–36.

Saklofske, D. H., & Schwean, V. L. (1991, August). *Cognitive and intellectual performance of ADHD children.* Unpublished paper presented at the annual convention of the American Psychological Association, San Francisco.

Saklofske, D. H., & Schwean-Kowalchuk, V. L. (1992). Influences on testing and test results. In M. Zeidner & R. Most (Ed.), *Psychological testing: An inside view* (pp. 89–118). Palo Alto, CA: Consulting Psychologists Press.

Saklofske, D. H., & Schwean, V. L., Yackalic, R. A., & Quinn, D. (1994). WISC-III and SB:FE performance of children with Attention Deficit Disorder. *Canadian Journal of School Psychology, 10,* 167–171.

Sattler, J. M. (1992). *Assessment of children* (3rd ed.). San Diego, CA: Author.

Schaughency, E. A., Lahey, B. B., Hynd, G. W., Stone, P. A., Piacentini, J. C., & Frick, P. J. (1989). Neuropsychological test performance and the attention deficit disorders: Clinical utility of the Luria-Nebraska Neuropsychological Battery-Children's Revision. *Journal of Consulting and Clinical Psychology, 57,* 112–116.

Schwean, V. L., Saklofske, D. H., Yackulic, R. A., & Quinn, D. (1993). WISC-III performance of ADHD children. *Journal of Psychoeducational Assessment, WISC-III Monograph,* 56–70.

Schwean, V. L., Saklofske, D. H., Yackulic, R. A., & Quinn, D. (1995). Aggressive and nonaggressive ADHD boys: Cognitive, intellectual, and behavioral comparisons. *Journal of Psychoeducational Assessment, Special ADHD Issue Monograph,* 6–21.

Semrud-Clikeman, M., & Lorys-Vernon, A. (1988, July). *Discriminate validity of neurocognitive measures in diagnosing children with attention deficit disorder/hyperactivity.* Paper presented at the Annual European Meeting of the International Neuropsychological Society, Finland. (ERIC Document Reproduction Service No. ED308688).

Shaywitz, B. A., Fletcher, J. M., & Shaywitz, S. E. (1994). A conceptual framework for learning disabilities and attention-deficit/hyperactivity disorder. *Canadian Journal of Special Education, 9,* 1–31.

Shaywitz, S. E., & Shaywitz, B. A. (1988). Attention deficit disorder: Current perspectives. In J. F. Kavanagh & T. J. Truss, Jr. (Eds.), *Learning disabilities: Proceedings of the national conference* (pp. 369–546). Parkton, MD: York Press.

Stewart, K. J., & Moely, B. E. (1983). The WISC-R third factor: What does it mean? *Journal of Consulting and Clinical Psychology, 51,* 940–941.

Still, G. F. (1902).The Coulsonian lectures on some abnormal physical conditions in children. *Lancet, 1:* 1008–1012, 1077–1082, 1163–1168.

Strauss, A. A., & Lehtinen, L. E. (1947). *Psychopathology and education of the brain-injured child.* New York: Grune & Stratton.

Szatmari, P. (1992). The epidemiology of attention-deficit hyperactivity disorders. In G. Weiss (Ed.), *Child and adolescent psychiatry clinics of North America: Attention deficit disorder* (pp. 361–372). Philadelphia: W. B. Saunders.

Teeter, P. A., & Smith, P. L. (1993). WISC-III and WJ-R: Predictive and discriminant validity for students with severe emotional disturbance. *Journal of Psychoeducational Assessment, WISC-III Monograph,* 114–124.

Thorndike, R. L, Hagen, E. P., & Sattler, J. M. (1986). *Stanford-Binet Intelligence Scale: Fourth Edition*. Chicago: Riverside.

Traver, M. A., & Hallahan, D. P. (1974). Attention deficit in children with learning disabilities: A review. *Journal of Learning Disabilities, 9,* 36–45.

Webster, R. E. (1988). Statistical and temporal stability of the WISC-R for cognitively disabled adolescents. *Psychology in the Schools, 25,* 365–372.

Wechsler, D. (1974). *Wechsler Intelligence Scale for Children—Revised* [manual]. New York: Psychological Corp.

Wechsler, D. (1991). *Wechsler Intelligence Scale for Children* (3rd ed.). San Antonio, TX: Psychological Corporation.

Weiss, G., & Hechtman, L. (1993). *Hyperactive children grown up.* New York: Guilford Press.

Wender, P. H. (1971). *Minimal brain dysfunction in children.* New York: Wiley.

Whalen, C. K., & Henker, B. (1991). Social impact of stimulant treatment for hyperactive children. *Journal of Learning Disabilities, 24,* 231–241.

Wielkiewicz, R. M. (1990). Interpreting low scores on the WISC-R Third Factor: It's more than distractibility. *Journal of Consulting and Clinical Psychology, 2,* 91–97.

Worland, J., North-Jones, M., & Stern, J. A. (1973). Performance and activity of hyperactive and normal boys as a function of distraction and reward. *Journal of Abnormal Child Psychology, 1,* 363–377.

Zagar, R., Arbit, J., Hughes, J. R., Busell, R. E., & Busch, K. (1989). Development and disruptive behavior disorders among delinquents. *Journal of the American Academy of Child and Adolescent psychiatry, 28,* 437–440.

Zentall, S. S. (1995). Modifying classroom tasks and environments. In S. Goldstein (Ed.), *Understanding and managing children's classroom behavior* (pp. 356–374). New York: Wiley.

Zentall, S. S., & Javorsky, J. (1995). Functional and clinical assessment of ADHD: Implications of DSM-IV in the schools. *Journal of Psychoeducational Assessment, ADHD Monograph Series,* 22–41.

Zentall, S. S., & Smith, Y. S. (1993). Mathematical performance and behavior of children with hyperactivity with and without coexisting aggression. *Behavior Research and Therapy, 31,* 701–710.

6

ASSESSMENT OF EMOTIONALLY DISTURBED CHILDREN WITH THE WISC-III

PHYLLIS ANNE TEETER AND RICHARD KORDUCKI

Department of Educational Psychology
University of Wisconsin—Milwaukee
Milwaukee, Wisconsin

INTRODUCTION

An estimated 6 to 10% of school-aged children and adolescents exhibit serious and persistent emotional and behavioral difficulties (Juul, 1986), which include low-incidence problems, such as autism, as well as the more common internalizing (e.g., anxiety, depression) and externalizing (e.g., oppositional/defiant, conduct) disorders. *The Diagnostic and Statistical Manual of Mental Disorders* (*DSM-IV;* American Psychiatric Association, 1994) contains an extensive nosology of children's emotional problems. *The DSM-IV's* breadth extends to rare disorders and to those that are identified on the basis of a single symptom (e.g., anorexia nervosa; Achenback & McConaughy, 1996). In the educational setting, terms such as emotional handicap, behavioral disturbance (BD), severe emotional disturbance (SED), emotional and behavioral disturbance (EBD), and emotional disturbance (ED) have been used more or less interchangeably to encompass this heterogeneous group of children.

The myriad problems and long-term social consequences associated with childhood ED point to the importance of assessment practices that lead to accurate identification and effective interventions. For example, antisocial behaviors associated with conduct disorder (CD), the most prevalent form of childhood disorder (Quay, 1986) and the most frequently occurring problem among children identified as BD or ED in American schools (Epstein, Kauffman, & Cullinan, 1985; McGinnis

& Forness, 1988), constitute one of the most serious public health challenges in American society (Earls, 1989; Prinz & Miller, 1991). Children with these EDs are at increased risk for later substance abuse (Short & Shapiro, 1993), delinquency, occupational, and health problems (Kazdin, 1987).

Comprehensive approaches to evaluation are indicated by the complex and diverse problems of children referred due to suspected ED. This chapter addresses the use of the WISC-III within the framework of a multimethod–multisource conceptualization of assessment. The contribution of the WISC-III to assessment will be considered in light of research regarding the relationship of intelligence and EDs, and the extent to which various patterns of performance on the WISC-III are helpful for understanding children's strengths as well as the nature of their emotional and cognitive disorders. A number of clinical case studies are presented as examples of how the WISC-III can be used in ED assessment and intervention planning. Future research directions are considered including the need for multimethod, longitudinal assessment, a developmental-ecological perspective for studying ED, and linking cognitive factors to intervention planning for children with ED. Finally, the notion of cognitive–intellectual functions as a protective or mediating factor for long-term outcome and for treating ED is discussed. First, categorical versus dimensional approaches for defining ED in children and adolescents are discussed.

CATEGORICAL VERSUS EMPIRICAL APPROACHES FOR DEFINING EMOTIONAL DISTURBANCES IN CHILDREN

Both *DSM-IV-* (categorical) and empirically (standardized rating scales) based approaches are widely used in the evaluation of ED children. In their detailed discussion, Achenbach and McConaughy (1996) elaborate the similarities and differences between the two approaches. Similarities among the two approaches include explicit specification of criterial problems, content similarity between some *DSM-IV* diagnostic categories and empirically based syndromes, and statistically significant agreement between some *DSM-IV* diagnoses and syndrome scores. A fundamental distinction between the two approaches is the nosological model in which symptoms or problems are judged to be present or absent in the *DSM-IV* model (i.e., categorical classification), while the psychometric model of the empirically based approach uses quantitative data to measure the degree to which a child manifests particular problems (i.e., dimensional classification). Measures associated with the empirically based approach typically include questionnaires and rating scales that are standardized and normed according to both the informants' status (e.g., teacher, parent, child) and the age and gender of the population of interest. Thus, syndrome, problem, and competence scales are devised and empirically tested to discriminate children with various behavioral and emotional problems. The *DSM-IV* approach does not concern itself with how clinicians determine the presence or absence of particular symptoms. Empirically based methods could, for example, be used to confirm the presence of symptoms for making *DSM-IV* diagnosis. The extent to which one or the other approach, or a combination of the two, is utilized may depend on factors such as the nature of the child's problem, the treatment setting, and the clinician's orientation.

Although the empirically based approach is generally associated with multiple measures and informants, either approach can be utilized within the context of multimethod–multisource assessment. Given the complexity of children's emotional difficulties and the variability in behavior across different contexts, sound assessment will, in most cases, favor a comprehensive approach that considers multiple sources of data. These sources should include norm-based behavior ratings obtained from multiple sources, such as parents and teachers, as well as from children's self-report questionnaires; structured and semistructured interviews; other clinical interviews; behavioral observations; and projective data. Cognitive and achievement assessment should also be incorporated into a comprehensive evaluation to determine the impact of ED on intellectual and academic performance.

Many ED children present concerns seemingly unrelated to intelligence. In fact, intellectual functioning is not even considered among the criteria for the most frequently diagnosed *DSM-IV* disorders (CD, Oppositional Defiant Disorder). Kamphaus (1993) notes that in these cases intelligence test scores are used primarily to rule out comorbid conditions in which the role of intelligence is more central (e.g., learning disabilities and mental retardation). Emphasizing the fundamental role intelligence plays in a child's adaptation in every facet of life, Cooper (1995) advocates the inclusion of formal assessment of intellectual functioning in the evaluation of every child and adolescent. Intellectual assessment may help to isolate targets for remediation and to identify strengths upon which to build interventions. Furthermore, in a longitudinal study of children who were identified at high or low risk for delinquent behaviors, White, Moffitt, and Silva (1989) suggest that high IQ may serve as a mitigating factor for the development of delinquent behaviors. Intellectual assessment merits inclusion in the comprehensive evaluation of ED.

RELATIONSHIP OF IQ
TO EMOTIONAL DISTURBANCE

Overall, the literature suggests an inverse relationship between intelligence and children's emotional and behavioral difficulties; however, the magnitude, exact nature, and clinical relevance of this association remains ambiguous. Some studies suggest an extremely modest relationship. For example, Glutting, Youngstrom, Oakland, and Watkins' (1996) quantitative synthesis of 11 investigations of associations between children's IQ and their home and school behavior found a low negative overall correlation (−.19)

Although children with emotional difficulties tend to perform less well on intelligence measures than their nondisturbed peers, their scores vary considerably across studies. Vance, Fuller, and Ellis (1983) and Paget (1982) reported IQ scale scores in the 89–91 and 86–90 ranges, respectively, for their samples of ED children. Stone (1981) reported that children with IQs in the 70–80 range were more likely to show conduct and personality problems than children with IQs above 100. Scott (1994) found that children with IQs in the retarded range (<70) were at increased risk of psychiatric disorders.

Lefkowitz and Tesiny (1985) reported that children of both sexes who scored in the lower quartile on an IQ measure, were at greater risk for severe depression than those scoring in the upper quartile. They noted that their finding of an inverse relationship of depression to cognitive functioning was consistent with prior investigations (Kaslow, Tanenbaum, Abramson, Peterson, & Seligman, 1983; Lefkowitz & Tesiny, 1980; Schwartz, Friedman, Lindsay, & Narrol, 1982; Tesiny, Lefkowitz, & Gordon, 1980) but inconsistent with others (Kashani et al., 1983; Weinberg & Rehmet, 1983).

In their investigation of the intellectual abilities of 300 ED children, Zimet, Farley, Shapiro-Adler, and Zimmerman (1994) reported that ED children scored significantly lower on the WISC-R ($M = 94.91$) than the standardization sample, but questioned the clinical significance of this difference as well as differences reported in other studies. However, in their epidemiological study of 411 13-year-olds of normal intelligence, Goodman, Dimonoff, and Stevenson (1995) found lower intelligence to be associated with increased psychopathology, supporting the clinical significance of even relatively small differences in intelligence vis-à-vis emotional functioning. Furthermore, their findings supported IQ-as-cause and IQ-as-marker explanations for ED as more plausible than IQ as a consequence of increased psychopathology.

Teeter and Smith (1993) note that the severity/chronicity of emotional and behavior problems of ED groups vary across studies, that this may be a factor in conflicting results, and that lower IQs are associated with more chronic, severe difficulties. In their study, chronically ED adolescents with a history of serious CDs, attention deficit hyperactivity disorder (ADHD) or other related behavior disorders, scored markedly lower on the WISC-III (Full Scale $M = 79.10$) than a group of matched controls (Full Scale $M = 104.40$). Citing Work by Weiss and Hechtman (1986), they note that mixed attention deficit disorder (ADD)/conduct children tend to have particularly poor cognitive and academic outcomes. In contrast, Zimet et al. (1994) found no significant differences in intellectual competence on the WISC-R between children in day treatment and presumably more severely disturbed psychiatric inpatients. However, Zimet et al. (1994) did find a small group of children (9.4%) that showed below normal performance on all subtests of the WISC-R (<8.0 subscale scores). Taken together, these two studies suggest that for a small number of ED children, severity, chronicity, and IQ may be related. However, the extent to which lower intelligence is associated with or causal to more severe or chronic disturbance needs further exploration. Differences between the WISC-R and the WISC-III should also be investigated.

APPROPRIATENESS OF WISC-III
FOR EMOTIONALLY DISTURBED CHILDREN

Important considerations in the selection of an intelligence measure include psychometric qualities, interpretability, appropriateness for the population of interest, and breadth of abilities sampled. The WISC-III (Wechsler, 1991) is recommended since it samples a broad range of specific content areas and problem-solving capacities (Cooper, 1995). Its immediate predecessor, the WISC-R (Wechsler, 1974), has been thoroughly researched with well over 1100 research studies in the literature (Kamphaus, 1993). The WISC-R has been shown to be a valid predictor of academic achievement for a variety of populations, including low socioeconomic status groups (Hartlage & Steele, 1977) and various minority groups (Reschly & Reschly, 1979; Reynolds & Gutkin, 1980). The WISC-III (1991 revision) shares the basic structure of the WISC-R. The most significant change to the WISC-III was the addition of new, complementary subtests, Symbol Search, and updated norms. In light of substantial correlations between the WISC-R and the WISC-III (excluding Symbol Search, approximately 80% of the items on the WISC-III were taken from the WISC-R), existing evidence regarding the validity of the WISC-R is felt to support the validity of the WISC-III (Cooper, 1995).

Not unexpectedly, available studies generally support the validity of the WISC-III for ED children. Lavin (1996) examined the relationship between WISC-III IQs and the Kaufman Test of Educational Achievement (K-TEA; Kaufman & Kaufman, 1985) for a sample of 72 emotionally handicapped children (aged 7–16) with primary diagnoses of CD or oppositional defiant disorder, and a smaller number with dissociative disorders. Scores on both instruments fell within the low to average range. Significant correlations of moderate magnitude were found between WISC-III Full Scale IQ (FSIQ) and Verbal IQs (VIQs) and all K-TEA subtests. Performance IQs (PIQs), however, were significantly related only to K-TEA mathematics subtests. B. Vance, Mayes, Fuller, and Abdullah (1994) reported similar findings regarding the WISC-III and the Wide Range Achievement Test-3 (WRAT-3; Wilkinson, 1993) with a varied population referred for special education. Hishinuma and Yamakawa (1993) reported correlations from .51 to .78 between WISC-III IQs and WRAT-R scores for a sample of gifted and handicapped children. A study by Teeter and Smith (1993) provided support for the predictive and discriminant validity of the WISC-III cognitive scores for an ED and a control group.

Whether it is used with ED or nondisturbed children, the WISC-R appears to measure similar constructs. Dixon and Anderson (1995) found that for psychiatric inpatients as well as normal adolescents the three-factor structure of the WISC-R proposed by Kaufman (1979) provided the best fit. In general, factor analytic research on the WISC-R has found (a) strong support for an overarching general intelligence or "g" factor associated with the FSIQ; (b) strong support for a Verbal Comprehension (VC) factor (Information, Similarities, Vocabulary, and Comprehension subtests) and Perceptual Organization (PO) factor (Picture Completion, Picture Arrangement, Block Design, Object Assembly, Mazes); (c) strong support for a smaller third factor (Arithmetic, Digit Span, Coding) but little agreement as to what it measures; and (d) some subtests (Coding, Picture Arrangement, Digit Span) frequently emerge as "deviant" or difficult to interpret (Kamphaus, 1993). The factor structure of the WISC-III is similar in many respects to that of the WISC-R; however, the addition of the Symbol Search subtest along with the Coding subtest create a fourth factor labeled Processing Speed (PS) (Kamphaus, 1993). The WISC-III third factor label, Freedom from Distractibility (FD), remains controversial, and is comprised of but two subtests, Arithmetic and Digit Span (Kamphaus, 1993). The two versions of the WISC are sufficiently similar so that much of the WISC-R research can be applied to the WISC-III. Dixon and Anderson (1995) investigated covariance structures of the normative samples for the WISC-R and WISC-III and concluded that for all practical purposes, covariation among WISC-III subtests does not differ from covariation among WISC-R subtests.

PERFORMANCE OF EMOTIONALLY DISTURBED CHILDREN ON THE WISC-R AND WISC-III

Various studies have examined the performance and differentiating characteristics of ED children on the WISC-R/WISC-III. In some studies ED children could be discriminated from other populations on the basis of their performance on the Wechsler scales (e.g., Fuller & Goh, 1981; Vance et al., 1983; Teeter & Smith, 1993). Many studies have reported significant findings for one or another aspect of WISC-R performance, and there have been some fairly consistent findings as well. However, in general there appears to be a consensus in the literature that there are no distinctive Wechsler patterns that can provide reliable, discriminative information about a child's behavior or emotional condition (Cooper, 1995; Gluting et al., 1996; Hale & Landino, 1981; Lufi & Cohen, 1988).

Lufi and Cohen (1988) assessed the utility of various factor structures of the WISC-R in differentiating boys (aged 6–16) with LD from those with ED and found that only two modifications of Kaufman's (1975) factor structure differentiated between the two groups and though statistically significant, the difference was not good enough to render it a valid method of assessment. The authors agreed with Vance et al. (1983) in decrying reliance on WISC-R subtest scatter in diagnosing LD or ED children.

Typically, ED children have shown higher PIQ versus VIQ, but not significantly higher (e.g., Finch et al., 1988; Hodges & Plow, 1990; Ipsen, McMillan, &

Fallen, 1983; Paget, 1982; Paramesh, 1982; Schooler, Beebe, & Koepke, 1978; Teeter & Smith, 1993; Vance et al., 1983). Dean (1977) likewise reported that CD adolescents exhibited a depression in their verbal functioning and also more sub-test scatter than normals but found no direct connection between any particular subtest pattern and distinct nosological category. Paget (1982) reported that ED children obtained highest scores on WISC-R nonverbal tasks requiring spatial skills—especially on those tasks that did not involve a fine motor component, and performed most poorly on tasks that drew on abilities in long and short-term memory. Their performance on verbal conceptualization and comprehension tasks occupied a middle ground between those extremes (Paget, 1982).

When compared to the WISC-R standardization sample, ED children from in-patient and day treatment settings scored significantly lower in the IQ scale scores (FSIQ, VIQ, PIQ) and in 7 of the 10 subtests; however, with the exception of the Arithmetic and Coding subtests, these differences were so small they were not considered to be clinically meaningful (Zimet et al., 1994). Zimet et al. (1994) found no significant differences between ED children and the standardization sample in Similarities, Picture Arrangement, or Object Assembly. Emphasizing that ED children exhibit a wide range of intellectual abilities, Zimet et al. (1994) identified three profiles on the WISC-R: In one profile (47.5% of children) depressed scores were noted on Information, Coding, and Arithmetic, with the re-maining seven subtests within the normal range. In another profile (43.1%), all scores were in the normal range, with the exception of Similarities, which was el-evated. Finally, in the third (less than 10%), ED children exhibited a flat profile with depressed scores on all subtests.

Wielkiewicz (1990) reported that, although children with ADD, learning disabil-ities (LDs), and behavioral problems all tend to perform poorly on the WISC-R's FD or third factor, distractibility does not explain poor performance in and of it-self. Wielkiewicz (1990) notes that besides being able to attend to the stimuli, per-formance on the third factor is thought to be related to executive function (i.e., planning, reasoning, judgment) plus short-term (working) memory. Therefore children who perform poorly on the third factor and poorly on just about all other subtests probably have deficits in executive function. However, children who per-form poorly on the third factor but perform well on other subtests (e.g., Block De-sign) that tap executive processing, probably have deficits in working memory (Wielkiewicz, 1990).

Semrud-Clikeman, Hynd, Lorys, and Lahey (1993) reported that the WISC-R third factor (Arithmetic, Coding, Digit Span) did not differentiate groups of chil-dren with ADHD from those with dual diagnoses of ADHD and CD, and a group of clinic controls with internalizing disorders. However, they found that the ADHD and CD group performed significantly poorer on the Verbal Comprehension (VC) factor than both the ADHD group and controls, whereas there was no difference between the ADHD and control groups on VC. Semrund-Clikeman et al. (1993) note that this is significant in light of the fact that 30–50% of the cases in epi-demiological studies find co-occurrence of ADHD and CD.

CONTRIBUTIONS OF THE WISC-III
TO ASSESSMENT OF CHILDREN
WITH EMOTIONAL DIFFICULTIES

As previously noted, the WISC-III provides a valid and reliable measure of a child's cognitive functioning, which can help identify or rule out comorbid conditions, such as LD or mental retardation, for children presenting with emotional difficulties. It can also provide information regarding a particular child's cognitive strengths or weaknesses that can be useful in designing academic or instructional interventions. Such information is also likely to be of value in choosing a particular therapy, for example, embarking on therapy that relies to a greater or lesser extent on verbal mediation (Cooper, 1995).

A child's responses on the WISC-III can help examiners to gain insight into the child's personality. Kamphaus (1993) notes that the open-ended nature of the Vocabulary subtest allows the child to express information of clinical importance. The Comprehension subtest assesses both knowledge of and conformity to societal conventions and can elicit rich clinical cues about a child's personality (Zimmerman & Woo-Sam, 1985).

Observations of child's behavior during administration of the WISC-III may also provide some insight into, for example, the manner in which a child handles challenges and frustration. However, one must interpret a child's behavior during testing with great caution. Although there is a significant relationship between a child's behavior during testing and their performance on the WISC-III, there is little relationship between children's test-taking behavior and behavior in other contexts (Gluting et al., 1996).

CASE STUDIES

Two case studies are presented to show how various children and adolescents with ED perform on the WISC-III. In each case, a brief background is given and other test scores (i.e., rating scales, academic screening, etc.) are provided when available. These cases were taken from typical referrals of two school psychologists in a large urban school district.

CASE #1

Background

Donald is an African-American boy referred for psychoeducational evaluation by his classroom teacher who expressed concern about his socioemotional functioning and achievement. Donald is described as moody. His teacher says that he is frequently oppositional and often looks sad. With the exception of a few classmates, most of his peers stay clear of Donald because he has been physically aggressive and is easily provoked.

Donald is the second of three children. He has an older brother in middle school and a younger brother in K-5. Both of Donald's parents are employed. His mother is a clerical worker and his father is an unskilled laborer who holds two jobs. Donald's father works virtually 6–7 days a week and his average work day with both jobs is approximately 14 hours. The family, particularly Donald's mother, is very religious, and the children attend church every Sunday. They view themselves as loving parents. They are extremely protective and do not allow their children to roam the neighborhood or even participate in organized recreational activities that will have them arriving home after dark. Spanking is the primary mode of discipline in the home.

Both parents downplayed Donald's difficulties. When told that Donald appeared depressed, his father commented that Donald seemed like any other kid and that he was happy at home most of the time. Donald's mother acknowledged conflicts with brothers at home and some sulking and moodiness, but said she felt that Donald was a pretty happy kid at home, and that most of his difficulties must be related to the school environment. Yet on the mother's version of the Child Behavior Checklist (CBCL), Donald's behavior was rated in the clinically significant range for anxiety and depression and in the borderline ranges for withdrawn behavior, attention problems, and aggressive behavior.

WISC-III				*IQ*	*Percentile*	*Confidence interval*
Information	5	Picture Completion	8	Verbal	74	4	71–81
Similarities	2	Coding	9	Perform	90	25	72–86
Arithmetic	10	Picture Arrangement	8	Full Scale	80	9	70–80
Vocabulary	5	Block Design	7	VC	69	2	73–84
Comprehension	5	Object Assembly	10	PO	90	25	74–88
(Digit Span)	8	(Symbol Search)	6	FD	96	39	68–83
		(Mazes)	14	PS	88	21	72–89

Bender Visual/Motor Gestalt Test

Developmental age range 5–6 to 5–11 (Koppitz Scoring System). Primarily rotation and integration errors and an unusual perseveration error.

WRAT-3	*Std. S.*	*Percentile*	*Grade S.*
Reading	88	21	2
Spelling	84	14	1
Arithmetic	95	37	2

Reynolds Child Depression Scale

RS 101   %ile: 99

Achenback Behavior Rating Scales

CBCL (Father) INT T: 48; EXT T: 54 (rated in normal range for all areas)
CBCL (mother) INT T:73; EXT T: 68 (clinically significant range for anxious/depressed; borderline range for withdrawn, attention problems, aggressive behavior)
TRF (classroom teacher) INT T: 78; EXT T: 83 (clinically significant range for withdrawn, anxious/depressed, attention problems, aggressive behavior; borderline range for social problems and delinquent behavior.)

KINETIC FAMILY DRAWING AND CLINICAL INTERVIEW

Projective data suggest Donald sees his parents as preoccupied with their adult lives and concerns. He feels he is treated unfairly at home and at school. He feels he is not a competent student.

IMPLICATIONS FOR INTERVENTIONS

Donald's profile of cognitive-intellectual and psychological strengths and weaknesses shows a young student with high levels of depression, anxiety and withdrawal, and physical aggressiveness in conjunction with verbal language delays and relative strengths in nonverbal, PO abilities. Slightly depressed achievement scores were also obtained in the reading and spelling area, with average skills in arithmetic.

Although his clinical profile shows that Donald displays signs of depression and aggression, these may be exasperated by his academic, school-related difficulties. Interventions should focus on a combination of socioemotional and academic adjustment strategies. A functional analysis of his classroom should be conducted to determine the following: (a) the degree to which verbal-language delays interfere with comprehension of written and verbal material; (b) the extent to which reading and spelling difficulties interfere with completing and comprehending classwork; and (c) the appropriateness of the present instructional level given apparent verbal-language weaknesses.

Consultation with teachers might focus on designing accommodations in the classroom including the following: utilize high-interest and motivating instructional materials; utilize multisensory strategies; and encourage active participation with choices that maximize Donald's PO strengths. Utilize graphic organizers to increase meaning making when reading. These may include techniques such as storyboards, where the sequence of the story events are drawn in separate boxes; story charts, where characters, story plots, sequences of story events, and story problems and endings are arranged; plot profiles, where story events are reviewed by the class and each child selects the most exciting part of the story—these are plotted on a large graph; circle stories, where the main events of a story with a cyclical theme (e.g., If You Give a Mouse a Cookie) are arranged around a circle according to the sequence—students then retell the story and draw pictures; or character webs, where the name of the main character is put in the center of web and descriptions of the character are filled in to attaching circles. Efforts should be made to increase reading, vocabulary, and language abilities using reciprocal teaching strategies. These include questioning strategies where the student is taught how to use questioning and answering techniques while reading. Students learn how to use self-monitoring skills when reading after modeling from teacher-generated questions.[1]

---

[1] See Reif's (1993) handbook entitled, "How to Reach and Teach ADD/ADHD Children" for these and other practical techniques for children. Although the title targets ADD/ADHD children, this book is filled with many useful strategies for teachers.

Therapeutic efforts to address depressive and aggressive tendencies may include strategies that allow for active participation (e.g., role playing and modeling), the use of natural social situations, where problem solving can be discussed and the student can practice new skills, and the use of group-oriented projects and games (e.g., Ropes Curriculum where small groups of children work, play, or do a project together). When using cognitive-behavioral or talk-therapy techniques, reduce the complexity and length of verbal interchanges. Keep it simple, direct, and repetitious. Utilize behavior management techniques in the classroom to increase effective anger control. Help alter Donald's "bad boy" status among his peers by assigning important helping tasks, giving him verbal praise for a job well done, increasing learning or free-time choices for completed work and compliance, allowing him to regain lost points by self-correcting within 1–2 minutes of his infraction, and using nonverbal or private cues to avoid problem areas. Avoid using feedback where Donald's academic and/or behavioral weaknesses are made in public.

CASE #2: ADHD WITH CONDUCT-RELATED DIFFICULTIES

This is a second-grade (9.5 years old) student who was referred due to concerns about hyperactivity, impulsivity, impatience, and inappropriate social behavior.

Background

Henry repeated the first grade after being administratively transferred to another school because of inappropriate touching. His first-grade teachers reported that Henry had trouble distinguishing "good" from inappropriate touching, and was within the clinically elevated range for aggressive behavior and inattention (Achenbach Scales). Elevated scores were also obtained on the Conner's scale for inattention/impulsivity. These behaviors were highly resistant to a classroom-based management system, extensive teacher consultation with the school psychologist, and psychoeducational therapy on a weekly basis for an academic year. Therapy focused on social skills building and aggression management. Although he was referred to an outside agency for further evaluation and treatment for ADHD, his mother was unable to follow-up on the recommendation.

In the following year (second grade), Henry was referred for an evaluation for ED, after 50 referrals to the office for a variety of severely disruptive, destructive, and aggressive behaviors. During this timeframe, Henry's teacher was concerned that he was dangerous to himself and to others in the classroom. Henry was also performing well below grade level in all academic areas of functioning.

At present Henry lives at home with his mother and a younger sibling. His mother describes him as extremely active and angry when he doesn't get his way. Henry's mother endorsed attentional problems, aggressive behavior, delinquency, and social problems all within a clinically elevated range. A clinical diagnosis of

ADHD was made at a community-based clinic, and Henry was placed on stimulant medication. Although Henry has been more on-task and has shown improvement in the areas of impulsivity and disruption, he still has serious trouble controlling his aggression and has frequent temper outbursts. Oppositional defiance and social interaction difficulties also persist, and are most pronounced in settings where there is little structure (e.g., the playground)

Behavioral Observations

Henry was observed on multiple occasions since the beginning of the school year, as well as during small group, one-to-one counseling, and in testing sessions. Regardless of the setting, Henry tends to be extremely verbal and displays a high level of activity (i.e., bounces, fidgets, squirms, and out-of-seat). He is highly impulsive and has trouble restraining himself from grabbing other student's or the teacher's materials. When his classmates express their displeasure in his behaviors, Henry typically reacts in an angry, confrontational, or violent manner. During testing, he was generally cooperative, although he required frequent redirection and encouragement.

Intellectual and Academic Functioning

Henry's intellectual functioning was initially shown (2 years ago) to fall within the extremely lower limits of the low–average range. Current cognitive assessment is consistent with this estimate.

WISC-III				IQ	Percentile	Confidence interval
Information	4	Picture Completion	4	Verbal	75	5	71–81
Similarities	5	Coding	6	Perform	77	6	72–86
Arithmetic	5	Picture Arrangement	8	Full Scale	74	4	70–80
Vocabulary	6	Block Design	8	VC	77	6	73–84
Comprehension	8	Object Assembly	5	PO	79	8	74–88
(Digit Span)	5	(Symbol Search)	5	FD	72	3	68–83
		(Mazes)	7	PS	77	6	72–89

Academically, Henry shows achievement at the pre-first-grade level in word recognition. At present, he is able to identify most letter-sounds and has learned a few sight words. Overall, Henry's academic performance is consistent with measured levels of cognitive-intellectual abilities.

Socioemotional Functioning

Observations, projective data, and parent–teacher reports suggest that Henry has significant emotional difficulties that when combined with his marked ADHD characteristics (impulsivity and hyperactivity) have resulted in a long-standing pattern of aggressive, destructive, and disruptive behaviors. Henry's apparent cognitive delays also appear to be contributing to his overall behavioral difficulties.

Major concerns have been expressed over Henry's aggression, and he has been frequently sent out of the classroom because of dangerous behaviors. He often hits, kicks, and throws objects at other students. Teachers have also expressed serious concerns about Henry's inappropriate touching and behavior toward female classmates. Recently these behaviors have decreased and no incidents have been reported since the beginning of the school year.

Projective and interview data also suggest that Henry has some difficulty understanding the consequences of his misbehavior. Furthermore, Henry's version of events typically varies substantially from the perceptions of others. He also has trouble comprehending the interpersonal consequences of his actions. Although Henry reports that he has many friends at school, his teachers report that it is difficult to find children who are willing to work or play with Henry. While he typically reacts with anger or aggression when limits are placed on him, Henry otherwise appears quite personable in a one-to-one relationship with adults. Despite a well-documented history of conduct problems, Henry appears to enjoy school. He has shown improvement in impulse control and attention to task subsequent to medication. However, Henry continues to respond to limits with forceful opposition. His defiance often escalates to temper outbursts. Finally, Henry also continues to behave aggressively toward peers generally without substantive or apparent provocation.

Implications for Interventions

Many of the same strategies described for Donald might also be appropriate for Henry. However, a highly structured management plan should be implemented immediately. Henry might benefit from a highly structured classroom with predictable routines and clear, concise expectations. Consequences should be fair and follow-through should be consistent. Attempts to prevent behavioral problems should be ongoing. Use of color-coded cards to monitor emotions and behaviors is recommended. The student starts out with a pink card, is verbally warned after a rule infraction, and after another misbehavior, the card is changed to yellow (warning), which results in a prearranged consequence (5-minute time-out). If the child misbehaves again, the card is changed to the next card (blue then red) and a more serious consequence is given. Allow the class to help make up consequences. This system allows the child several opportunities to correct himself and also allows for a clean slate at the beginning of every day. See Reif (1993) for more details. (It is important to note that some psychologists have cautioned against using reductive and time-out procedures for children with serious EDs particularly when interpersonal and social maladjustment is an issue). Attempts to improve social bonding, attachment, and relationships should be incorporated into management programs focusing on behavioral control.

Preventive cuing to prevent and/or reduce behavioral problems in the classroom should be considered. Proximity control may be helpful where the teacher circulates through the class and places a hand on the target student's shoulder or stays within close proximity to the child to help maintain focus and on-task behaviors.

The teacher should develop a crisis plan for times when Henry loses control, such as having another adult available so calming strategies are done; the remaining classmates can be moved to another room until the crisis is over. Techniques for allowing the tantrum to run its course while avoiding injury to Henry or others should be utilized. Use a calm and soothing voice, avoid a confrontational style, and use special holding techniques during rage periods. Once Henry has gained some control allow a period of time for him to regain his composure before returning to work.

SUMMARY OF CASE STUDIES

In both these cases, different emotional problems were accompanied by rather significant verbal-language problems. In Henry's case, he showed a more severe range of ED problems and also had lower overall IQ. Techniques that address these basic cognitive weaknesses should be considered along with other therapeutic interventions (e.g., behavior management, role playing and modeling of appropriate social behaviors, and self- and anger control). Clinicians are advised to consider the cognitive and academic profiles of children with ED when planning therapeutic interventions. Care should also be taken to avoid highly verbal, talk therapy for children with low verbal language skills. There are numerous other therapeutic strategies that incorporate more natural social situations where self-control and problem solving can be taught in "real-life" scenarios.

In the following section, considerations for future use of the WISC-III when assessing and treating children with ED are discussed.

FUTURE RESEARCH DIRECTIONS

Future research must address the need for multimethod, longitudinal assessment, a developmental–ecological perspective, and linking cognitive factors to intervention planning for studying ED in children. This includes the notion of cognitive-intellectual functions as a protective or mediating factor for long-term outcome and for treating children with ED. Methods for improving cognitive functioning as part of a comprehensive intervention plan for children and adolescents with ED are briefly discussed next.

MULTIMETHOD, LONGITUDINAL RESEARCH

Although assessment and diagnosis of ED in children often focuses on observational, rating scales, and interviewing methods, there are a number of reasons why measures of intelligence should be incorporated into a comprehensive assessment. First, there is sufficient evidence that children with low cognitive abilities are at risk for developing academic and behavioral problems. Given its strong psychometric properties, the WISC-III may serve an important role in research investigating these relationships.

Second, EDs and BDs are associated with a myriad of cognitive, neuropsychological, and neurodevelopmental anomalies that directly or indirectly impact on the child's adjustment in academic, psychosocial, and family settings. Teeter and Semrud-Clikeman (1995, 1997) argue that assessment and intervention planning for children with various psychiatric, psychosocial, and behavioral problems should be conducted within a transactional, integrated paradigm. Furthermore, by more carefully delineating these associated features, intervention and prevention research may be significantly advanced by integrated models.

Third, there may be different developmental pathways for children with various EDs depending on the presence of other cognitive and/or neurodevelopmental disorders. It is important to determine the developmental course of ED in children and to investigate how various factors commingle to produce negative outcomes in children. For example, how do emotional and/or behavioral problems interact with low cognitive abilities to affect academic underachievement in children? Research with the WISC-R suggests that this is potentially fruitful, and may help us understand the long-term outcome of children with various externalized disorders of childhood (Frick et al., 1991). It would be important to determine this relationship using the WISC-III. Do ED children with higher verbal abilities remain more academically engaged than ED children with significant difficulties? To what extent are difficulties in reading emotions, understanding complex socioemotional interactions, and picking up subtle psychosocial cues in one's environment related to verbal or nonverbal intellectual abilities in children with ED? These factors warrant more careful study.

Furthermore, a need to conduct longitudinal research within an ecological framework is needed.

DEVELOPMENTAL–ECOLOGICAL PERSPECTIVE

A number of theories argue for a developmental framework for predicting and preventing EDs and other psychosocial behavioral problems. These theoretical paradigms emphasize the importance of the interplay of normal developmental challenges and risks, the interaction of multiple causal factors (e.g., parental psychopathology, biological vulnerabilities) that impact differentially depending on the age of the child, the determination of different developmental or risk pathways, and the cumulative risk over a child's life span (Teeter, in press; Teeter & Semrud-Clikeman, 1997).

Research investigating the developmental course of ED and BD in children is important for a number of reasons. First, major paradigms emphasize a developmental–ecological perspective for predicting, intervening, and/or preventing serious delinquency and substance abuse (Guerra, Huesmann, Tolan, Acker, & Eron, 1995) and antisocial BD (Tremblay et al., 1995). Barkley (1990) and Teeter (in press) also argue for a developmental perspective for treating ADHD in children and adolescents, where biological vulnerabilities can be managed and serious disturbances can be reduced when interventions and modifications also focus on the child's home and school environment.

Second, the extent to which cognitive abilities interact with ED and further predict a developmental pathway or particular outcome needs further research. A number of important questions could be better answered with such studies. For example, do children with ED differ in terms of outcome based on their cognitive and academic performance? See Zimet et al. (1994) for a review of the three cognitive profile patterns for children with ED. Would we expect different outcomes in children with more cognitive resources to deal with or cope with problems, particularly in interpersonal, social, and academic domains?

Third, the study of cultural and ethnic differences within an ecological, developmental framework may prove important, where effects of environmental stress (e.g., socioeconomic status, neighborhood violence, etc.), family resources (e.g., extended family support, parental psychological health), and school environment (e.g., school climate, levels of violence) interact with child variables (e.g., cultural background, cognitive abilities, academic engagement, self-control, etc.) to produce positive academic, behavioral, and psychosocial outcomes. Often we address these individual child factors in isolation when an ecological model is both more accurate and potentially more beneficial. For example, by only addressing child factors in therapy, we might not affect other critical stress factors that might even have more impact (e.g., decreasing violence in the school environment) if they too were the focus of intervention. These studies may also shed light on how producing healthy environments impacts the child in positive ways.

LINKING COGNITIVE FACTORS TO INTERVENTION PLANS

There is a need to determine the extent to which cognitive strengths and weaknesses can be factored into research studies investigating therapeutic intervention efficacy. Intervention efficacy might be enhanced when programs consider a combination of factors including the child's psychosocial, cognitive, and academic profile within an ecological perspective where home and school environments are also a target of intervention. The extent to which verbal strengths or weaknesses facilitated or interfere with traditional psychotherapy also needs further investigation.

Research might also examine how cognitive factors interact with various EDs and BDs to determine if meaningful patterns emerge for children with depression and low verbal abilities or for children with conduct disorders and low verbal abilities. Furthermore, investigation into the impact of different profiles of cognitive impairment on early versus late emergence of ED also may be useful. For example, do children with early verbal-language impairments with accompanying academic delays place the child at significant risk for developing secondary emotional and self-esteem issues and more internalized disorders? Can cognitive and academically based interventions significantly reduce this cycle when instruction is done within a therapeutic, supportive classroom environment? Are children with high verbal abilities and low nonverbal reasoning skills at-risk for depression and social withdrawal due to difficulty interpreting nonverbal cues? Are children with lower cognitive abilities more at-risk for developing emotional problems in school?

Further, do ED children with low verbal abilities show a different course or outcome than children with higher verbal abilities? Do ED children with higher verbal abilities show better long-term outcome because these cognitive skills are so useful in academic settings? Success in the academic area may be a way in which a child with emotional problems can gain positive reinforcement from teachers and increased self-esteem from this interaction. Do children with higher verbal abilities have better cognitive skills for understanding and expressing complex emotions (i.e., pride, guilt, joy, nervousness, etc.) than children without these cognitive resources? The ability to understand and express emotion and to negotiate and compromise in conflict situations are important social as well as cognitive skills. Would we expect a better outcome for children if interventions targeted both emotional as well as cognitive abilities in enriched language-based and therapeutic environments when these problems first appear? We need more data to sufficiently answer these important questions.

In effect, the extent to which intelligence serves as a mediating factor improving the long-term outcome for ED children needs further investigation. The relationship between the severity and chronicity of ED and overall cognitive developmental appears to be a fruitful area of inquiry. However, White et al. (1989) caution that we must be careful in how we formulate these studies, and suggest that "the important question then becomes, what characteristics differentiate low-IQ children who do not develop antisocial behavior patterns from those who do?" (p. 723). It might be important to also determine if the child's maladaptive coping strategies (i.e., internalized versus externalized responses) are related to various cognitive profiles (e.g., high/low IQ or high/low verbal IQ). Thus, the WISC-III should play an important role in developmental, ecological models for SED in children.

SUMMARY

The WISC-III has been shown to have utility in understanding the full range of problems of children with ED. Initial studies generally have shown that ED children do score in the low–average range of ability, although no discernible pattern of cognitive performance has been found. Further research is needed to answer important questions about the relationship between cognitive abilities and ED, particularly within a developmental, ecological model. These studies will also shed light on how cognitive strengths and weaknesses can be incorporated into intervention programs to reduce the negative impact of emotional problems. Future research should also clarify the relationship among various classification systems (e.g., psychiatric vs. educational models, categorical vs. empirical) and treatment strategies. Finally, more research is needed to determine the extent to which children with more severe BDs and EDs also have other associated cognitive and academic difficulties. The issue of comorbidity may be helpful in this light, as children with more than one psychiatric disorder often have a more guarded outcome.

REFERENCES

Achenback, T. M., & McConaughy, S. H. (1996). Relations between DSM-IV and empirically based assessment. *School Psychology Review, 25,* 329–341.

American Psychiatric Association. (1994). *Diagnostic and statistical manual of mental disorders* (4th ed.). Washington, DC: Author.

Barkley, R. A. (1990). *Attention deficit hyperactivity disorder,* New York, NY: Guilford Press.

Cooper, S. (1995). *The Clinical Use and Interpretation of the Wechsler Intelligence Scale for Children-3rd Edition,* Springfield, IL: Charles C. Thomas.

Dean, R. S. (1977). Patterns of emotional disturbance on the WISC-R. *Journal of Clinical Psychology, 33* (2), 486–490.

Dixon, W. E. & Anderson, T. (1995). Establishing covariance continuity between the WISC-R and the WISC-III. *Psychological Assessment, 7,* 115–117.

Earls, F. (1989). Epidemiology and child psychiatry: Entering the second phase. *American Journal of Orthopsychiatry, 59,* 279–283.

Epstein, M. H., Kauffman, J. M., & Cullinan, D. (1985). Patterns of maladjustment among the behaviorally disordered, II: Boys aged 6–11, boys aged 12–18, girls aged 6–11, and girls aged 12–18. *Behavioral Disorders, 10,* 12–13.

Finch, A. J., Jr., Blount, R. L., Saylor, C. F., Wolfe, V. V., Pallmeyer, T. P., McIntosh, J. A., Griffin, J. M., & Carh, D. J. (1988). Intelligence and emotional/behavioral factors as correlates of achievement in child psychiatric inpatients. *Psychological Reports, 63,* 163–170.

Frich, P. J., Kamphaus, R. W., Lahey, B. B., Loeber, R., Christ, M. A., Hart, E. L., Tannebaum, L. E. (1991). Academic underachievement and the disruptive behavior disorders. Journal of *Consulting and Clinical Psychology, 59,* 289–294.

Fuller, G., & Goh, D. (1981). Intelligence, achievement, and visual-motor performance among learning disabled and emotionally impaired children. *Psychology in the Schools, 18,* 261–268.

Glutting, J. J., Youngstrom, E. A., Oakland, T., & Watkins, M. W. (1996). Situational specificity and generality of test behaviors for samples of normal and referred children. *School Psychology Review, 25,* 94–107.

Goodman, R., Dimonoff, E., & Stevenson, J. (1995). The impact of child IQ, parent IQ and sibling IQ on child behavioral deviance scores. *Journal of Child Psychology and Psychiatry, 36,* 409–425.

Guerra, N. G., Huesmann, R., Tolan, P. H., Acker, R. V. & Eron, L. D. (1995). Stressful events and individual beliefs as correlates of economic disadvantage and aggression among urban children. *Journal of Consulting and Clinical Psychology, 63,* 518–528.

Hale, R. L., & Landino, S. A. (1981). Utility of WISC-R subtest analysis in discriminating among groups of conduct problem, withdrawn, mixed, and nonproblem boys. *Journal of Consulting and Clinical Psychology, 1,* 91–95.

Hartlage, L. C., & Steele, C. T. (1977). WISC and WISC-R correlates of academic achievement. *Psychology in the Schools, 14,* 15–18.

Hishinuma, E. S., & Yamakawa, R. (1993). Construct and criterion-related validity of the WISC-III for exceptional students and those who are at risk. *Journal of Psychoeducational Assessment: WISC-III Monograph* (pp. 94–104). Cordova, TN: The Psychoeducational Corporation.

Hodges, K., & Plow, J. (1990). Intellectual ability and achievement in psychiatrically hospitalized children with conduct, anxiety, and affective disorders. *Journal of Consulting and Clinical Psychology, 58,* 589–595.

Ipsen, S. M., McMillan, J. H., & Fallen, N. H. (1983). An investigation of the reported discrepancy between the Woodcock-Johnson Tests of Cognitive Ability and the Wechsler Intelligence Scale for Children—Revised. *Diagnostique, 9,* 32–44.

Juul, K. D. (1986). Epidemiological studies of behavior disorders in children: An international survey. *International Journal of Special Education, 1,* 1–20.

Kamphaus, R. W. (1993). *Clinical Assessment of Children's Intelligence: A Handbook for Professional Practice.* Boston: Allyn & Bacon.

Kashani, J. H., McGee, R. O., Clarkson, S. E., Anderson, J. C., Walton, L. A., Williams, S., Silva, P. A., Robins, A. J., Cytryn, L., & McKnew, D. H. (1983). Depression in a sample of 9-year-old children. *Archives of General Psychiatry, 40,* 1217–1223.

Kaslow, N. J., Tannenbaum, R. L., Abramson, L. Y., Peterson, C., & Seligman, M. E. P. (1983). Problem-solving deficits and depressive symptoms among children. *Journal of Abnormal Child Psychology, 11,* 497–502.

Kaufman, A. S. (1975). Factor analysis of the WISC-R at eleven age levels between 6.5 and 16.5 years. *Journal of Clinical and Consulting and Psychology, 43,* 135–147.

Kaufman, A. S. (1979). *Intelligent testing with the WISC-R.* New York: Wiley-Interscience.

Kaufman, A. S., & Kaufman, N. L. (1985). *Kaufman Test of Educational Achievement—Comprehensive Form.* Circle Pines, MN: American Guidance Service.

Kazdin, A. E. (1987). *Conduct disorders in childhood and adolescence.* Beverly Hills, CA: Sage.

Lavin, C. (1996). The relationship between the Wechsler Intelligence Scale for Children-Third Edition and the Kaufman Test of Educational Achievement. *Psychology in the Schools, 33,* 119–123.

Lefkowitz, M. M., & Tesiny, E. (1980). Assessment of childhood depression. *Journal of Consulting and Clinical Psychology, 48,* 43–50.

Lefkowitz, M. M., & Tesiny, E. (1985). Depression in children: Prevalence and correlates. *Journal of Consulting and Clinical Psychology, 53,* 647–656.

Lufi, D., & Cohen, A. (1988). Differential diagnosis of learning disability versus emotional disturbance using the WISC-R. *Journal of Learning Disabilities, 21,* 515–516.

McGinnis, E., & Forness, S. (1988). Psychiatric diagnosis: A further test of the special education eligibility hypothesis. *Severe Behavior Disorders Monograph, 11,* 3–10.

Paget, K. D. (1982). Intellectual patterns of conduct problem children on the WISC-R. *Psychology in the Schools, 19,* 439–445.

Paramesh, C. R. (1982). Relationship between Quick Test and WISC-R and reading ability as used in a juvenile setting. *Perceptual and Motor Skills, 55,* 881–882.

Prinz, R. J., & Miller, G. E. (1991). Issues in understanding and treating childhood conduct problems in disadvantaged populations. *Journal of Clinical Child Psychology, 20,* 379–385.

Quay, H. C. (1986). Conduct disorder. In H. C. Quay & J. S. Werry (Eds.), *Psychopathological disorders of early childhood* (3rd ed., pp. 35–72). New York: Wiley.

Reif, S. (1993). *How to reach and teach ADD/ADHD children.* West Nyack, NY: The Center for Applied Research in Education.

Reschly, D., & Reschly, J. E. (1979). Validity of WISC-R factor scores in predicting achievement and attention for four sociocultural groups. *Journal of School Psychology, 17,* 355–361.

Reynolds, C. R., & Gutkin, T. B. (1980). A regression analysis of test bias on the WISC-R for Anglos and Chicanos referred to psychological services. *Journal of Abnormal Child Psychology,* 237–243.

Schooler, D. L., Beebe, M. C., & Koepke, T. (1978). Factor analysis of WISC-R scores for children identified as learning disabled, educable mentally impaired, and emotionally impaired. *Psychology in the Schools, 15,* 478–485.

Schwartz, M., Friedman, R., Lindsay, P., & Narrol, H. (1982). The relationship between conceptual tempor and depression in children. *Journal of Consulting and Clinical Psychology, 50,* 488–490.

Scott, S. (1994). Mental handicap. In M. Rutter, E. Taylor, & L. Hersov (Eds.), *Child and adolescent psychiatry* (3rd ed., pp. 616–646). Oxford: Blackwells.

Semrud-Clikeman, M., Hynd, G. W., Lorys, A. R. & Lahey, B. B. (1993). Differential diagnosis of children with ADHD and ADHD/with Co-occurring conduct disorder. *School Psychology International, 14,* 361–370.

Short, R. J., & Shapiro, S. K. (1993). Conduct disorders: A framework for understanding and intervention in schools and communities. *School Psychology Review, 22,* 362–375.

Stone, F. B. (1981). Behavior problems of elementary-school children. *Journal of Abnormal Child Psychology, 9,* 407–418.

Teeter, P. A. (in press). *A developmental perspective for ADHD: Therapeutic interventions through the lifespan.* New York: Guilford Press.

Teeter, P. A., & Semrud-Clikeman, M. (1995). Integrating neurobiological, psychosocial, and behavioral paradigms: A transactional model for the study of ADHD. *Archives of Clinical Neuropsychology.*

Teeter, P. A., & Semrud-Clikeman, M. (1997). *Child neuropsychology: Assessment and interventions for neuropsychiatric and neurodevelopmental disorders of childhood.* Needham Heights, MA: Allyn & Bacon.

Teeter, P. A., & Smith, P. L. (1993). WISC-III and WJ-R: predictive and discriminant validity for students with severe emotional disturbance. *Journal of Assessment: Advances in Psychoeducational Assessment: WISC-III Monograph* (pp. 114–124). Cordorva, TN: The Psychoeducational Corporation.

Tesiny, E. P., Lefkowitz, M. M., & Gordon, N. H. (1980). Childhood depression, locus of control, and school achievement. *Journal of Educational Psychology, 34,* 506–510.

Tremblay, R. E., Pagani-Kurtz, L., Masse, L. C., Pihl, R. O. (1995). A bimodal preventive intervention for disruptive kindergarten boys: Its impact through mid-adolescence. *Journal of Consulting and Clinical Psychology, 63,* 560–568.

Vance, B., Mayes, L., Fuller, G. B., & Abdullah, A. A. (1994). A preliminary study of the relationship of the WISC-III and WRAT-3 with a sample of exceptional students. *Diagnositque, 19,* 15–21.

Vance, H. B., Fuller, G. B., & Ellis, R. (1983). Discriminant function analysis of LD/BD scores on the WISC-R. *Journal of Clinical Psychology, 39,* 749–753.

Wechsler, D. (1974). *Manual for the Wechsler Intelligence Scale for Children-Revised.* New York: The Psychological Corporation.

Wechsler, D. (1991). *Manual for the Wechsler Intelligence Scale for Children-Third Edition.* San Antonio, TX: The Psychological Corporation.

Weinberg, W., & Rehmet, A. (1983). Childhood affective disorder and school problems. In D. P. Cantwell & G. A. Carlson (Eds.), *Affective disorders in childhood and adolescence—An update* (pp. 109–128). New York: Spectrum.

Weiss, R., & Hechtman, L. (1986). *Hyperactive children grown up.* New York: Guilford Press.

Wielkiewicz, R. M. (1990). Interpreting low scores on the WISC-R third factor: It's more than distractibility. *Journal of Consulting and Clinical Psychology, 2* (1), 91–97.

White, J. L., Moffitt, T. E., & Silva, P. A. (1989). A prospective replication of the protective effects of IQ in subjects at high risk for juvenile delinquency. *Journal of Consulting and Clinical Psychology, 57,* 719–724.

Wilkinson, G. S. (1993). *Wide Range Achievement Test-3.* Wilmington, DE: Widerange Inc.

Zimmerman, I. L., & Woo-Sam, J. M. (1985). Clinical applications. In B. B. Wolman (Ed.), *Handbook of intelligence: Theories, measurements, and applications* (pp. 873–898). New York: Wiley.

Zimet, S. G., Farley, G. K., Shapiro-Adler, S., & Zimmerman, T. (1994). Intellectual competence of children who are beginning inpatient and day psychiatric treatment. *Journal of Clinical Psychology, 50,* 866–877.

7

SIGNIFICANCE

OF VERBAL–PERFORMANCE

DISCREPANCIES

FOR SUBTYPES OF CHILDREN

WITH LEARNING DISABILITIES:

OPPORTUNITIES FOR THE WISC-III

BYRON P. ROURKE

Department of Psychology
University of Windsor
Windsor, Ontario, Canada
and
School of Medicine
Yale University
New Haven, Connecticut

In this chapter an attempt is made to chart the course for some potentially interesting and contributory studies relating to the development of the concurrent, predictive, and construct validity of the WISC-III. The focus of the chapter is on a particular clinical group: children and young adolescents with learning disabilities (LD).

We begin with a generic definition of LD. Next, there is a consideration of our studies of Verbal IQ–Performance IQ (VIQ–PIQ) discrepancies in children and young adolescents with LD using the forerunners of the WISC-III. Included are considerations relating to the neuropsychological significance of these findings as well as their psychosocial dimensions. Then, some considerations regarding the dimensionality of the WISC-III in some other populations of interest are presented. Throughout the chapter, an agenda for future studies is proposed.

GENERIC DEFINITION
OF LEARNING DISABILITIES

LEARNING DISABILITIES:
GENERICALLY AND SPECIFICALLY

The following is a working definition of LD considered from a generic perspective that we have found useful:

> LD is a generic term that refers to a heterogeneous group of disorders manifested by significant difficulties in the mastery of one or more of the following: listening, speaking, reading, writing, reasoning, mathematical, and other skills and abilities that are traditionally referred to as "academic." The term LD is also appropriately applied in instances where persons exhibit significant difficulties in mastering social and other adaptive skills and abilities. In some cases, investigations of LD have yielded evidence that would be consistent with hypotheses relating central nervous system dysfunction to the disabilities in question. Even though a learning disability may occur concomitantly with other handicapping conditions (e.g., sensory impairment, mental retardation, social and emotional disturbance) or environmental influences (e.g., cultural differences, insufficient/inappropriate instruction, psychogenic factors), it is not the direct result of those conditions or influences. However, it is possible that emotional disturbances and other adaptive deficiencies may arise from the same patterns of central processing assets and deficits that generate the manifestations of academic and social LD. LD may arise from genetic variations, biochemical factors, events in the pre- to peri-natal period, or any other subsequent events resulting in neurological impairment. (Rourke, 1989, p. 215).

Note especially that this is a *generic* definition that, although including the notion of heterogeneity, does not specify the nature of the subtypes that are inferred. Of critical importance within the present context is that specific subtypes of LD have been identified, some of which can be defined rather precisely, have excellent reliability, and have been shown to have concurrent and predictive validity with respect to a number of important neurodevelopmental and psychosocial dimensions (Rourke, 1985, 1991). These can be more fruitfully addressed within the context of the following discussions.

CRITERIA FOR DESIGNATION
OF CHILDREN AS LEARNING DISABLED

It is important to note that, except where specified to the contrary, the participants employed in the series of investigations to be reviewed in this chapter met a fairly standard definition for children with LD (Rourke, 1975, 1978). That is, these children

1. performed in a markedly deficient manner in at least one academic subject area;
2. obtained WISC Full Scale IQs (FSIQ) within the roughly normal range;
3. were free of primary emotional disturbance;
4. had adequate visual and auditory acuity;
5. lived in homes and communities where socioeconomic deprivation was not a factor;
6. had experienced only the usual childhood illnesses;
7. had attended school regularly since the age of 5½ or 6 years;
8. spoke English as their native language.

Of course, it should be noted that the generalizability of the results of the studies to be discussed in this chapter must be viewed within the context of the "exclusionary" criteria that were employed in the selection of subjects for them.

WISC VERBAL IQ–PERFORMANCE IQ DISCREPANCIES: NEURODEVELOPMENTAL DIMENSIONS

Presented in this section is a review of our studies that focused on the concurrent validity of VIQ and PIQ discrepancies on the WISC (Wechsler, 1949) for children with LD.

STUDY 1

The first study in the series (Rourke, Young, & Flewelling, 1971) involved children with LD who were chosen for study on the basis of VIQ and PIQ discrepancies on the WISC (Wechsler, 1949). It was designed to assess the relationships between such discrepancies and selected verbal, auditory-perceptual, visual-perceptual, and problem-solving abilities. Three groups, each containing 30 children with LD, were formed on the basis of the relationship between their VIQ and PIQ scores on the WISC. One group (HP-LV) consisted of subjects whose PIQ was at least 10 points higher than their VIQ; a second group (V = P) was composed of subjects with VIQ and PIQ within 4 points of each other; and the third group (HV-LP) had VIQ values at least 10 points higher than their PIQ. All participants fell within a FSIQ range between 79 to 119 and an age range of 9 to 14 years; there were no significant differences in either WISC FSIQ or age between the three groups.

As expected, the performance of the HV-LP group was superior to that of the HP-LV group on those tasks that involved verbal and auditory-perceptual skills: Peabody Picture Vocabulary Test (PPVT; Dunn, 1965); Aphasia Screening, Speech-Sounds Perception, and Seashore Rhythm Tests (Reitan & Davison, 1974); Reading, Spelling, and Arithmetic subtests of the Wide Range Achievement Test (WRAT; Jastak & Jastak, 1965). The differences on all but the PPVT were statistically significant.

The performances of the HP-LV group were, as expected, superior to those of the HV-LP group on tasks that primarily involve visual-perceptual skills: Trail Making Test (TMT), Part A, and Target Test (Reitan & Davison, 1974). Also as expected, the performances of the V = P group were roughly intermediate between those of the other two groups over most of the dependent measures. Although the difference was not statistically significant, the HP-LV group did somewhat better than the HV-LP group on the Category Test (Reitan & Davison, 1974).

Of particular importance in the present context were two additional findings of this study that had not been anticipated. First, the HV-LP group did well on the TMT, Part B, relative to Part A, whereas the HP-LV group did poorly on TMT, Part B, relative to Part A. This was thought to be the case because children in the HV-LP group, although relatively deficient in the visual-perceptual abilities necessary for success on both parts of the TMT, were relatively more adept than were those in the HP-LV group at the verbal and symbolic abilities necessary for success on TMT, Part B.

Second, an a posteriori comparison of the Reading, Spelling, and Arithmetic subtests of the WRAT within each of the three groups indicated a striking, statistically significant difference between Reading and Spelling (high) on the one hand and Arithmetic (low) on the other hand for the HV-LP group. Although no such statistically significant differences in performance on these three subtests of the WRAT were evident in either of the other two groups, there was an opposite trend observed in the performance of children in the HP-LV group on these WRAT measures—that is, a tendency toward higher performance on the WRAT Arithmetic subtest relative to performance on the WRAT Reading and Spelling subtests.

One important implication of the results of this investigation is that, for older (9- to 14-year-old) children, the WISC VIQ–PIQ relationship appeared to be a far more important consideration with regard to the neuropsychological ramifications of LD than is general level of psychometric intelligence. That is, although the three groups of children with LD were *equated* for WISC FSIQ, their vastly different patterns of relative cognitive strengths and weaknesses became evident when a more complex type of "IQ" characterization was employed: VIQ–PIQ discrepancies. Indeed, although we did not emphasize this point at the time, it appeared that the groups of children with LD formed on the basis of WISC VIQ–PIQ discrepancies might very well constitute unique subtypes within the LD population. This appeared to be so not only for independent measures of verbal, auditory-perceptual, and visuospatial abilities, but also for patterns of performance on the Reading, Spelling, and Arithmetic subtests of the WRAT.

One further note regarding these findings. The pattern of relative abilities (verbal and auditory-perceptual) and deficits (visuospatial) exhibited by the HV-LP group is similar to what would be expected in adults who are experiencing the debilitating effects of a significant lesion confined to the right cerebral hemisphere. Furthermore, the opposite pattern of relative abilities and deficits exhibited by the HP-LV group is similar to what would be expected in adults who are experiencing the debilitating effects of a significant lesion confined to the left cerebral hemisphere. Because these groups of children with LD with different configurations of VIQ–PIQ discrepancies exhibited patterns of performance that might suggest differential impairment of skills ordinarily thought to be subserved primarily by one or other of the two cerebral hemispheres, it was thought advisable to carry out a subsequent investigation including dependent variables from a very different adaptive domain so as to shed some additional light on this interesting theoretical question.

STUDY 2

Thus, three groups of subjects who exhibited patterns of VIQ–PIQ discrepancies virtually identical to those in the Rourke et al. (1971) investigation were selected in order to compare their performances on motor and psychomotor tasks that allowed for separate assessments of right-hand and left-hand efficiency (Rourke & Telegdy, 1971). The motor and psychomotor tasks used in this study were chosen in terms of what seemed to be varying degrees of two dimensions: (a) complexity and (b) visuospatial skills. Thus, the dependent measures ranged from relatively simple motor tasks (e.g., strength of grip, speed of tapping) to relatively complex psychomotor tasks (e.g., timed placement of grooved pegs into holes). The children with LD were chosen for study in terms of the same VIQ–PIQ criteria that were employed in the Rourke et al. (1971) investigation. The 45 male children with LD (15 in each of the HP-LV, V = P, and HV-LP groups) selected for study were between the ages of 9 and 14 years, and their WISC FSIQs fell within the range of 85 to 115. There were no statistically significant differences between the groups in terms of age or WISC FSIQ.

The performances of these three groups on 25 measures indicated clear superiority of the HP-LV group (especially in comparison to the HV-LP group) on most measures on complex motor and psychomotor abilities, regardless of the hand employed. The clearest separation of the groups was observed on the most complex psychomotor measure employed (Grooved Pegboard Test; Klove, 1963); on this task, the differences were evident for both right- and left-hand trials, with the following pattern of relative superiority between groups obtaining: HP-LV > V = P > HV-LP. There were nonsignificant trends in evidence favoring the right-hand over the left-hand performances of the HV-LP group on the Finger Tapping Test (Reitan & Davison, 1974) and the Tactual Performance Test (Reitan & Davison, 1974), with the opposite pattern of right-hand and left-hand results for the HP-LV group.

These findings, in addition to the superior performance of the HP-LV over the HV-LP group on the Location component of the Tactual Performance Test (Reitan & Davison, 1974) offered support for one of the alternative hypotheses of the study: That is, that the HP-LV group, because of relative superiority in visual-perceptual skills, would do better than the HV-LP group on tasks involving complex visual-motor coordination and spatial visualization and memory. Although expectations involving differential hand superiority of the HP-LV and HV-LP groups were not supported, the results were considered consistent with the view that WISC VIQ–PIQ discrepancies reflect the differential integrity of the two cerebral hemispheres in older children with LD.

CONCLUSIONS: STUDY 1 AND STUDY 2

The important conclusions and hypotheses formulated at this point in our research program were as follows:

1. It was apparent that older (9- to 14-year-old) children with LD did not constitute a homogenous group. There were clearly significant differences between the patterns of abilities and deficits exhibited by these three groups of youngsters with LD. However, there was still a need to determine the reliability of these apparent subtypes.

2. Simply separating these children with LD for study on the basis of WISC VIQ–PIQ discrepancies suggested strongly that one subtype within this group (HV-LP) seemed to be relatively efficient in skills and abilities ordinarily thought to be subserved primarily by the left cerebral hemisphere (e.g., speech-sounds discrimination), whereas another subtype (HP-LV) appeared to be much more efficient in skills and abilities ordinarily thought to be subserved primarily by the right cerebral hemisphere (e.g., visual-spatial-organizational skills). (This hypothesis was to be subjected to several different tests throughout the course of this research program.)

3. The consequences of the separation of the groups in terms of WISC VIQ–PIQ discrepancies vis-à-vis differences in levels and patterns of performance in reading, spelling, and arithmetic appeared to be important. At this point, it seemed reasonable to investigate the possible neuropsychological significance of such patterns of academic achievement.

Before pursuing these implications further, however, we felt it necessary to investigate the correlates of VIQ–PIQ discrepancies among younger children with LD. It was thought that some developmental implications regarding the emerging abilities and deficits of children with LD might be revealed thereby. Although the patterns of abilities and deficits exhibited by the 9- to 14-year-olds studied to this point appeared to be interpretable in terms of fairly well-established principles of brain–behavior relationships that had been generated in the study of adults, we were not so sanguine as to assume that such would be the case for children at more tender age levels. Indeed, there appeared to be rather sound reasons for thinking otherwise, including those of a psychometric (i.e., higher variability in performance on the versions of the tests used at younger ages) and a developmental (i.e., less "differentiation" of abilities at younger ages) nature.

STUDY 3

In the third study of this series (Rourke, Dietrich, & Young, 1973), 82 5- to 8-year-old children with LD were divided into three groups using virtually the same criteria as those employed in the Rourke et al. (1971) and Rourke and Telegdy (1971) investigations. The children had WISC FSIQs ranging from 79 to 120; there were no significant differences between the groups with respect to age and FSIQ. The study employed as dependent variables measures within the following two categories: (a) the verbal, auditory-perceptual, visual-perceptual, and problem-solving tests similar to those employed in the Rourke et al. (1971) study; and (b) the motor and psychomotor tests similar to those employed by Rourke and Telegdy (1971).

In contrast to the findings of Rourke et al. (1971) and Rourke and Telegdy (1971), there were few significant differences in performance evident between or among the three groups in the Rourke et al. (1973) study. However, the pattern of group differences on the PPVT, WRAT, Speech-Sounds Perception Test, Seashore Rhythm Test, Category Test, and Target Test closely resembled that exhibited by the 9- to 14-year-old children in the Rourke et al. (1971) study. The only statistically significant differences evident among the motor and psychomotor measures indicated superiority of the HP-LV over the HV-LP group on selected aspects of the Mazes (Klove, 1963), Grooved Pegboard, and Tactual Performance Tests. Given the large number of comparisons carried out, the latter differences may have emerged by chance.

Although the pattern of performances on the verbal, auditory-perceptual, and visual-perceptual measures exhibited by these 5- to 8-year-old subjects was of interest because of its similarity to results obtained with older children with LD, the absence of any strong indications of differences in motor and psychomotor patterns and the relatively large variability of performances across the majority of measures at this age level suggested strongly that meaningful developmental patterns would be difficult to determine with these data. However, one thing was abundantly clear: There was an emerging differentiation of abilities in children with LD similar to that seen with great regularity in normal children. In addition, this progressive differentiation of abilities appeared to be accompanied by an emerging differentiation of selective deficits in these subtypes of youngsters with LD.

GENERAL CONCLUSIONS AND NEURODEVELOPMENTAL DIMENSIONS ARISING FROM STUDIES 1, 2, AND 3

The studies reviewed to this point would suggest that the following general conclusions are tenable:

1. There are subtypes of children with LD that can be identified and studied in a reliable fashion. These appear to be related to particular patterns of VIQ–PIQ discrepancies on the WISC.

2. Some distinct patterns of "cognitive" abilities" and deficits are associated with equally distinct patterns of sensorimotor abilities and deficits in different subtypes of children with LD. These are especially evident among older (9- to 14-year-old) children with LD who exhibit particular patterns of VIQ–PIQ discrepancies on the WISC.

3. There are significant developmental differences in the manifestations of LD and in the associations between and among these manifestations. Specifically, manifestations of LD in 9- to 14-year-old children are rather consistent with expectations based upon models of brain–behavior relationships derived from studies of normal and brain-damaged adults, as reflected in VIQ–PIQ discrepancies on the adult Wechsler scales. Neuropsychological manifestations in 5- to 8-year-old children are, for the most part, not in line with such expectations.

It is clear that the aforementioned studies should be "replicated" using the WISC-III for the designation of subgroups of children with LD. This would allow for an assessment of the extent to which these important neurodevelopmental dimensions can be generalized.

WISC VERBAL IQ–PERFORMANCE IQ DISCREPANCIES: PSYCHOSOCIAL DIMENSIONS

For some time, we have been interested in the investigation of an hypothesis that proposes a causal connection between particular patterns of central processing abilities and deficits on the one hand and particular subtypes of both LD and psychosocial functioning on the other (Rourke & Fisk, 1981). Examples of the testing of this hypothesis involve an explanation of the results of several LD-subtype investigations aimed at the determination of patterns of central processing abilities and deficits that characterize such subtypes and the patterns of psychosocial responsivity that appear to be related to them, as follows.

PATTERNS OF READING, SPELLING, AND ARITHMETIC

The results of studies by Rourke and Finlayson (1978), Rourke and Strang (1978), and Strang and Rourke (1983) demonstrated that 9- to 14-year-old children with LD who exhibit a pattern of impaired reading (word recognition) and spelling within a context of significantly better, though still impaired, level of performance in mechanical arithmetic differ markedly in their patterns of neuropsychological abilities and deficits from those who exhibit a pattern of above-average reading and spelling and an outstandingly deficient level of mechanical arithmetic performance.

After investigating other dimensions of these two groups of children, we now refer to the first group as having a Basic Phonological Processing Disorder (BPPD) and the latter as exhibiting the syndrome of Nonverbal Learning Disabilities (NLD; Rourke, 1989, 1995). As summarized in Rourke (1989), these differences cover a wider range of skills and abilities: Specifically, children with NLD exhibit below-normal performances on tasks requiring visual-spatial-organizational, psychomotor, tactile-perceptual, and conceptual skills and abilities, within a context of normal performances on verbal tasks that require rote, overlearned verbal skills; they also have difficulties on measures that involve novel task requirements, whether these are "verbal" or "nonverbal" in nature. Children with BPPD exhibit the virtually opposite pattern of neuropsychological skills and abilities: mild to moderate difficulties in many areas of complex linguistic endeavors and marked problems in auditory-perceptual tasks that tax their capacities for exact hearing of speech-sounds, within a context of normal visual-spatial-organizational, psychomotor, tactile-perceptual, and nonverbal concept-formation skills and abilities. In addition, complex problem solving, hypothesis testing, and concept formation in situations where verbal instructions and response requirements are kept to a minimum pose no difficulties for them. Both subtypes of children have significant difficulties with mechanical arithmetic.

Within the present context, it is important to point out that, on the WISC and WISC-R, children with BPPD exhibit a pattern of HP-LV, whereas those with NLD exhibit a pattern of HV-LP. Also, it should be noted that their equally impaired levels of mechanical arithmetic appear to arise from radically different sources, as reflected in their markedly different VIQ–PIQ patterns (Rourke, 1993; Rourke & Conway, 1997).

We turn now to an examination of studies that have shed some light on the psychosocial correlates of such VIQ–PIQ discrepancies.

STUDY 4

When the average Personality Inventory for Children (PIC; Wirt, Lachar, Klinedinst, & Seat, 1984) profiles of children chosen to approximate the characteristics of these two subtypes of children with LD were compared (Strang & Rourke, 1985), it was clear that the profile for the NLD group was similar to that exhibited by the "emotionally disturbed" group in a study by Porter and Rourke (1985), whereas the profile for BPPD children was virtually identical to that exhibited by the "normal" group in that study. Additional examination of three factor scores derived from the PIC revealed that children with BPPD and NLD did not differ significantly on the concern over academic achievement factor, but that they differed sharply on the factors of "personality deviance" and "internalized psychopathology." In both of the latter cases, the levels of deviation were significantly higher (i.e., more pathological) for children with NLD than for those with BPPD.

The results of Studies 1 through 4, taken together, offer support for the hypothesis that particular patterns of central processing assets and deficits can, at one and the same time, eventuate in markedly different subtypes of LD (BPPD and NLD) and in markedly different patterns of psychosocial functioning (one characterized by normalcy; the other by an internalized form of psychopathology and personality deviance). Because such group results can be deceiving when applied to the individual case, it should be emphasized that there was very little variance evident in the PIC protocols of the children classified into Groups 2 and 3 in these studies. Furthermore, the interested reader may wish to consult case studies of such youngsters in works dealing with the neuropsychological assessment of children

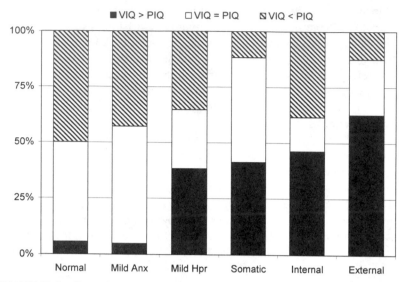

FIGURE 7.1   Proportions of subjects with Verbal IQ greater than Performance IQ (VIQ > PIQ), VIQ = PIQ, and VIQ < PIQ, in each subtype. (ANX = anxiety; HPR = hyperactive; SOMATIC = somatic concern; INTERNAL = internalized psychopathology; EXTERNAL = externalized psychopathology (From Fuerst et al., 1990.)

(Rourke et al., 1983; Rourke, Fisk, & Strang, 1986) for evidence of such consistent differences in psychosocial manifestations.

STUDY 5

As a further exploration of the psychosocial significance of VIQ–PIQ discrepancies, Fuerst, Fisk, and Rourke (1990) selected children with LD to comprise three (equal-sized) groups with distinctly different patterns of VIQ and PIQ. One group had VIQ greater than PIQ by at least 10 points (VIQ > PIQ); a second had VIQ less than PIQ by at least 10 points (VIQ < PIQ); and a third had VIQ and PIQ scores within 9 points of each other (VIQ = PIQ). The application of several cluster-analytic techniques in this study yielded a reliable solution, suggesting the presence of six distinct personality subtypes. The frequencies of the three VIQ–PIQ groups within each of these psychological subtypes were calculated and compared (see Figure 7.1).

We found that within the Normal subtype, children with VIQ > PIQ occurred at a much lower frequency (roughly 6% of the subtype) than did either children with the opposite pattern (VIQ < PIQ) or those with no significant difference between VIQ and PIQ. This was also the case in the Mild Anxiety subtype, in which subjects with VIQ > PIQ were found at a rate significantly below expectation (about 5% of the subtype). In the Mild Hyperactivity subtype, the frequencies of subjects from the three VIQ–PIQ groups were approximately equal. These results indicated that, overall, within normal and mildly disturbed psychosocial subtypes of children with LD, there was a tendency for VIQ > PIQ children to occur at lower frequencies than did VIQ = PIQ or VIQ < PIQ children. There were only about half as many VIQ > PIQ children in these three groups as there were VIQ = PIQ or VIQ < PIQ children.

In the Internalized Psychopathology subtype, subjects with VIQ = PIQ were found at frequencies significantly lower than expected (about 15% of the subtype). On the other hand, subjects with VIQ > PIQ were found at a higher frequency than would be expected (roughly 46% of the subtype), and at a higher frequency than VIQ < PIQ subjects (39%). Within the Externalized Psychopathology subtype, subjects with VIQ > PIQ were found at a much higher frequency (about 63% of the group) than were children with either VIQ = PIQ or VIQ < PIQ. Thus, unlike the normal and mildly disturbed subtypes, subtypes characterized by severe psychosocial disturbance showed a strong tendency to include VIQ > PIQ subjects at higher frequencies then either the VIQ = PIQ or VIQ < PIQ subjects. In total, there were about twice as many VIQ > PIQ children in these two "severe" groups as there were VIQ = PIQ or VIQ < PIQ children.

Refinements of these findings and some theoretical explanations of their interrelationships are contained in several works (e.g., Ozols & Rourke, 1988; Rourke, 1982, 1987; Rourke & Fisk, 1988; Strang & Rourke, 1985). For example, the propensity of children with NLD to develop a particular configuration of academic learning difficulties and a specific type of severe psychosocial disturbance has been characterized in terms of the interaction between (a) their *deficiencies* in neuropsychological dimensions (such as visual-spatial, tactile-perceptual, psychomotor, and concept-formation skills and abilities) and (b) their *excessive reliance upon* one area of strength (language). This interaction, in conjunction with their difficulties in dealing with novel and otherwise complex situations, is thought to lie at the root of both sets of adaptive difficulties.

Finally, two studies that were designed to determine the developmental outcome for children with NLD are relevant in this context.

STUDY 6

Rourke, Young, Strang, and Russell (1986) compared the performances of children exhibiting the NLD syndrome and a group of clinic-referred adults on a wide variety of neuropsychological variables. The adults presented with Wechsler VIQ–PIQ discrepancies and WRAT patterns that were virtually identical to the analogous patterns in children with NLD. It was demonstrated that the patterns of age-related performances of the adults and the children on the neuropsychological variables were remarkably identical. In addition, the adults were characterized by internalized forms of psychopathology that bore a striking resemblance to those exhibited by children with NLD.

STUDY 7

In a related study, Del Dotto, Fisk, McFadden, and Rourke (1991) administered a variety of neuropsychological and personality tests to five adolescents and young adults who exhibited the NLD syndrome, all of whom had undergone neuropsychological and personality assessments a minimum of 5 years previously. The results of this study confirmed the stability of the neuropsychological and personality characteristics of this NLD subtype over time.

CONCLUSIONS RELATING TO THE PSYCHOSOCIAL DIMENSIONS OF VIQ–PIQ DISCREPANCIES FOR CHILDREN WHO EXHIBIT TWO SUBTYPES OF LD

In summary, it would appear that children who exhibit the NLD profile of neuropsychological assets and deficits are very likely to be described by parents as emotionally or behaviorally disturbed. In contrast, children with BPPD are so described at a much lower frequency. More generally, it would appear that the profile of neuropsychological assets and deficits (including a HV-LP pattern) that constitutes the NLD syndrome is a sufficient condition for the development of some sort of psychosocial disturbance that tends to remain stable or worsen over time, whereas the profile of central processing assets and deficits (including a HP-LV pattern) exhibited by the BPPD subtype does not constitute the same sufficient basis for such an outcome.

This is not meant to imply that children in the BPPD subtype will never experience psychosocial disturbance. Indeed, clinical experience (e.g., Rourke et al., 1983; Rourke et al., 1986) suggests that many do. Rather, these results suggest that, for the child with BPPD, something *in addition to* psycholinguistic deficiency is necessary for disturbed psychosocial functioning to occur. Such "additional" factors may include teacher–pupil personality conflicts, unrealistic demands by parents and teachers, and inappropriate motivation and social expectancies. Others would appear to include the presence of salient antisocial models, selective reinforcement of nonadaptive and socially inappropriate behaviors, and any number of other factors that have the potential for encouraging problems in the psychosocial functioning of youngsters who are free of any type of LD.

It is clear that Studies 5, 6, and 7 should be "replicated" using the WISC-III as one of the variables for the designation of subgroups of children with LD. This would allow for an assessment of the extent to which these important psychosocial dimensions that seem closely related to WISC and WISC-R VIQ–PIQ discrepancies also obtain when the WISC-III is used for this purpose.

COMPARABILITY OF THE SUMMARY MEASURES OF THE WECHSLER SCALES FOR CHILDREN WITH LEARNING DISABILITIES

Issues relating to the comparability of summary measures of the WISC and WISC-R for children with LD were evaluated in a study by Fisk and Rourke (1987). In this investigation, children with LD who had been referred for neuropsychological evaluation were administered either the WISC or WISC-R in order to determine the comparability of the two tests. The results indicated no significant differences between the WISC and WISC-R with respect to VIQ, PIQ, and FSIQ. Examination of groups of children exhibiting various patterns of Reading, Spelling, and Arithmetic also yielded nonsignificant differences between WISC and WISC-R VIQ, PIQ, and FSIQ. These results suggested that the summary IQ scores of these two tests have the same concurrent validity for this population of children with LD.

A similar comparison of the summary measures of the WISC-III with those of the WISC R and/or WISC would add to our knowledge of the generalizability of all of the findings discussed in this chapter.

CLINICAL IMPLICATIONS OF FINDINGS WITH THE WECHSLER SCALES

In a survey of the results of 90 children with LD whom we had chosen carefully to exhibit the BPPD ($n = 45$) and NLD ($n = 35$) subtypes, the following rules were generated for classifying children into these two subtypes. Note that some of the rules include reference to the WISC or the WISC-R which, as a result of the Fisk and Rourke (1987) study outlined above, we know are equivalent measures for children whom we define as having LD. All of the rules are included below so that the clinician may have access to the entire decision-making process. Descriptions of all of the tests mentioned are contained in Rourke et al. (1986).

RULES FOR CLASSIFYING CHILDREN WITH BPPD: 9–15 YEARS

1. WISC VIQ < PIQ by at least 10 points.
2. Two of the WISC or WISC-R Block Design, Object Assembly, and Picture Arrangement subtests are the highest of the Performance scaled scores.
3. Two of the WISC or WISC-R Vocabulary, Digit Span, and Information subtests are the lowest of the Verbal scaled scores.
4. Trail Making Test, Part B performance is more than 1 SD below the mean.
5. Performance on three of subtests 9, 10, 11, and 12 of the Underlining Test are outstandingly poor.
6. Category Test performance is within 1 SD of the mean.
7. WRAT Standard Scores for Reading and Spelling are below 80.
8. WRAT Standard Score for Arithmetic exceeds that for Reading + Spelling/2 by at least 15.
9. TPT Right, Left, and Both hand scores become progressively better vis-à-vis norms.
10. No or very minimal simple tactile imperception and suppression, finger agnosia, or astereognosis for coins versus poor finger dysgraphesthesia.
11. Evidence of a preponderance of somatosensory errors on the right side.

12. Normal grip strength and Grooved Pegboard Test performance.

13. Below average performance on all of the following tests: Speech-Sounds Perception, Auditory Closure, Sentence Memory, and Phonemically Cued Verbal Fluency.

  1. It should be clear that not all of these rules are mutually exclusive.
  2. It would seem reasonable to assert the following:

A youngster who exhibits: 11–13 of these = Definite BBPD
                             9–10 of these = Very Probable BBPD
                             7–8 of these = Possible BBPD
                             4–6 of these = Questionable BBPD
                             1–3 of these = Low Probability of BBPD

RULES FOR CLASSIFYING CHILDREN WITH NLD: 9–15 YEARS

1. WISC VIQ > PIQ by at least 10 points.

2. Two of the WISC or WISC-R Vocabulary, Similarities, and Information are the highest of the Verbal scaled scores.

3. Two of the WISC or WISC-R Block Design, Object Assembly, and Coding are the lowest of the Performance scaled scores.

4. Target Test is at least 1 SD below the mean.

5. WRAT Standard Score for Reading is at least 8 points greater than Arithmetic.

6. TPT Right, Left, and Both hand scores become progressively worse vis-à-vis norms.

7. No or very minimal simple tactile imperception and suppression versus very poor finger agnosia, finger dysgraphesthesia, astereognosis composite.

8. Normal to superior grip strength versus mildly to moderately impaired Grooved Pegboard.

9. Evidence of a preponderance of somatosensory or psychomotor errors on the left side.

10. Normal to superior Speech-Sounds Perception and Auditory Closure versus somewhat poorer Sentence Memory and very poor Phonemically Cued Verbal Fluency.

  1. It should be clear that not all of these rules are mutually exclusive.
  2. It would seem reasonable to assert the following:

A youngster who exhibits: 9 or 10 of these = Definite NLD
                             7 or 8 of these = Probable NLD
                             5 or 6 of these = Possible NLD
                             1 to 4 of these = Low Probability of NLD

If the clinician applies these rules to the test results of children of this age group who meet our generic definition for LD, it would be expected that the hit rate for classification in the Definite and Probable categories for both BPPD and NLD would be above 90%.

It would be well to cross-validate these findings to determine if the same rules for the WISC and the WISC-R (the first three for each subtype) obtain for the WISC III. There is very good reason to infer that such will be the case.

A NOTE REGARDING THE USE OF THE WECHSLER SCALES FOR CHILDREN AND ADOLESCENTS WHO EXHIBIT SOME TYPES OF NEUROLOGICAL DISEASE OR DISORDER

We and others have found that there are a number of types of pediatric neurological diseases and disorders wherein the NLD pattern of neuropsychological assets and deficits is very evident. These include Williams syndrome (Anderson & Rourke, 1995), early hydrocephalus (Fletcher, Brookshire, Bohan, Brandt, & Davidson, 1995; Fletcher et al. 1992), Asperger syndrome (Klin, Sparrow, Volkmar, Cicchetti, & Rourke, 1995), congenital hypothyroidism (Rovet, 1995), and a number of other diseases and disorders (see Rourke, 1995). Of importance within the present context is the salience of the pattern of the Wechsler scale results, as specified in the classification rules for NLD, that these children and adolescents exhibit. It is also important to note that many of the studies of these forms of pediatric neuropathology utilized the WISC-R and/or the WISC-III.

SUBTYPES OF LEARNING DISABILITIES: FINDINGS FROM OTHER LABORATORIES

Although we have concentrated on the findings emerging from our own laboratory in this chapter, it should be pointed out that many other investigators have arrived at conclusions that are very similar—even identical—to our own with respect to the external validity of the BPPD and NLD subtypes. Some of these studies have involved electrophysiology indices (e.g., Grunau & Low, 1987; Loveland, Fletcher, & Bailey, 1990; Mattson, Sheer, & Fletcher, 1992; Stelmack & Miles, 1990; for a summary of these and related studies, see Dool, Stelmack, & Rourke, 1993). Others have used approaches that could be characterized as behavioral/ experimental and psychometric with children and adolescents (e.g., Fletcher, 1985; Share, Moffitt, & Silva, 1988; White, Moffitt, & Silva, 1992). There have been studies of such subtypes of adults (e.g., McCue & Goldstein, 1991; Morris & Walter, 1991) and the subtypes have been cross-validated in at least one other culture (van der Vlugt, 1991). It is important to emphasize that the subtypes under investigation—which are obviously quite reliable and that have been shown to have considerable external validity—are constituted to a considerable extent by the use of measures derived from the WISC and WISC-R (in the case of adults, such indices from the adult Wechsler scales are often used).

This would suggest strongly that it would be worthwhile to determine the reliability and validity of similar indices from the WISC-III for these subtypes in children and adolescents.

REFERENCES

Anderson, P., & Rourke, B. P. (1995). Williams syndrome. In B. P. Rourke (Ed.), *Syndrome of nonverbal learning disabilities: Neurodevelopmental manifestations* (pp. 138–170). New York: Guilford Press.

Del Dotto, J. E., Fisk, J. L., McFadden, G. T., & Rourke, B. P. (1991). Developmental analysis of children/adolescents with nonverbal learning disabilities: Long-term impact on personality adjustment and patterns of adaptive functioning. In B. P. Rourke (Ed.), *Neuropsychological validation of learning disability subtypes* (pp. 293–308). New York: Guilford Press.

Dool, C. B., Stelmack, R. M., & Rourke, B. P. (1993). Event-related potentials in children with learning disabilities. *Journal of Clinical Child Psychology, 22,* 387–398.

Dunn, L. M. (1965). *Expanded manual for the Peabody Picture Vocabulary Test.* Minneapolis, MN: American Guidance Service.

Fisk, J. L., & Rourke, B. P. (1987). WISC/WISC-R comparisons in a learning-disabled population: Equivalence of summary IQ measures. *The Clinical Neuropsychologist, 1,* 47–50.

Fletcher, J. M. (1985). External validation of learning disability typologies. In B. P. Rourke (Ed.), *Neuropsychology of learning disabilities: Essentials of subtype analysis* (pp. 187–211). New York: Guilford Press.

Fuerst, D. R., Fisk, J. L., & Rourke, B. P. (1990). Psychosocial functioning of learning-disabled children: Relations between WISC Verbal IQ–Performance IQ discrepancies and personality subtypes. *Journal of Consulting and Clinical Psychology, 58,* 657–660.

Fuerst, D. R., & Rourke, B. P. (1995). Psychosocial functioning of children with learning disabilities at three age levels. *Child Neuropsychology, 1,* 38–55.

Grunau, R. V. E., & Low, M. D. (1987). Cognitive and task-related EEG correlates of arithmetic performance in adolescents. *Journal of Clinical and Experimental Neuropsychology, 9,* 563–574.

Jastak, J. F., & Jastak, S. R. (1965). *The Wide Range Achievement Test.* Wilmington, DE: Guidance Associates.

Klin, A., Sparrow, S. S., Volkmar, F., Cicchetti, D. V., & Rourke, B. P. (1995). Asperger syndrome. In B. P. Rourke (Ed.), *Syndrome of nonverbal learning disabilities: Neurodevelopmental manifestations* (pp. 93–118). New York: Guilford Press.

Klove, H. (1963). Clinical neuropsychology. In F. M. Forster (Ed.), *The medical clinics of North America.* New York: Saunders.

Loveland, K. A., Fletcher, J. M., & Bailey, V. (1990). Nonverbal communication of events in learning-disability subtypes. *Journal of Clinical and Experimental Neuropsychology, 12,* 433–447.

Mattson, A., J., Sheer, D. E., & Fletcher, J. M. (1992). Electrophysiological evidence of lateralized disturbances in children with disabilities. *Journal of Clinical and Experimental Neuropsychology, 14,* 707–716.

McCue, M., & Goldstein, G. (1991). Neuropsychological aspects of learning disability in adults. In B. P. Rourke (Ed.), *Neuropsychological validation of learning disability subtypes* (pp. 311–329). New York: Guilford Press.

Morris, R. D., & Walter, L. W. (1991). Subtypes of arithmetic-disabled adults: Validating childhood findings. In B. P. Rourke (Ed.), *Neuropsychological validation of learning disability subtypes* (pp. 330–346). New York: Guilford Press.

Ozols, E. J., & Rourke, B. P. (1988). Characteristics of young children with learning disabilities classified according to patterns of academic achievement: Auditory-perceptual and visual-perceptual disabilities. *Journal of Clinical Child Psychology, 17,* 44–52.

Porter, J. E., & Rourke, B. P. (1985). Personality and socioemotional dimensions of learning disabilities in children. In B. P. Rourke, (Ed.), *Neuropsychology of learning disabilities: Essentials of subtype analysis* (pp. 257–280). New York: Guilford Press.

Reitan, R. M., & Davison, L. A. (Eds.) (1974). *Clinical neuropsychology: Current status and applications.* New York: Wiley.

Rourke, B. P. (1975). Brain–behavior relationships in children with learning disabilities: A research program. *American Psychologist, 30,* 911–920.

Rourke, B. P. (1978). Reading, spelling, arithmetic disabilities: A neuropsychologic perspective. In H. R. Myklebust (Ed.), *Progress in learning disabilities* (Vol. 4, pp. 97–120). New York: Grune & Stratton.

Rourke, B. P. (1982). Central processing deficiencies in children: Toward a developmental neuropsychological model. *Journal of Clinical Neuropsychology, 4,* 1–18.

Rourke, B. P. (Ed.) (1985). *Neuropsychology of learning disabilities: Essentials of subtype analysis.* New York: Guilford Press.

Rourke, B. P. (1989). *Nonverbal learning disabilities: The syndrome and the model.* New York: Guilford Press.

Rourke, B. P. (Ed.) (1991). *Neuropsychological validation of learning disability subtypes.* New York: Guilford Press.

Rourke, B. P. (1993). Arithmetic disabilities, specific and otherwise: A neuropsychological perspective. *Journal of Learning Disabilities, 26,* 214–226.

Rourke, B. P. (Ed.) (1995). *Syndrome of nonverbal learning disabilities: Neurodevelopmental manifestations.* New York: Guilford Press.

Rourke, B. P., Bakker, D. J., Fisk, J. L., & Strang, J. D. (1983). *Child neuropsychology: An introduction to theory, research, and clinical practice.* New York: Guilford Press.

Rourke, B. P., & Conway, J. A. (1997). Disabilities of arithmetic and mathematical reasoning: Perspectives from neurology and neuropsychology. *Journal of Learning Disabilities, 30,* 34–46.

Rourke, B. P., Dietrich, D. M., & Young, G. C. (1973). Significance of WISC verbal-performance discrepancies for younger children with learning disabilities. *Perceptual and Motor Skills, 36,* 275–282.

Rourke, B. P., & Finlayson, M. A. J. (1978). Neuropsychological significance of variations in patterns of academic performance: Verbal and visual-spatial abilities. *Journal of Abnormal Child Psychology, 6,* 121–133.

Rourke, B. P., & Fisk, J. L. (1981). Socio-emotional disturbances of learning disabled children: The role of central processing deficits. *Bulletin of the Orton Society, 31,* 77–88.

Rourke, B. P., & Fisk, J. L. (1988). Subtypes of learning-disabled children: Implications for a neurodevelopmental model of differential hemispheric processing. In D. L. Molfese & S. J. Segalowitz (Eds.), *Brain lateralization in children: Developmental implications* (pp. 547–565). New York: Guilford Press.

Rourke, B. P., Fisk, J. L, & Strang, J. D. (1986). *Neuropsychological assessment of children: A treatment-oriented approach.* New York: Guilford Press.

Rourke, B. P. & Fuerst, D. R. (1991). *Learning disabilities and psychosocial functioning.* New York: Guilford Press.

Rourke, B. P., & Strang, J. D. (1978). Neuropsychological significance of variations in patterns of academic performance: Motor, psychomotor, and tactile-perceptual abilities. *Journal of Pediatric Psychology, 3,* 62–66.

Rourke, B. P., & Telegdy, G. A. (1971). Lateralizing significance of WISC verbal-performance discrepancies for older children with learning disabilities. *Perceptual and Motor Skills, 33,* 875–883.

Rourke, B. P., Young, G. C, & Flewelling, R. W. (1971). The relationships between WISC verbal-performance discrepancies and selected verbal, auditory-perceptual visual-perceptual, and problem-solving abilities in children with learning disabilities. *Journal of Clinical Psychology, 27,* 475–479.

Rourke, B. P., Young, G. C., Strang, J. D., & Russell, D. L. (1986). Adult outcomes of central processing deficiencies in childhood. In I. Grant & K. M. Adams (Eds.), *Neuropsychological assessment in neuropsychiatric disorders; Clinical methods and empirical findings,* (pp. 244–267). New York: Oxford University Press.

Rovet, J. (1995). Congential hypothyroidism. In B. P. Rourke (Ed.), *Syndrome of nonverbal learning disabilities: Manifestations in neurological disease, disorder, and dysfunction.* New York: Guilford Press.

Sparrow, S. S. (1991). Case studies of children with nonverbal learning disabilities. In B. P. Rourke (Ed.), *Neuropsychological validation of learning disability subtypes* (pp. 349–355). New York: Guilford Press.

Share, D. L., Moffitt, T. E., & Silva, P. A. (1988). Factors associated with arithmetic-and-reading disability and specific arithmetic disability. *Journal of Learning Disabilities, 21,* 313–320.

Stelmack, R. M., & Miles, J. (1990). The effect of picture priming on event-related potentials of normal and disabled readers during a word recognition memory task. *Journal of Clinical and Experimental Neuropsychology, 12,* 887–903.

Strang, J. D., & Rourke, B. P. (1983). Concept-formation/non-verbal reasoning abilities of children who exhibit specific academic problems with arithmetic. *Journal of Clinical Child Psychology, 12,* 33–39.

Strang, J. D., & Rourke, B. P. (1985). Adaptive behavior of children with specific arithmetic disabilities and associated neuropsychological abilities and deficits. In B. P. Rourke (Ed.), *Neuropsychology of learning disabilities: Essentials of subtype analysis* (pp. 302–328). New York: Guilford Press.

van der Vlugt, H. (1991). Neuropsychological validation studies of learning disability subtypes: Verbal, visual-spatial, and psychomotor abilities. In B. P. Rourke (Ed.), *Neuropsychological validation of learning disability subtypes* (pp. 140–159). New York: Guilford Press.

Wechsler, D. (1949). *Wechsler Intelligence Scale for Children.* New York: Psychological Corporation.

White, J. L., Moffitt, T. E., & Silva, P. A. (1992). Neuropsychological and psychosocial correlates of specific-arithmetic disability. *Archives of Clinical Neuropsychology, 7,* 1–16.

Wirt, R. D., Lachar, D., Klinedinst, J. K., & Seat, P. D. (1984). *Multidimensional description of child personality: A manual for the Personality Inventory for Children Revised 1984.* Los Angeles: Western Psychological Services.

8

UTILITY OF THE WISC-III FOR CHILDREN WITH LANGUAGE IMPAIRMENTS

LeADELLE PHELPS

Department of Counseling and
Educational Psychology
State University of New York at Buffalo
Buffalo, New York

OVERVIEW

There exists considerable confusion among professionals and laypersons alike regarding the definition and etiology of language impairment (LI), as well as its differentiation from and relationship to other childhood handicapping conditions such as learning disabilities (LDs), dyslexia, and mental retardation. The definition of LI is one of exclusion, requiring a significant discrepancy (at least 1 SD) between standardized, individually administered measures of language and *nonverbal* intellectual capacity, which is *not accounted for* by (a) mental retardation; (b) a pervasive development disorder, such as autism, Rett's, or childhood disintegrative disorder; (c) physical abnormalities, such as a hearing impairment or cleft palate; or (d) environmental depravation (American Psychiatric Association [APA], 1994). Youngsters meeting these criteria, and thus diagnosed as LI, should not be confused with the many children who attend preschool and self-contained classes *for which delayed language is the sole criterion for admission* (i.e., no required discrepancy with nonverbal IQ). Such programs serve numerous children who have global developmental delays of which language is simply the most obvious manifestation. These two groups of children differ significantly in a number of ways, the more notable being (a) early prognosis for improvement, and (b) long-term outcomes (Bishop & Edmundson, 1987; Field, Fox, & Radcliffe, 1990).

WISC-III Clinical Use and Interpretation:
Scientist–Practitioner Perspectives

Research substantiates a probable genetic etiology of LI, with between 53 and 77% of children so diagnosed having at least one first-degree relative similarly affected (Felsenfeld, Broen, & McGue, 1992; Tallal, Ross, & Curtiss, 1989; Tomblin, 1989). In a longitudinal study evaluating the prevalence of language disorders in the *children* of adults who had been diagnosed as LI 28 years earlier (at 4–6 years of age), Felsenfeld, McGue, and Broen (1995) reported that 33% of *the offspring* had LI. In another study surveying *male* monozygotic (MZ) and dizygotic (DZ) twin pairs, Bishop, North, and Donlan (1995) reported a 70% language disorder concordance rate for MZ and 46% for DZ. Finally, studies have generally reported a higher occurrence in males with an approximate 4:1 male to female ratio (Robinson, 1991). Similar familial and gender prevalence data have been reported since the 1950s (Richardson, 1992).

It is likely that the inheritability configuration depends on more than one gene or on a complex interaction of alleles (gene sites), as the familial pattern does not follow a simple Mendelian model. Whatever the mechanism, there is evidence via magnetic resonance imaging (MRI) studies of lower regional cerebral blood flow in the left temporofrontal brain region of children with language disorders (Lou, Henriksen, & Bruhn, 1990). Likewise, children with LI perform quite poorly on tasks that require sequential and analytical processing, often linked with left-hemisphere functioning, yet achieve significantly better on nonverbal simultaneous tasks, which are most often linked to the right hemisphere (Allen, Lincoln, & Kaufman, 1991). Finally, the processing and production of language as well as the visual recognition of *written words* are clearly dependent upon left temporal functioning (Nobre, Allison, & McCarthy, 1994; Nobre & McCarthy, 1995; Shaywitz, 1996). By comparison, the visual processing of symbols, designs, and complex multicolored patterns, as well as the recognition of faces and *single letters* are contingent upon occipital lobe performance (Nobre et al., 1994; Shaywitz, 1996).

Language disorders are generally viewed as resulting from auditory perceptual deficits. When appropriate research designs and comparable comparison groups are utilized, children with LI do not differ significantly from children with *hearing* impairments in such areas as: (a) significant Verbal IQ < Performance IQ (VIQ < PIQ) contrasts; (b) type and frequency of errors committed in grammatically complex sentences regardless of whether communicated orally, in written form, or through total communication; and, (c) notable sequential < simultaneous discrepancies (Bishop, 1992). Such commonalities suggest that distinctive patterns of impairment can arise because of auditory perceptual limitations. Likewise, such data lend support to the left hemisphere neurological model for LI.

Language disorders have historically been divided into four subtypes: (a) phonological, (b) receptive, (c) expressive, and (d) pragmatic. Current research, however, is indicating that there is considerable overlap among these traditional diagnostic categories (Bishop et al., 1995; Robinson, 1991). Likewise, there is a paucity of valid methods for assessing each subtype *exclusively* (for a review, refer to Sommers, 1989). For example, when evaluating the complex pragmatic subtype, how can one be assured errors are not committed as a result of receptive–expressive involvement? How can one assess day-to-day expressive language functioning without recognizing the prerequisite receptive component? Finally, numerous studies have validated these concerns by consistently finding only one general "cross-modality" language factor when subjecting tests purporting to provide independent measures of each subtype to factor analysis (Dale & Henderson, 1987; Sommers, Erdige, & Peterson, 1978). Likewise, studies have generally reported that the large preponderance of school-aged children demonstrate dual or multiple subtype comorbidities (Bishop et al., 1995; Robinson, 1991). Nonetheless, the groupings continue to be used for want of a better system.

It should be noted that articulation errors are *not* a subtype of LI, but considered to be subsumed within the domain of *speech impairments*. Such pronunciation difficulties are quite common in preschoolers and are not indicative, in and of themselves, of later language difficulties. Likewise, isolated articulation problems in preliterate children are not predictive of later reading difficulties (Bishop & Adams, 1990). Articulation errors only assume importance in scholastic acquisition when they occur simultaneously with phonological, receptive, and/or expressive impairments.

PHONOLOGICAL SUBTYPE

This diagnostic category includes delays in linking specific sounds to letters as well as in blending such sounds together to decode new or unusual words. Although good letter-sound knowledge in preschool may predict which children will be unusually good readers, the converse is not true. That is, phonological deficits become diagnostically significant only when such errors are atypical for the developmental age of the child. As stated by Allen (1989):

> A child is considered phonologically (i.e., linguistically) impaired if we observe sound substitutions, omissions, or distortions which are unusual, inconsistent, or unpredictable. The deficits stand in distinction to patterns of developmental misarticulations of younger or linguistically immature children. (p. 443)

With older children, phonological deficits are clearly evident in word attack skills and nonword decoding, such as "pheeg, gacku, philodron, conflanugate" (Conti-Ramsden, Donlan, & Grove, 1992). Written language difficulties focus on (a) disparate spelling and meaning for words that are phonologically identical (e.g., there, their, they're; to, too, two); and, (b) dissimilar spelling for words that are phonetically similar (e.g., bee, sea, key). During adolescence and/or adulthood, the deficits became more subtle and may include written or verbal substitutions of highly similar words (e.g., causal vs. casual; discriminate vs. discriminant; though vs. through) and omission of syllables (e.g., "historally" for historically; "narsistic" for "narcissistic").

RECEPTIVE SUBTYPE

Receptive competencies reflect comprehension of spoken language. Deficits can range from severe cases comparable to aphasia, wherein the child has great difficulty understanding *anything* that is said to her or him, to such subtle nuances as not comprehending the *context* of language. For example, consider the statement: "The boy who hit the girl was crying." A child with a moderate receptive language impairment may be able to report that there were two children involved, yet have difficulty determining who was crying. The choice is often based on proximity (e.g., as "girl" is closer to "crying" than "boy," the child concludes that the girl was crying) rather than on the correct analysis of modifiers (Bishop, 1992). (No doubt this brings to mind memories of sentence diagramming!) Likewise, active versus passive confusion is common. For example, consider the difference between: "The girl was chasing the dog" as compared to: "The girl was chased by the dog." Such minor word alternations result in major modifications in meaning. These grammatical complexities are far more important than sentence length as a determinant of difficulty for children with a receptive disorder (Bishop, 1992). Finally, it is important to note that it is very rare for a child to have notable receptive impairment, yet score within the normal range on expressive language tests (Bishop et al., 1995). As stated in the *DSM-IV,* "Because the development of expressive language in childhood relies on the acquisition of receptive skills, a pure receptive language disorder (analogous to a Wernicke's aphasia in adults) is virtually never seen" (APA, 1994, p. 59).

EXPRESSIVE SUBTYPE

Expressive language proficiencies include the use of language to effectively convey information as well as the formulation of more complex grammatical sentences. As with articulation errors, studies indicate that many preschool children with limited vocabularies have normalized by school age (Aram & Eisele, 1992; Eisele & Aram, 1993). It should be noted that by 2 years of age, a vocabulary of over 300 words is expected (Aram & Eisele, 1994). Of more diagnostic significance, however, is nonverbal gesturing, limited vocabulary, and use of simple three- and four-word sentences by children in the primary grades. With older children evidencing an expressive language disorder, verbal interactions contain hesitations, word selection difficulties, overuse of simple declarative sentences (e.g., "The milk is sour" vs. "The milk, which has been in the refrigerator since Sunday, is sour"), omission of pivotal words or phrases, and the use of unusual word order (e.g., "I will be with them friends"). The more pervasive the problems, the less likely positive outcomes (Beitchman et al., 1994). As the child ages, impairment in verbal reasoning and problem solving, drawing conclusions not explicitly stated, and making inferences becomes apparent. For example, a child is asked: "Kambri was riding her bicycle. She ran over some broken glass. She has to walk her bicycle home. Why did she walk home?" In this instance, the child must infer a flat tire. For a more complex illustration, consider the following stimulus appropriate for adolescents: "This is a boy named Poc. This is Poc's jed. Poc likes to play with his jed. Look at Poc gib. Poc is gibbing with his jed." The student is then asked: "What are possible real words that could replace Poc, jed, gib, and gibbing? (Acceptable sample answers: a boy's name such as Rhett, Ricardo; an animal/object/person with which/whom the boy can play such as dog, bike, sister; any active verb such as run, jump, read; the -ing form of the selected active verb such as running, jumping, reading). Note the complex language-based hypothetical-deductive reasoning that is required to solve this problem.

PRAGMATIC SUBTYPE

This subtype refers to the appropriate use of language in social situations. It involves the knowledge of social conventions that govern interpersonal communications as well as the application of complex word relationships. Thus, it requires the use of perspective taking and self-monitoring procedures. Examples of pragmatic deficits during verbal exchanges include interjecting irrelevant comments, frequently interrupting others, not following the topic of conversation, and violating other unspoken social rules of language. Likewise, pragmatic understanding requires sophisticated discrimination between word forms. For example, consider that in the English language, the noun *men* can refer (at least historically) to either (a) all persons, regardless of sex, or (b) to the male gender exclusively. Thus, the statement: "All men are created equal" is pragmatically distinct from: "The men are required to wear hats." To illustrate a more subtle nuance of pragmatic reasoning, Abbeduto and Nuccio (1989) gave the choice between "Sign this" vs. "Would you mind very much signing this" when an employee is approaching the company president. In order to select the better alternative, the employee must posses a social understanding of status and politeness. Finally, recognition of the social *context* of language is essential. That is, although using baby talk with an infant is acceptable, it is not appropriate with the infant's mother. Likewise, jokes are admissible at parties but quite improper at funerals.

ACADEMIC OUTCOMES OF LANGUAGE IMPAIRMENTS

An estimated 5 to 10% of preschool children meet the strict discrepancy criteria for an LI diagnosis. By school age, this proportion has dropped to 3 to 5% (Aram & Hall, 1989). Yet as those figures suggest, 50 to 60% of preschool children with documented language disorders continue to evidence impairment. Are there discriminating factors that can identify those children most at risk?

As previously noted, there is substantial evidence that *isolated* phonological errors as well as *limited* vocabulary competencies in the preschool years are not prognostic indicators of long-term difficulties. By comparison, early *global* (i.e., presence of two or more subtypes), *moderate to severe* manifestations of LI that *do not respond quickly* to remediation are significantly related to later verbally mediated academic complications. For example, longitudinal studies have substantiated that such language disorders in preschool children are highly predictive of reading, spelling, and language competencies at 7 through 12 years of age (Beitchman et al.,

1994; Bishop & Adams, 1990; Scarborough & Dobrich, 1990; Silva, Williams, & McGee, 1987). Thus, the key prognostic indicators are depth, breadth, and responsivity to treatment.

As an illustration, Bishop and Adams (1990) followed a prospective sample of 83 children diagnosed as LI at 4 years of age, who were later reassessed at ages 5 and 8. The researchers indicated that if resolution of the language problems had occurred by 5½ years of age, the children continued to make good progress and had proficient phonetic and reading competencies at age 8. Yet children who still evidenced global phonological, receptive, and/or expressive language deficits at 5½ years were likely to have significant reading difficulties and continued language impairment at age 8. With regard to reading competencies, Bishop and Adams reported that reading comprehension scores were disproportionately poor relative to reading accuracy. That is, although the children made some omission and substitution errors, the notable impairment was in little recollection of or insight about the material they had studied.

Such academic deficits continue throughout the schooling years and into adulthood. For example, Aram, Ekelman, and Nation (1984) followed a group of preschool children diagnosed LI for 10 years, and documented academic difficulties that persisted with middle and high school enrollment. Likewise, in spite of employing considerable compensatory strategies, adults with such handicaps continue to be hampered in competitive academic and occupational ventures (Shaywitz, 1996).

LANGUAGE IMPAIRMENTS, LEARNING DISABILITIES, AND DYSLEXIA

Many children who are initially diagnosed in preschool as LI are later classified as LD in school systems and/or dyslexic in medical settings. It is seldom the case that the language deficits have mitigated; rather, the foci of "identified problem(s)" and treatment regime(s) have altered to reflect the primary concern of academic failure. This has led researchers such as Tallal and Curtis (1988) to conclude: "Language impairment and reading impairment may be the same disorder, manifesting itself differently in the same child at different stages of development" (p. 19). Other authors agree (Catts, 1989c; Kamhi & Catts, 1989). As summarized by Kamhi (1992):

> Dyslexia is a developmental language disorder whose defining characteristic is a life-long difficulty processing phonological information. This difficulty involves encoding, retrieving, and using phonological codes in memory as well as deficits in phonological awareness and speech production. The disorder, which is often genetically transmitted, is generally present at birth and persists throughout the lifespan. A prominent characteristic of the disorder is spoken and written language deficiencies (p. 50).

The developmental pattern of children diagnosed as dyslexic follows the familiar LI paradigm. As toddlers, they have delays in language acquisition (Scarborough & Dobrich, 1990). During the elementary years, such children demonstrate deficiencies in phonological awareness, word recognition, spelling and writing competencies, as well as in reading comprehension. The understanding of complex sentences (i.e., receptive), and the verbal communication of sequential directions, messages, stories, and/or events (i.e., expressive) are likewise impaired (Catts, 1989a; Conti-Ramsden et al., 1992). As adults, they may be able to read adequately, but continue to show phonological deficits in rapid naming tasks (e.g., magazine pronounced as "mazagine") and in repeating phonologically complex words (e.g., amblyopia, episcopal, statistical; Catts, 1989b).

It is uncertain what percentage of children classified in school systems as LD are actually LI. As most professionals who are employed by or consult with school districts can attest, the LD classification is frequently the "dumping ground" for children who are experiencing academic failure, regardless of the causal model. For example, parents will accept/support an LD classification far more readily than one suggesting emotional disturbance or impaired intellectual functioning (e.g., slow learner, mental retardation). Even the Federal Register (1992), which outlines the classification categories and related diagnostic criteria relevant to the Individuals with Disabilities Education Act (IDEA), lists significant discrepancies in oral expression or listening comprehension as examples of a specific LD.

Rose, Lincoln, and Allen (1992) suggested that differentiation of LD/LI children from LD/nonLI youngsters could be based on (a) history of language disorder(s) in preschool/early primary grades; and (b) current status of phonological, receptive, expressive, and/or pragmatic competencies. By comparing two such groups, the authors reported that (a) the LD/LI children had significantly lower WISC-R VIQs than did the LD/nonLI group: (b) likewise the WISC-R Verbal Comprehension factor score differed, with the LD/LI mean notably lower; (c) the LD/LI children had pervasive language deficits in such broad areas as word knowledge and selection, length and complexity of spoken sentences, understanding of implied meanings (e.g., "What is likely to happen next?"), as well as in verbally mediated hypothetical-deductive reasoning (e.g., "Who committed the crime?"); and, (d) the LD/LI children had far more deficits in arithmetic, especially story problems. Thus, the two groups were closely matched on impaired reading and spelling skills, but differed considerably in history of language development, current verbal abilities, and level of functioning in language development, current verbal abilities, and level of functioning in language-mediated math competencies.

INTELLIGENCE TESTING AND LANGUAGE IMPAIRMENTS

Assessing the cognitive abilities of children with language impairments can prove difficult for professionals. Because intelligence tests historically have been weighted heavily with items that require verbal mediation (e.g., McCarthy Scales of Children's Abilities, Stanford-Binet L-M), children with language handicaps often appeared to have global cognitive deficits. Currently, there is a consensus among psychologists to use nonverbal, performance-based tests that do not discriminate against the language disabilities of these children (Aram & Hall, 1989; Phelps, Leguori, Nisewaner, & Parker, 1993; Sattler, 1988). Likewise, the current definition of LI requires the use of *nonverbal* IQ in the discrepancy formula.

KAUFMAN ASSESSMENT BATTERY FOR CHILDREN

Since its publication in 1983, the Kaufman Assessment Battery for Children (K-ABC; Kaufman & Kaufman, 1983) has gained popularity as a measure of intellectual functioning with children diagnosed as language disordered (Allen et al., 1991; Phelps et al., 1993; Ricciardi, Voelker, Carter, & Shore, 1991). Because the Mental Processing subtests emphasize problem-solving tasks and exclude items that assess acquired verbal knowledge, the test is viewed as less discriminatory. Likewise, the subtests have no or liberal time limits which do not handicap these children because of their impoverished reaction time or processing speed competencies (Bishop, 1992; Sininger, Klatzky, & Kirchner, 1989). Thus, the K-ABC appears to circumvent many psycholinguistic deficiencies.

With the LI population, the K-ABC has been compared to the McCarthy Scales of Children's Abilities (MSCA; McCarthy, 1972), the WISC-R (Wechsler, 1974), and the WISC-III, (Wechsler, 1991). For the K-ABC/McCarthy contrast, Ricciardi, et al. (1991) used preschoolers identified as LI and reported a significant difference of *14.42* points between the McCarthy's Global Cognitive Index (GCI mean = 64.75) and the K-ABC's Mental Processing Composite (MPC mean = 79.17). As restandardization and concurrent validity data consistently have documented *lower* scores on *newer* tests, this large disparity is in the wrong direction. For example, mean scores on the WISC-III were 2, 7, and 5 points lower on the VIQ, PIQ, and FSIQ when compared to the comparable WISC-R values for a nondisabled sample (Wechsler, 1991). Doll and Boren (1993) reported similar WISC-R–WISC-III comparisons for children diagnosed as LI, with the WISC-III VIQ, PIQ, and FSIQ scores lower by 5, 6, and 7 points, respectively. Likewise, Newby, Recht, Caldwell, and Schaefer (1993) reported differences of 5, 3, and 5 points, respectively, with a sample of children diagnosed as reading disordered. But the McCarthy–K-ABC differential of nearly *1 SD* is substantial and counterdirectional, thus suggesting that the two tests are measuring very different aspects of intelligence. Whereas the MSCA emphasizes language competencies as well as school-related acquired information, the K-ABC minimizes language requirements and attempts to assess cognitive abilities less influenced by previously acquired knowledge. Thus, the K-ABC may be viewed as providing a more nonverbal and, as such, less biased indication of intellectual competency.

For a K-ABC/WISC-R comparison, Allen et al. (1991) assessed 20 LI children ranging from 7 to 12 years of age (M = 9.3) and found a 8.6-point differential between the WISC-R PIQ (M = 97.10) and the K-ABC MPC (Mean = 88.45). Historically, the WISC-R PIQ has been interpreted as a valid measure of cognitive ability with deaf, hearing impaired, and language disordered children (Phelps & Branyan, 1988, 1990; Stark, Tallal, Kellman, & Mellits, 1983; Vernon & Andrews, 1990). There exists, however, controversy over the use of timed items with the LI population. Past research has demonstrated that these children do not differ significantly from normal youngsters in terms of accuracy of visual-spatial judgment. However, they process such information very slowly and require considerably more reaction time (Bishop, 1992; Sininger et al., 1989). Therefore, nonverbal measures of intelligence that have strict time limits (e.g., Wechsler Performance subtests) may be viewed as more discriminatory than tests with liberal or untimed items (e.g., K-ABC Nonverbal subtests). This study, however, calls this concern into question, for the WISC-R PIQ was *higher* by over ½ of a standard deviation. Some portion of this disparity, however, may be accounted for by the WISC-R standardization date, which was 9 years *earlier* than the K-ABC (WISC-R, 1974; K-ABC, 1983).

In contrast, Phelps et al. (1993) compared concurrent assessments of the *K-ABC Nonverbal Scale* (K-ABC NV) to the WISC-III PIQ with 40 children diagnosed with severe language disorders. The K-ABC NV score is recommended for use as the cognitive ability score because (a) it requires even less language than the MPC, (b) the directions may be pantomimed, (c) it has only one timed subtest, and (d) the numerous samples ensure the child's comprehension of tasks (Phelps & Branyan, 1988, 1990). The NV–PIQ comparison resulted in only a 4.4-point discrepancy, with the K-ABC NV *higher* (K-ABC NV mean = 81.13; WISC-III PIQ mean = 76.73). Given the 8-year differential between the two test standardizations (K-ABC, 1983; WISC-III, 1991), such a minor difference was expected and in the *correct direction.*

From these K-ABC studies, several conclusions can drawn. First, nonverbal performance-based scales are preferred over verbally mediated tests such as the McCarthy. Second, the K-ABC NV and WISC-III PIQ provide comparable assessments of nonverbal intellectual capacity. Third, the debate over timed versus untimed items for the LI population appears resolved and without cause. Finally, it should be noted that all K-ABC studies using LI school-age samples documented the notable sequential < simultaneous paradigm, further validating the left hemisphere neurological model for language disorders.

WISC-R

Numerous studies have reported WISC-R profile patterns for school-age children diagnosed as LI. First, the WISC-R VIQ < PIQ discrepancy was ubiquitous and varied from 11 (Doll & Boren, 1993) to 15 points (Allen et al., 1991; Rose et al., 1992). Such consistent findings with this population suggested that (a) WISC-R FSIQ scores should *never* be calculated or reported, as they are meaningless and reflect neither cognitive ability nor learning potential; and, (b) profile analyses should be conducted *within* a scale (i.e., Verbal vs. Performance) rather than across scales, as such comparisons using all 11 WISC-R subtests only greatly confounded interpretation. Second, although some authors identified specific WISC-R verbal subtests that especially were difficult for children (e.g., Comprehension—Bishop & Adams, 1990; Digit Span and Vocabulary—Rose et al., 1992), the *variability* within the six WISC-R Verbal subtests was never statistically significant, regardless of whether one employed the Kaufman or Wechsler discrepancy model. In short, the verbal profiles generally were quite flat. Finally, a similar conclusion was reached for the five WISC-R Performance subtests. Although Coding and Picture Arrangement were identified as arduous for LI children because of the sequential reasoning requirements (Bishop & Adams, 1992), no statistically significant weaknesses were ever identified using either the Kaufman or Wechsler models. Thus, there was no empirical support for WISC-R profile interpretations with the LI population beyond the Verbal–Performance discrepancy.

The use of the WISC-R PIQ as an index of academic potential for *hearing-impaired* students has had reasonable support (e.g., Kelly & Braden, 1990; Phelps & Branyan, 1990). Yet no studies reporting achievement/WISC-R PIQ correlations backed such a notion when LI samples were utilized (e.g., Doll & Boren, 1993). Schery (1985) did, however, report that WISC-R PIQ was a significant predictor of language performance and improvement over a 2–3-year time period for 718 severely LI children attending a special day school intervention program.

WISC-III

Only two studies have evaluated the WISC-III with LI samples (Doll & Boren, 1993; Phelps et al., 1993). In both investigations, the VIQ < PIQ discrepancy was maintained. Thus, the recommendation of never calculating or reporting the FSIQ is maintained. Even presenting the various verbal scores is considered hazardous because such findings may be misinterpreted as indices of cognitive ability by professionals, teachers, and parents alike. Thus, statements clearly specifying the VIQ, Verbal Comprehension Index, and Verbal subtests as indices of *receptive/ expressive competencies* are appropriate.

Neither study provided evidence of a "distinct" WISC-III subtest profile for this population; subtest variance within each scale (Verbal vs. Performance) was nonsignificant. Therefore, as with the WISC-R data, there is no empirical support for WISC-III subtest interpretations with children diagnosed as LI. Even with normal populations, there is considerable debate over the appropriate method and interpretive use of scatter or profile analysis based on subtest variance (Maccow & Laurent, 1996). Further studies are clearly warranted.

The Doll and Boren (1993) study reported no significant correlations between the WISC-III PIQ and the Woodcock-Johnson Tests of Achievement scores in Reading, Mathematics, Language, or Knowledge (W-J; Woodcock & Johnson, 1977). Interestingly, two correlations with the WISC-III VIQ were significant: Mathematic (.71) and Knowledge (.75). As no conclusions based on one study are appropriate, further evaluations of *both* the WISC-III VIQ and PIQ as predictors of *academic potential* are sorely needed for this population.

Phelps et al. (1993) reported on factor score comparisons. The Freedom from Distractibility Index (FDI) was the lowest and differed from the WISC-III PIQ by 7.93 points. One should consider the processing requirements of the two subtests loading on this factor (i.e., Arithmetic and Digit Span). Recent research has documented notable memory deficits with language disordered children that result from diminished phonological functioning and increased memory retrieval time (Gathercole & Baddeley, 1990; Sininger et al., 1989; von der Lely & Howard, 1993). Given that the Arithmetic and Digit Span items require verbal responses, short-term memory, and quick processing time, it is doubtful that the significantly impaired FD functioning of this sample was due to "distractibility." Perhaps the term *verbal memory* might better reflect the required competencies.

Subtests comprising the PIQ are divided into two factor scores: (a) Perceptual Organization (PO) which consists of Picture Completion, Picture Arrangement, Block Design, and Object Assembly; and, (b) Processing Speed (PS) which contains Coding and Symbol Search. Given the concerns regarding delayed response time for LI youngsters, it was not unusual that the PS Index was lower than PO by 6.85 points. In fact, the PO Index (POI) was the highest of the factor scores (Phelps et al., 1993). Whereas, the POI was 3.92 points *higher* than the PIQ, the PS Index was 2.93 points *lower.* Such findings suggest that the POI (as compared to PIQ) may be an even less discriminatory measure of cognitive ability for the LI population.

Studies evaluating the factor *structure* (i.e., factor analysis) of the WISC-III with the LI population have not been published. Likewise, the stability of the four factors (i.e., VC, PO, PS, and FD) has not been well established for any special education population. For example, using a sample of LD children with the majority having severe discrepancies in two or more areas of eligibility (e.g., reading, math, and written language), Kush (1996) reported construct validity for the Verbal Comprehension (VC) and PO factor scores but little or no support for the PS and FD WISC-III factor scores. Given such findings, caution against overinterpretation of factor score differences is warranted. Clearly, future research examining possible deferential factor structures across different special education classifications (e.g., autistic, hearing impaired, LI, LD/nonLI) is sorely needed.

CASE STUDY

Dylan Z. (pseudonym), a 12-year-old male starting the sixth grade, was referred for a neuropsychological evaluation by his pediatrician to determine appropriate psychopharmacological and educational recommendations. The following tests or procedures were administered or completed: (a) WISC-III; (b) Wide

Range Assessment of Memory and Learning (WRAML); (c) Woodcock-Johnson Tests of Achievement-Revised (WJ-R); (d) portions of the Halstead-Reitan Neuropsychological Test Battery for Older Children; (e) Test of Adolescent and Adult Language (TOAL-3); (f) developmental history; and (g) review of school records.

BACKGROUND INFORMATION

A parental interview and review of school records indicated that Dylan was referred for a complete evaluation (i.e., cognitive, speech, language, adaptive behavior, motor) by his pediatrician at 3 years of age due to "general developmental immaturity." Mrs. Z estimated Dylan's vocabulary consisted of approximately 100 words at that time, with most vocalizations being one word (e.g., wa-wa, go, no). He communicated primarily by gestures. The assessment results indicated Dylan had "significant delays in all areas." The Stanford-Binet L-M (S-B: L-M) IQ was 57. Brain stem auditory evoked response audiometry (BAER), which determines whether sounds are being adequately transmitted to the brain stem, indicated normal hearing. (Since BAER testing does not require a conscious response, uncommunicative children can be accurately examined.)

Dylan was enrolled in a full-day preschool program from 3 to 5 years of age. Services included cognitively oriented classroom instruction as well as speech/language, occupational, and physical therapy. The preschool teachers noted considerable inattentiveness. Although some improvements in attending behaviors, cooperativeness, articulation, receptive language, and fine-motor skills were documented, his general language and academic readiness skills were so delayed as to justify self-contained placement from kindergarten through the third grade, with a classification of Speech/Language Impaired. At 6 years of age, the S-B: L-M was readministered, resulting in a IQ score of 72. During this self-contained portion of his education, he was retained 1 year (e.g., completed the first grade twice).

In the fourth grade, his classification was changed to LD, and he was placed in a regular classroom with pull-out resource room assistance in reading (45 min per day). Considerable behavioral, social, and academic difficulties were noted by the regular classroom teacher. In a referral to the school psychologist, this teacher indicated that resource services at 45 min a day were not adequate to meet "Dylan's diverse needs." Mrs. Z reported that this teacher "thought Dylan was retarded." To sort out these diverse opinions, Dylan was referred to a licensed psychologist for further evaluation. As a result, he was diagnosed as having Attention Deficit Hyperactivity Disorder (ADHD) and medicated with Ritalin. When the school reported considerable levels of irritability and crying seemingly related to the Ritalin, he was switched to Cylert.

The fifth grade was most difficult for Dylan. In spite of being on 75 mg. of Cylert, the school noted random variability in his behavior. Some days he was reported to have considerable motor hyperactivity and severe levels of distractibility; however, on other days, his behavior was appropriate. School personnel questioned whether Mrs. Z was administering the morning dosage of Cylert consistently. In addition, Dylan received failing grades in the regular classroom instruction in science and social studies.

BEHAVIORAL OBSERVATIONS DURING TESTING

Dylan was evaluated during the summer months before starting the sixth grade. As he had been taken off Cylert for the summer, all testing was completed medication-free. Although he was cooperative at all times, his behavior vacillated from attentive, quiet, and task-oriented to notable levels of inattentiveness, impulsivity, and motor hyperactivity. For example, while completing *novel nonverbal* activities he found quite intriguing (e.g., Finger Tapping, Finger-tip Number Writing, and the Category Test from the Halstead-Reitan; Picture Completion and Object Assembly from the WISC-III; Finger Windows from the WRAML), he demonstrated age-appropriate movement, task vigilance, hypothetical-deductive reasoning, and executive planning. Yet during the Arithmetic and Vocabulary subtests of the WISC-III, and for most of the WJ-R (academic testing) and TOAL-3 (language assessment), he fidgeted, played with pencils, showed considerable interest in irrelevant items in the testing room, made frequent random guesses, and attempted to terminate the activities. When more complicated verbal interchanges were required, he appeared confused frequently and asked for clarification. Finally, his use of language was limited primarily to simple declarative sentences.

WISC-III RESULTS

Verbal subtests	Score	Performance subtests	Score
Information	7	Picture Completion	13
Similarities	7	Coding	5
Arithmetic	6	Picture Arrangement	11
Vocabulary	3	Block Design	10
Comprehension	6	Object Assembly	13
Digit Span	9	Symbol Search	7

Factor indices	Standard score	Percentile rank
Verbal Comprehension	77	6
Perceptual Organization	111	77
Freedom from Distractibility	87	19
Processing Speed	80	9

IQ indices	Standard score	Percentile rank
Verbal	76	5
Performance	103	58

These results validate the continued presence of LI. Given Dylan's difficulty with speeded responses (PS Index), a common element among language disordered children, it is suggested that the *less discriminatory* nonverbal index of cognitive ability is the POI score. Even if the PIQ is employed, it is apparent that the earlier S-B IQ scores of 57 and 72 reflected his language disorder and not intellectual potential. Likewise recall that the Verbal subtests, VC Index, and VIQ scores all reflect receptive and expressive competencies, not cognitive ability. Finally, Dylan's FDI score should not be used as validation of the ADHD diagnosis. Such a diagnosis requires a multidimensional assessment focusing on consistency of behaviors across numerous environments (e.g., home, school, psychologist's office), divergent tasks (e.g., verbal vs. nonverbal, novel vs. mundane, structured vs. open-ended), and varying sources (e.g., parent, teacher, psychologist). Recall that Dylan's behavior did vary across nonverbal/verbal domains.

TOAL-3 RESULTS

Area	Standard score	Percentile rank
Receptive Language	84	14
Expressive Language	69	2

Dylan continues to evidence significant language deficits in word knowledge and selection, length and complexity of verbal interchanges, and verbally mediated problem solving. It is possible his inattentiveness, impulsivity, and motor hyperactivity evidenced throughout the TOAL-3 evaluation reflect his frustration with verbally mediated tasks *rather than ADHD*.

HALSTEAD-REITAN RESULTS

This test battery documents neuropsychological impairment limited to the left temporofrontal area responsible for language and reading processing. For example, procedures assessing motor, sensory, nonverbal auditory discrimination, and nonverbal executive functioning (i.e., Finger Tapping, Finger-tip Number Writing, Tactile Form Recognition, Tactile Performance Test, Seashore Rhythm Test, and Category Test) were all within the normal range. By comparison, mildly impaired scores occurred on the Speech-sounds Perception Test (phonological discrimination), and the Trail Making Tests A and B (speeded scanning tasks requiring skills comparable to WISC-III Coding). Likewise, spelling dyspraxia, dyslexia, and central dysarthria (i.e., omission, addition, or transposition of syllables in enunciation) were evident on the Aphasia Screening Test.

WRAML

Subtest scores have a mean of 10 and standard deviation of 3.

Verbal memory subtests	Score	Visual memory subtests	Score
Story Memory	10	Picture Memory	11
Sentence Memory	5	Design Memory	11
Number/Letter	8	Finger Windows	11

Memory indices	Standard score	Percentile
Verbal Memory	85	16
Visual Memory	104	53

All items on this test assess short-term memory competencies. The subtests Story Memory (recollection of details within a short paragraph), Sentence Memory (word-for-word repetition), Number/Letter (reiteration of mixed numbers and letters similar to WISC-III Digit Span), and Finger Windows (replication of a visual dot-to-dot pattern) evaluate sequential processing. Picture Memory (recollection of details within an illustration) and Design Memory (reproduction of intricate patterns) reflect simultaneous processing. In agreement with the previous findings, the WRAML illustrates Dylan's ubiquitous language deficiencies.

WJ-R RESULTS

As Dylan was retained in the first grade, standard scores are based on grade norms.

Area	Standard score	Percentile rank
Word Identification	81	10
Reading Comprehension	85	16
Math Calculation	103	58
Math Applied Problems	96	39
Writing Samples	85	16
Spelling	84	14
Word Attack	75	5

Phonological impairment is manifested in both real and non-word decoding competencies (i.e., Word Identification, Spelling, and Word Attack). For example, Spelling and Word Attack errors included omissions, substitutions, and transpositions reflecting little blended letter-sound knowledge. Dylan's reading was laborious and hesitant. Word omissions and substitutions (e.g., "largest" for "longest") were frequent. Finally, he did not use contextual clues or inferential processing to comprehend the "gist" of a story.

Math was the only academic area within the normal range. Yet note the difference between Math Applied Problems (i.e., story problems requiring language mediation) and Math Calculations (i.e., computations presented in numerical form wherein no language is involved).

All language-based academic competencies (i.e., Word Identification, Reading Comprehension, Writing Samples, Spelling, and Word Attack) have grade-equivalent scores ranging for 2.5 (Work Attack) to 3.3 (Writing Samples). Recall that Dylan will be starting the sixth grade in the fall and has received two years of preschool service, five years of self-contained placement, and two years of resource room support. Clearly, acknowledgment of the LI genesis of his academic difficulties and, perhaps, ADHD behaviors is imperative. (For an excellent review of the relationship between ADHD and language disorders, refer to Kavanagh & Lyon, 1996.) Likewise, academic instruction reflecting *empirically validated* cognitive strategies and directed practice in phonetic decoding and drilling are essential. (Refer to Swanson, Carson, & Sachse-Lee, 1996, for a meta-analysis of instructional procedures appropriate for LD students.) Finally, the Committee for Special Education serving Dylan's school would be well advised to consider placement options and provision of services that reflect the depth and breadth of this student's special needs.

REFERENCES

Abbeduto, L., & Nuccio, J. (1989). Evaluating the pragmatic aspects of communication in school-age children and adolescents: Insights from research on atypical development. *School Psychology Review, 18,* 502–512.

Allen, D. A. (1989). Developmental language disorders in preschool children: Clinical subtypes and syndromes. *School Psychology Review, 18,* 442–451.

Allen, M. H., Lincoln, A. J., & Kaufman, A. S. (1991). Sequential and simultaneous processing abilities of high-functioning autistic and language-impaired children. *Journal of Autism and Developmental Disorders, 21,* 483–502.

American Psychiatric Association. (1994). *Diagnostic and statistical manual of mental disorders* (4th ed.). Washington, DC: Author.

Aram, D. M., & Eisele, J. A. (1992). Plasticity and recovery of higher cognitive functions following early brain injury. In I. Rapin & S. J. Segalowitz (Eds.), *Handbook of neuropsychology* (Vol. 6, pp. 73–92). Amsterdam: Elsevier.

Aram, D. M., & Eisele, J. A. (1994). Limits of a left hemisphere explanation for specific language impairment. *Journal of Speech and Hearing Research, 37,* 824–830.

Aram, D. M., Ekelman, B. L., & Nation, J. E. (1984). Preschoolers with language disorders: 10 years later. *Journal of Speech and Hearing Research, 27,* 232–244.

Aram, D. M., & Hall, N. E. (1989). Longitudinal follow-up of children with preschool communication disorders: Treatment implications. *School Psychology Review, 18,* 487–501.

Beitchman, J. H., Brownlie, E. B., Inglis, A., Wild, J., Mathews, R., Schachter, D., Kroll, R., Martin, S., Ferguson, B., & Lancee, W. (1994). Seven year follow-up of speech/language impaired and control children: Speech/Language stability and outcome. *Journal of the American Academy of Child and Adolescent Psychiatry, 33,* 1322–1330.

Bishop, D. V. M. (1992).The underlying nature of specific language impairment. *Journal of Child Psychology, Psychiatry, and Allied Disciplines, 33,* 3–66.

Bishop, D. V. M., & Adams, C. (1990). A prospective study of the relationship between specific language impairment, phonological disorders, and reading retardation. *Journal of Child Psychology, Psychiatry, and Allied Disciplines, 31,* 1027–1050.

Bishop, D. V. M., & Adams, C. (1992). Comprehension problems in children with specific language impairment: Literal and inferential meaning. *Journal of Speech and Hearing Research, 35,* 119–129.

Bishop, B. V. M., & Edmundson, A. (1987). Language-impaired 4-year-olds: Distinguishing transient from persistent impairment. *Journal of Speech and Hearing Disorders, 52,* 156–173.

Bishop, D. V. M., North T., & Donlan, C. (1995). Genetic basis of specific language impairment: Evidence from a twin study. *Development Medicine and Child Neurology, 37,* 56–71.

Catts, H. (1989a). Phonological processing deficits and reading disabilities. In A. Kamhi and H. Catts (Eds.), *Reading disabilities: A developmental language perspective* (pp. 101–133). Austin, TX: Pro-Ed.

Catts, H. (1989b). Speech production deficits in developmental dyslexia. *Journal of Speech and Hearing Disorders, 54,* 422–428.

Catts, H. (1989c). Defining dyslexia as a developmental language disorder. *Annals of Dyslexia, 39,* 50–67.

Conti-Ramsden, G., Donlan, C., & Grove, J. (1992). Characteristics of children with specific language impairment attending language units. *European Journal of Disorders of Communication, 27,* 325–342.

Dale, P. S., & Henderson, V. L. (1987). An evaluation of the Test of Early Language Development as a measure of receptive and expressive language. *Language, Speech, and Hearing Services in Schools, 18,* 179–187.

Doll, B., & Boren, R. (1993). Performance of severely language-impaired students on the WISC-III, language scales, and academic achievement measures. *Journal of Psychoeducational Assessment Monograph: Wechsler Intelligence Scale for Children: Third Edition, 11,* 77–86.

Eisele, J. A., & Aram, D. M. (1993). Differential effects of early hemisphere damage on lexical comprehension and production. *Aphasiology, 5,* 513–523.

Federal Register (1992). *Rules and regulations.* (Vol. 57, No. 189). Washington, DC: U.S. Government Printing Office.

Felsenfeld, S., Broen, P. A., & McGue, M. (1992). A 28-year follow-up of adults with a history of moderate phonological disorder: Linguistic and personality results. *Journal of Speech and Hearing Research, 35,* 1114–1125.

Felsenfeld, S., McGue, M., & Broen, P. A. (1995). Familial aggregation of phonological disorders: Results from a 28-year follow-up. *Journal of Speech and Hearing Research, 38,* 1091–1107.

Field, M., Fox, N, & Radcliffe, J. (1990). Predicting IQ changes in preschoolers with developmental delays. *Developmental and Behavioral Pediatrics, 11,* 184–189.

Gathercole, S. E., & Baddeley, A. D. (1990). Phonological memory deficits in language disordered children: Is there a causal connection? *Journal of Memory and Language, 29,* 336–360.

Kamhi, A. G. (1992). Response to historical perspective: A developmental language perspective. *Journal of Learning Disabilities, 25,* 48–52.

Kamhi, A. G., & Catts, H. (Eds.). (1989). *Reading disabilities: A developmental language perspective.* Austin, TX: Pro-Ed.

Kaufman, A. S., & Kaufman, N. L. (1983). *Kaufman Assessment Battery for Children.* Circle Pines, MN: American Guidance Service.

Kavanagh, J. F., & Lyon, G. R. (Eds.). (1966). ADD and its relationships to spoken and written language (Special Issue). *Topics in language disorders, 14.*

Kelly, M., & Braden, J. P. (1990). Criterion validity of the WISC-R Performance Scale with the Stanford Achievement Test-Hearing Impaired Edition. *Journal of School Psychology, 28,* 147–151.

Kush, J. C. (1996). Factor structure of the WISC-III for students with learning disabilities. *Journal of Psychoeducational Assessment, 14,* 32–40.

Lou, H. C., Henriksen, L, & Bruhn, P. (1990). Focal cerebral dysfunction in developmental learning disabilities. *Lancet, 335,* 8–11.

Maccow, G., & Laurent, J. (1996). Analyzing WISC-III profiles: A comparison of two approaches. *Journal of Psychoeducational Assessment, 14,* 20–31.

McCarthy, D. (1972). *McCarthy Scales of Children's Abilities.* San Antonio, TX: Psychological Corporation.

Newby, R. F., Recht, D. R., Caldwell, J., & Schaefer, J. (1993). Comparison of WISC-III and WISC-R IQ changes over a 2-year time span in a sample of children with dyslexia. *Journal of Psychoeducational Assessment, Wechsler Intelligence Scale for Children: Third Edition* (Monograph), *11,* 87–93.

Nobre, A. C., Allison, T., & McCarthy, G. (1994). Word recognition in the human inferior temporal lobe. *Nature, 372,* 260–263.

Nobre, A. C., McCarthy, G. (1995). Language-related field potentials in the anterior-medial temporal lobe: Effects of word type and semantic priming. *Journal of Neuroscience, 15,* 1090–1098.

Phelps, L., & Branyan, B. J. (1988). Correlations among the Hiskey, K-ABC Nonverbal Scale, Leiter, and WISC-R Performance Scale with public school deaf children. *Journal of Psychoeducational Assessment, 6,* 354–358.

Phelps, L., & Branyan, B. J. (1990). Academic achievement and nonverbal intelligence in public school hearing-impaired children. *Psychology in the Schools, 23,* 138–141.

Phelps, L., Leguori, S., Nisewaner, K., & Parker, M. (1993). Practical interpretations of the WISC-III with language-disordered children. *Journal of Psychoeducational Assessment, Wechsler Intelligence Scale for Children: Third Edition* (Monograph), *11,* 71–76.

Ricciardi, P. W. Voelker, S., Carter, R. A., & Shore, D. L. (1991). K-ABC sequential-simultaneous processing and language-impaired preschoolers. *Developmental Neuropsychology, 7,* 523–535.

Richardson, S. O. (1992). Historical perspectives on dyslexia. *Journal of Learning Disabilities, 25,* 40–47.

Robinson, R. L. (1991). Causes and associations of severe and persistent specific speech and language disorders in children. *Developmental Medicine and Child Neurology, 33,* 943–962.

Rose, J. C., Lincoln, A. J., Allen, M. H. (1992). Ability profiles of developmental language disordered and learning disabled children: A comparative analyses. *Developmental Neuropsychology, 8,* 413–426.

Sattler, J. M. (1988). *Assessment of children* (3rd ed.). San Diego, CA: Author.

Scarborough, H., & Dobrich, W. (1990). Development of children with early language delay. *Journal of Speech and Hearing Research, 33,* 70–84.

Schery, T. K. (1985). Correlates of language development in language disordered children. *Journal of Speech and Hearing Disorders, 50,* 73–83.

Shaywitz, S. E. (1996). The neurobiology of reading. *Scientific American, 275,* 98–104.

Silva, P. A., Williams, S. M., & McGee, R. (1987). A longitudinal study of children with developmental language delays at age three: Later intelligence, reading, and behaviour problems. *Developmental Medicine and Child Neurology, 29,* 630–640.

Sininger, Y. S., Klatzky, R. L., Kirchner, D. M. (1989). Memory scanning speed in language-disordered children. *Journal of Speech and Hearing Research, 32,* 289–297.

Sommers, R. K. (1989). Language assessment: Issues in the use and interpretation of tests and measures. *School Psychology Review, 18,* 452–462.

Sommers, R. K., Erdige, S., & Peterson, M. K. (1978). How valid are children's language tests? *The Journal of Special Education, 12,* 394–407.

Stark, R. E., Tallal, P., Kellman, C., & Mellits, E. D. (1983). Cognitive abilities of language-delayed children. *Journal of Psychology, 114,* 9–19.

Swanson, H. L., Carson, C., & Sachse-Lee, C. M. (1996). A selective synthesis of intervention research for students with learning disabilities. *School Psychology Review, 25,* 370–391.

Tallal, P., & Curtis, S. (1988). From developmental dysphasia to dyslexia: A neurodevelopmental continuum. *Journal of Clinical and Experimental Neuropsychology, 10,* 19.

Tallal, P., Ross, R., & Curtiss, S. (1989). Familial aggregation in specific language impairment. *Journal of Speech and Hearing Disorders, 54,* 167–173.

Tomblin, J. B. (1989). Familial concentration of developmental language impairment. *Journal of Speech and Hearing Disorders, 54,* 287–295.

Vernon, M., & Andrews, J. F. (1990). *The psychology of deafness: Understanding deaf and hard-of-hearing people.* New York: Longman.

von der Lely, H. K. J., & Hoard, D. (1993). Children with specific language impairment: Linguistic impairment or short-term memory deficit? *Journal of Speech and Hearing Research, 36,* 1193–1207.

Wechsler, D. (1974). *Wechsler Intelligence Scale for Children—Revised.* San Antonio, TX: Psychological Corporation.

Wechsler, D. (1991). *Wechsler Intelligence Scale for Children—III.* San Antonio, TX: Psychological Corporation.

Woodcock, R. W., & Johnson, M. B. (1977). *Woodcock-Johnson Psycho-Educational Battery.* Allen, TX: DLM.

9

ASSESSMENT OF HEARING-IMPAIRED AND DEAF CHILDREN WITH THE WISC-III

JEFFERY P. BRADEN AND JOSEPH M. HANNAH

Department of Educational Psychology
University of Wisconsin—Madison
Madison, Wisconsin

The WISC-III in its various editions is the most widely used test of intelligence with hearing-impaired and deaf children[1] in North America. In fact, it is probably the most widely used test of intelligence with deaf children in the world. The Wechsler scales are extremely popular with clinicians and researchers interested in measuring the intellectual abilities of deaf children. Furthermore, experts in deafness consistently recommend the Wechsler scales, and in particular, the Performance Scales, as being among the best ways to assess intelligence. Indeed, the Performance Scale of the Wechsler in all its versions has generated more studies on deaf children than any other measure of intelligence (Braden, 1994).

Therefore, it is no surprise that new versions of the Wechsler should attract substantial attention among those who are interested in its use with deaf children. This is true for the WISC-III (Wechsler, 1991). The WISC-III is the first Wechsler scale to include a clinical study of the use of the test with deaf students (see Wechsler, 1991, p. 216). Furthermore, this clinical study was elaborated in detail in a subsequent publication (Maller & Braden, 1993). Therefore, even before its publication, the WISC-III was likely to be a tool for assessing the intelligence of deaf children.

---

[1] We realize that American Psychological Association style recommends person-first usage (e.g., children who are deaf or hard-of-hearing). However, we use the term "deaf children" to be consistent with the way in which deaf people in North America define themselves. Consequently, we refer to children who have normal hearing as "normal-hearing children." We hope that our usage does not offend or confuse readers.

This book is intended to address practitioner and scientific perspectives. The professional literature presents both perspectives when describing the use of the Wechsler scales in deaf populations. The first perspective is that of the practitioner. That literature explores the use of the Wechsler scales for assessing deaf children's intelligence, and for differentially diagnosing cognitive deficits within deaf children. For example, substantial literature is available on "profile analysis" with earlier versions of the Wechsler (Braden, 1990). Additionally, there is substantial literature on how the Wechsler Performance Scale can differentially diagnose average, gifted, and mentally retarded deaf children. The primary clinical purpose of the Wechsler is to differentially diagnose the impact of deafness from the possible impact of mental retardation. That is, most deaf children also have significant language delays and deficits in acquired knowledge and other culturally relevant (i.e., crystallized abilities) cognitive skills. Experts frequently argue that these deficits are due not to a lack of intellectual ability, but to lack of opportunity to acquire the dominant language. Therefore, deaf children appear to be retarded if one only examines traditional measures of language development, academic achievement, and the like. However, deaf children as a whole appear to have average intellectual abilities when assessed using language-reduced measures of cognitive ability (Braden, 1994; Vernon, 1967). Therefore, the primary use of the Wechsler scales is to differentially diagnose mental retardation from deafness as a cause of poor academic and language performance in deaf children. Additionally, the Wechsler is occasionally used to diagnose learning difficulties within deaf children. That is, just because a child is deaf does not mean the child does not have additional cognitive deficits that might interfere with learning. This tradition has historically been pursued with the Wechsler through the use of profile analysis, in which it has been found that the Coding subtest is especially sensitive to academic deficits in deaf children (Braden, 1990; Ensor, 1988).

In contrast, the research or empirical tradition of work with deafness has focused on the adequacy of the Wechsler scales from a technical point of view. In other words, there is a fair amount of research attempting to demonstrate the reliability and validity of the Wechsler scales (again, primarily the Performance Scales) for their use with deaf populations. These studies of previous versions of the Wechsler have been summarized elsewhere (see Braden, 1992, 1994). The most important feature of this research is that the previous versions of the Wechsler have generally been found to have adequate technical characteristics when applied to populations of deaf people. However, this general conclusion can be challenged on some specific issues including the variability of correlations between IQ and measures of achievement.

All the issues addressed in previous versions of the Wechsler remain as important issues for the WISC-III. That is, there is still a strong interest in clinical traditions and in particular how effective the WISC-III will be for differentially diagnosing the impact of hearing impairment from the potential impacts of conjoint cognitive impairments. Secondarily, there will be interest in the degree to which Wechsler subtest profiles will be able to be used to differentially diagnose (or be sensitive to) academic deficits in deaf children.

Likewise, all of the issues about the technical integrity of the WISC-III are critical and must be reestablished. Although it is a good bet that many of the characteristics that were true for previous versions of the Wechsler will be true for this version, findings must be replicated to establish adequate reliability and validity for the WISC-III. Therefore, our chapter will address clinical and research issues that have been critical to the use of Wechsler scales with deaf children. In particular, we will identify those issues we see as critical and will bring to bear available research using the WISC-III to address them. We will often illustrate the issue or describe it by citing research on previous versions of the Wechsler scales.

ADMINISTRATION ISSUES

METHODS OF TRANSLATION

Wechsler (1991) cautions examiners that deviations from the standard administration procedures can reduce the validity of test results. Given that caution, however, the WISC-III manual states that "some flexibility may be necessary to balance the needs of the particular child with the need to maintain standard procedures" (p. 38). Regarding children who are deaf, the manual suggests that modifications, such as translation of the test into signs or the use of additional visual aids, be noted on the record form. This will allow those who are evaluating the child's functioning to weigh the impact of any modifications made.

When assessing deaf or hard-of-hearing children whose primary mode of communication is American Sign Language (ASL), Pidgin Signed English (PSE), or a sign system such as Signing Exact English (SEE), psychologists have an ethical responsibility to administer tests in the child's primary language. Ideally, the psychologist would be skilled in the method of sign language used by the child. When this is not feasible, a certified sign language interpreter may be secured to interpret instructions to the child. Examiners should observe the child in various settings and consult with the child's parents and teacher prior to assessing a child who is deaf or hard of hearing to identify the child's communication needs.

The most common procedure for administering the Wechsler scales is to translate the directions from speech to another (visual) form to allow the deaf child to understand the tasks at hand. In some cases, the directions are supplemented with gestures or a written transcription of directions. In other cases, the directions are given concurrently in sign language and speech. The range of methods used to supplement directions include the following:

- careful oral enunciation
- supplementing oral directions with written transcripts of the directions
- finger-spelling directions
- signing directions in English signs
- concurrently saying the directions orally and signing them in an English-type sign dialect
- translating directions into ASL without concurrent voice

- gestures
- supplemented examples/demonstrations of subtests.

The most popular of these adaptations has historically been concurrent presentation of task directions in voice and sign (Braden, 1992, 1994).

The impact of administrative adaptations varies. Some adaptations produce higher scores in deaf children than do others. Literature reviews find concurrent administration of Wechsler subtests using voice and sign directions as yielding higher PIQs than any of the other methods (Braden, 1992, 1994), although any individual study may fail to achieve statistical significance for the comparison (e.g., Sullivan & Montoya, in press). Generally, oral administration (and oral administration supplemented with written directions) produces lower Performance IQs (PIQs). Most experts encourage examiners to use concurrent voice and sign administrations, although some experts (e.g., Ray, 1982) also recommend supplemental examples and demonstrations.

Often experts recommend simultaneous administration of directions in voice and signs because this method produces higher scores. This is incorrect reasoning from a research perspective, as one cannot assume higher scores are necessarily "better" at estimating deaf children's intelligence. In other words, it would probably also be true that if we gave deaf children the answers to questions before giving them the test they would get higher scores. Yet few would argue that such an adaptation would be appropriate for assessing deaf children's intelligence. Therefore, the finding that deaf children get higher IQs when given tests concurrently in voice and signs is insufficient to support its use. Advocates of concurrent voice and sign methods draw on another argument to support the use of that administration method. That argument is that deaf children should be assessed in their native communication or dominant communication method. Because most deaf children in North America are instructed using a simultaneous approach (concurrent presentation of information in voice and signs), it would make sense that they should also be assessed in a concurrent voice and sign approach. However, this may be changing. The bilingual/bicultural movement in deafness is encouraging educators to teach deaf children using ASL before introducing English. In situations where deaf children are fully immersed in an ASL environment, it would make the most sense to administer the WISC-III using ASL directions. That is, the psychologist would administer the test without using concurrent voice, as ASL cannot be concurrently voiced in English.

A final note on adaptations for administration is the use of interpreters. There has been very little systematic research on the impact of interpreters in the assessment situation. However, the available research (e.g., Sullivan, 1978; Sullivan & Montoya, in press; Sullivan & Schulte, 1992) suggests that interpreter use generally yields scores equal to those that are produced when the test is administered by a psychologist who is fluent in sign and voice communication. That is, when the psychologist gives the directions orally and an interpreter translates those oral directions into sign, deaf children generally do about as well as deaf children who get the tests administered by a psychologist fluent in sign language. However, the impact of interpreters on assessment outcomes is not well understood, especially with respect to ASL. Most previous studies use signed English systems rather than ASL. Preliminary evidence suggests that deaf psychologists who administer the WISC-III to normal-hearing children can use an interpreter and get reasonably accurate results (Kostrubala, 1996). Likewise, the accuracy of an ASL version of the WISC-III was demonstrated using blind back-translation (Maller, 1996). These results are encouraging in suggesting that careful, comprehensive procedures for translation can provide accurate ASL versions of the Wechsler scales. However, with one exception (Maller, 1996), none of the previous research has explicitly defined the procedures used to translate the Wechsler scales from English to ASL. The process should follow procedures for translating tests between oral languages, and include blind back-translation accuracy checks. The process for effective translation is provided in Figure 9.1 (from Kostrubala, 1997).

NONLINGUISTIC ADAPTATIONS

Sattler (1992) summarizes many nonlinguistic modifications of the WISC-III recommended for use for children who are deaf. On the Verbal Scale, these include typing the questions for the Information, Comprehension, Similarities, and Vocabulary subtests, and allowing written or typed responses if the child cannot respond orally. He warns that visually administering the Arithmetic and Digit Span subtests may be difficult due to the nature of these tasks. Modifications for the Performance Scale are presented in Appendix D (Sattler, 1992; pp. 896–899). These include pantomime and various visual adaptations to subtest instructions. Examiners are warned, however, that the use of pantomimed instructions or visual aids may produce lower PIQs than those obtained from sign language administration (Braden, 1985a; Sullivan, 1982). Sattler (1992) too cautions that scores obtained using these modifications should be viewed only as estimates of what the child's score would be had standardized procedures been followed. Table 9.1 summarizes the various modifications to the Wechsler subtests for administration to deaf children. Note that few of these recommendations are recent; the trend in the past 10–20 years has been to translate the test directions into the child's primary language rather than emphasize nonlinguistic modifications to subtest administration.

TECHNICAL ADEQUACY OF THE WISC-III WITH DEAF CHILDREN

RELIABILITY

The reliability of the Wechsler scales has not been as widely studied as other characteristics. However, some previous studies suggest that the internal consistency of the Wechsler scales is similar in deaf and hearing samples. That is, the

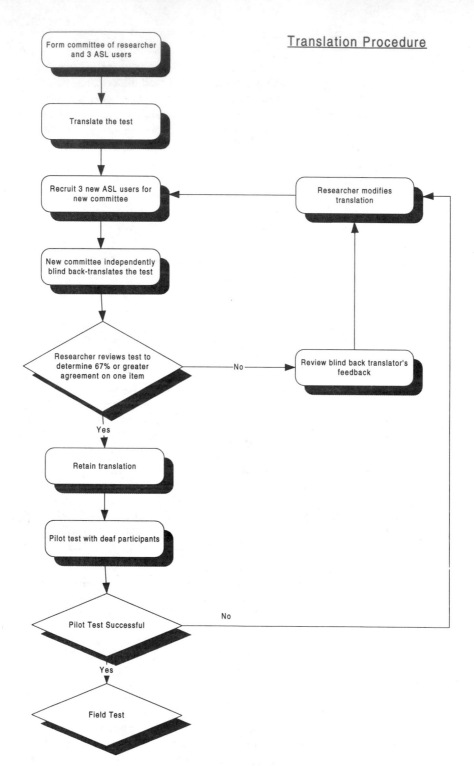

FIGURE 9.1   Steps for effective translations of the Wechsler Scales.

TABLE 9.1   Nonlinguistic Modifications to Wechsler Performance Scale Subtests for Deaf Children[a]

Subtest	Adaptation
Picture Completion (Neuhaus, 1967)	Three sample pictures are drawn on separate cards, a complete picture on one side and the same picture with a missing detail on the other. Each card is presented by showing the incomplete side first, then the complete side while indicating the detail.
Coding (Murphy, 1957)	Examiner models completion of sample items using Coding protocol from previous version of the Wechsler. A card with the words "Do this quickly" is laid beside the child's protocol.
Picture Arrangement (Reed, 1970)	Two sets of three cards are used, one with the numbers 1, 2, and 3, and one with the letters, A, B, and C, as well as the sample item. Cards are presented out of sequence and the examiner models arranging them in order then motions for the child to do the same.
Block Design (Murphy, 1957)	Four blocks are laid out in a line each with the red side on top, followed by the white, and red/white sides. Designs are then presented as is a card with the words "Make one like this."
Object Assembly (Neuhaus, 1967)	Three pictures are drawn on cards representing the sample item and first two test items. Pieces are arranged behind the shield and when exposed, the corresponding picture is laid next to the pieces as a model.
Mazes (Sullivan, 1978)	Examiner models completion of sample items using Mazes protocol from previous version of the Wechsler. A card with the words "Start in the middle. Find your way out" is laid beside the child's protocol.

[a]Summarized from Sattler, 1992; pp. 896–899.

Wechsler Performance Scale subtest scores and PIQ are equally precise in deaf and hearing samples (Braden, 1994). Additional research on the stability of previous versions of the Wechsler suggest good stability over 1 year to multiyear intervals (Braden, Maller, & Paquin, 1993). However, carefully controlled test–retest research is not available on either previous versions of the Wechsler or the WISC-III. Therefore, the stability of WISC-III IQs and subtests is unknown. We will discuss comparisons between the WISC-R and WISC-III with deaf children in the following (Validity) section.

Estimates of internal consistency suggest that the WISC-III is equally accurate for deaf and normally hearing children (Maller & Braden, 1993). Unfortunately, there have been no replications of internal consistency studies with the WISC-III using deaf participants. We conclude that the available evidence does not show reliability differences when the WISC-III is used with deaf children, but we also note there is not much evidence to show that reliabilities are the same. The best verdict for the case of whether WISC-III reliability is consistent within deaf children is the Scottish Law verdict of "not proven." Scientists and practitioners will need additional replications of reliability studies, particularly for temporal stability, before they can adequately judge the reliability of the WISC-III with deaf children.

JEFFERY P. BRADEN AND JOSEPH M. HANNAH

TABLE 9.2   Mean WISC-III Scale and Index Scores from Studies of Deaf Children[a]

Study	N	VIQ M	PIQ M	FSIQ M
Wechsler (1991)	30	81.10 (20.30)	105.80 (20.80)	92.20 (19.80)
Braden, et al. (1994)	19	81.63 (18.74)	102.32 (11.03)	90.68 (12.54)
Slate & Fawcett (1995)	47		88.00 (18.10)	
Sullivan & Montoya (1997)	106	75.35 (17.55)	100.63 (19.48)	86.22 (17.37)

[a]Values enclosed in parentheses represent standard deviations. VIQ = Verbal Intelligence Quotient; PIQ = Performance Intelligence Quotient; FSIQ = Full Scale Intelligence Quotient.

VALIDITY

The WISC-III manual (Wechsler, 1991; p. 216) presents one study regarding the validity of the WISC-III with a sample of deaf children. The sample, as described by Maller and Braden (1993), consisted of 30 children who had severe to profound hearing losses. Etiology of hearing loss was attributed to unknown or suspected genetic causes for the majority of the sample. The median age at which hearing loss was diagnosed was 2 years. Twenty-seven children had parents with normal hearing, and 3 had parents who are deaf. Administration procedures were modified by using ASL or PSE, depending on the child's primary mode of communication. The results indicated mean scale and index scores in the expected direction (e.g., PIQ > VIQ). These results provide tentative evidence that the WISC-III, much like its predecessors, is a useful measure with deaf children (Wechsler, 1991).

Since the publication of the WISC-III, other studies have investigated its validity with samples of deaf children. First, we examine the mean Scale and Index scores reported in various studies. Table 9.2 presents Scale and Index means and standard deviations.

The data in Table 9.2 replicate previous studies of the Wechsler Scales by noting that deaf children consistently demonstrate lower scores on subtests from the Verbal Scale (i.e., VIQ, VC, FFD) than scores drawn from Performance Scale subtests (i.e., PIQ, PO, PS). The exception to this generalization is the Processing Speed (PS) Index score. Research with previous Wechsler tests found a pattern of lower Coding scores (Braden, 1990), thus raising the question of lower speed of information-processing abilities. The current research is inconsistent in defining whether lower scores are limited to the Coding subtest (e.g., Maller & Braden, 1993; Sullivan & Montoya, in press) or generalize to the PS factor (Slate & Fawcett, 1995).

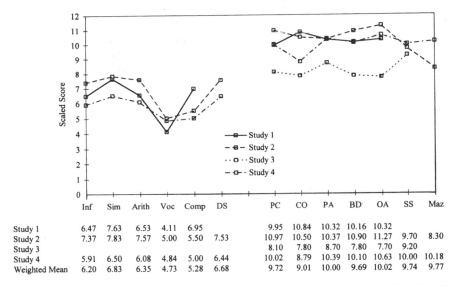

	Inf	Sim	Arith	Voc	Comp	DS		PC	CO	PA	BD	OA	SS	Maz
Study 1	6.47	7.63	6.53	4.11	6.95			9.95	10.84	10.32	10.16	10.32		
Study 2	7.37	7.83	7.57	5.00	5.50	7.53		10.97	10.50	10.37	10.90	11.27	9.70	8.30
Study 3								8.10	7.80	8.70	7.80	7.70	9.20	
Study 4	5.91	6.50	6.08	4.84	5.00	6.44		10.02	8.79	10.39	10.10	10.63	10.00	10.18
Weighted Mean	6.20	6.83	6.35	4.73	5.28	6.68		9.72	9.01	10.00	9.69	10.02	9.74	9.77

FIGURE 9.2   WISC-III subtest means and standard deviations reported in studies of deaf children.

The second issue we address is the variability among WISC-III subtest scores reported in these studies. Figure 9.2 presents the means and standard deviations of WISC-III subtests from those studies and depicts the mean scores for each study as a graphic psychometric profile.

There are two striking features of Figure 9.2: (a) the mean Performance Scale scores are higher than the mean Verbal Scale scores, and (b) there are substantial differences in average scores among studies. That is, all studies that included both Verbal and Performance Scales reported higher Performance Scale subtest means, but among the Performance subtests, the most striking variability is between studies, not between subtests. Thus, it is difficult to identify a "characteristic" psychometric profile for deaf children.

The factor structure of the WISC-III was examined in two studies. Sullivan and Montoya (in press) included all of the WISC-III subtests, whereas Slate and Fawcett (1995) only included Performance Scale subtests. Sullivan and Montoya found two factors, which clearly corresponded to the Verbal and Performance Scales. This replicates previous factor analyses of the WISC-R (Sullivan & Schulte, 1992). In contrast, Slate and Fawcett found Performance subtest loadings consistent with PO and PS factors. It is not clear whether the differences in these studies are due to differences in factor analytic procedures, the variables included in the analyses (i.e., Performance versus Full Scale subtests), or differences in the participants (e.g., Sullivan & Montoya, in press, use a much larger and less heterogeneous cohort than Slate & Fawcett, 1995). Therefore, psychologists can be reasonably certain that Verbal and Performance factors are replicated within samples

TABLE 9.3   Correlations of the WISC-III with Other Psychological Tests[a]

Study	WISC-III IQ		
	VIQ	PIQ	FSIQ
Braden et al. (1994)			
K-TEA Math	.48	.14	.47
K-TEA Reading	.60	.16	.56
K-TEA Spelling	.54	−.04	.43
K-TEA Composite	.58	.11	.53
Maller & Braden (1993)			
SAT-HI Total Reading	.80	.46	.71
SAT-HI Total Language	.85	.54	.77
SAT-HI Total Math	.83	.63	.81
Slate & Fawcett (1995)			
WISC-R PIQ		.93	
WRAT-R Reading		.41	
WRAT-R Spelling		.48	
WRAT-R Arithmetic		.64	

[a]K-TEA = Kaufman Test of Educational Achievement; SAT-HI = Stanford Achievement Test (7th edition) using norms for Hearing-Impaired children; WISC-R = Wechsler Intelligence Scale for Children-Revised; WRAT-R = Wide Range Achievement Test-Revised.

of deaf children, but it is not clear whether additional Index factors (e.g., Processing Speed) are also present.

Finally, we turn our attention to relationships between the WISC-III and other tests. Again, the data are limited, but generally supportive of the WISC-III. Slate and Fawcett (1995) examined the relationships between the WISC-III and WISC-R PIQ and subtests, and the relationship between WISC-III PIQ and subscales of the Wide Range Achievement Test-Revised (WRAT-R). The gap between WISC-R and WISC-III testing was about 3 years, whereas the WISC-III and WRAT-R were administered concurrently. Maller and Braden (1993) examined the relationship between WISC-III IQs and subtests of the Seventh Edition of the Stanford Achievement Test, which was normed on a large national sample of deaf children (SAT-HI). Finally, Braden, Reed, and Kostrubala (1994) reported correlations between concurrent administrations of the WISC-III and the Kaufman Test of Educational Achievement (K-TEA). The results of these studies are summarized in Table 9.3.

These findings generally support the use of the WISC-III with deaf children. By finding strong correlations between the WISC-III and WISC-R, Slate and Fawcett (1995) support generalization of research with the WISC-R to the WISC-III. Correlations between the WISC-III and tests of achievement are also moderate to high. However, the finding that VIQs and Indexes correlate higher with achievement than PIQs and Indexes suggests a dilemma in the assessment of deaf children. That is, the WISC-III Verbal Scale offers greater predictive accuracy, but confounds language knowledge with the estimation of intelligence. We will return to this issue in our concluding section.

ISSUES IN USING AND INTERPRETING RESULTS

There are many issues that test users and researchers should address when using the WISC-III with deaf children. Many of these issues are controversial, with experts in stark disagreement. We will address seven issues in this section, including the following:

- Special norms based on deaf children
- VIQ versus PIQ
- Differential item functioning (i.e., item bias) in Verbal subtests
- The mean IQ of deaf children of deaf parents versus deaf children of hearing parents
- Differences in IQ among deaf children in different educational settings
- Differences among other subgroups of deaf children
- Interpretation of Performance Scale profiles

Each of these issues has a history with previous versions of the Wechsler, and we believe these issues will continue to challenge scientists and practitioners who use the WISC-III with deaf children.

SPECIAL NORMS

Many experts in deafness (e.g., Sullivan & Vernon, 1979; Vernon & Brown, 1964) strongly recommend the use of special norms based on deaf children when assessing deaf children. These norms, often called "deaf norms" because they are based on deaf children, are available for at least five intelligence tests (Braden, 1992), including the WISC-R Performance Scale (Anderson & Sisco, 1977). Proponents of deaf norms do not clearly articulate the reasons why such norms are preferable to those based on normal-hearing children, but at least three reasons might be advanced: (a) norms based on normal-hearing children exclude deaf children, and therefore reduce the validity of those norms for deaf children, whereas norms based on deaf children are valid for use with deaf children; (b) deaf norms would better reflect how a deaf child compares to other deaf peers; and (c) deaf norms provide data demonstrating the reliability and validity of a test with deaf children.

The value of these arguments varies. The first reason, that deaf norms are intrinsically more valid than norms that exclude deaf children, is the most popular. However, it is the least legitimate. Believing that representation (or lack thereof) in a norm group affects the validity of a test for the group is a classic example of the "normative fallacy" (Jensen, 1980, Chap. 9). The validity of a test for a particular group is independent of its norm group. For example, the primary British measure of height was normed on one male Saxon ruler (i.e., a "foot" is literally the length of King Charlemagne's foot), yet it is a valid measure of height for women, non-Britons, and others not included in the norm group. Conversely, a test of intelligence composed of Swahili vocabulary would be invalid for English-speaking undergraduates, even if the test was normed on English-speaking undergraduates. Therefore, the case for deaf norms cannot be justified by arguing that norms based on deaf children are intrinsically better than norms excluding deaf children. The case for deaf norms must rest on other criteria.

Another criterion often invoked to justify deaf norms is the argument that one should compare deaf children to other deaf children, not to hearing children, to best describe their cognitive abilities. This argument presumes that deaf children have different cognitive abilities than hearing children; otherwise, why use different norms? Ironically, the evidence with respect to PIQ overwhelmingly shows the distribution of PIQ in deaf and hearing populations to have similar parameters (Braden, 1994). This in itself argues against the value of deaf norms (Braden, 1985b). However, even if there were differences between deaf and hearing children, we would argue against the exclusive use of deaf norms. Our reasoning is based on clinical practice and scientific theory. Clinically, special deaf norms would obscure differences between deaf and normal-hearing samples. These differences are useful for identifying additional disabling conditions (see the discussion of profile analysis later in this section). Scientifically, the use of norms to obscure between-group differences may encourage the "egalitarian fallacy" (Jensen, 1980, Chap. 9), in which differences between groups are attributed solely to some form of test bias. That is, there is a temptation to think that, by referencing scores only to deaf children (and thus eliminating the differences in scores between deaf and hearing children), one has successfully removed the bias inherent in the test (see Vonderhaar & Chambers, 1975, for an example of this argument). This is flawed reasoning that serves neither the child nor the research community (see Braden, 1994, for an extensive discussion of this issue).

Finally, one might argue in favor of deaf norms because the data from those norms would delineate the test's technical adequacy and validity for use with deaf children. In our opinion, this is a logical argument—if data are collected and retained at the item level to allow for reliability, differential item functioning, and other studies. However, few studies that develop special deaf norms collect or retain such data, and none of the studies have conormed achievement batteries (to allow for large-scale criterion validity studies). Also, a single large-scale norm study is more expensive (and statistically less powerful) than a series of independent, small-scale research efforts. Therefore, we question the scientific and practical value of special norms for deaf children. Given the available evidence, we would echo the need for more information on the reliability and validity of the WISC-III with deaf children, but we suspect development of special deaf norms for theWISC-III would do little to enhance effective assessment, and could possibly erode effective interpretation of test outcomes.

VIQ VERSUS PIQ

The PIQ of Wechsler Scales, as well as other language-reduced tests of intellectual abilities, have traditionally been administered to children who are deaf and hard of hearing. As mentioned previously, deaf children as a group have been found to score in the average range on PIQ. Additionally, Braden (1994) reports that the distribution of IQ in deaf people, as assessed by language-reduced measures, is almost identical to the distribution in normal-hearing people. This allows for the use of the PIQ as a means (though certainly not the sole means) to differentially diagnose the effects of deafness from the effects of cognitive delays (Braden, 1992; Maller & Braden, 1993).

The use of the Wechsler Verbal Scales with deaf and hard-of-hearing children has received relatively limited study (Maller & Braden, 1993). A meta-analysis of available studies reported a mean VIQ of approximately 1 SD below the mean of the standardization sample (Braden, 1992). Because VIQ is dependent on the acquisition of spoken English as well as on incidental knowledge gained through language, the Verbal Scale cannot necessarily be viewed as a valid measure of a deaf person's cognitive ability (Maller & Braden, 1993). Sattler (1992) suggests that the Verbal and Performance Scales can be compared to evaluate the level of a child's verbal language deficit, but that the Verbal Scale should not be used in the computation of IQ.

Sullivan and Schulte (1992) argue that because most deaf children attend school with normal-hearing peers, and engage in tasks that require language-related abilities, the use of the Verbal Scale may enhance one's ability to predict academic performance. This is concordant with Maller and Braden's (1993) finding that VIQ correlated with achievement significantly higher than did PIQ and achievement using the WISC-III. Maller and Braden (1993) caution examiners to carefully present Verbal Scale results, because low Verbal scores may be misconstrued as evidence of low cognitive ability.

DIFFERENTIAL ITEM FUNCTIONING

The debate between those who condemn the use of Verbal subtests with deaf children, and those who argue its use may be valuable for more accurate prediction of success, has taken a new twist. Maller (1996) examined differential item functioning (DIF) with Verbal Scale items in deaf samples. That is, rather than simply asking whether deaf children were more or less likely to get the items right or wrong, or asking whether the score on items was better predictive of achievement outcomes than other (nonverbal) item scores, she asked the question, "Do the items function the same way in deaf and hearing groups when deaf and hearing children are equated for overall scaled score?" If this question is not answered in the affirmative, it provides evidence that Verbal subtests are biased measures of ability. That is, the Verbal subtests are inaccurate because deaf children and hearing children who have the same overall score are more or less likely to get specific items right or wrong. Evidence of DIF suggests that items sample verbal knowledge differently within deaf and normal-hearing children. This is a statistical definition of item bias, because DIF implies the item does not measure the same construct with equal accuracy in both groups.

Maller's research found that Verbal subtests of the WISC-III (e.g., Vocabulary, Information) had numerous items demonstrating DIF. That is, she provided evidence to show that the Verbal Scales of the Wechsler do not measure the same construct with equal accuracy in deaf and hearing samples. Therefore, rather than rejecting Verbal subtests on the basis of a philosophical argument, or accepting them on the basis of an empirical statement, psychologists might be wise to avoid the use of Verbal subtests with deaf children because they are less accurate for measuring intelligence. However, the degree to which this inaccuracy, or DIF, actually influences the viability of the Verbal Scale as a predictor of success is not well established. Although Verbal subtests may show evidence of item bias, they still predict academic achievement better than Performance Scale scores. Therefore, additional research on the WISC-III is needed to clarify the degree to which DIF may contribute to inappropriate conclusions from a clinical, not just a research, perspective.

DEAF CHILDREN OF DEAF PARENTS
VERSUS DEAF CHILDREN OF HEARING PARENTS

The meta-analysis reported by Braden (1994) indicated that deaf children who have two deaf parents (DP) have higher mean PIQs than deaf children of hearing parents. DP (who comprise about 4% of all deaf children) also display consistently higher scores on measures of academic achievement than deaf children of hearing parents. Several hypotheses have been offered to explain these findings. Most of these hypotheses invoke the linguistic and emotional support that DP enjoy relative to their other deaf peers. That is, DP are raised in homes where deafness is accepted, sign language is used naturally and consistently by all family members for all communication, and where their parents understand, accept, and participate in the deaf community. In contrast, deaf children with normal-hearing parents experience disadvantages on all of these dimensions (i.e., their parents are less likely to understand and accept deafness, consistently use sign language for communication, and understand and participate in the deaf community).

Although the relative superiority of DP to other deaf children on cognitive and academic tests is widely noted in the deafness literature, it is often overlooked that DP have higher mean PIQs than normal-hearing children (Braden, 1987, 1994). This finding challenges family-based explanations for higher DP scores, because normal-hearing children presumably enjoy all of the same advantages (i.e., acceptance, native language use, and participation in the broader community). This has led some to hypothesize that DP have higher PIQs because of genetic, not social, factors (e.g., Braden, 1987, 1994; Kusche, Greenberg, & Garfield, 1983; cf. Conrad & Weiskrantz, 1981). Although there is evidence (Paquin, 1992) to support kinship correlations, and higher PIQs among deaf parents, scholars do not yet agree on a common explanation for the above-average PIQs of DP.

COMPARISONS BETWEEN DEAF CHILDREN IN DIFFERENT EDUCATIONAL PROGRAMS

Since the early part of this century, psychologists who work with deaf children have attempted to compare deaf children who attend programs in residential settings to their counterparts who attend commuter schools (i.e., programs in which children return home every night and return to school the following morning). Early comparisons between deaf children in these educational groups found that, deaf children who attended residential schools generally had lower IQs. However, the interpretation of this finding has been a matter of dispute. Some (e.g., Raviv, Sharan, & Strauss, 1973) interpret this finding as evidence that residential school environments are less cognitively stimulating for deaf children than the more customary home and school environments provided in commuter settings. In contrast, others interpret the difference in IQs between residential and day programs as evidence of selection bias (that is, children with lower IQs are generally sent to residential schools, whereas children with higher IQs are more successful and can be retained in commuter schools). Research to address this question was conducted using the WISC-R. In two longitudinal studies (Braden & Paquin, 1985; Braden et al., 1993), it was found that deaf children who were in residential programs had lower IQs than deaf children in commuter programs. However, over 3- and 6-year periods, the IQs of deaf children in residential programs steadily rise, whereas those of deaf children in commuter programs are stable. Therefore, contrary to popular belief, the residential school appeared to have a positive impact on IQ. This study should be replicated in other samples using other instruments such as the WISC-III. As it stands, the study suggests long-term residential placement facilitates development of higher PIQ. The available data on the WISC-III suggest there are no differences in FSIQ, PIQ, nor VIQ between students attending residential versus mainstream settings (Sullivan & Montoya, in press).

COMPARISONS AMONG OTHER SUBGROUPS OF DEAF CHILDREN

Contrasts between younger versus older deaf children, moderate to severe versus profoundly deaf children, and children using signs versus those using speech showed no differences in WISC-III PIQ, VIQ, nor FSIQ (Sullivan & Montoya, in press). Contrasts between boys versus girls are less consistent. Whereas Slate and Fawcett (1996) reported substantial gender differences (based on a small, nonrepresentative sample), Sullivan and Montoya (in press) report no gender differences (based on a larger, more representative sample). We were not able to find any study investigating ethnic group differences on the WISC-III within samples of deaf children, but we note that previous research with the WISC-R shows ethnic group differences quite similar to those reported in samples of normal-hearing children (Braden, 1994). Currently, there is little research investigating the similarities and differences among subgroups of deaf children on the WISC-III; clearly, psychologists need more research to draw firm conclusions regarding differences among groups of deaf children.

PROFILE ANALYSIS

The issue of whether and how to interpret Wechsler subtest profiles has received somewhat limited attention in the deafness literature. Whereas WISC-III profile analysis has been vigorously challenged in the literature regarding normal-hearing children (e.g., Glutting, McDermott, & Konold, 1997), it has received little attention in the literature regarding deaf children. We were unable to find any studies of profile interpretation using the WISC-III with deaf children, and we found no studies attempting profile analysis with any Wechsler version of the Verbal Scales.

Researchers have consistently noted that Wechsler PS profiles discriminate between deaf children who have relatively few academic difficulties, and deaf children with significant academic impairments (i.e., poor achievement in comparison to other deaf children). A review of this literature (Braden, 1990) shows that scores on the WISC-R Coding subtest are particularly sensitive to academic and neurological deficits in deaf children. That is, deaf children who have academic deficiencies, learning disabilities, and the like often exhibit low Coding scores relative to their other PS subtest scores. Although other interpretations of profile constellations have been suggested (e.g., Vonderhaar & Chambers, 1975, suggested depressed Picture Arrangement scores indicate reduced social awareness and judgment), the only characteristic of profile analysis that consistently emerges in deaf children is a link between depressed Coding subtest scores and psychoeducational difficulties (Braden, 1990). Also, there may be a sufficiently large number of such children that they depress the mean Coding score in large, representative samples of deaf children.

We note that the data in Figure 2 fail to show any clear or consistent profiles on the WISC-III PS. However, there appears to be consistency among studies in showing substantially lower Vocabulary scores relative to other Verbal Scale subtests. We cannot draw conclusions about the clinical sensitivity of WISC-III subtest profiles until researchers generate clinical studies that use WISC-III PS subtests to compare academically "successful" and "unsuccessful" deaf children.

WISC-III users should consider three additional factors with respect to profile analysis with deaf children. First, the use of special norms based on deaf children reduces or eliminates depressed Coding scores in many children, and thus may reduce the sensitivity of the instrument to psychoeducational difficulties (Braden, 1990). Second, none of the research on deaf children has used the large samples and sophisticated analysis techniques that are used by profile analysis studies in studies of normal-hearing children (e.g., Glutting et al., 1997). Third, the available factor analyses of the WISC-III PS with deaf children are not consistent in supporting the separation of PS subtests into PO and PS factors. That is, the Coding and Symbol Search subtests may form a factor independent of other PS subtests, but they may not. We suspect that PSI (rather than Coding alone) may be sensitive to psychoeducational deficits in deaf children (as it is in hearing children), but we have no direct evidence to support our prediction at this time.

GUIDELINES FOR USING THE WISC-III WITH DEAF CHILDREN

Research on the WISC-III and other Wechsler scales suggests practical guidelines for scientists and practitioners who use the WISC-III with deaf children. We suggest guidelines for researchers (scientists) and practitioners in the final section of this chapter. Although we encourage the successful combination of scientist and practitioner perspectives, we realize that researchers and practitioners have different interests and orientations to the use of the WISC-III with deaf children.

RESEARCH GUIDELINES

Researchers should consider three distinct issues when using the WISC-III for research with deaf children. These issues are as follows:

- Assessment of test bias
- Selection of an achievement metric for validity studies
- Test translation and accommodation

TEST BIAS

Assessment of test bias must move beyond studies of differences between groups (e.g., deaf and normal-hearing children). Sadly, the literature describing the Wechsler with deaf children shows a marked lack of sophistication with respect to test bias. Most researchers simply compare means for deaf samples to normative means, and conclude there is bias when those means are different. This does not demonstrate test bias, because it invokes the "egalitarian fallacy" (see Jensen, 1980, Chap. 9; Reynolds, 1995). Instead, researchers must strive to examine genuine forms of test bias. These should include DIF studies (see Maller, 1996), direct comparisons of factor structures between deaf and hearing samples, and differential reliability and validity studies. Unfortunately, researchers have difficulty recruiting the large samples required for DIF and factor analytic comparisons. Failing such large-sample studies, small studies that report WISC-III PS reliabilities, stabilities, and correlations with other measures are useful in building a body of evidence regarding the degree to which the WISC-III may function differently in deaf children (i.e., the degree to which the WISC-III exhibits bias when used with deaf populations).

SELECTION OF ACHIEVEMENT METRIC

One of the issues that has dogged previous versions of the Wechsler is the relationship between Wechsler scores and scores on achievement tests within samples of deaf children. Many studies report that these correlations are lower for deaf children than they are for hearing children. Three possible explanations for this phenomenon have been provided. First is the nonverbal nature of the Performance Scales (the most widely used part of the Wechsler to estimate deaf children's intelligence) overlaps less with the linguistic and verbal requirements of achievement tests. Therefore, the correlations between PIQ and academic achievement are low primarily because they sample distinct domains. A second argument that has been advanced is that the Wechsler is less effective at measuring the cognitive abilities that are needed for success in deaf individuals (Hirshoren, Hurley, & Kavale, 1977). A third argument is that the metric that is used for describing deaf children's achievement is inappropriate. That is, studies correlating IQ and achievement in hearing children typically convert IQ and achievement to age-based standard scores and then calculate correlations. In contrast, studies with deaf children typically calculate IQ but convert achievement scores into grade equivalents. The difference in metric is quite likely to lead to lower estimates of IQ–achievement correlations (Braden, Wollack, & Allan, 1995; cf. Kishor, 1995a, 1995b). This is frankly less an issue of the WISC-III and more an issue of how achievement metrics are selected to validate the WISC-III. However, readers of research using the WISC-III should carefully consider the metric that is used in the study when evaluating the outcomes. If the metric uses some form of age-adjusted score (where achievement measures are preferably normed on other deaf children), the correlation of that study is more likely to be comparable to studies of hearing children than when a grade equivalent or non-age-adjusted score is used to describe deaf children's achievement. Thus, it is likely that existing literature significantly underestimates the correlation between IQ and achievement that actually exists between Wechsler scales and tests of achievement because of inappropriate selection (see Braden et al., 1995, for more details).

TEST TRANSLATION AND ACCOMMODATION

Two factors may invalidate assessment results: construct underrepresentation, and construct-irrelevant variance (Messick, 1995). Construct underrepresentation means the test samples the domain of interest too narrowly; that is, the test excludes important samples of behavior to represent the domain of interest. Construct-irrelevant variance means the test includes task characteristics that are unrelated to the relevant domain. This irrelevant sampling increases or decreases the difficulty of the test for a person or group. Researchers should consider the degree to which each of these factors may affect the use of the WISC-III with deaf children.

Construct underrepresentation is an issue when deciding whether to include Verbal Scale subtests with deaf children. One might argue that intelligence is broadly defined, and therefore one must include verbal abilities in any broad representation of intelligence. Conversely, construct-irrelevant variance argues against using Verbal Scale subtests with deaf children. Use of verbal items increases the difficulty of the task for deaf people by including a task characteristic (knowledge of English) that is unrelated to the domain of interest (i.e., depressed English language skills—not depressed intelligence—may lower deaf children's scores). We agree with other experts that there is more risk in introducing construct-irrelevant variance than there is risk for underrepresenting cognitive domains, but we note that the argument for exclusive use of nonverbal or performance tests with deaf children may excessively narrow the breadth of the domain sampled (i.e., PIQ, PO indexes, and other Performance Scale scores may not adequately reflect broad intellectual abilities).

Test administration modifications can also introduce construct-irrelevant test variance. Generally, the literature focuses on the degree to which test modifications create "a level playing field" for deaf children. For example, by administering the WISC-III in ASL, the deaf child has the opportunity to respond to items with the same degree of understanding that hearing children enjoy. However, it is also possible that test modifications may decrease task difficulty for deaf people. For example, the ASL sign for "conflagration" is the same as the sign for "fight." If a psychologist signs "fight" while asking the child to define "conflagration," that psychologist has made the item significantly easier for that deaf child than for a hearing child.

This discussion highlights the issues surrounding testing modifications. We are aware of only two studies that used appropriate translation to blind back-translation techniques to ensure that sign translations did not significantly alter the nature of Wechsler Scale content (Kostrubala, 1997; Maller, 1996). There are no formal studies to evaluate the degree to which other recommended test modifications (e.g., supplemental instruction, practice items) reduce construct-irrelevant variance. Rather, it is implicitly assumed that any accommodation that increases deaf children's scores is "good." This assumption may be warranted in many cases (e.g., oral administration of the WISC-III to a profoundly deaf ASL user would certainly introduce construct-irrelevant difficulty), but researchers must invoke appropriate objective techniques to ensure that modifications do not inappropriately introduce construct-irrelevant variance (e.g., make the items excessively easy or change the nature of the task).

PRACTITIONER GUIDELINES

Practitioners vary in their exposure to and experience with deaf children. Practitioners who administer the WISC-III should remember that there are many test administration issues to consider beyond the communication method. Ideally, practitioners will gain expertise in methods of sign language communication and in understanding the unique, and varied, characteristics deaf children may display. Deaf children do not form a homogeneous group; etiologies vary, as does age of onset, severity of hearing loss, presence of additional disabilities, degree of exposure to sign language, family characteristics, and so on. Psychologists may pursue numerous avenues to acquire expertise in working with deaf children. Resources are listed annually in the April issue of the *American Annals of the Deaf*. The National Information Center on Deafness at Gallaudet University in Washington, D.C., is another resource (internet address: http://www.gallaudet.edu:80/~nicd/). For psychologists who do not have expertise in deafness, we offer the following recommendations:

- Obtain the services of a qualified psychologist who has deafness expertise. Psychologists may contact state residential schools for the deaf, state departments of education, or review resources in the April issue of the *American Annals of the Deaf* to identify local resources.
- If an expert psychologist is not available, use a sign language interpreter. We recommend psychologists use qualified, nationally certified interpreters (i.e., not parents, educational aides, or teachers). The psychologist should meet with the interpreter before the evaluation to review testing and administration procedures. Interpreters are bound by a code of ethics that prohibits revealing the content of sessions with clients; psychologists should remind the interpreter that the content of the intelligence test is included in this confidential mandate. If the psychologist plans to administer the Vocabulary subtest, we recommend that the first administration of verbal items use finger spelling and/or printed cards to present specific items. Later testing-of-limits could readminister failed items using sign translations. We discourage the use of signs for standard administration, because some translations may render the item easier, or harder, than it would be for normal-hearing children. We refer readers to examples of translation problems, and recommended solutions, in Table 9.4. We also recommend that psychologists schedule a posttesting session with the interpreter to review response translations, and to tap the interpreter's cultural expertise in deafness (e.g., a psychologist may view a deaf child's affect as excessively labile, whereas the interpreter may perceive it as appropriate within deaf culture).
- Determine the child's preferred mode of communication, and administer the WISC-III in that mode. Observe the child in a natural setting, and consult with the child's parent(s) and teacher(s) to establish communication preferences.
- In most cases, interpret PIQ as the best indicator of the child's underlying cognitive ability. To the degree that the examiner believes the test administration yielded reliable and valid results, and the deaf child is free from additional disabilities (e.g., coordination problems) that might affect PIQ, the

TABLE 9.4   Examples of Administration Modifications for Use with Deaf Children

Problem	Solution
Oral directions assume client can listen while looking at materials. Deaf people cannot "listen" and "look" at the same time.	Simplify directions, refer to visual aspects of materials, and pause to allow client to look to materials, then look back.
The query "Show me where you mean" fails to capitalize on spatial parameters of ASL.	Sign "Where?" with a questioning expression and point towards the picture.
Because the sign for "dozen" in ASL is the same as "12," signing "How many are in a dozen?" provides the answer to the client.	Fingerspell the word "dozen" when asking the question.
The signs for "tribe" and "family," are variants of the same root ("group"), so the signs signify the similarity between the two words.	Fingerspell the words "tribe" and "family" when asking the question.
The ASL translation for "If you have 3 and I have 3, how many are there altogether?" literally shows the answer with the fingers.	Translate this item into signed English so that the numbers are presented in serial, not parallel, order.
The ASL translations of rare English words usually substitute a more common signs (e.g., "conflagration" would be signed "fight," thus making the ASL version easier).	Fingerspell and/or write the words.

PIQ is the best index of general ability. PIQ is one means of differentiating deafness from mental retardation (i.e., a PIQ >70 generally rules out a diagnosis of mental retardation). However, placement decisions must not be made based solely on the use of PIQ. Other data, from other sources, settings, and respondents, must be included in any assessment.

- If desired, use VIQ to estimate the deaf child's incidental acquisition of language and knowledge; do not use VIQ to estimate underlying cognitive ability.
- Do not assume special ("deaf") norms are superior to norms based on normal-hearing children. Special norms may reduce the sensitivity of the WISC-III to differentiating psychoeducational difficulties, and may have few practical benefits. Consider carefully the use of special norms if they become available for the WISC-III.
- Consider administering a motor-free nonverbal test to supplement WISC-III Performance Scale results. Deaf children's scores may be lower on motor-free tests as compared to the WISC-III Performance Scale, but motor-free nonverbal tests may tap reflective thinking better than performance tasks.
- Compare the deaf child's performance across tasks that are speeded (e.g., Coding, Block Design) and those that are not (e.g., Picture Completion, motor-free nonverbal tests). Some experts argue that deaf children may be penalized on speeded tasks because they do not understand the time-limited nature of the test; also, motor coordination difficulties are more common

among deaf children than among normal-hearing peers. Therefore, examiners should consider the possible effects of communication and psychomotor disabilities on deaf children's Performance Scale scores.

CASE EXAMPLE: WISC-III

We have included a fictionalized case study to illustrate and apply the themes in this chapter. This case presents the report a psychologist produced in the context of an adolescent female who is seeking admission to the state residential school for the deaf. The report specifically touches on issues of test administration, selection of norms, the use and interpretation of Verbal Scale subtests, the value of the WISC-III for differential diagnosis, and the integration of intelligence, achievement, and adaptive behavior data to form a coherent presentation. Subsequent to this case study, a multidisciplinary team recommended Teresa be placed at the residential school. A follow-up suggested a dramatic improvement in social and interpersonal relationships, but no significant gains (nor losses) in academic achievement.

Name: Teresa　　　　　　　　　　　**School:** Mainstream middle
Date of birth: 2-6-82　　　　　　　　**Grade:** 7
Date of assessment: 12-6-95　　　　　**Parents:** Tom & Toni
Age: 13 years, 10 months　　　　　　　**Ethnicity:** Caucasian

REASON FOR REFERRAL

Teresa was referred for this assessment as part of the intake process at the residential school for the deaf. She has expressed dissatisfaction with her current educational setting, and she and her parents are exploring the possibility of placement in the residential school.

BACKGROUND INFORMATION

Teresa lives with her parents and two younger brothers in a small urban area. She is the only deaf member of her family. Teresa was diagnosed with a profound, bilateral hearing loss at the age of 2 years, although the loss is believed to be congenital. The etiology of her deafness is unknown and she has no additional physical concerns.

Teresa communicates using PSL with her family and with a normal-hearing friend who lives in her neighborhood. At school she communicates using ASL with several other deaf students, but her interpreter and support teacher use Signed English.

Academically, Teresa receives language arts instruction in a self-contained classroom with five other children who are deaf. She attends all of her other classes with her peer with the assistance of a sign language interpreter. Her grades have been Bs and Cs thus far this year.

PREVIOUS ASSESSMENTS

Teresa's most recent psychoeducational evaluation was completed nearly 3 years ago as part of the triennial review process. She obtained a score within the Average range on the Performance Scale of the WISC-III, and scores within the Well Below Average range in Reading and the Below Average range in Mathematics on the Brief Form of the K-TEA.

CURRENT ASSESSMENT TECHNIQUES

WISC-III
K-TEA
Vineland Adaptive Behavior Scales, Survey Form
Parent and Child Interview

OBSERVATIONS

Teresa was pleasant, although initially somewhat shy, throughout the assessment. She communicated with me predominantly via ASL signs in English word order. As the evaluation began, Teresa became more animated. Test items were presented in sign language and, when using signs would change the difficulty level of the task (i.e., Verbal Scale and Achievement tests), in written or finger-spelled form Teresa responded to task demands as if she understood directions without difficulty. She was persistent in her approach to most tasks, although when presented with more difficult verbal items she tended to respond quickly that she didn't know the answer. Given Teresa's motivation and her understanding of the tasks presented, I believe that the results obtained are reliable and valid indicators of her current level of functioning in the areas assessed.

ASSESSMENT RESULTS

WISC-III Scale and Index scores

Verbal Scale = 88 (83–94 at the 90% confidence level); Low Average–Average range
Performance Scale = 102 (95–109); Average range

Verbal Comprehension = 85 (80–92)
Perceptual Organization = 104 (97–111)

WISC-III Subtest Scores

Verbal Scale		Performance Scale	
Information	9	Picture Completion	13
Similarities	9	Coding	9
Arithmetic	10	Picture Arrangement	8
Vocabulary	4	Block Design	10
Comprehension	7	Object Assembly	11

K-TEA Brief Form Subtest and Composite Scores

Math = 87 (19th percentile)
Reading = 76 (5th percentile)
Spelling = 82 (12th percentile)
Battery Composite = 78 (7th percentile)

Vineland Adaptive Behavior Scales, Survey Form
(Teresa's mother provided responses)

Communication = 85 (74–96 at 90% confidence level); Adequate–
  Moderately Low range
Daily Living Skills = 106 (98–114); Adequate range
Socialization = 85 (74–96); Adequate–Moderately Low range
Adaptive Behavior Composite = 96 (89–103); Adequate range (the Maladaptive Behavior Domain was not assessed; norms are in reference to normal-hearing age mates, not special deaf norms).

IMPRESSIONS

Teresa's score on the Verbal Scale of the WISC-III should be interpreted as an indicator of her incidental knowledge and language acquisition—*not* her underlying cognitive ability. Her score on this scale is within the Low Average to Average range, reflecting performance between the 13th and 34th percentiles when compared to normal-hearing children her own age. Subtest scores are generally within the average range, with the exception of the Vocabulary subtest, which is significantly below average and is an area of relative weakness compared to Teresa's level of performance on this scale.

On the Performance Scale, Teresa's scores are in the Average range, reflecting performance between the 37th and 73rd percentiles when compared to normal-hearing age mates. Her score on the Picture Completion subtest is above average, and may reflect an area of relative strength for Teresa; all other subtest scores are within the average range.

The 14-point difference between Teresa's VIQs and PIQ is sufficiently large to suggest her nonverbal abilities are stronger than those requiring English. However, differences this size are not rare in normal-hearing children (28% of the WISC-III standardization sample showed a difference of the same size or larger), and higher PIQs over VIQs are common in deaf children. A similar pattern is shown by the 19-point discrepancy between her VC and PO indexes, which is met or surpassed by only 15% of the standardization sample. Again, such differences are common in deaf children, because deaf children often do not acquire English language fluency (and consequently get lower verbal scores).

Teresa's scores on the K-TEA reflect performance in the Well Below Average to Below Average range in Reading and Spelling, and the Below Average to Average range in Mathematics. These scores are commensurate with her actual classroom performance relative to normal-hearing children. However, scores in this range are common for deaf children.

Teresa's Adaptive Behavior Composite is within the Adequate range, between the 23rd and 58th percentiles compared to children her own age. Her Communication and Socialization domain scores are in the Adequate to Moderately Low range. The Written Communication subdomain is significantly lower than the other areas within the Communication domain, as is the Interpersonal Relationships subdomain within the Socialization area. One possible account of the depressed Interpersonal Relationships subdomain score is Teresa's limited access to friends and peers who can communicate easily with her via signs. An informal interview with Teresa indicates that her dissatisfaction with her current educational setting is mainly due to social factors. She reports that she has few friends in school and that it is difficult for her to interact with her peers, the vast majority of which do not know sign language. She also reports that she is reluctant to participate in classroom discussions, because she must depend on an interpreter to express her thoughts. She feels she is becoming more and more isolated socially as the school year goes on.

SUMMARY AND RECOMMENDATIONS

Teresa is a 13-year 10-month-old girl who was referred for this evaluation as part of the intake process for admission into this residential school. Although she is generally performing at acceptable academic levels in her current school setting, she reports feeling socially isolated. Teresa's cognitive abilities are within the average range as assessed with the WISC-III Performance Scale. Her WISC-III Verbal Scale score reflects an acquired language and knowledge level within the low average to average range. Teresa has difficulty in reading and spelling, and in her ability to define various vocabulary words. Adaptive behavior scores in communication, daily living skills, and socialization suggest adequate adaptation to her community environment. Items relating to reading and written communication, and to interpersonal relations, suggest limited interpersonal opportunities.

1. A multidisciplinary team, including Teresa, her parents, and representatives from Teresa's current school placement and district and the residential school for the deaf, should convene to discuss most appropriate placement for Teresa. A critical focus of the team should be to evaluate the degree to which the two settings can meet Teresa's academic and social development needs.

2. Regardless of setting, Teresa's educational placement should provide instruction (and, to the degree possible, social opportunities) in Teresa's primary mode of communication (i.e., PSE, with ASL and English sign features).

3. These assessment results suggest no other educational disabilities at this time. That is, there is no evidence of cognitive disabilities, nor is there evidence that the gap between Teresa's achievement and her (nonverbal) intellectual ability is due to any condition other than deafness. However, Teresa's lack of peers with whom to communicate could contribute to motivational and emotional difficulties in the future.

REFERENCES

Anderson, R. J., & Sisco, F. H. (1977). *Standardization of the WISC-R Performance Scale for deaf children* (Office of Demographic Studies Publication Series T, No. 1). Washington, DC: Gallaudet College.

Braden, J. P. (1985a). Futile gestures: A reply to Courtney, Hayes, Couch, and Frick regarding pantomimed administration of the WISC-R Performance Scale. *Journal of Psychoeducational Assessment, 3,* 181–185.

Braden, J. P. (1985b). WISC-R deaf norms reconsidered. *Journal of School Psychology, 23,* 375–382.

Braden, J. P. (1987). An explanation of the superior Performance IQs of deaf children of deaf parents. *American Annals of the Deaf, 132,* 263–266.

Braden, J. P. (1990). Do deaf persons have a characteristic psychometric profile on the Wechsler Performance Scales? *Journal of Psychoeducational Assessment, 8,* 518–526.

Braden, J. P. (1992). Intellectual assessment of deaf and hard-of-hearing people: A quantitative and qualitative research synthesis. *School Psychology Review, 21* (1), 82–94.

Braden, J. P. (1994). *Deafness, deprivation, and IQ.* New York: Plenum Press.

Braden, J. P., Maller, S. J., & Paquin, M. M. (1993). The effects of residential versus day placement on the Performance IQs of children with hearing impairment. *Journal of Special Education, 26,* 423–433.

Braden, J. P., & Paquin, M. M. (1985). A comparison of the WISC-R and WAIS-R Performance Scales in deaf adolescents. *Journal of Psychoeducational Assessment, 3,* 285–290.

Braden, J. P., Reed, J., & Kostrubala, C. E. (1994, April). *Separating verbal ability from language exposure with speed of information processing tasks.* Paper presented at the Annual Meeting of the Western Psychological Association, Kona, HI.

Braden, J. P., Wollack, J. A. & Allen, T. E. (1995). Reply to Kishor: Choosing the right metric. *Journal of Psychoeducational Assessment, 13,* 250–265.

Conrad, R., & Weiskrantz, B. C. (1981). On the cognitive ability of deaf children with deaf parents. *American Annals of the Deaf, 126,* 995–1003.

Ensor, A. (1988). *WAIS-R Performance as a predictor of achievement for deaf adolescents.* Paper presented at the annual meeting of the National Association of School Psychologists, Boston, MA.

Glutting, J. J., McDermott, P. A., & Konold, T. R. (1997). Ontology, structure, and diagnostic benefits of a normative subtest taxonomy from the WISC-III standardization sample. In D. P. Flanagan, J. L. Genshaft, & P. L. Harrison (Eds.), *Contemporary intellectual assessment: Theories, tests, and issues* (pp. 349–372). New York: Guilford Press.

Hirshoren, A., Hurley, O. L., & Kavale, K. (1979). Psychometric characteristics of the WISC-R Performance Scale with deaf children. *Journal of Speech and Hearing Disorders, 44,* 73–79.

Jensen, A. R. (1980). *Bias in mental testing.* New York: Free Press.

Kishor, N. (1995a). Evaluating predictive validity: a rejoinder to Braden et al. (1995). *Journal of Psychoeducational Assessment, 13,* 266–270.

Kishor, N. (1995b). Evaluating predictive validity by using different scales of the Stanford Achievement Test for the Hearing Impaired. *Journal of Psychoeducational Assessment, 13,* 241–249.

Kostrubala, C. E. (1996, August). Using interpreters for language-minority psychologists. In L. Ford & J. P. Braden (chairs), *Equitable psychological assessment for language-minority learners: Theory, research, and practice.* Symposium presented at the meeting of the American Psychological Association, Toronto, Canada.

Kostrubala, C. E. (1997). *Translation of the WAIS-III into American Sign Language.* Unpublished master's thesis, University of Wisconsin—Madison.

Kusche, C. A., Greenberg, M. T., & Garfield, T. S. (1983). Nonverbal intelligence and verbal achievement in deaf adolescents: An examination of heredity and environment. *American Annals of the Deaf, 128,* 458–466.

Maller, S. J. (1996). WISC-III verbal item invariance across samples of deaf and hearing children of similar measured ability. *Journal of Psychoeducational Assessment, 14*(2), 152–165.

Maller, S. J., & Braden, J. P. (1993). The construct and criterion-related validity of the WISC-III with deaf adolescents. *Journal of Psychoeducational Assessment, Advances in Psychoeducational Assessment, Wechsler Intelligence Scale for Children: Third Edition [Monograph], 11,* 105–113.

Messick, S. (1995). Validity of psychological assessment. *American Psychologist, 50* (9), 741–749.

Murphy, K. P. (1957). Tests of abilities and attainments. In A. W. G. Ewing (Ed.), *Educational guidance and the deaf child* (pp. 213–251). Manchester, UK: Manchester University Press.

Neuhaus, M. (1967). Modifications in the administration of the WISC Performance subtests for children with profound hearing losses. *Exceptional Children, 33,* 573–574.

Paquin, M. M. (1992). *The superior nonverbal intellectual performance of deaf children of deaf parents: An investigation of the genetic hypothesis.* Unpublished doctoral dissertation, California School of Professional Psychology, Alameda, CA.

Raviv, S., Sharan, S., & Strauss, S. (1973). Intellectual development of deaf children in different educational environments. *Journal of Communication Disorders, 6,* 29–36.

Ray, S. (1982). Adapting the WISC-R for deaf children. *Diagnostique, 7,* 147–157.

Reynolds, C. R. (1995). Test bias and the assessment of intelligence and personality. In D. H. Saklofske & M. Zeidner (Eds.), *International handbook of personality and intelligence* (545–576). New York: Plenum.

Sattler, J. M. (1992). *Assessment of children* (3rd ed.). San Diego, CA: Author.

Slate, J. R., & Fawcett, J. (1995). Validity of the WISC-III for deaf and hard of hearing persons. *American Annals of the Deaf, 140* (4), 250–254.

Slate, J. R., & Fawcett, J. (1996). Gender differences in Wechsler Performance scores of school-age children who are deaf or hard of hearing. *American Annals of the Deaf, 141* (1), 19–23.

Sullivan, P. M. (1978). *A comparison of administration modifications on the WISC-R Performance Scale with different categories of deaf children.* Unpublished doctoral dissertation, University of Iowa.

Sullivan, P. M. (1982). Administration modifications on the WISC-R Performance Scale with different categories of deaf children. *American Annals of the Deaf, 127,* 780–788.

Sullivan, P. M., & Montoya, L. A. (in press). Factor analysis of the WISC-III with deaf and hard-of-hearing children. *Psychological Assessment.*

Sullivan, P. M., & Schulte, L. E. (1992). Factor analysis of WISC-R with deaf and hard of hearing children. *Psychological Assessment, 4* (4), 537–540.

Sullivan, P. M., & Vernon, M. (1979). Psychological assessment of hearing impaired children. *School Psychology Digest, 8,* 271–290.

Vernon, M. (1967). Relationship of language to the thinking process. *Archives of General Psychiatry, 16,* 325–333.

Vernon, M., & Brown, D. W. (1964). A guide to psychological tests and testing procedures in the evaluation of deaf and hard-of-hearing children. *Journal of Speech and Hearing Disorders, 29,* 414–423.

Vonderhaar, W. F., & Chambers, J. F. (1975). An examination of deaf students' Wechsler Performance subtest scores. *American Annals of the Deaf, 120,* 540–543.

Wechsler, D. (1991). *Wechsler Intelligence Scale for Children—Third Edition.* San Antonio, TX: The Psychological Corporation.

10

NEUROPSYCHOLOGICAL BASIS OF INTELLIGENCE AND THE WISC-III

GEORGE W. HYND

*Center for Clinical
and Developmental Neuropsychology
The University of Georgia
Athens, Georgia*

CYNTHIA A. RICCIO

*Department of Educational Psychology
College of Education
Texas A & M University
College Station, Texas*

MORRIS J. COHEN

*Child Neuropsychology
Medical College of Georgia
Augusta, Georgia*

JANET M. ARCENEAUX

*Professional Studies
University of Alabama
Tuscaloosa, Alabama*

INTRODUCTION

The WISC-R (Wechsler, 1974) has been the most widely used individual intelligence test for children for a number of years. However, it was increasingly criticized as being out of date (Witt & Gresham, 1985). As a result, The Psychological Corporation revised and updated the test in 1991 (Wechsler, 1991).

Although little doubt exists that the Wechsler scales will continue to be the most frequently employed measures of intelligence, there remain misconceptions as to what constitutes the neurobiological bases of intelligence and how these measures of general ability should be interpreted with respect to revealing clinically meaningful variability in brain–behavior relationships in children and adolescents. It is our contention that psychometric 'g' cannot be localized in the brain but that associated subprocess may be differentially localized within the brain. Wechsler (1958) has well expressed this view himself. As he has suggested,

*WISC-III Clinical Use and Interpretation.
Scientist–Practitioner Perspectives*

203

> One cannot expect anything like fixed centers of intelligence for purely logical reasons. In-
> telligence deals not with mental representations but with relations that may exist between
> them, and the relations cannot be localized. . . . For effective functioning intelligence may
> depend more upon the intactness of some rather than other portions of the brain, but in no
> sense can it be said to be mediated by any single part of it. Intelligence has no locus. (p. 20)

Although this indeed seems like a reasonable perspective at face value, it does challenge us to develop a better understanding of the neurobiological bases of intelligence because intelligence is so very sensitive to the effects of brain impairment (Boll, 1974; Seinberg, Giordani, Berent, & Boll, 1983). Thus, one might ask, how can something not localized within the brain in turn be so sensitive to brain impairment?

The answer lies in the notion that intelligence, or psychometric g, is a reflection of our ability to perceive relations, or as Spearman and Jones (1950) suggest, the ability to engage in the "education of correlates." Thus, although the various subtests or scales on intelligence tests may be useful in revealing some aspects of impairment in correlated neurological systems that may be more localized in the brain, a general intelligence quotient such as that provided by a full scale measure will be less useful in specific clinical interpretation.

So, where does this leave researchers conducting neuropsychological evaluations with respect to employing tests of intelligence or their scales or subtests, such as the Wechsler scales? Why might they be useful and what interpretations about neuropsychological functioning can one make from data provided by tests of intelligence such as the WISC-III?

In order to address these questions and reach conclusions supported by the literature, we first need to address the validity of the factor structure of the Wechsler scales. Then we will address the validity of using verbal–performance discrepancies in arriving at neuropsychological interpretations. Although much of the research relevant to this discussion is derived from studies employing the WISC-R, some pertinent new studies also exist. As will be seen, a number of studies do support the notion than some neuropsychological interpretations can be made employing tests of intelligence, especially with more well-researched populations. Finally, we will attempt to draw some conclusions that are supported by the extant literature and provide some preliminary data that illustrate the notion that certain subprocesses assessed on the WISC-III may indeed have some association with theoretically consistent neurological systems. We remain convinced, however, that general intellectual ability, or psychometric g, has no specific locus in the brain, only perhaps its associated subcomponents.

FACTOR STRUCTURE OF THE WISC-III

Factor analytic research with the WISC-R yielded strong support for the Full Scale (FSIQ), Verbal (VIQ) and Performance IQ (PIQ) scores along with a three-factor solution comprised of a Verbal Comprehension (VC) factor, a Perceptual

Organization (PO) factor, and a Freedom from Distractibility (FD) factor (Kamphaus, 1993). Factor analysis of the WISC-III (Wechsler, 1991) as reported in the examiner's manual, continues to demonstrate support for the FSIQ, VIQ, and PIQ scores as well as the VC and PO factors. With the addition of the Symbol Search subtest, however, the factor analysis now yields two additional factors rather than just one. The third and fourth factors are identified as FD and Processing Speed (PS). The new FD factor includes only two subtests, both auditory; the fourth factor (PS) is also composed of two subtests, both visual and involving a motor speed component.

VERBAL-PERFORMANCE DISCREPANCY

Research has been done relating performance on the WISC (Wechsler, 1949) specific to localizing brain dysfunction. There is some correlative evidence to support that the VIQ reflects left-hemisphere functioning whereas the PIQ reflects right-hemisphere functioning (e.g., Fedio & Mirsky, 1969; Rourke, Young, & Flewelling, 1971). Similar types of conclusions, with implications for clinical diagnosis, have been offered for the VIQ PIQs on the WISC-R (Wechsler, 1974), with particular importance attributed to discrepancies between VIQ and PIQ scores (e.g., Kaufman, 1979). These hypotheses are based on the distinction between verbal and nonverbal abilities that is historically evidenced in factor analytic support (Kaufman, 1979) and continue to be applicable for the WISC-III (Kamphaus, 1993).

DISCREPANCY IN HETEROGENEOUS LD SAMPLES

It has been argued that a significant VIQ–PIQ discrepancy (PIQ > VIQ) is suggestive of an LD (e.g., Kavale, & Forness, 1984) and/or the presence of a speech or language impairment (Kamphaus, 1993). There are numerous studies that support the use of VIQ–PIQ discrepancy as a characteristic of LDs. For example, Newman, Wright, and Fields (1989) found that students with a reading disability demonstrated a significant VIQ–PIQ difference. Further, Clampit and Silver (1990) concluded that a large VIQ–PIQ difference had considerable face validity in identifying children with LDs based on the WISC-R standardization sample. Cheng, Dai, and Liu (1994) investigated the pattern of VIQ–PIQ discrepancy for Chinese children using the Chinese version of the WISC-R. Results suggested that children with LD showed a larger mean VIQ–PIQ discrepancy than that of controls. Cheng et al. concluded that the factor pattern for the children with learning disabilities was consistent with the pattern described by Bannatyne (1968).

In contrast, other researchers have not found the use of WISC-R VIQ–PIQ discrepancy patterns to be useful in the differentiation of children with LDs from other groups of children (e.g., Clampit & Silver, 1990; Humphries & Bone, 1993; Newman et al., 1989). In many studies, the VIQ–PIQ discrepancy found on the

WISC-R was small (Kamphaus, 1993), and similar results have been found with the WISC-III. In a study of 202 children with specific LDs (115 children with mental retardation and 159 children who were referred but not classified), Slate (1995) found that all three groups of children demonstrated a higher PIQ than VIQ on the WISC-III. The VIQ–PIQ discrepancy for the children in this study was smaller than that found in the normative sample. In a study of 40 children identified as language impaired, VIQ–PIQ discrepancies on the WISC-III were also found to be small (Phelps, Leguori, Nisewaner, & Parker, 1993).

DISCREPANCY AND THE GIFTED

Furthermore, a number of researchers have examined the profiles of children with FSIQs greater than 120 with results suggesting that large subtests scatter, VIQ–PIQ discrepancy (VIQ > PIQ), and high variability are relatively frequent for bright children (Saccuzzo, 1992; Taylor, Ziegler, & Partenio, 1984; Wilkinson, 1993). There is also some indication that the higher VIQ generally found with these students may be associated with higher achievement motivation (Kamphaus, 1993).

It has been noted that among bright students, gender differences with regard to profile variability were evident (Wilkinson, 1993). Cultural differences have also been found in the studies of gifted children. For example, Saccuzzo (1992) found that a significant VIQ–PIQ discrepancy (VIQ > PIQ) was common for gifted White children, but the opposite pattern (PIQ > VIQ) was evident for gifted children who were Filipino. Furthermore, Taylor et al. (1984) found that gifted children of Hispanic origin were likely to have a greater VIQ–PIQ (PIQ > VIQ) than White children. Other studies have also found that the frequency or extent of a VIQ–PIQ discrepancy was no higher in gifted children than in children with FSIQs in the average range (Patchett & Stansfield, 1992).

DISCREPANCY AND EMOTIONAL OR BEHAVIORAL PROBLEMS

Evidence to support a VIQ–PIQ discrepancy (PIQ > VIQ) on the WISC-R as predictive of delinquent behavior is also equivocal (Cornell & Wilson, 1992; Walsh, 1992; Walsh & Beyer, 1986). For example, Walsh (1992) found no correlation between the magnitude of the VIQ–PIQ discrepancy and measures of delinquency. Results suggested, however, that the presence of such a discrepancy may predict the severity of delinquent behavior once the youth has become a delinquent. Discrepancies between VIQ and PIQ (VIQ > PIQ) have also been attributed to depression; however, as with LDs and delinquency, the results of clinical studies have been mixed (Mokros, Poznanski, & Merrick, 1989).

DISCREPANCY AND CULTURAL DIFFERENCES

Various studies have demonstrated a higher frequency of VIQ–PIQ discrepancies in children for whom English is their second language (Gerken, 1978; Saccuzzo, 1992; Taylor et al., 1984). Variations of English usage may also impact not only on the child's ability to understand the task and respond, but also the clinician's ability to interpret the response (Kamphaus, 1993). Other factors (e.g., lack of exposure) may also result in a VIQ–PIQ discrepancy. For example, it has been suggested that African-American children may have difficulty with some of the Performance Scale tasks due to the novelty of these tasks (Reynolds, 1981).

In summary, research has not supported the validity of reliance on VIQ–PIQ discrepancies for clinical purposes with the WISC-R. With regard to diagnosis or classification, it has been argued that reliance solely on the presence of a specific VIQ–PIQ discrepancy on the WISC-III is of no value (Kamphaus, 1993) and may result in misclassification (Prifitera & Dersh, 1993).

In interpreting a VIQ–PIQ difference, a variety of confounding factors should be addressed. These include the presence of speech or language problems, hearing problems, motor problems, achievement motivation, and linguistic and cultural differences as accounting for the VIQ–PIQ discrepancy (Kamphaus, 1993). Thus, although a VIQ–PIQ discrepancy may be used for hypothesis generation, the presence or absence of such a discrepancy should not be viewed as conclusive evidence for the presence or absence of a disability.

THE THIRD AND FOURTH FACTORS OF THE WISC-III

In the early studies of the WISC-R, the FD factor has been used as a clinical indicator of attention deficit/hyperactivity disorder (ADHD) (Barkley, 1990); however, a variety of studies have questioned its validity for this purpose (e.g., Cohen, Becker, & Campbell, 1990; Kamphaus, 1993; Kostura, 1993; Stone, 1992). Various studies have, for example, failed to support a correlation between the FD factor and attention of hyperactivity subscales of frequently used rating scales for ADHD (e.g., Cohen, Becker, et al., 1990). Cohen and colleagues found that the FD factor correlated in the expected direction only with the Anxiety subscale on the Conners Teacher Rating Scale (Conners, 1969, 1973; Goyette, Conners, & Ulrich, 1978). Cohen et al. concluded that the FD factor was not a reliable indicator of ADHD. They further surmised that the high correlation between the FD factor and the VC factor ($r = .70, p < .001$), and FD factor and the PO factor ($r = .60, p < .001$) suggested that the FD factor was actually measuring some other cognitive function such as numerical facility, working memory, or sequencing ability.

Similarly, Kostura (1993) concluded that the WISC-R FD factor was not a pure indicator of attention and should not be used when making ADHD diagnoses. He cited several studies (e.g., Barkely, DuPaul, & McMurray, 1990; Brown & Wynne, 1982; Milich & Loney, 1979) that concluded that factor scores on the WISC-R do not adequately differentiate children with ADHD from other groups. Stone (1992) also questioned the utility of the FD factor, suggesting that it was never a specific entity, but the result of psychometric underfactoring. Furthermore, Woodcock (1990) found a lack of any combination of loadings to support the WISC-R FD factor. He suggested that the three subtests comprising the FD factor are single markers of separate and specific abilities (short-term memory, processing speed, and quantitative ability) as opposed to a common factor underlying the subtests.

The validity of the FD factor continues to be an issue with the WISC-III. The WISC-III manual includes data suggesting that both learning-disabled (LD) and ADHD children earn lower scores on both the FD and PS factors. However, similar to previous studies of the WISC-R FD factor with regard to ADHD diagnoses, Anastopoulos, Spisto, and Maher (1994) questioned this factor's diagnostic utility. Although they found that the FD factor on the WISC-III was a more valid indicator of the construct of inattention than the FD factor on the WISC-R, its use as a diagnostic measure for an ADHD diagnosis was also rejected. They found that as many as 78% of children who met stringent criteria for an ADHD diagnosis did not demonstrate any significant discrepancy between the FD factor score and other factor scores.

Kamphaus, Benson, Hutchinson, and Platt (1994) concluded that the four-factor structure was "somewhat supported" but that the "theoretical or clinical importance of the additional factors and the Index scores is unclear" (p. 185). Furthermore, they concluded that the distractibility label for the third factor was not supportable and that the PS factor lacked empirical support as well. More recently, the factor structure of the WISC-III was examined for a sample of 140 children with LDs, (e.g., reading disorders), ADHD, or both (Smith & Gfeller, 1995). Both confirmatory and exploratory factor analyses were employed and both a three-factor model (VC, PO, and PS) as well as the four-factor model provided in the WISC-III manual emerged. Furthermore, Woodcock (1990) noted that for effective measurement of a specific ability (i.e., processing speed) a battery requires at least three subtests.

In a recent study of 126 children referred due to academic and/or behavioral difficulty (mean age of 9.24 years; $SD = 2.33$), a battery of neuropsychological tests was administered in order to further explore the meaningfulness and utility of the FD and PS factors (Riccio, Cohen, Hall, & Ross, in press). The FD and PS factors were found to correlate significantly with the VC and PO factors, as well as with each other. Neither the FD nor PS factors correlated significantly with visual and auditory continuous performance measures, and correlations of the FD and PS factors with the Wisconsin Card Sorting Test (Heaton, 1981) were low at best. In addition, correlations with behavioral rating scales (parent and teacher) did not consistently support an association of the FD or PS factors with inattention or hyperactivity. Rather, results suggests that the FD or PS factor scores may be influenced by a myriad of abilities, including but not limited to attention and concentration.

The study by Riccio and colleagues did, however, yield a significant association between the FD factor and measures of immediate memory. This was evident not only for performance on the Sentence Imitation subtest of the Detroit Tests of Learning Aptitude-2 (DTLA-2; Hammill, 1985), but also for the Spatial Memory and Hand Movements subtests of the Kaufman Assessment Battery for Children

(K-ABC, Kaufman & Kaufman, 1983). Specific to the PS factor, significant correlations ($p < .001$) were found with the Spatial Memory and Hand Movements subtests only, and were not as robust as the correlations between the immediate memory measures and the FD factor.

Finally, to assess the utility of the third and fourth factors in determining the presence or absence of ADHD in a clinical population, analysis of variance (ANOVA) was computed for the three clinical groups that did not have a co-occurring diagnosis: LD/no ADHD ($n = 30$), ADHD Predominantly Inattentive ($n = 31$), and ADHD Combined Type ($n = 47$). The finding of no significant between-group differences suggests that the FD and PS factors do not provide information that facilitates differential diagnosis within a heterogeneous clinical sample of children with developmental disabilities (Riccio et al., in press).

In another study, Slate (1995) examined the performance of children diagnosed with specific learning disability, mental retardation, and children who were referred but not diagnosed. Results indicated that children with specific learning disability scored higher on the FD factor than the PO factor, whereas children with mental retardation and undiagnosed children demonstrated a higher PO factor score relative to the FD factor score. Between-group differences were not evident on the FD factor or VC factor.

Kamphaus (1993) asserted that further research is required to provide clearer guidelines for the interpretation and use of the third and fourth factors. Kaufman (1993) also noted the lack of empirical support for the third and fourth factors and recommended that the clinical value of the four-factor model be studied further. Based on research completed thus far, the clinical validity of the FD and PS factors remains questionable. Although these two factors may emerge in factor analysis, the results of studies to date do not support any clinical or theoretical importance of the FD and PS factors for differential diagnosis of ADHD. Neither of these factors appears to measure attention or concentration in a manner similar to other measures used to assess attention (behavior rating scales; continuous performance tests).

Of most interest from the early research with the WISC-III is the association between the FD factor and measures of both auditory–verbal and visual–spatial immediate–working memory. Additional research specific to the relationship between the FD factor and immediate–working memory appears warranted. The PS factor also correlated significantly with measures of visual–spatial immediate–working memory, however, to a lesser degree. The PS factor may be better explained by Kaufman's (1993) assertion that there is greater emphasis on speed with the WISC-III and/or the incorporation of a motor component. Thus, this factor may be assessing immediate–working memory and fine motor skills in combination with PS. Given the apparent relationship between FD–PO factors and immediate–working memory, it would appear reasonable for clinicians to evaluate as child's ability to learn and remember new material (e.g., California Verbal Learning Test for Children; Delis, Kramer, Kaplan, & Ober, 1994; The Children's Memory Scale; Cohen, 1997) when the child exhibits poor performance on either of these factors.

WISC-III AND THE
NEUROPSYCHOLOGICAL EVALUATION

It is beyond the scope of this chapter to discuss the various batteries and eclectic approaches that are currently being used in the neuropsychological assessment of children and adolescents. The reader is referred to chapters by Hynd and Willis (1988), Teeter (1986), and Tramontana and Hooper (1987) for such discussion. Regardless of which approach to assessment is applied, the goal of the evaluation is to analyze the integrity of the child's higher cortical functioning in order to (a) determine the child's present pattern of strengths and weaknesses, (b) characterize future patterns of functioning that might be expected as the child matures, and (c) develop appropriate remedial and compensatory programs in order to assist the child so that he or she can perform at their maximum capability (Cohen, Branch, Willis, Weyandt, & Hynd, 1992).

According to Luria's (1980) functional system approach to assessment, a given behavior is the product of several interrelated cortical and subcortical components functioning in concert. Therefore, if any one or more of the components become dysfunctional, the functional system is effected in such a way that one sees not only a quantitative but also a qualitative deviation from normal performance. The dysfunction also affects other functional systems that require the particular component in question. Those functional systems that do not require the particular component remain unaffected. Thus, a child neuropsychologist must not only be proficient in test administration and interpretation from a quantitative (norm-referenced) perspective, but also skilled at qualitative analysis (observation) of how a child or adolescent passes or fails certain test items.

Perhaps the best place to begin the neuropsychological assessment is with intelligence testing. The intelligence test affords a reference point for all higher cortical functions in that it provides an estimate of a child's intellectual potential or psychometric g. Furthermore, intelligence testing provides the child neuropsychologist with a cross-sectional panorama of the child's higher cortical functioning. Thus, by combining the "seven-step" quantitative approach to WISC-III interpretation as described by Kaufman (1994), and the qualitative approach offered by Kaplan (Appendix, Chapter 1, this volume), the examiner can use the WISC-III to begin developing hypotheses concerning the child's higher cortical strengths and weaknesses, which will require further verification. The remaining portion of the chapter will focus on the clinical research findings related to the WISC-R and WISC-III in various clinical groups commonly referred for child neuropsychological assessment.

EPILEPSY

It is estimated that 100,000 new cases of epilepsy are diagnosed in the United States each year (Kurtzke & Kurland, 1984), and of these cases, approximately 70% experienced their first seizure during childhood (Dreisbach, Ballard, Russo, &

Schain, 1982). Indeed, within the pediatric population, epilepsy is considered by many to be the most prevalent chronic neurologic disorder (Bolter, 1986) and is estimated to occur in 4 to 8 children per 1,000 (Blom, Heijbel, & Bergfors, 1978).

Specifically, epilepsy is a disorder that is characterized by two or more unprovoked seizures. Often, the words, "seizures" and "epilepsy" are used interchangeably, however they are two distinct entities. Epilepsy is a disorder that is the result of two or more unprovoked epileptic seizures, whereas a seizure is a sudden electrical discharge of neurons from the brain resulting in impaired functioning (Henrikson, 1990). Impaired functioning within the areas of behavior, emotion, cognition, and academic performance have long been recognized as a result of epilepsy, and some authors have postulated that subclinical seizure activity may result in specific types of LDs (Hynd & Willis, 1988). In addition, a relationship between cognitive impairment and the effects of antiepileptic medications, and the epileptic focal point has also been recognized (Chaudry, Najam, DeMahieu, Raza, & Ahmed, 1992). Therefore, given the immense annual growth rate of this population, in conjunction with the resulting impairments that occur, the need to address the intellectual functioning of school children that fall within this population is vital.

Several investigators have examined the relationship between intelligence and epilepsy in children. In general, four major findings have repeatedly surfaced. First, the intelligence of children with epilepsy is skewed toward the lower end of normal functioning (Bolter, 1986; Farwell, Dodrill, & Batzell, 1985; Giordiani, Berent, Sackellares, et al., 1985; O'Leary et al., 1983; O'Leary, Seidenberg, Berent, & Boll, 1981). Specifically, 40–48% of the children evaluated in these studies had FSIQ scores below 90. In a study of epileptic children using the WISC-R, Bolter (1986) found that as a group the children fell within the average range. However, only 13% had above-average FSIQ scores, whereas 48% were below average.

Cohen, Branch, Riccio, and Hall (1991) studied the intellectual performance of children followed in a tertiary care medical center for epilepsy. Analysis of their performance on the WISC-R and the WISC-III indicated that this population generally functioned in the borderline to low average range across the VIQ, PIQ, and the FSIQ, as well as on the Factor/Index scores. In addition, like the standardization sample, children with epilepsy scored slightly lower on the WISC-III than the WISC-R. However, this decline was found to be significantly ($p < .05$) greater for VIQ and FSIQ in the sample of children with epilepsy as compared with that reported for the standardization sample. Furthermore, it is felt that the slightly lower mean scores obtained for this particular sample of children with epilepsy may be explained by the fact that this sample was taken from a population of children being treated at a tertiary care epilepsy center. In general, children treated at such a center tend to have more severe and more difficult-to-control seizure disorders that may result in lower intellectual functioning (Holmes, 1987). This interpretation is further supported by studies evaluating the intellectual performance of institutionalized children or children with severe epilepsy that have reported IQs in the borderline to mentally handicapped range (Kugelmass, Poull, & Rudnich, 1938; Tenny, 1955).

The second major finding reported by several authors (e.g., Bourgeois et al., 1983; Farwell et al., 1985; O'Leary et al., 1983) but not all (Ellenberg, Kirtz, & Nelson, 1986) indicates that the onset of seizures in early childhood is associated with a higher risk for intellectual impairment than when seizures began in late childhood or adolescence. Third, children with symptomatic epilepsy have a higher risk for intellectual impairment than children with idiopathic epilepsy (Bourgeois et al., 1983; Ellenberg et al., 1986). Fourth, children with typical absence, generalized tonic clonic, and partial seizures tend to score higher on IQ tests than children with atypical absence, akinetic, and myoclonic seizures (Farwell et al., 1985; Giordiani et al., 1985; Sofijanov, 1982).

Finally, there appears to be few antiepileptic medications that have positive effects on cognitive functioning. In a review by Holmes (1987), the author concludes that most of the antiepileptic medications used to treat seizure disorders impede intellectual functioning, especially when there drugs are used in combination. Perhaps the worst offenders are phenobarbital (barbiturates) and dilantin (phenytoin), which have been shown to consistently produce negative effects on attention and concentration, motor speed, and processing speed. Thus, children with epilepsy should be carefully monitored for drug toxicity and associated functional deficits. Furthermore, the use of antiepileptic medication in combination should be avoided whenever possible.

HYDROCEPHALUS

Within the normal brain, there is a stable balance between the production and absorption of cerebral spinal fluid (CSF) maintaining suitable size of the ventricles. When a disruption of this balance occurs, hydrocephalus is often times the result. Hydrocephalus is a condition by which an increase of cerebral spinal fluid occurs in the ventricles of the brain resulting in an increase of intracranial pressure (Hynd & Willis, 1988). This increase of CSF is the result of obstruction of the CSF flow, that is, the overproduction or malabsorption of CSF (Bigler, 1988). The increased intraventricular pressure produces a compression, especially concerning the white matter, which in turn results in a thinning of the cortical mantle (Rowland, 1981).

Hydrocephalus often develops in conjunction with other neurological disorders or postnatal insult, thereby making it difficult to provide an accurate estimate of the incidence of true hydrocephalus. However, as a congenital disorder, it is estimated that the incidence rate ranges from .9 to 1.5 per 1,000 births (Milhorat, 1982). The incidence rate for hydrocephalus in association with spina bifida and myelomeningocele rises to 1.3 to 2.9 per 1,000 births (Myrianthopoulos & Kurland, 1961).

Hydrocephalus appears not only to have physical ramifications but cognitive ramifications as well (Bigler, 1988). Cognitive characteristics of hydrocephalic patients are low intelligence and poor academic performance (spelling, reading, and arithmetic). Even in patients with mild hydrocephalus, IQ and academic achievement is reported to be approximately one standard deviation below the mean for the normal population. In addition, poor abstract reasoning, poor visual-perceptual skills, and a higher verbal than nonverbal IQ were also so noted (Hurley, Dorman, Laatsch, Bell, & D'Avignon, 1990).

Several studies (e.g., Anderson, 1975; Lorber, 1971; Tew & Laurence, 1975) have noted that on intellectual testing, verbal performance is typically higher than nonverbal performance. The verbal performance of hydrocephalic patients is one that is characterized by good form and structure producing adequate verbal fluency, but poor substance and monitoring of output, that is, a poor understanding of language. The speech of hydrocephalic patients has been described as lacking substance (Spain, 1974), with their conversation containing a high proportion of improper words (Swisher & Pinsker, 1971). Indeed, this verbal characteristic is one of several characteristics that in combination have been described as the "cocktail party syndrome." This syndrome is characterized by good fluency and articulation, verbal perseveration and trivial loquaciousness, overuse of social phrases, and an apparent overfamiliarity with the listener. Thus, the elevated VIQ typically seen in hydrocephalic patients may reflect these verbal abilities, which are emphasized on the verbal portion of IQ testing (Holler, Fennell, Crosson, Boggs, & Mickle, 1995).

Based on the type of nonverbal deficits exhibited by this population, some researchers have suggested right-hemisphere white matter lesions (Harnadek & Rourke, 1994; Hurley et al., 1990; Rourke, 1989). Another area that is hypothesized to be effected based on the observed cognitive patterns is the frontal lobes (Hagberg & Sjorgen, 1966).

TRAUMATIC BRAIN INJURY

In 1985, the National Head Injury Foundation estimated that 1 in 80 people born in that year would receive a brain injury from an auto accident. Indeed, traumatic brain injury (TBI) is so prevalent that it has become the second leading cause of death within the pediatric population (Annegers, 1983). Automobile accidents account for ⅓ to ½ of all TBIs within the adolescent population (Filley, Cranberg, Alexander, & Hart, 1987), whereas pedestrian auto accident accounts for the majority of TBIs in younger children (Chadwick, Rutter, Thompson, & Shaffer, 1981). Falls are the second leading cause of TBI (Field, 1979). While TBIs are not uncommon in infants from birth to 2 years of age (Goldstein & Levin, 1987), child abuse is the major cause of TBI in children under 1 year of age (Lange-Cosack & Tepfer, 1973). Finally, although there is little disagreement that males experience a higher frequency of TBI as opposed to females, ratio estimations vary from 2:1 to 3:1 (Goldstein & Levin, 1987; Rimel & Jane, 1983).

In nearly all children with TBI, residual motor deficits have been observed (Dalby & Obrzut, 1991). These include paresis (Filley et al., 1987), unsteadiness of gate, mild tremors, fine motor incoordination, difficulties with copying tasks, difficulty with rapidly alternating movements, and clonus (Dimitrijevic, Dimitrijevic,

Kinalski, McKay, & Sherwood, 1987; Fuld & Fisher, 1977; Rourke, Fisk, & Strang, 1986). However, a review (Levin, Eisenberg, & Miner, 1983) suggests that the most significant impairments in children with TBI involve motor skills, motor speed, and memory.

Persistent speech and language impairments do occur, but are most influenced by the etiology and extent of the lesion (Chadwick, 1985). Acquired aphasia in children is most often the result of brain trauma (Dalby & Obrzut, 1991), involving the left hemisphere. However, right-hemisphere lesions have been reported to produce linguistic deficits in 3½- to 6-year-olds (Hecaen, 1976). Expressive language difficulties include anomia for objects, decreased performance in verbal fluency, describing functions of objects, sentence repetition, and verbal associative fluency (Dalby & Obrzut, 1991). Receptive language deficits include poor linguistic comprehension (Levin & Eisenberg, 1979) and difficulties comprehending lengthy or multipart oral directions (Fuld & Fisher, 1977). Written expression deficits appear more evident in children than adolescents (Hecaen, Perenin, & Jennerod, 1984). Such writing difficulties occurred more frequently in right-handed children, 10 years of age and younger with left-hemisphere lesions.

Case studies by Fuld and Fisher (1977) have revealed that in general, intelligence scores are lower when compared to the preinjury estimates. However, some controversy does exist on WISC VIQ–PIQ discrepancies. Some studies have indicated a lower PIQ in relation to the VIQ (Chadwick, Rutter, Thompson, & Shaffer, 1981; Levin, Benton, & Grossman, 1982). Nevertheless, no significant VIQ–PIQ differences have also been reported (Fuld & Fisher, 1977). It has been suggested that lower PIQs may actually be the result of deficits in visual-spatial perception or reduced processing speed (Dalby & Obrzut, 1991). Furthermore, because attention span, memory, and motor skill or speed are frequently effected, any one or combination of these deficits could result in decreased performance on the PIQ subtests.

A greater number of children in comparison to adolescents are more effected in their cognitive functioning. In one study, (Levin, Eisenberg, Wigg, & Kobayashi, 1982) after a 6-month follow-up, it was found that 33% of the children (12 years and younger) in the sample had WISC-R VIQs lower than 80 compared to their matched adolescents who were all above 80. Similarly, 40% of children demonstrated WISC-R PIQ deficits, whereas no adolescent scored below 80.

There is still debate as to whether the preinjury condition of children with TBI is ever fully restored (Dalby & Obrzut, 1991). The foundation of this debate is based on the lack of accuracy in establishing preinjury estimation of intellectual functioning. A review by Ewing-Cobbs, Fletcher, and Levin (1986) suggests that children with severe TBI do not achieve preinjury intellectual functioning. Thus, data from previous studies indicate that premorbid intellectual functioning does not occur in children with TBI resulting in bilateral generalized damage.

UNILATERAL LESION

Neuropsychologists should be careful when inferring lateralized brain dysfunction based upon VIQ–PIQ discrepancies on the Wechsler scales. Based on the oversimplistic notion that the left hemisphere primarily mediates linguistic functions whereas the right hemisphere is typically involved in the mediation of visual-spatial or nonverbal functions, it is tempting to conclude that individuals with unilateral lesions involving the left cerebral hemisphere should demonstrate VIQ–PIQ discrepancies in favor of PIQ. Similarly, individuals with unilateral lesions involving the right cerebral hemisphere should exhibit VIQ–PIQ discrepancies in favor of VIQ. However, this notion finds little support in the adult literature. For example, Kaufman (1990) reviewed 33 studies (30 WAIS and 3 WAIS-R) reporting VIQ–PIQ discrepancies in samples of adults with unilateral brain insult due to various etiologies. If one insisted upon at least a 6-point difference between mean VIQ and PIQ in the predicted direction, only 9 of the 33 samples (27%) exhibited the predicted VIQ–PIQ discrepancy pattern.

Research within the pediatric population is even more equivocal than that which is reported in the adult literature. In a study by Lewandowski and DeRienzo (1985), the authors investigated the WISC-R performances of children with hemiplegia who were 6 to 12 years of age. They reported a significant association between right-hemisphere insult and depressed PIQ, contrasted by a nonsignificant relationship between left-hemisphere insult and depressed VIQ. Shapiro and Doltan (1986) reported a nonsignificant relationship between location of lesion and VIQ–PIQ discrepancy on the WISC-R in their sample of children with unilateral brain damage. Morris and Bigler (1987) investigated the WISC-R performance of children (6 to 12 years of age) with unilateral brain damage and found a more substantial relationship between left-hemisphere insult and depressed VIQ than between right-hemisphere insult and depressed PIQ. Finally, Cohen, Branch, McKie, and Adams (1994) reported the neuropsychological test performance of a small group of children (6 to 16 years of age) with sickle cell anemia who experienced a single stroke in the left or right cerebral hemisphere. Results indicated that children with left-hemisphere insult demonstrated a global decline on intelligence testing with a very small VIQ–PIQ discrepancy in favor of PIQ (4 points). In contrast, children with right-hemisphere insult demonstrated a marked decline in PIQ only, which resulted in a large (13 points) VIQ–PIQ discrepancy in favor of VIQ.

In order to comprehend the disparity of the results concerning VIQ–PIQ discrepancy in children, one must consider the notion of plasticity in the developing brain. Although the exact physiological mechanisms underlying the recovery of functioning remain unclear, numerous physiological mechanisms, including axonal regeneration, collateral sprouting, and denervation supersensitivity have been postulated to account for the recovery processes. Furthermore, factors such as premorbid level of functioning, age at lesion onset, the type, size, and location of lesion, and subsequent habilitation efforts must also be considered (Cohen, Branch, Willis, Weyandt, & Hynd, 1992).

Specifically, there are two general theoretical perspectives regarding recovery of function following early brain insult. Isaacson (1976) proposes that early brain insult must be considered more detrimental than insults occurring later in life. This speculation is based on the fact that the infant brain often shows a reduction in size following insult, whereas the adolescent brain typically does not show a similar reduction. Consequently, loss of function in the adolescent tends to be more highly localized. This contention is supported by a study conducted by Reitan (1981), which examined the learning potential of children experiencing brain insult at different ages. Results indicated that younger children demonstrated a reduction in overall learning potential as compared with children who experienced brain insult at an older age.

Based upon the work of Kennard (1936, 1942), who compared the effects of unilateral motor cortex lesions in infant and adult monkeys, the concepts of "sparing of function" and "brain plasticity" were developed. Specifically, Kennard found that lesions in the infant monkey brain resulted in milder deficits than those occurring within the adult monkey brain. These concepts encompass two major postulates (Fletcher & Satz, 1983): (a) younger organisms exhibit better outcomes following brain injury, and (b) there is greater plasticity in the immature brain, which explains the better outcomes. For example, studies by Rasmussen and Milner (1977), and Woods and Teuber (1973) indicate that early damage to the language centers of the left hemisphere lead to a functional shift in language abilities to the right hemisphere. However, this transfer is typically not complete in that subtle deficits in linguistic ability are often evident later in life (Dennis & Whitaker, 1976, 1977). Furthermore, children experiencing early left-hemisphere insult typically exhibit evidence of "crowding" in which deficits in visual-spatial functioning are also evident (Lansdell, 1962, 1969). Thus, it is common to see higher VIQs, as opposed to PIQs, in children who have experienced early (prior to 5 years of age) left-hemisphere insults (Cohen, Hynd, & Hartlage, 1983). In contrast, children who experience early right-hemisphere insults tend to demonstrate impairment of both VIQ and PIQ (Nass, Koch, Janowsky, & Stiles-Davis, 1985; Woods, 1980). Woods interpreted this finding as being consistent with an early right-hemisphere contribution to linguistic functions.

The concepts of "sparing of function" and "brain plasticity" can be used to help explain the large disparity of results regarding VIQ–PIQ discrepancies in children with unilateral brain damage. In addition, they also serve to emphasize the fact that statements regarding brain dysfunction based solely upon WISC-III VIQ–PIQ discrepancies are not warranted (Hynd & Willis, 1988).

DEVELOPMENTAL DYSLEXIA

Historically, developmental dyslexia (severe LD in reading) has been conceptualized as a homogeneous clinical entity in which researchers directed their efforts in search of a single cause for the disorder. However, during the last 30 years, considerable research has been accumulated that indicates that developmental dyslexia is best conceptualized as a heterogeneous disorder with multiple etiologies. This conceptualization makes sense, if one assumes that the development of reading skills requires the complex integration of various higher order processes, which work together to form a higher cortical functional system for reading. Dysfunction in any one of these component processes will disrupt the total mechanism and result in a qualitatively different subtype of developmental dyslexia

(Hynd & Cohen, 1983). Thus, it is possible for children with developmental dyslexia to experience reading failure for a variety of reasons including deficits in the areas of phonological processing, expressive/receptive language, auditory/verbal memory, visual/spatial perception, and visual/nonverbal memory.

Review of the dyslexic subtyping literature indicates that clinically reproducible subtypes do exist. Although there are several subtyping approaches in this area of literature, one approach is to use WISC VIQ–PIQ discrepancies as a clinical criteria for subtyping inclusion. For example, Kinsbourne and Warrington (1963) developed a subtyping model based upon a child's performance on the WISC or the WAIS. Employing this rationale, they found two distinct subgroups of reading-disabled children. Group 1 was composed of children with at least a 20-point discrepancy between verbal and nonverbal performance (VIQ < PIQ). In addition, this group also exhibited delays in speech acquisition, verbal comprehension, and verbal expression. Group 2 also demonstrated a 20-point discrepancy but in the opposite direction (VIQ > PIQ). Furthermore, this group exhibited significant deficits in right–left confusion, arithmetic, and constructional abilities. Group 2 was labeled the "developmental" Gerstmann Group as reflected by similar symptoms seen in adults with Gerstmann Syndrome.

Using a neuropsychological model that involved the administration of a comprehensive neuropsychological battery that included the WISC-R, Pirozzolo (1979, 1981) was also able to identify two clinically distinct dyslexic subtypes. Subtype 1 (auditory-linguistic) exhibited the following pattern of test performance; average to above average PIQ, VIQ < PIQ, developmentally delayed onset of language, expressive speech deficit, anomia, agrammatism, phonological errors in reading, phoneme-to-grapheme association errors in spelling, a letter-by-letter decoding strategy, normal eye movements, and intact visual–spatial abilities. In contrast, Subtype 2 (visual–spatial) exhibited the following test performance pattern; average to above average VIQ, PIQ < VIQ, right-left confusion, early evidence of mirror or inverted writing, spelling errors reflecting letter/word reversals and omissions, finger agnosia, spatial dysgraphia (e.g., poor handwriting, poor use of space), visual type errors in reading, a phonetic decoding strategy, faulty eye movements during reading, and intact oral language abilities.

Finally, support for the use of VIQ–PIQ discrepancies in the clinical subtyping of children with dyslexia is derived from the work of Cohen and colleagues (Cohen, Hynd, & Hugdahl, 1992; Cohen, Krawiecki, & DuRant, 1987). In the first study, the dichotic listening performance of subtypes of children with developmental dyslexia was examined. In the second study, the effectiveness of the neuropsychological approach to remediation was examined. In both studies, children with dyslexia were diagnostically classified into three subtypes; language disorder, visual–spatial, and mixed. These children were then placed into two groups. Examination of the VIQ–PIQ discrepancy patterns of the three groups indicated that in both studies the language-disorder group demonstrated a significant VIQ–PIQ discrepancy in favor of PIQ, whereas the visual–spatial group demonstrated a significant VIQ–PIQ discrepancy in favor of VIQ.

Although there is still much work to be done in the area of diagnosis and treatment of children with developmental dyslexia, that is, subtype validation to ensure that the subtypes are clinically distinct and reproducible, this area of research has resulted in the educational and medical communities viewing dyslexia as a heterogeneous clinical entity with multiple etiologies.

CONCLUSIONS

What can be concluded about the usefulness of the WISC-III in terms of complementing information gathered from the comprehensive neuropsychological evaluation of children and adolescents? Based on our review, a number of conclusions seems warranted.

First, considerable scientific evidence points to the validity of the WISC-III Verbal and Performance scales. Furthermore, these scales may indeed differentially tap left- and right-hemispheric process, respectively. Consequently, in a child with a left-hemispheric lesion one might expect depressed VIQ relative to relatively intact PIQ. However, as we have noted, there are considerable factors that mediate the confidence one can employ in using these scales in isolation in determining the locus of a lesion. As a result, one should only employ these scales in differentiating hemispheric impairment if other collaborative evidence attests to the locus of a lesion (e.g., neuroimaging [CT/MRI] evidence, etc.).

Second, numerous studies attest to the validity of the VC and PO factors both with the WISC-R and WISC-III. In fact, since these factor scales are relatively more "pure" in a psychometric sense, one might expect that they could be more useful in confirming the presence of intact or impaired VC or PO abilities.

Some experimental evidence, in fact, supports this notion. For example, Morgan, Hynd, Hall, Novey, and Eliopulos (1997) reported a correlation of .63 ($p < .05$) between the length of the left temporal bank of the planum temporale and the VC factor score from the WISC-III among normal children. Figure 10.1 illustrates the location of the left planum temporale, which has historically been associated with Wernicke's area, known to be vitally linked to language comprehension. In a larger sample of normal, ADHD, and dyslexic children, Morgan et al. (1997) found that irrespective of group, as plana asymmetry increased in favor of the left plana (L > R), so did ability on VC factor on the WISC-III. Figure 10.2 illustrates how the more normal pattern of left greater than right plana asymmetry increased when the VC factor score is >100. It can be seen that among children scoring <100 standard score on the VC factor, only 25% had L > R plana asymmetry. However, 61% of children scoring >100 standard score on the VC factor had left plana greater than the right. Thus, it might be concluded tentatively that the VC factor score may have a link with the length of the left-hemispheric language cortex such that better ability is associated with a larger left planum temporale.

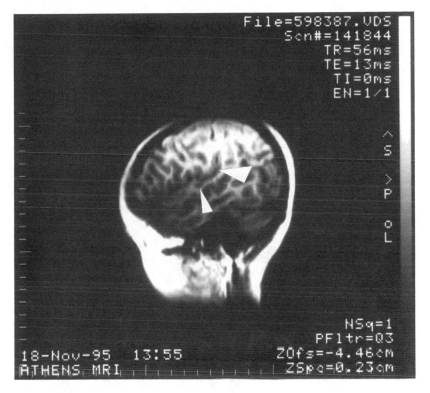

FIGURE 10.1 A magnetic resonance imaging scan showing a lateral sagittal view of the left cerebral hemisphere. The region of the planum temporale lies in the posterior end of the Sylvian fissure between the two white arrowheads.

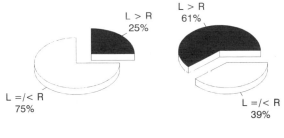

FIGURE 10.2 Plana asymmetry and the WISC-III Verbal-Comprehension (VC) factor. The incidence of greater left over right (L > R) asymmetry increases when the VC score is >100 standard score (based on N = 47 children). This may support the notion that left plana length is positively associated with greater verbal comprehension abilities in children.

Third, it is clear that insufficient research exists regarding the usefulness of the third and fourth factors of the WISC-III. Thus, in a neuropsychological context, clinicians should not make statements regarding the process these factors and their associated subtests assess in relation to neuroanatomy. Rather, they should be interpreted as revealing process abilities which to date have not been related to specific brain regions. This seems an appropriate caution considering the lack of validation regarding these third and fourth factors on the WISC-III.

Overall then, we must reiterate that the VIQ and PIQ scores as well as the VC and PO factors may have relevance in revealing the intactness of neurological systems associated with the right and left hemispheres but that caution should be applied in making statements regarding the integrity of neurological regions or structures.

General ability, or psychometric g, has no locus as it reflects the ability to perceive associations across neuropsychological abilities and processes as well as more localized subprocesses. However, because general ability may be impacted by dysfunctional processes, general ability may be sensitive to the intactness of the functioning of the brain and its associated processes. Clearly, as more advanced forms of neuroimaging, such as functional magnetic resonance imaging, become more widely used by the community of scholars, future research may reveal more about the locus of all of the mental subprocess assessed on tests of intelligence, such as the WISC-III.

ACKNOWLEDGMENTS

Supported in part by a grant (RO1-HD26890-03) awarded to the first author (GWH) from the National Institute of Child Health and Human Development (NICHHD), National Institutes of Health (NIH).

REFERENCES

Anastopoulos, A. D., Spisto, M. A., & Maher, M. C. (1994). The WISC-III freedom from distractibility factor: Its utility in identifying children with attention deficit hyperactivity disorder. *Psychological Assessment, 6,* 368–371.

Anderson, E. M. (1975). Cognitive deficits in children with spina bifida and hydrocephalus: A review of the literature. *British Journal of Educational Psychology, 45,* 257–268.

Annegers, J. F. (1983). The epidemiology of head trauma in children. In K. Shapiro (Ed.), *Pediatric head trauma.* New York: Futura.

Bannatyne, A. (1968). Diagnosing learning disabilities and writing remedial prescriptions. *Journal of Learning Disabilities, 1,* 242–249.

Barkley, R. A. (1990). *Attention deficit hyperactivity disorder: A handbook for diagnosis and treatment.* New York: Guilford.

Barkley, R. A., DuPaul, G., & McMurray, M. B. (1990). Comprehensive evaluation of attention deficit disorder with and without hyperactivity as defined by research criteria. *Journal of Consulting and Clinical Psychology, 58,* 775–789.

Bigler, E. D. (1988). The neuropsychology of hydrocephalus. *Archives of Clinical Neuropsychology, 3*, 81–100.

Boll, T. J. (1974). Behavioral correlates of cerebral damage in children aged 9 through 14. In R. M. Reitan & L. A. Davidson (eds.), *Clinical Neuropsychology* (pp. 91–120). Washington, DC: V. H. Winston & Sons.

Blom, S., Heijbel, J., & Bergfors, P. G. (1978). Incidence in epilepsy in children. *Epilepsia, 19,* 343–350.

Bolter, J. F. (1986). Epilepsy in children: Neuropsychological effects. In J. E. Obruzt & G. W. Hynd (Eds.), *Child neuropsychology: Vol 2: Clinical practice* (pp. 127–165). New York: Academic Press.

Bourgeois, B. F. D., Prensky, A. L., & Palkes, H. S. (1983). Intelligence in epilepsy: A prospective study in children. *Annals of Neurology, 14,* 438–444.

Chadwick, O. (1985). Annotations: Psychological sequelae of head injury in children. *Development Medicine and Child Neurology 27,* 72–75.

Chadwick, O., Rutter, M., Thompson, J., & Shaffer, D. (1981). Intellectual performance and reading skills after localized head injury in children. *Journal of Child Psychology and Psychiatry, 22,* 117–139.

Chaudry, H. R., Najam, N., De Mahieu, C., Raza, A., & Ahmed, N. (1992). Clinical use of Piracetam in epileptic patients. *Current Therapeutic Research, 52*(3), 355–360.

Cheng, Z., Dai, X., & Liu, S. (1994). The patterns of intellectual functioning in Chinese children with learning disability. *Bulletin of the Hong Kong Psychological Society,* (32–33), 60–71.

Clampit, M. K., & Silver, S. J. (1990). Demographic characteristics and mean profiles of Learning Disability Index subtests of the standardization sample of the Wechsler Intelligence Scale for Children–Revised. *Journal of Learning Disabilities, 23,* 263–264.

Cohen, M. J. (1997). *The Children's Memory Scale.* San Antonio, TX: The Psychological Corporation.

Cohen, M. J., Becker, M. G., & Campbell, R. (1990). Relationships among four methods of assessment of children with attention deficit-hyperactivity disorder. *The Journal of School Psychology, 28,* 189–202.

Cohen, M. J., Branch, W. B., McKie, V. C., & Adams, R. J. (1994). Neuropsychological impairment in children with sickle cell anemia and cerebrovascular accidents. *Clinical Pediatrics,* 517–524.

Cohen, M. J., Branch, W. B., Riccio, C. A., & Hall, L. L. (1991, August). *Intellectual functioning of children with epilepsy: Comparison of performance on the WISC-III and WISC-R.* Paper presented at the 99th Annual Convention of the American Psychological Association, San Francisco, CA.

Cohen, M. J., Branch, W. B., Willis, W. G., Weyandt, L. L., & Hynd, G. W. (1992). Childhood. In A. E. Puente & R. J. McCaffrey (Eds.), *Handbook of neuropsychological assessment* (pp. 49–79). New York: Plenum Press.

Cohen, M. J., Holmes, G. L., Campbell, L. R., Smith, J. R., & Flanigin, H. F. (1990). Memory performance following unilateral electrical stimulation of the hippocampus in a child with right temporal lobe epilepsy. *Journal of Epilepsy, 3,* 115–122.

Cohen, M. J., Hynd, G. W., & Hartlage, L. C. (1983). A shift in language lateralization: One case for and one case against. *Clinical Neuropsychologist, 5,* 187–202.

Cohen, M. J., Hynd, G. W., & Hugdahl, K. (1992). Dichotic listening performance in subtypes of developmental dyslexia and a left temporal lobe tumor contrast group. *Brain and Language, 42,* 187–202.

Cohen, M. J., Krawiecki, N., & DuRant, R. H. (1987). The neuropsychological approach to the remediation of dyslexia. *Archives of Clinical Neuropsychology, 2,* 163–173.

Conners, C. K. (1969). A teacher rating scale for use in drug studies with children. *American Journal of Psychiatry, 126,* 884–888.

Conners, C. K. (1973). Rating scales for use in drug studies with children. *Psychopharmacology Bulletin* (special issue), 24–84.

Cornell, D. G., & Wilson, L. A. (1992). The PIQ > VIQ discrepancy in violent and nonviolent delinquents. *Journal of Clinical Psychology, 48,* 256–261.

Dalby, P. R., & Obrzut, J. E. (1991). Epidemiologic characteristics and sequelae of closed head-injured children and adolescents: A review. *Developmental Neuropsychology, 7* (1), 35–68.

Delis, D. C., Kramer, J. H., Kaplan, E., & Ober, B. A. (1994). *California Verbal Learning Test—Children's Version*. San Antonio, TX: The Psychological Corporation.

Dennis, M., & Whitaker, H. A. (1976). Language acquisition following hemidecortication: Linguistic superiority of the left over the right hemisphere. *Brain and Language, 3,* 404–433.

Dennis, M., & Whitaker, H. A. (1977). Hemispheric equipotentiality and language acquisition. In S. J. Segalowitz & F. A. Gruber (Eds.), *Language development and neurological theory* (pp. 93–107). New York: Academic.

Dimitrijevic, M. M., Dimitrijevic, M. R., Kinalski, R., McKay, W. B., & Sherwood, A. M. (1987). Neuropsychological assessment of motor disorders in patients with brain injury. In M. E. Miner & K. A. Wagner (Eds.), *Neurotrauma: Treatment rehabilitation and related issues No. 2* (pp. 413–473). Boston: Butterworths.

Dreisbach, M., Ballard, M., Russo, D. C., & Schain, R. J. (1982). Educational intervention for children with epilepsy. *Journal of Special Education, 16,* 341–353.

Ellenberg, J. H., Kirtz, D. G., & Nelson, K. B., (1986). Do seizures cause intellectual deterioration? *New England Journal of Medicine, 314,* 1085–1088.

Ewing-Cobbs, L., Fletcher, J. M., & Levin, H. S. (1986). Neurobehavioral sequelae following head injury in children: Educational implications. *Journal of Head Trauma Rehabilitation, 1,* 57–65.

Farwell, J. R., Dodrill, C. B., & Batzell, L. W. (1985). Neuropsychological abilities of children with epilepsy. *Epilepsia, 26*(5), 395–400.

Fedio, P., & Mirsky, A. F. (1969). Selective intellectual deficits in children with temporal lobe or centrencephalic epilepsy. *Neuropsychological, 7,* 287–300.

Field, J. H. (1979). *Epidemiology of head injury in England and Wales.* London: H. M. Stationery Office.

Filley, C., Cranberg, L. D., Alexander, M., & Hart, E. (1987). Neurobehavioral outcome after closed head injury in childhood and adolescence. *Archives of Neurology, 44,* 194–198.

Fletcher, J. M., & Satz, P. (1983). Age, plasticity and equipotentiality: A reply to Smith. *Journal of Consulting and Clinical Psychology, 51,* 763–767.

Fuld, P. A., & Fisher, P. (1977). Recovery of intellectual ability after closed head injury. *Developmental Medicine and Child Neurology, 19,* 495–502.

Gerken, K. C. (1978). Performance of Mexican American children on intelligence tests. *Exceptional Children, 44,* 438–443.

Giordiani, B., Berent, S., Sackellares, J. C., Kirtz, D., & Boll, T. (1985). Intelligence test performance of patients with partial and generalized seizures. *Epilepsia, 26,* 37–42.

Goldstein, F. C., & Levin, H. S. (1987). Epidemiology of pediatric closed head injury: Incidence, clinical characteristics, and risk factors. *Journal of Learning Disabilities, 20,* 518–525.

Goyette, C. H., Conners, C. K., & Ulrich, R. F. (1978). Normative data on revised Conners Parent and Teacher Rating Scales. *Journal of Abnormal Child Psychology, 6,* 221–236.

Hagberg, B., & Sjorgen, I. (1966). The chronic brain syndrome of infantile hydrocephalus. *American Journal of Disease of Children, 112,* 189–196.

Hammill, D. D. (1985). *Detroit Tests of Learning Aptitude* (2nd ed.). Austin, TX: Pro-Ed.

Harnadek, M. C. S., & Rourke, B. P. (1994). Principal identifying features of the syndrome of nonverbal learning disabilities in children. *Journal of Learning Disability, 27,* 144–154.

Heaton, R. H. (1981). *Wisconsin Card Sorting Test manual.* Odessa, FL: Psychological Assessment Resources.

Hecaen, H. (1976). Acquired aphasia in children and the ontogenesis of hemispheric functional specialization. *Brain and Language, 3,* 114–134.

Hecaen, H., Perenin, M. T., & Jennerod, M. (1984). The effects of cortical lesions in children: Language and visual functions. In C. R. Almli & S. Finger (Eds.), *Early brain damage, Vol 1: Research orientations and clinical observations* (pp. 229–261). New York: Academic.

Henrikson, O. (1990). Education and epilepsy: Assessment and remediation. *Epilepsia, 31*(Suppl. 4), S21–S25.

Holler, K. A., Fennell, E. B., Crosson, B., Boggs, S. R., & Mickle, J. P. (1995). Neuropsychological and adaptive functioning in younger versus older children shunted for early hydrocephalus. *Child Neuropsychology, 1*(1), 63–73.

Holmes, G. L. (1987). *Diagnosis and management of seizures in children* (pp. 112–114). Philadelphia: W. B. Saunders.

Humphries, T., & Bone, J. (1993). Use of IQ criteria for evaluating the uniqueness of the learning disability profile. *Journal of Learning Disabilities, 26,* 348–351.

Hurley, A. D., Dorman, C., Laatsch, L., Bell, S., & D'Avignon, J. (1990). Cognitive functioning in patients with spina bifida, hydrocephalus, and the "cocktail party" syndrome. *Developmental Neuropsychology, 6*(2), 151–172.

Hynd, G. W., & Cohen, M. J. (1983). *Dyslexia.* New York: Grune & Stratton.

Hynd, G. W., & Willis, W. G. (1988). *Pediatric neuropsychology.* Orlando, FL: Grune & Stratton.

Isaacson, R. L. (1976). Recovery "?" from early brain damage. In T. D. Tjossem (Ed.), *Intervention strategies for high risk infants and young children* (pp. 176–197). Baltimore: University Park Press.

Kamphaus, R. W. (1993). *Clinical assessment of children's intelligence.* Needham Heights, MA: Allyn & Bacon.

Kamphaus, R. W., Benson, J., Hutchinson, S., Platt, L. O. (1994). Identification of factor models for the WISC-III. *Educational and Psychological Measurement, 54,* 174–186.

Kaufman, A. S. (1979). *Intelligent testing with the WISC-R.* New York: Wiley.

Kaufman, A. S. (190). *Assessing adolescent and adult intelligence.* Boston, MA: Allyn & Bacon.

Kaufman, A. S. (1993). King WISC the third assumes the throne. *Journal of School Psychology, 31,* 345–354.

Kaufman, A. S. (1994). *Intelligence testing with the WISC-III.* New York: A Wiley-Interscience Publication.

Kaufman, A. S., & Kaufman, N. L. (1983). *Kaufman Assessment Battery for Children.* Circle Pines, MN: American Guidance Service.

Kavale, K. A., & Forness, S. R. (1984). A meta-analysis of the validity of Wechsler Scale profiles and recategorizations: Patterns or parities. *Learning Disabilities Quarterly, 7,* 136–156.

Kennard, M. (1936). Age and other factors in motor recovery from precentral lesions in monkeys. *Journal of Neuropsychology, 1,* 447–496.

Kennard, M. (1942). Cortical reorganization of motor function: Studies on series of monkeys of various ages from infancy to maturity. *Archives of Neurology and Psychiatry, 47,* 227–240.

Kinsbourne, M., & Warrington, E. (1963). Developmental factors in reading and writing backwardness. *British Journal of Psychology, 54,* 145–156.

Kostura, D. D. (1993). Using the WISC-R freedom from distractibility factor to identify attention deficit hyperactivity disorder in children referred for psychoeducational assessment. *Canadian Journal of Special Education, 9,* 91–99.

Kugelmass, I. N., Poull, L. E., & Rudnich, J. (1938). Mental growth of epileptic children. *American Journal of Diseases in Children, 55,* 295–303.

Kurtzke, J. F., & Kurland, L. T. (1984). The epidemiology of neurological disease. In A. B. Baker & L. H. Baker (Eds.), *Clinical neurology.* Philadelphia: Harper & Row.

Lansdell, H. (1962). Laterality of verbal intelligence in the brain. *Science, 135,* 922–923.

Lansdell, H. (1969). Verbal and nonverbal functions in right-hemisphere speech. *Journal of Comparative and Physiological Psychology,* 734–738.

Lange-Cosack, H., & Tepfer, G. (1973). *Das hirntrauma im kinder-und jugendalter* [Brain trauma in children and adolescents]. New York: Springer.

Levin, H. S., Benton, A. L., Grossman, R. G. (1982). *Neurobehavioral consequences of closed head injury.* New York: Oxford University Press.

Levin, H. S., & Eisenberg, H. M. (1979). Neuropsychological impairment after closed head injury in children and adolescents. *Journal of Pediatric Psychology, 4,* 389–402.

Levin, H. S., Eisenberg, H. M., & Miner, M. E. (1983). Neuropsychologic findings in head injured children. In K. Shapiro (Ed.), *Pediatric head trauma.* New York: Futura.

Levin, H. S., Eisenberg, H. M., Wigg, N. R., & Kobayashi, K. (1982). Memory and intellectual ability after head injury in children and adolescents. *Neurosurgery, 11,* 668–673.

Lewandowski, L. J., & DeRienzo, P. J. (1985). WISC-R and K-ABC performance of hemiplegic children. *Journal of Psychoeducational Assessment, 3,* 215–221.

Lorber, J. (1971). Results of treatment of myelomeningocele. *Developmental Medicine and Child Neurology, 13,* 279–303.

Luria, A. R. (1980). *Higher cortical functions in man.* New York: Basic Books.

Milhorat, T. H. (1982). Hydrocephalus: Historical notes, etiology, and clinical diagnosis. In R. C. McLaurin (Ed.), *Pediatric neurosurgery: Surgery of the developing nervous system* (pp. 197–210). Orlando, FL: Grune & Stratton.

Mokros, H. B., Poznanski, E. O., & Merrick, W. A. (1989). Depression and learning disabilities in children: A test of an hypothesis. *Journal of Learning Disabilities, 22,* 230–233.

Morgan, A. E., Hynd, G. W., Hall, J., Novey, E. S., & Eliopulos, D. (1997). *Planum temporale morphology and linguistic abilities.* Manuscript submitted for publication.

Morris, J. M., & Bigler, E. D. (1987). Hemispheric functioning and the Kaufman Assessment Battery for Children: Results in the neurologically impaired. *Developmental Neuropsychology, 3,* 67–79.

Myrianthopoulos, N. C., & Kurland, L. T. (1961). Present concepts of the epidemiology and genetics of hydrocephalus. In W. S. Fields & M. M. Desmonds (Eds.), *Disorders of the developing nervous system* (pp. 83–106). Springfield, IL: Charles C. Thomas.

Nass, R. D., Koch, D. A., Janowsky, J., & Stiles-Davis, (1985). Differential effects on intelligence of early left versus right brain injury. *Annals of Neurology, Abstracts, 18,* 393.

Newman, S., Wright, S., & Fields, H. (1989). Identifying subtypes of reading and spelling disorders by discrepancy scores. *The Irish Journal of Psychology, 10,* 647–656.

O'Leary, D. S., Lovell, M. R., Sackellares, J. C., et al. (1983). Effects of age onset of partial and generalized seizures on neuropsychological performance in children. *Journal of Nervous and Mental Disease, 171,* 624–629.

O'Leary, D. S., Seidenberg, M., Berent, S., & Boll, T. J. (1981). Effects of age onset of tonic–clonic seizures on neuropsychological performance in children. *Epilepsia, 22,* 197–204.

Patchett, R. F., & Stansfield, M. (1992). Subtest scatter on the WISC-R with children of superior intelligence. *Psychology in the Schools, 29,* 5–11.

Phelps, L., Leguori, S., Nisewaner, K., & Parker, M. (1993). Practical interpretations of the WISC-III with language disordered children. *Journal of Psychoeducational Assessment,* WISC-III Monograph, 71–76.

Pirozzolo, F. J. (1979). *The neuropsychology of developmental reading disorders.* New York: Praeger Press.

Pirozzolo, F. J. (1981). *Language and current status and application.* Washington, DC: Hemisphere.

Prifitera, A., & Dersh, J. (1993). Base rates of WISC-III diagnostic subtest patterns among normal, learning disabled, and ADHD samples. *Journal of Psychoeducational Assessment,* WISC-III Monograph, 43–55.

Rasmussen, T., & Milner, B. (1977). The role of early left brain injury in determining lateralization of cerebral speech functions. *Annals of the New York Academy of Science, 299,* 255–369.

Reitan, R. M. (1981, July). *Effects of age of onset of brain damage on later development.* Paper presented at the Reitan Neuropsychological Workshop, Chicago, IL.

Reynolds, C. R., (1981). Neuropsychological assessment and the habilitation of learning: Considerations in the search for aptitude X treatment interaction. *School Psychology Review, 10,* 343–349.

Riccio, C. A., Cohen, M. J., Hall, J., & Ross, C. M. (in press). The third and fourth factors of the WISC-III: What they don't measure. *Journal of Psychoeducational Assessment.*

Rimel, R. W., & Jane, J. A. (1983).Characteristics of the head-injured patient. In M. Rosenthal, M. R. Bond, J. D. Miller, & E. R. Griffith (Eds.), *Rehabilitation of the head injured adult* (pp. 347–356). Philadelphia: Davis.

Rourke, B. P. (1989). *Nonverbal learning disabilities: The syndrome and the model.* New York: Guilford.

Rourke, B. P., Fisk, J. L., & Strang, J. D. (1986). *Neuropsychological assessment of children: A treatment-oriented approach.* New York: Guilford.

Rourke, B. P., Young, G. C., & Flewelling, R. W. (1971). The relationship between WISC verbal performance discrepancies and selective verbal, auditory-perceptual, visual-perceptual, and problem solving abilities in children with learning disabilities. *Journal of Clinical Psychology, 27,* 465–479.

Rowland, L. P. (1981). Blood–brain barrier, cerebrospinal fluid, brain edema and hydrocephalus. In E. C. Kandel & J. H. Schwartz (Eds.), *Principles of neural science* (pp. 651–659). New York: Elsevier.

Saccuzzo, D. P. (1992). Verbal versus performance IQ's in gifted African American, Caucasian, Filipino, and Hispanic children. *Psychological Assessment, 4,* 239–244.

Seidenberg, M., Giordani, B., Berent, S., & Boll, T. J. (1983). IQ level and performance on the Halstead-Reitan Neuropsychological Test Battery for older children. *Journal of Consulting and Clinical Psychology, 51,* 406–413.

Shapiro, E. G., & Doltan, N. (1986). The Kaufman Assessment Battery for Children and neurologic findings. *Developmental Neuropsychology, 2,* 51–64.

Slate, J. R. (1995). Discrepancies between IQ and index scores for a clinical sample of students: Useful diagnostic indicators? *Psychology in the Schools, 32,* 103–108.

Smith, B. P., & Gfeller, J. D. (1995, November).*The WISC-III factor structure in a clinical population: Will the real factors please stand up?* Presented at the 15th Annual Conference of the National Academy of Neuropsychology, San Francisco, CA.

Sofijanov, N. G. (1982). Clinical evolution and prognosis of childhood epilepsy. *Epilepsia, 23,* 61–91.

Spain, B. (1974). Verbal and performance ability in children with spina bifida. *Developmental Medicine and Child Neurology, 16,* 773–780.

Spearman, C., & Jones, L. (1950). *Human abilities.* London: MacMillan.

Stone, B. J. (1992). Joint factor analysis of the DAS and WISC-R. *Diagnostique, 17,* 176–184.

Swisher, L. P., & Pinsker, E. J. (1971).The language characteristics of hyperverbal, hydrocephalic children. *Developmental Medicine and Child Neurology, 13,* 746–755.

Taylor, R. L., Ziegler, E. W., & Partenio, I. (1984). An investigation of WISC-R verbal-performance differences as a function of ethnic status. *Psychology in the Schools, 21,* 437–441.

Teeter, P. A. (1986). Standard neuropsychological batteries for children. In G. W. Hynd & J. E. Obrzut (Eds.), *Child neuropsychological: Vol. 2. Perspective in neurolinguistics, neuropsychology, and psycholinguistics: A series of monographs and treatises* (pp. 187–227). New York: Academic Press.

Tenney, J. W. (1955). Epileptic children in Detroit's special school program: A study. *Exceptional Children, 21,* 162–167.

Tew, B., & Laurence, K. M. (1979). The clinical and psychological characteristics of children with the "cocktail party" syndrome. *Zeitschrift fur Kinderchirurgie, 28,* 360–367.

Tramontana, M., & Hooper S. (1987). *Neuropsychological assessment of children.* New York: Plenum Press.

Walsh, A. (1992). The P > V sign in corrections: Is it a useful diagnostic tool? *Criminal Justice and Behavior, 19,* 372–383.

Walsh, A., & Beyer, J. A. (1986). Wechsler performance–verbal discrepancy and anti-social behavior. *Journal of Social Psychology, 126,* 419–420.

Wechsler, D. (1949). *Manual for the Wechsler Intelligence Scale for Children.* San Antonio, TX: The Psychological Corporation.

Wechsler, D. (1958). *The measurement and appraisal of adult intelligence (4th ed.).* Baltimore, MD: Williams & Wilkins.

Wechsler, D. (1974). *Manual for the Wechsler Intelligence Scale for Children—Revised.* New York: The Psychological Corporation.

Wechsler, D. (1991). *Manual for the Wechsler Intelligence Scale for Children—Third Edition.* New York: The Psychological Corporation.

Wilkinson, S. C. (1993). WISC-R profiles of children with superior intellectual ability. *Gifted Child Quarterly, 37,* 84–91.

Witt, J. C., & Gresham, F. M. (1985). Review of the Wechsler Intelligence Scale for Children—Revised. In J. V. Mitchell (Ed.), *Ninth mental measurement yearbook* (pp. 1716–1719). Lincoln, NE: University of Nebraska Press.

Woodcock, R. W. (1990). Theoretical foundations of the WJ-R measures of cognitive ability. *Journal of Psychoeducational Assessment, 8,* 231–258.

Woods, B. T. (1980). The restricted effects of right hemisphere lesions after age one: Wechsler test data. *Neuropsychologia, 18,* 65–70.

Woods, B. T., & Teuber, H. L. (1973). Early onset of complementary specialization of cerebral hemispheres in man. *Transactions of the American Neurological Association, 98,* 113–117.

11

ASSESSMENT OF MINORITY
AND CULTURALLY DIVERSE
CHILDREN

ANTONIO E. PUENTE AND GABRIEL D. SALAZAR

Department of Psychology
University of North Carolina at Wilmington
Wilmington, North Carolina

INTRODUCTION

"Are the inferior races really inferior, or are they merely unfortunate in their lack of opportunity to learn? Only intelligence tests can answer these questions" (Terman, 1916, p. 20). By 1932, alternative suggestions for addressing the issue began to appear in the psychological literature. Sanchez (1932), often considered the founder of Chicano psychology, published in the *Journal of Applied Psychology* that mental testing biases existed against Mexican children. Well over half a century later these questions remain unanswered, but the debates continue in the public and professional sectors. The role of culture, ethnicity, and race are central and controversial issues in both the definition and measurement of intellectual functions. One need not look further than the recent publication of Herrnstein and Murray's (1994) *The Bell Curve* for illustrations of the importance and timeliness of this topic. The relevance of these variables in the unbiased assessment of intellectual and general cognitive abilities is critical (Betancourt & Lopez, 1993) and are highlighted in the most recent American Psychological Association (APA) guidelines on this topic. In 1993, APA published the "Guidelines for Providers of

Parts of this chapter, including the section on Aboriginal and Native American Children, were written by D. H. Saklofske.

227

Psychological Services to Ethnic, Linguistic, and Culturally Diverse Populations" (APA, 1993). Interestingly, the focus of those guidelines appear to be centered more around intervention rather than assessment practices.

The purpose of this chapter, despite the importance of addressing more central issues of the role of ethnicity, race, and related variables on testing (see Puente, in press, for a broader review), will be to examine the relationship between ethnicity and race and the three Wechsler scales for assessing children's intelligence, especially the earlier versions of this test where much of the research on this issue is found. Furthermore, as a means to better understand the role of these complex variables on cognitive functions as measured by the Wechsler tests, special emphasis will be placed not on race but on ethnicity. If Lewontin, Rose, and Kamin (1984) are correct, race accounts for approximately 6% of genetic variability. Hence, it is difficult to account for large-scale differences between groups using race as a factor. Indeed, within-race variability, if different ethnic-racial group configurations are considered, is greater than between-race variability, especially if no large-scale cultural variation (e.g., adding Whites from two different countries such as United States and Russia) is introduced.

Here it will be assumed that whatever differences exist in intelligence and cognition are more culturally than racially determined. This assumption does not negate or even presuppose the existence of racial differences in intellectual functions. What it does do is help to reconfigure reported racial differences based on cultural rather than biological variables. Thus we believe that culture may have a greater impact on cognitive functions than race. Further, it could be that what is measured on standardized tests of cognitive abilities when race is an independent variable is simply the culture associated with the race rather than race itself. In other words, even though data are sparse on this topic, we believe that Blacks from two quite different cultures (e.g., USA and Zaire) may be more dissimilar than Caucasians and Blacks both living in similar geographic regions of the United States. This issue has been raised in descriptions of Aboriginal children where the belief may be held that there is, for example, only one type of hunting-gathering society. In contrast, the socioecological context of Aboriginal children is most important in describing their intellectual, behavioral, and social characteristics. Murdoch (1988) contends that whether Aboriginal children are from "hunter-gathering," "pastoral," or "agrarian" backgrounds has critical implications for the types of sociocultural adaptations they manifest. Furthermore, "the cultural and linguistic experiences of most Native American children, however, differ considerably from those of the middle-class, monolingual, English-speaking students upon whom most standardized intelligence tests were normed" (Tanner-Halverson, Burden, & Sabers, 1993, p. 125).

The pioneering studies of Scarr (e.g., Scarr & Weinberg, 1976) also suggest that culture may be more critical than race in determining differences on tests. This view has been further elaborated by Moore (1987), who found not only that the ethnicity of the family but also the ethnic milieu help explain IQ score differences. It is not only the family culture but the culture in which the child interacts daily that help to explain cognitive test differences. Further support for this departure from conventional thinking is warranted based on the overstating of race as a salient factor in intellectual functioning (Rowe, 1994) and the understating of the impact of culture on basic cognitive functions (Ardila, 1995). The work of Ardila (Ardila, Rosselli, & Puente, 1994) has also suggested that culture plays a critical role in the measurement of basic neuropsychological functions.

This readjustment from a racial to a cultural perspective may help further clarify some of the existing literature on this topic. However, an initial step in this approach is to define the differences between race, ethnicity, and culture. The next section of the chapter outlines the definition of culture, race, and ethnicity, especially as it pertains to the issue of how children from a nonmajority group (e.g., African Americans) fit into a majority group (e.g., White, Anglo-Saxon).

DEFINING RACE, ETHNICITY, AND CULTURE

Besides the fact that these variables have traditionally not been well researched in psychology, there is a general confusion about their differences. Although Jones (1991) has argued that race is difficult to operationalize, there is some agreement as to how to generally describe races. Obvious biological characteristics include skin color, facial features, and hair type (Betancourt & Lopez, 1993). However, other variables might include size and other related physical characteristics. According to Brislin (1989), there are three races; Caucasian, Negroid, and Indian (with two subcomponents, Asian and American).

Ethnicity is more diffuse and is behaviorally rather than biologically based. Specifically, ethnicity refers to a set pattern of behaviors that might include rituals, beliefs, customs, common ancestry, as well as family, social, and even marital restrictions. In contrast, culture is a wider defined pattern of behavior, which is generally more widely accepted across a number of ethnic groups. These patterns are more ingrained, socially less questioned, and often considered to be universal in scope. For example, Western culture is very focused on time, and more ethnic groups in the Western culture consider time to be of critical importance in everyday life. However, different ethnic groups view time in different ways. Ethnic groups in northern climates, especially with European ancestry, consider time a critical component in a variety of factors, ranging from intelligence to common courtesy. In contrast, ethnic groups closer to the Equator view time as something that occurs, and secondary to the enjoyment of the activity in question. Thus, it is not surprising that when time, namely speed, plays an important role in arriving at a conclusion regarding cognitive ability, people with ethnic origins close to the Equator may appear less intelligent than those with ancestry in northern climates.

It is important to emphasize that these three variables are not necessarily unique or independent. Indeed, the opposite may be more true than the principles of experimental methodology would allow to be easily detected. For example, there are Blacks that have their ancestry in the warm climates just as there are several

TABLE 11.1   Ethnicity and Race According to the 1990 U.S. Census Data: Origin, Total
Numbers, and Subgroups

Spanish/Hispanic/Latin Background or Origin
  Origin = Latin America or Spain; Total = 22,354,059
  Cuban
  Mexican/Mexican-American/Chicano
  Puerto Rican
  Hispanic Latin American (e.g., Panamanian, Peruvian, Venezuelan, Ecuadorian, Guatemalan, etc.)
  Spaniard
African American/Black/Negro
  Origin = African or Caribbean; Total = 29,986,060
Asian or Pacific Islander
  Origin = Far East, Southeast Asia, Indian Subcontinent, or Pacific Islands; Total = 7,273,662
  Asian Indian
  Chinese
  Japanese
  Korean
  Vietnamese
  Filipino
  Hawaiian
Indian (American) or Alaska Native
  Origin = North America; Total = 1,959,234
  Aleut
  American Indian
  Eskimo
White
  Origin = Europe, North America, Middle East; Total = 199,686,070

---

generations of Hispanics that have been raised strictly in northern climates (e.g., New York, Chicago). Furthermore, there is the complication of socioeconomic status. Laosa (1984), among others, reported that economic status is often not controlled for or measured, but when it is this variable has a critical impact in explaining the effects of race, ethnicity, and culture. This important issue has also been raised in chapter 1 of this book.

Another issue raised above that is rarely addressed is that of subgroup heterogeneity. Not all Whites have similar ethnic backgrounds. This is best illustrated with Hispanics. According to the Census Bureau, there are at least five different types of Hispanics. Cuban, Mexican/Mexican-American/Chicano, Puerto Rican, Hispanic Latin American (e.g., Panamanian, Peruvian, Venezuelan, Ecuadorean, Guatemalan), and Spaniard (originally from Spain). Table 11.1 provides a more specific breakdown according to the different ethnic groups as well as the 1990 Census data. As this table indicates, blacks outnumber other groups but only by a relatively small amount when compared with Hispanics. When considering the different subgroups, the question arises as to whether within-group heterogeneity could tend to obscure between-group differences. For example, when Hispanics are subdivided into smaller groups (e.g., Puerto Ricans, Cubans, etc.) it appears that Cubans parallel the general majority culture, whereas Puerto Ricans show the most differences (Garcia & Marotta, 1977).

CONTROVERSIAL ISSUES

Underlying the potential differences in performance on intellectual tests, in general, and the Wechsler tests in particular, are a host of variables that differentially affect cognitive functions and functioning. These variables have been the focus of two major if not controversial reports in recent years. In the highly controversial book, *The Bell Curve,* Herrnstein and Murray (1994) present some provocative ideas and interpretations that warrant attention when attempting to identify ethnic group differences in intellectual performance. A major premise is the rise of the "cognitive elite." This social class, highly predicted by intelligence test scores, are physically segregated through educational and vocational channels and institutions. Their review of the literature suggests that Asians have higher IQs, whereas Hispanics score ½ to 1 standard deviation, and Blacks about 1 standard deviation below Whites. Intelligence test findings for North American Aboriginal samples often show further that score differences exist not only in culturally loaded items but also in more neutral items. For example, differences are evident in both digit span forward and backward, and more so on the backward items. Such differences, according to Herrnstein and Murray, are due to motivation, knowledge of standard English, success and failure expectations on these tests, and so forth. The authors argue that up to 60% of the variance in intelligence test scores appears to be inherited and, thus, intelligence may not be that malleable through environmental interventions. To complicate matters, the authors propose that individuals with social problems are heavily represented in the lower portion of the cognitive ability distribution. Without actually resolving matters, this book has spurred active discussions on the historically controversial topics discussed by Galton during the 19th century and by Terman at the beginning of this century.

Probably the major and most official response from the psychological community was the report "Intelligence: Knowns and Unknowns" published by a Task Force appointed by the Board of Scientific Affairs of the American Psychological Association (Neisser et al., 1995). In this report, a number of major topic areas were reviewed, including the concept of intelligence, intelligence tests and their correlates, genetics and intelligence, environmental effects on intelligence, and group differences. In a particularly important section of this paper, ethnic group differences were considered. One possible way to explain the apparent differences between ethnic groups was to consider socioeconomic and related cultural factors. The authors concluded, "Thus the issue ultimately comes down to a personal judgement," (p. 35) and they add that at present scientific answers for these differences are still elusive.

However, the Neisser et al. report and the Herrnstein and Murray book have had critics and criticism. According to Lane (1994), the sources cited in *The Bell*

Curve, appear to be "tainted," thus resulting in biased and incorrect conclusions. Lane stated that a large number of sources are from individuals associated with the periodical *The Mankind Quarterly* and the Pioneer Fund, both associated with "race betterment," presumably of the white race. A number of in-depth reviews of this book were published in the *School Psychology Review* (volume 24, number 1) in 1995. The Neisser et al. report has similarly been critiqued, though not as aggressively. For example, as part of series of commentaries in the *American Psychologist,* Rushton and Yee (1997) suggested that IQ differences need to be considered as a function of not just environmental but hereditary issues. Yee also (1997) described the suggested links between IQ and socioeconomic status and race.

TECHNICAL ISSUES

The proposed differences between different ethnic groups may be partially or even largely attributable to methodological issues in research. It could be that such differences exist not because of internal variables that are neurologically and genetically based determinants of cognitive capacity but because of external variables, such as test content or administration. For example, Terrell and Terrell (1983) reported that race of examiner appears to have an effect on Black children's performance on standardized cognitive tasks. Saklofske and Janzen (1990) have described the potential problems that might arise when tests developed and standardized in one country are then used in another country. Cicchetti (1994) provided an interesting perspective on how to evaluate normed and standardized instruments in psychology. His approach included careful attention to standardization procedures, norming procedures, test reliability, and test validity. However, no reference in the text nor in the citations is made to potential issues of bias so comprehensively discussed in the psychological literature (e.g., Reynolds, 1995). However, the usual criteria for evaluating the efficacy of instruments appears a good one from which to begin the difficult task of examining the efficacy of intellectual tests for ethnic-minority children. This section attempts to address some of the more salient methodological issues that could help account for the differences described in *The Bell Curve* and the journal article, "Intelligence: Knowns and Unknowns" but which are often ignored in the applied world of assessment (a particularly thorough assessment of test validity as applied to Hispanics is found in Geisinger, 1992).

Padilla (1988, 1995) Olmedo (1981), and Westmeyer (1987) are modern pioneers following in the footsteps of Garcia, who in the 1930s suggested that people from minority groups (e.g., linguistic, racial, etc.) have to be understood from a different vantage point. To do otherwise would confound "abnormality" (statistical or clinical) with culture-based behavior patterns or communication difficulties. According to Olmedo (1981), when linguistic minorities are tested several factors are often ignored: type of test used, socioeconomic class, degree of bilingualism, language-based factors, ability to communicate in the nonmajority language, acculturation, and cultural equivalence. Pragmatic factors in these circumstances include language proficiency, language of test examiner, language used in the evaluation, translations, translators, etc. For example, Hanley and Barclay (1979) reported that race of the child and the tester interacted negatively on WISC and WISC-R scores. Cross-cultural researchers have sensitized psychologists to these observations. "Emic" and "etic" were coined by Pike (1966) to represent two viewpoints in the study of human behavior. The "etic" viewpoint seeks to discover universals in a system, but when universals are assumed, this is termed "imposed etic." It may be argued that "great risk attends the use of an imposed etic, since there would be no way of knowing whether it makes any sense to use it in any culture than that of its origin" (Berry, Poortinga, Segall, & Dasen, 1992, p. 54).

The "emic" viewpoint studies behavior from within the cultural system. Here it is recognized that understanding can only occur in reference to the context in which behavior takes place. Thus an intelligence test that is rooted in one culture but used as though it was valid for some other culture may result in very inaccurate and even tragic conclusions. Examples of potential item bias on the WISC-III for Native American children is described by Tanner-Halverson et al. (1993) and for Canadian Aboriginal Children by Greenough-Olson (1993). The assumption that mainstream culture, socialization, and language are the same for Native children as for the White children is an imposed etic. In fact, the research literature shows some quite consistent findings for the performance of Native children on the WISC-R and WISC-III, with the general trend being lower Verbal IQ (VIQ) than Performance IQ (PIQ) scores (e.g., McShane & Plas, 1984; Scaldwell, Frame, & Cookson, 1985; Wilgosh, Mulcahy, & Walters, 1986), as well as lower Full-Scale IQs (FSIQs) in relation to the standardization data (ie., $\bar{x} - 100$, $SD = 15$); (e.g., Tanner-Halverson et al., 1993).

From these complex set of variables, possibly a common factor could be extracted. Beyond the obvious problems of communication (especially when English is not the original language) is the underlying issue of cultural equivalence. Although much attention has been given to addressing the issue of test bias, whether due to socioeconomic status, language, or whatever, the question of intent still remains. Specifically, what is the goal or purpose of intelligence testing. Helms (1992) has argued that ethnic differences in cognitive ability are actually differences in culture, and no necessarily due to either biological or environmental determinants. In other words, if the goal is to measure the intellectual ability of the child, then testing a Spanish-speaking child in English, or an Aboriginal child from a remote northern settlement by a White examiner from the 'deep' south, may result in a less than contextually sensitive assessment. In contrast, the alternative might be to test a Spanish-speaking child's ability to understand the intellectual demands of the Anglo-Saxon culture. The second intention would not reflect a bias but rather a different and more difficult goal.

Defining the goal of assessment establishes a direction and a set of guidelines from which one can carry out the necessary testing. If the question is one of intellectual acculturation, then testing variations such as the use of English IQ tests for Spanish children might be appropriate. If the question relates more to an assessment of intellectual ability, then matching the test to a larger set of intellectual concepts that are global rather than cultural would appear to make more sense. La Frambroise, Coleman, and Gerton (1993) provide support for a psychological viewpoint on biculturalism and a perspective from which to address this problem. Thus an initial and critical issue is to determine what the goal of the intellectual testing might be. In most cases, the location or position of the child within an intellectual spectrum as defined by the majority culture would be one obvious choice. However, underlying this criterion would be an important secondary question; what capabilities does the child have that will enable him or her to assimilate and accommodate critical 'data' from the majority culture?

Several important technical variables may influence our description of the child within a cognitive framework. Regardless of ethnic background, these variables have received some attention in the literature. The variables addressed here include samples tested, language and communication, and acculturation.

SAMPLES

It is often assumed that is a child does not belong to a majority group (i.e., the reference group), they belong to a homogeneous minority group. Homogeneity is often associated with limited variation in a host of variables, including race, language, socioeconomic background, and even religion in some instances. Such an approach is fraught with problems. Chrisjohn and Lanigan (1986) have commented on the frequent presence of "Pan-Indianism" in the research literature. Pan-Indianism refers to the treatment of members of different native nations as a homogeneous group. However, they argue against this viewpoint by stating that not a single study has demonstrated a universal Aboriginal cognition. It is this tremendous variability in intelligence test scores that has led Brandt (1984) to state that "the high degree of variability of scores in Native American populations is the major reason researchers have little confidence in the WISC-R as an assessment instrument" (p. 75).

To further illustrate this point, Hispanics are a nonmajority group composed of a variety of subgroups, including Mexicans, Puerto Ricans, Central Americans, Cubans, and so on. Furthermore, these individuals may either be black or white, yellow, or some combination thereof (most often seen in the Caribbean). Finally, these individuals may be monolingual, bilingual, or mixed. Thus, when a test is normed on Hispanics, African Americans, or Aboriginal peoples in either Canada or the United States, for example, a number of problems are bound to arise. An African American who lives in affluent America with an ancestry going back several generations in the United States would be more likely to perform like a White person with an affluent background than a newly emigrated Haitian Black with limited resources and a different cultural history. Thus, it is extremely important to sort through these kinds of variables when considering the appropriateness of both the test and the test norms.

Many of the issues raised throughout this chapter mainly focus on black and Hispanic children, in part due to the large numbers they represent in the WISC-R and WISC-III standardization samples and in the general population of the United States. However, it is important to note that these issues in intelligence testing probably apply to other ethnic minority groups as well. Further, studies are now available (e.g., Yang, Su, Qhang, & Ta, 1995, see also chapter 1, by Prifitera et al., this volume) that have examined the Wechsler test performance of children in different countries and even translated the WISC-R and WISC-III into other languages.

COMMUNICATION AND LANGUAGE

The assumption is made in any testing situation that meaningful communication has been effectively established between the examiner and the test taker. Furthermore, when communication has not been established an assumption may be made that language differences exist (e.g., the English-speaking psychologist is testing a Spanish-speaking child), which may then hinder the meaningful communication of instructions and concepts (Malgady, Rogler, & Constantinio, 1987). This communication, which is most frequently verbally established, is not the sole means of transmitting information. A host of other communication variables exist; social boundaries, use of slang, eye and physical contact, and the relationship between the tester and the examinee when cultural and linguistic differences are present. Thus, communication is obviously multifaceted, with far-reaching effects on the measurement of intellectual functions. One such effort to address this issue was the somewhat controversial publication of *The Black Intelligence Test of Cultural Homogeneity,* which contained 100 vocabulary words used mainly in African-American settings (Williams, 1975).

Bilingualism may also present a problem when assessing some children. It is often commonly assumed that if a child can speak enough English to take an IQ test, then they should be proficient in that language. Laosa (1975) suggested that this is an oversimplification of a more complicated situation. In interviewing nearly 300 Hispanic children and their families, he found the following patterns of communication; English is the single most frequently used language, Spanish is the single most frequently used language, both English and Spanish were used without mixing, and English and Spanish were equally used with mixing.

Thus assumptions that are made about a child's proficiency in one or more languages could actually be wrong. Hickey (1972) tested two groups of 100 students, monolingual (Spanish and English) and bilingual. He reported that Mexican-American children had difficulty associating English verbal nouns with pictures because of the differences between the two languages. Manuel-Dupont, Ardila, Rosselli, and Puente (1992) have argued that bilingualism is a complex concept rooted both in sociocultural traditions and in neurological substrates. Such variables as the method of language acquisition, age and sequence of acquisition, and the structure of the languages in question all affect the 'imprinting' of language in the brain and subsequent use (e.g., speaking, comprehension).

Finally, it is important to appreciate that bilingualism is not restricted only to obvious differences in the language. In other words, subtle differences in verbal communication (e.g., standard and black English) are probably sufficient to result in some of the problems and issues outlined in this section. As early as the mid-part of this century language differences between Welsh and English-speaking children in the United Kingdom had been reported (Jones, 1952). A recently published statement on conducting assessments of non-English individuals (de Jesus, Perrin, and Blackwood, 1996) provides an overview of general principles of communication with individuals of a nonmajority group culture.

ACCULTURATION

Perhaps the most salient factor that is related to all the previous variables discussed above is that of acculturation. Acculturation in this instance is not considered in the classical sense but instead is viewed in a broader context, as described by Laosa (1991). He identified the problem of construct validity in the testing of minority population as a critical ethical problem. Specifically, the assumption is made that the intellectual domains of the test in question reflect a cultural 'g' of some sort. The test could therefore be biased in a very specific sense. For example, one of the WAIS-R Picture Completion items involves a map of the United States without the state of Florida. Even very impaired or culturally limited individuals living in Florida were able to obtain a correct response, whereas the same could not be said of similar individuals living in North Carolina. Similarly, Aboriginal children from remote settlements in northern Canada often give very different answers to test items, such as what they should do if they see a house on fire. Here there are no fire departments, police, or phones to call 911.

The question of what is intellectually salient may be more critical. This might include very basic questions involving some of the following variables: response to authority figure (tester), acknowledgment and manipulation of time as a critical element, expression of confidence as either an unwarranted coping mechanism or a lack of courtesy to others, and the understanding of complex cultural concepts. Also, the role of sociocultural variables needs to be considered. Barona, Santos de Barona, and Faykus (1993) reported that these variables accounted for a significant degree of the variance in Mexican-American students diagnosed with mental retardation.

Ellis (1990) examined cross-national comparisons of intelligence using translated versions of the Wilde Intelligence Test and the Career Ability Placement Survey. She concluded that cross-national comparisons of intelligence and abilities might result in incorrect conclusions when translation equivalence is not established. The question of what is important and relevant for one majority group versus another must also be considered together with the question of cultural equivalence. Understanding the basic concepts of the culture in question is essential to appreciating its similarities and differences with other cultures. For example, Nobles (1995) has provided an interesting background of what is called "African philosophy." This philosophy provides a critical backdrop from which to understand culturally based intellectual concepts.

The concept of equivalence is not restricted just to the words of a language but to a host of other factors all contained under the general rubric of culture. Casagrande (1954; in Bontempo 1993) has identified four types of translations. These include pragmatic, aesthetic-poetic, ethnographic, and linguistic. It is assumed that when a test is "translated" by a test administrator for a child, what is typically occurring is pragmatic translation. The question involves something like, "We need to obtain a general idea of the intellectual abilities of this child . . . do what you can." This approach reduces translation fidelity (Bontempo, 1993) and increases measurement error. It is for all of these reasons and more that different cultural and language groups contend that the commonly employed tests and testing practices in schools may provide an inaccurate and unfair assessment of particular examinees. For example, in Canada, the Saskatchewan Indian Institute of Technology (SIIT, 1990) recognized this problem in their Aboriginal Literacy Action Plan as follows:

> Most of the testing instruments are inappropriate. They are culturally irrelevant and geared toward white middle class society. Indian educators should be able to develop their own testing instruments using means and methods that will be relevant and familiar to Indian Students. The testing that our Indian students are presently being subjected to is another reason for their frustration and discouragement, because they do not do well on these tests. (p. 44).

ASSESSING CHILDREN'S INTELLIGENCE WITH THE WESCHLER SCALES

Before describing the findings from studies of the WISC performance of children from different groups, several relevant issues regarding such test findings will be raised here. First, the study of intelligence across cultural, ethnic groups may be viewed from within three broad paradigms described by Berry (1984). The general intelligence paradigm assumes that intelligence is a single construct that is common across all people so that comparing culturally different groups will indicate who has more or less of this general intelligence, if there are differences at all. The "specific abilities" paradigm reflects our emic perspective, in which the emphasis is on the culturally relative nature of cognition. Here there is no assumption relating to universal patterns of intelligence so that cross-cultural comparisons are not especially relevant or meaningful. The cognitive styles paradigm is also based on a position of cultural relativism but in addition searches for systematic connections among abilities. For example, More (1987) has outlined the cognitive style characteristics of Aboriginal children while also recognizing that there are many within-group differences. These differing paradigms remind us that studies of the WISC across cultural, ethnic, and even racial groupings reflects but one perspective in the study of cognition and intelligence.

Another major issue related to the cross-cultural study of intelligence is tied to the contentious problem of bias. While Jensen (1980) is often credited with "leading the charge" on the problem of bias and ethnic differences in intellectual tests and assessment, much had been written before him (Kaufman & Doppelt, 1976; Reschely, 1978; Sandoval, 1979). The early writings of Terman (Terman, 1916; Terman and Merril, 1937) provide an interesting insight into the difficulties surrounding this issue. More recently Sattler (1988) has summarized some of the key themes thought to underlie test bias. The finding of differences in mean scores between two groups has been suggested as evidence of test bias. However, Sattler contends that such differences are not indicative of test bias since differences between the test scores of a minority group and the majority group may reflect differences in socioeconomic status. Another suggestion that a test may be biased is related to how good a predictor it is of some criteria across two or more groups. A third criterion for evaluating test bias relates to whether the instrument measures the same abilities across different groups. The items or test content have been suggested as a cause of that bias. Reynolds and Wilson (1983) has also included examiner and language bias and inappropriate standardization samples among the reasons for suspected bias and criticism of intelligence tests.

Two of these points will be briefly commented on to illustrate how they relate to the Wechsler Scales for assessing intelligence in children. Although the WISC-III (Wechsler, 1991) was published in 1991, most studies involving ethnic-minorities are based on data from the WISC and the WISC-R. Hence, the majority of discussions center around these studies, although chapter 1 of this book reexamines the WISC-III performance of Black and Hispanic children. It is important to note that despite the relatively minimal bias that had been reported for earlier versions of the WISC, the WISC-III used item-bias statistics to eliminate potentially biased items (primarily restricted to Information, Vocabulary, and Comprehension subtests) and also obtained expert's reviews of items for potential bias.

The sample obtained for the WISC-III reflects the 1988 United States Census survey. A particularly interesting approach to ethnic identification involved the use of the parents of Hispanic children to identify their children as Hispanic or otherwise. Furthermore, Hispanic ethnicity was not confounded with race. Blacks were sampled in exact proportion to their representation by age group, whereas Hispanics were very closely sampled relative to their representation in the different age groups. Also, similar representation was noted for ethnicity by geographical region, which is a particularly difficult task in a large sampling study of this type. Furthermore, during standardization, an extra 400 minority children were used. This effort did not go unnoticed by Kaufman (1993), who reported that of the seven major changes in the WISC-III, one involved the new (and presumably comprehensive) standardization with a better definition of ethnicity.

AFRICAN AMERICANS

Based on allegations that inappropriate educational placements had occurred as a result of the test evaluation of two African-American girls in Chicago, the Chicago School Board and eventually Judge Grady ruled over a decade ago that tests of intelligence, including eight items from the WISC and WISC-R were so culturally biased that their use was considered inappropriate (Koh, Abbatiello, & McLoughlin, 1984). This was a particularly problematic issue in light of the fact that the revision of the WISC had taken into account perceived racial differences (Weschler, 1974). Yet, according to several studies by Munford and colleagues (e.g., Munford, Meyerowitz, and Munford, 1980), the differences had actually increased. However, in more refined studies with larger samples, alternative conclusions have been reached. For example, Koh et al. (1984) administered the eight alleged biased items in the Grady decision to 360 educable mentally handicapped (EMH) White and Black children. The results indicated that "the children who constituted this sample could not be discriminated on the basis of ethnicity" (p. 93). Factor analysis of the WISC-R have also been conducted for white and black children (Gutkin & Reynolds, 1981). The results suggested similar factor structures for both sets of children, and according to the authors provide support for the "growing body of research supporting the construct validity of the WISC-R across race" (p. 230).

These studies could be considered in direct contrast to those of other researchers. Kaufman and Kaufman (1983) reported up to 16-point differences between Black and White children on the WISC-R. Others (Naglieri, 1986) have reported somewhat smaller differences (i.e., 9 points). Slate and Jones (1995) recently reported on the validity of the WISC-III for African-American students undergoing special education evaluation. In general, and as expected, the results suggested lower scores for the WISC-III when compared to the WISC-R. A salient explanation for such discrepancies probably lies both in the questions asked and the methodologies used as well as the newer norms for the WISC-III. To compare studies of racial differences on the WISC by contrasting, say, the Kaufman and Kaufman (1983) with the Koh et al. (1984) results seems inappropriate at best. Indeed, in this instance one study uses the entire test, the other eight items; one uses "normal" children, the other uses EMH. Furthermore, other salient variables are not controlled. Considering the earlier discussions in this chapter, particularly important variables are not considered or even controlled for, such as socioeconomic status, parental educational achievement, race matching between tester and test taker, and so forth.

HISPANICS

According to Figeroa (1983), the argument that bias is not present in the WISC is due primarily to the adopted model and definition of bias and not the lack of bias itself. The assumption that underscores the item bias theory tested by Sandoval (1979) was that there is a specific and relatively inflexible learning curve of language and cultural knowledge across a society. Further, that learning curve is shared when others, including those with different language backgrounds, do not interact with the majority culture on an active and ongoing level. Jensen (1980) had already suggested that bias might occur when intelligence is measured in a language different than the original language of the test. Thus, one could argue that even if the tests themselves were equivalent, they would not be in other and presumably more important ways (e.g., knowledge of the culture in question). Hence, it is not surprising that despite the fact that the WISC-R was intended to be less biased than the WISC according to Wechsler (1974), that indeed the discrepancy between Hispanics and Anglos was actually greater with the WISC-R.

An alternative to this situation was to translate and standardize the WISC into Spanish (Rodriguez, de Torres, Herrans, & Aponte, 1994). This was done with varying results. In reviewing the literature, the work of Prewitt-Diaz, Rodrigues, and River (1986) provides a glimpse into the problems in question and reflects the difficulties previously outlined. The Escala de Inteligencia de Wechsler para Ninos was intended to be a test which could be used across all Spanish-speaking children. Unfortunately, the sample was based only on Puerto Rican children. A more recently published and updated version of this test reflects many of these same problems. Some of the questions did not appear to have wide generalizability to other Hispanic subcultures because the items were reflective of only indigenous Puerto Rican culture. However, the newer version of this test (Rodriguez et al., 1994) provides updated norms, alternative and better instructions for Similarities and Digit Backwards, as well as improvement on several specific items. For a historical analysis of mental testing with one group of Hispanic (Mexican) children, the reader is referred to Padilla (1988).

ABORIGINAL AND NATIVE AMERICAN CHILDREN

Although the research and clinical literature on the Wechsler test performance of Aboriginal children is relatively small, it does serve to raise issues related to differential test performance, test bias, and research methodology. Such findings are most relevant in the clinical interpretation and reporting of intelligence test data for children of Native ancestry.

A number of investigations have tended to report a pattern of lower VIQ in contrast to more average PIQ scores on the Wechsler scales (e.g., McShane & Plas, 1984). However this general finding must be further viewed within the context of other observations. St. John, Krichev, and Bauman (1976) tested 160 Cree and Ojibiway children and youth on the WISC and WAIS and found that VIQ ranged from 69.7 at 6–7 years to 91.1 at 18–20 years. In contrast PIQ ranged from 99.8 at 9–10 years to 103.4 at 18–20 years. This large Verbal-Performance (V-P) discrepancy was found among the youngest children and decreased with age. Language spoken at home was significantly related to VIQ scores. Seyfort, Spreen, and Lahmer (1980) administered the WISC-R to 177 Aboriginal children from three different West Coast Canadian bands. Again average PIQs and lower VIQs were reported but more important was the finding that a large number of test items did not contribute to the total test score or score variance. Similarly Mueller, Mulcahy, Wilgosh, Watters, and Mancini (1986) reported other item difficulty data suggesting "that these figures for the Inuit sample represent a significant increase in the overall WISC-R difficulty compared to that shown by majority children" (p. 35). Wilgosh, Mulcahy, and Walters (1986) also examined the WISC-R scores of 366 Inuit children and observed that 77% earned VIQs less than 70 in contrast to only 5.7% with PIQs less than 70. FSIQs of less than 70 were attained by 32% of the children. The Information and Vocabulary subtests accounted for the majority of items unanswered or answered incorrectly.

Turning to studies of the predictive validity of the WISC, St. John et al. (1976) found that the WISC-R VIQ and PIQ was significantly correlated with year-end school grades for only one of the four age groups in their study of Aboriginal children. A study comparing the predictive validity of the WISC-R for samples of Anglo, Black, Chicano, and Native American Papagos children found that FSIQ and the Verbal Comprehension factor were the best predictors of achievement defined by teacher ratings and the Metropolitan Achievement Test (Reschly & Reschley, 1979). However, the validity coefficients were lowest for the Native American children in comparison with the other three groups. These cumulative research findings led McCullough, Walker, and Diessner (1985) to conclude that

> caution is advised in the use of the WISC-R and WAIS with Native Americans. Significant Verbal–Performance deviations have been found across the tribes. The predictive validity of the Wechsler tests for academic achievement may vary across the Native American Cultures. (p. 29)

Several published reports have focused on the construct validity of the Wechsler Scales for children. Mulcahy and Marfo (1987) suggested that factor analytic studies of the WISC-R with Inuit children generally support the construct validity of the test for children aged 12 to 15 years but not for those 7 to 11 years of age. Chrisjohn and Lanigan (1986) argue that there is a lack of research substantiating the construct validity of the WISC-R when used with Aboriginal groups. They contend the following:

> The WISC-R may indeed measure intelligence in non-Indian populations, but fail to measure it in Indian groups. Or the Performance Subtests of the WISC-R may measure intellect well enough and the verbal subtests not. Or the WISC-R may work for "acculturated" Indians and not for less acculturated groups. Mean comparisons under the condition of not knowing whether the test behaves equivalently in experimental groups are largely meaningless. (p. 7)

Finally, the argument that factors outside of the test may impact on the WISC performance of Aboriginal children, as with other culturally different children, has been raised by various authors. Sattler (1988) states that

> whether the use of a particular test in a particular situation results in discrimination . . . will depend on such factors as the purpose to which the results are put, how the results are interpreted, and how the test is administered. (p. 568)

Many of the same factors that pertain to studies of the WISC performance of Black or Hispanic children may be raised in relation to Aboriginal children, such as the uniqueness of cultural experiences, linguistic differences, health issues, and factors associated with the testing experience. McShane (1983) cites the high incidence of otitis media as the "single leading identifiable disease among Indian populations" (p. 37), which in turn can compromise efficient language learning (Friel-Patti, 1990). McShane also notes the higher incidence of vision problems of Native children and the problem of fetal alcohol syndrome or fetal alcohol effect associated with the problem of alcoholism in some communities. Tanner-Halverson et al. (1993) argue that the cultural and linguistic experiences of Native-American children are quite different from the experiences of English-speaking, middle-class children. They contend that the WISC-III has certainly shown improvements over the WISC-R, but there is still the potential for other bias. Furthermore, they raise questions regarding the sampling strategies and test norms and contend that

> although this is the proper representation of these minority groups, the scores derived from the national standardization norm tables by no means assume that this will be unbiased for the minority group. (p. 126)

In order to address this issue, Tanner-Halverson et al. have suggested that local norms be generated for the WISC-III and provide data for 110 randomly selected Tohono O'Odham Native American children.

Insensitivity to cultural differences may not only impact on the integrity of test administration but also interpretation (Wilgosh, Mulcahy, & Walters, 1986). Saklofske and Schwean-Kowalchuk (1992) have discussed a number of factors that may impact on the test performance of children, ranging from race of examiner–examinee to test anxiety. Common and Frost (1988) conclude that misdiagnosis is an apparent danger when tests such as the WISC are used with Aboriginal students, because of the kind of factors described above. Although it may be argued that a "theory of Indian intelligence must eventually be constructed from within Indian ranks, with Indian perspectives and concerns reflected in its development" (Chrisjohn & Lanigan, 1986), it is imperative that research examining the test performance of Aboriginal children continues and that culturally sensitive test administration, scoring, and interpretation is "the order of the day."

CROSS-GROUP COMPARISONS

Considering that everything in science is relative and the efficacy of a comparison hinges on the integrity and representativeness of the group in question, an alternative to simply examining how single ethnic groups compare to Anglos would be to compare how different ethnic groups compare to each other as well. A study by Sandoval, Zimmerman, and Woo-Sam (1983) is reflective of the complexities and subtleties in cross-group comparisons. The WISC-R was administered to

7½ and 10½ year old Anglos, African Americans, Chicanos, and Bermudians. The results indicated that item difficulty curves were "remarkably parallel." In addition, similar patterns were reported when the factor structures were compared across different ethnic groups. For example, Reschly (1978), Reschly and Reschly (1979), and Sandoval (1979) reported that the factors do not vary much and that the correlation's between IQs and subtest scores were also generally similar. Another approach to addressing item bias was used by Sandoval and Whelan (1980), who tested 100 college students from different ethnic backgrounds to assess the face validity and item difficulty of the WISC items. No differences in cross-ethnic groups were found, suggesting that item difficulty was generally equally rated by the different groups of college students.

An alternative approach to cross-group comparison would be to control general IQ rather than ethnic group identity alone, and then to compare different ethnic groups. Taylor and Richards (1991) controlled overall IQ and then examined the intellectual patterns of African-American, Hispanic, and White children. In general, White children had the highest subtest test scores with African-American children scoring higher than Hispanics on the verbal subtests, and Hispanics scoring higher than African Americans on the performance subtests. When FSIQ was covaried, the Hispanic group was highest on Picture completion, Block Design, and Object Assembly, the White group on Information and Similarities, and the African-American group on Vocabulary This study underscores some very important issues. Children of different ethnic groups appear to have different general intellectual patterns before and after FSIQ is controlled, and the subtest patterns differ considerably. Thus, one could conclude that different ethnic groups seem to vary on both the overall IQ scores as well as in the score patterns (e.g., White children attain higher FSIQ scores than African Americans and Hispanics, African Americans are better at Verbal tasks, and Hispanics are better at Performance tasks. However, when FSIQ is covaried, the patterns are much more subtle, suggesting large within-group differences, which may often be masked by the perceived large between-group differences. These findings, however, may be tempered by the overall intellectual status of the student. The Taylor and Richards study compared ethnic groups composed of normal children. Will the same patterns exist with special needs children? Barona (1989) reported that for children with mental retardation no significant differences were found across the major WISC-R factors between African-American, Mexican, and White children. However, for learning-disabled children, White children score higher on the verbal scale while African Americans score lower on the perceptual organization factor.

Finally, it is worth noting that such differences appear to be stable over time. Elliott and Boeve (1987) reported that handicapped Anglo, African American, and Mexican-American children did not have large "clinically significant" changes in their score patterns over a 3-year period. It would be easy yet erroneous to simply say that either no differences exist between ethnic groups or that easy-to-understand differences are evident. The complex truth appears to lie somewhere in between. Furthermore, ethnic differences, though apparently reliable over time, appear to be modulated by intellectual status, and most likely by other variables not frequently measured nor considered (i.e., socioeconomic status, the educational attainment of parents, acculturation level, and so forth).

SUMMARY

Ethnic and race differences may best be explained not by speculation, popular opinion, or emotionally based arguments but through more of an anthropological or cultural understanding of the issues in question. The WISC-III is a measure of 'g,' which many psychologists accept as a universal description of intelligence. However, the content of intelligence tests and the normative data reflecting performance may not be universal but vary across as well as within groups. Foster and Cone (1995) discussed the importance of a cohesive hypothetical construct in assessment as well having a clear understanding of the purpose for which the test reflecting this construct is intended. Even though the WISC-R and the WISC-III may be used to assess the intelligence of American children, ethnic differences are still observed. The task will then be to determine exactly what those differences are, how are they manifested when important variables are controlled, and finally, what do these differences suggest. Even then, we must always appreciate the diversity of the children and the society we seek to understand and serve. In this context, the Wechsler scales can serve as useful measures of childrens' intelligence.

REFERENCES

American Psychological Association. (1993). Guidelines for providers of psychological services to ethnic, linguistic, and culturally diverse populations. *American Psychologist, 48,* 45–48.

Ardila, A. (1995). Directions of research in cross-cultural neuropsychology. *Journal of Clinical and Experimental Psychology, 17,* 143–150.

Ardila, A., Rosselli, M., & Puente, A. E. (1994). *Neuropsychological Evaluation of the Spanish Speaker.* New York: Plenum.

Barona, A. (1992). Effects of test administration procedures and acculturation level on achievement scores. *Journal of Psychoeducational Assessment, 10,* 124–132.

Barona, A. (1989). Differential effects of WISC-R factors on special education eligibility for three ethnic groups. *Journal of Psychoeducational Assessment, 7,* 31–38.

Barona, A., Santos de Barona, M., & Faykus, S. P. (1993). The simultaneous effects of sociocultural variables and WISC-R factors on MR, LD, and nonplacement of ethnic minorities in special education. *Education and Training in Mental Retardation, 28,* 66–74.

Betancourt, H., & Lopez, S. R. (1993). The study of culture ethnicity and race in American psychology. *American Psychologist, 48,* 629–637.

Berry, J., Poortinga, Y., Segall, M., & Dasen, P. (1992). *Cross-cultural Psychology: Research and Applications.* New York: Cambridge University Press.

Berry, J. (1984). Towards a universal psychology of cognitive competence. *International Journal of Psychology, 19,* 335–361.

Bontempo, R. (1993). Translation fidelity of psychological scales: An item response theory analysis of an individualism-collectivism scale. *Journal of Cross-Cultural Psychology, 24,* 149–166.

Brace, C. L. (1997). Intelligence. *Natural History, 6,* 12.

Brandt, E. (1984). The cognitive functioning of American Indian children: A critique of McShane and Plas. *School Psychology Bulletin, 13,* 74–81.

Brislin, R. W. (1989). Increasing awareness of class, ethnicity, culture and race by expanding on student's own experiences. In I. S. Cohen (Ed.) *The G. Stanley Hall Lecture Series* (Vol. 8). Washington, D.C. American Psychological Association.

Chrisjohn, R., & Lanigan, C. (1986). Research on Indian intelligence: Review and prospects. In selected papers from the First Mokakit Conference (1984) (pp. 50–57). Mokakit Indian Educational Research Association, University of British Columbia.

Cicchetti, D. (1994). Guidelines, criteria, and rules of thumb for evaluating normed and standardized assessment instruments in psychology. *Psychological Assessment, 6,* 1–7.

Common, R. & Frost, L. (1988). The implication of the mismeasurement of Indian students through the standardized intelligence tests. *Canadian Journal of Native Education, 15,* 18–30.

de Jesus, N., Perrin, G., & Blackwood, H. D. (1996). Conducting assessments of non-English speaking persons. *El Boletin, 2,* 3–6.

Elliott, S. N., & Boeve, K. (1987). Stability of WISC-R IQs: An investigation of ethnic differences over time. *Educational and Psychological Measurement, 47,* 461–465.

Ellis, B. (1990). Assessing intelligence cross-nationally: A case for differential functioning detection. *Intelligence, 14,* 61–78.

Figueroa, R. (1983). Test bias and Hispanic children. *The Journal of Special Education, 17,* 431–440.

Foster, S. L., & Cone, J. D. (1995). Validity issues in clinical assessment. *Psychological Assessment, 7,* 248–260.

Friel-Patti, S. (1990). Otitus media with effusion and the development of language: A review of the evidence. *Topics in Language Disorders, 11*(1), 11 23.

Garcia, J. G., & Marotta, S. (1997). In Jorge G. Garcia & Maria Cecilia Zea (Eds.), *Psychological interventions and research with Latino populations* (pp. 1–14). Needham Heights, MA: Allyn and Bacon.

Geisinger, K. F. (1992). Fairness and selected psychometric issues in the psychological testing of Hispanics. In K. F. Geisinger (Ed.), *Psychological testing of Hispanics* (pp. 17–42). Washington DC: American Psychological Association.

Greenough-Olson, S. C. (1993). *The influence of language on non-verbal intelligence test performance of Northern Saskatchewan Aboriginal children.* Unpublished Master's thesis, University of Saskatchewan, Canada.

Gutkin, T. B., & Reynolds, C. R. (1981). Factorial similarity of the WISC-R for white and black children from the standardization sample. *Journal of Educational Psychology, 73,* 227–231.

Hanley, J. H., and Barclay, A. G. (1979). Sensitivity of the WISC and WISC-R to subject and examiner variables. *The Journal of Black Psychology, 5,* 79–84.

Helms, J. E. (1992). Why is there no study of cultural equivalence in standardized cognitive ability testing? *American Psychologist, 47,* 1083–1101.

Herrnstein, R. J., & Murray, C. (1994). *The bell curve.* New York: The Free Press.

Hickey, T. (1972). Bilingualism and the measurement of intelligence and verbal learning ability. *Exceptional Children, 39,* 24–28.

Jensen, A. R. (1980). *Bias in mental testing.* New York: Free Press.

Jones, J. M. (1994). *Our similarities are different: Toward a psychology of affirmative diversity.* San Francisco, CA: Jossey Bass.

Jones, J. M. (1991). *Racism: A cultural analysis of the problem.* Berkeley, CA: Cobb & Henry.

Kaufman, A. S. (1993). King WISC the Third assumes the throne. *Journal of School Psychology, 31,* 345–54.

Kaufman, A. S., & Doppelt, J. E. (1976). Analysis of standardization data in terms of stratification variables. *Child Development, 47,* 165–171.

Kaufman, A. S., & Kaufman, N. L. (1983). *Kaufman Assessment Battery for Children.* Circle Pines, MN: American Guidance Service.

Koh, T., Abbatelio, A., & McLoughlin, C. S. (1984). Cultural bias in WISC subtest items: A response to Judge Brady's suggestion in relation to the PASE case. *School Psychology Review, 13,* 89–94.

La Fromboise, T., Coleman, H. L., & Gerton, J. (1993). Psychological impact of biculturalism: Evidence and theory. *Psychological Bulletin, 114,* 395–412.

Lane, C. (1994). The tainted sources of *The Bell Curve. The New York Review, 26,* 14–19.

Laosa, L. (1991). The cultural context of construct validity and the ethics of generalizability. *Early Childhood Research Quarterly, 6,* 313–321.

Laosa, L. (1984). Ethnic, socioeconomic, and home language influences upon early performance on measures of ability. *Journal of Educational Psychology.*

Laosa, L. (1975). Bilingualism in three United States Hispanic groups: Contextual use of language and children and adults in their families. *Journal of Educational Psychology, 67,* 617–627.

Lewontin, R. Rose, S., & Kamin, L. (1984). *Not in our genes.* New York: Penguin Books.

Malgady, R. D., Rogler, L. H., & Constantino, G. (1987). Ethnoculture and linguistic bias in mental health evaluation of Hispanics. *American Psychologist, 41,* 228–234.

Manuel-Dupont, S., Ardila, A. A., Rosselli, M., & Puente, A. E. (1992). Bilingualism. In Puente, A. E. & McCaffrey, A. J. (Eds.) *Handbook of neuropsychological assessment.* New York: Plenum.

Melnick, M. (1997). Methodological errors in the prediction of ability. *American Psychologist, 52,* 74–75.

McClelland, D. (1973). Testing for competence rather than for intelligence. *American Psychologist, 28,* 1–14.

McCullough, C., Walker, J., & Diessner, R. (1985). The use of the Wecshler scales in the assessment of Native Americans in the Columbia River Basin. *Psychology in Schools, 22,* 23–28.

McShane, D. (1983). Explaining achievement patterns of American Indian children: A transcultural and developmental model. *Peabody Journal of Education, 61,* 1, 34–48.

McShane, D., & Plas, J. (1984). The cognitive functioning of American Indian children: Moving from the WISC to the WISC-R. *School Psychology Review, 13,* 11, 61–73.

Moore, E. G. J. (1987). Ethnic, social milieu and black children's intelligence test measurement. *Journal of Negro Education, 56,* 44–52.

More, J. (1987). *Native American learning styles: A review for research.* Paper presented at "Meeting Their Needs," Winnepeg, Manitoba.

Mulcahy, R., & Marfo, K. (1987). Assessment of cognitive ability and instructional programming with Native Canadian children. In L. Stews & S. McCann (Eds.), *Contemporary education issues: The Canadian mosaic* (pp. 157–178). Toronto: Copp Clark Phman Ltd.

Mueller, H., Mulcahy, R., Wilgosh, L., & Watters, B., & Mancini, G. (1986). An analysis of WISC-R item responses with Canadian children. *Alberta Journal of Education Research, 32,* 12–36.

Munford, P. R., & Munoz, A. (1980). A comparison of the WISC and WISC-R on Hispanic children. *Journal of Clinical Psychology, 36,* 452–458.

Murdoch, J. (1988). Cree cognition in natural and educational context. In J. Berry, S. Irvine, & E. Hunt (Eds.), *Indigenous cognition: Functioning in cultural context* (pp. 231–255). Boston: Martinus Nijoff Publishers.

Naglieri, J. A. (1986). WISC-R and K-ABC comparison for matched samples of black and white children. *Journal of School Psychology, 24,* 81–88.

Neisser, U., Boodoo, G., Bouchard, T. J., Boykin, A. W., Brody, N., Ceci, S. J., Halpern, D. F., Loehlin, J. C., Perloff, R., Sternberg, R. J., & Urbina, S. (1995). *Intelligence: Knowns and unknowns.* Washington, DC: American Psychological Association.

Nobles, W. W. (1995). *Psychological research and black self-concept: A Cultural Review.* New York: University Press.

Olmedo, E. (1981). Testing linguistic minorities. *American Psychologist, 36,* 1078–1085.

Padilla, A. M. (1995). *Hispanic Psychology: Critical issues in theory and research.* Thousand Oaks, CA: Sage Publications.

Padilla, A. M. (1988). Early psychological assessments of Mexican-American children. *Journal of the History of the Behavioral Sciences, 24,* 111–117.

Pike, R. (1966). *Language in relation to a unified theory of the structure of human behavior.* The Hague: Morton.

Prewitt-Diaz, J., Rodriguez, M., & Rivera, D. (1986). The predictive study of the Spanish translation of the WISC-R (Eiwn-R) with Puerto Rican students in Puerto Rico and the United States. *Educational and Psychological Measurement, 46,* 401–407.

Rechsly, D. (1978). WISC-R factor structures among anglos, blacks, Chicanos, and Native American Papangos. *Journal of Consulting and Clinical Psychology, 46,* 417–422.

Rechsly, D. J., & Rechsly, J. E. (1979). Brief reports on the WISC-R. *Journal of School Psychology, 17,* 355–361.

Reynolds, C. R. (1995). Test bias and the assessment of intelligence and personality. In D. H. Saklofske & M. Zeidner (Eds.), *International handbook of personality and intelligence* (pp. 545–576). New York: Plenum.

Reynolds, C. R., & Wilson, V. L. (1983). *Methodological and statistical advances in the study of individual differences.* New York: Plenum.

Rodriguez, J. M., de Torres, I. R., Herrans, L., & Aponte, M. R. (1994). Comprehension of instructions and other critical issues in the test standardization process. *Revista Interamericana de Psicologia, 28,* 179–190.

Rowe, D. C. (1994). No more than skin deep. *American Psychologist, 49,* 215–216.

Rushton, J. P. (1997). Race, IQ, and APA report on *The Bell Curve. American Psychologist, 52,* 69–70.

Saklofske, D. H., & Janzen, H. Z. (1990). School-based assessment research in Canada. *McGill Journal of Education, 25,* 1, 5–23.

Saklofske, D. H., & Schwean-Kowalchuk, V. (1992). Influences on testing and test results. In M. Zeidner & R. Most (Eds.), *Psychological testing: An inside view* (pp. 89–119). Palo Alto, CA. Consulting Psychologist Press.

Sanchez, G. I. (1932). Group differences in Spanish-speaking children: A critical review. *Journal of Applied Psychology, 16,* 549–558.

Sandoval, J. (1979). The WISC-R and internal evidence of test bias with minority groups. *Journal of Consulting and Clinical Psychology, 47,* 919–927.

Sandoval, J., & Whelan, M. P. (1980). Accuracy of judgements of WISC-R item difficulty for minority groups. *Journal of Consulting and Clinical Psychology, 48,* 249–253.

Sandoval, J., Zimmerman, I. L., & Woo-Sam, J. (1983). Cultural differences on WISC-R verbal items. *Journal of School Psychology, 21,* 49–55.

Saskatchewan Indian Institute of Technology. (1990). *Aboriginal literary plan.* Saskatoon, Saskatchewan.

Sattler, J. (1988). *Assessment of children* (3rd ed.). San Diego: Jerome Sattler Publications.

Scaldwell, W., Frame, J., & Cookson, D. (1985). Individual assessment of Chippewa, Muncey, and Oneida children using the WISC-R. *Canadian Journal of School Psychology, I* (1), 15–21.

Scarr, S., & Weinberg, R. A. (1976). I. Q. test performance of black children adopted by white families. *American Psychologist, 31,* 726–739.

Seyfort, B., Spreen, D., & Lahmer, V. (1980). A critical look at the WISC-R with Native Indian children. *Alberta Journal of Educational Research, 26,* 1, 14–21.

Slate, J. R., & Jones, C. H. (1995). Preliminary evidence of the validity of the WISC-III for African American students undergoing special education evaluation. *Educational and Psychological Measurement, 55,* 1039–1046.

St. John, J., Kirchev, A., & Bauman, E. (1976). Northwestern Ontario Indian children and the WISC. *Psychology in the Schools, 13,* 407–411.

Tanner-Halverson, P., Burden, T., & Sabers, D. (1993). WISC-III normative data for Tohono O'Oodham Native American children. *Journal of Psychoeducational Assessment, WISC-III Monograph,* 125–133.

Taylor, R., & Richards, S. (1991). Patterns of intellectual differences of black, Hispanic, and white children. *Psychology in the Schools, 28,* 5–9.

Terman, L. M. (1916). *The measurement of intelligence.* Cambridge, MA: Riverside.

Terman, L. M., & Merrill, M. A. (1937). *Measuring intelligence.* Cambridge, MA: Houghton Mifflin.

Terrell, F., & Terrell, S. L. (1983). The relationship between the race of the examiner, cultural mistrust, and the intelligence test performance of black children. *Psychology in the Schools, 20,* 367–369.

U.S. Bureau of the Census. (1992). *Survey of Business Owners and Self-Employed Persons: Form MB-1.* Washington, D.C.: Department of Commerce.

Wechsler, D., (1974). *Wechsler Intelligence Scale for Children—Revised Edition.* New York: The Psychological Corporation.

Wechsler, D. (1991). *Wechsler Intelligence Scale for Children—Third Edition: Manual.* San Antonio: The Psychological Corporation.

Westermeyer, J. (1987). Cultural factors in clinical assessment. *Journal of Consulting and Clinical Psychology, 55,* 471–478.

Wilgosh, L., Mulcahy, R., & Walters, B. (1986). Assessing intellectual performance of culturally different Inuit children with the WISC-R. *Canadian Journal of Behavioral Science, 18,* 3, 270–277.

Williams, R. L. (1975). The BITCH-100: A culture-specific test. *Journal of Afro-American Issues, 3,* 103–116.

Yee, A. H. (1997). Ending the controversy. *American Psychologist, 52,* 70–71.

12

THE USE OF THE WISC-III
WITH ACHIEVEMENT TESTS

BETTY E. GRIDLEY

Department of Educational Psychology
Ball State University
Muncie, Indiana

GALE H. ROID

Graduate School of Clinical Psychology
George Fox University
Newberg, Oregon

INTRODUCTION

In this chapter, we discuss some general issues regarding the use of ability and achievement measures along with review of specific studies on the WISC-III and achievement tests. One goal was to introduce the reader to the research base from which decisions can be made. However, perhaps more importantly, we have tried to make the chapter practical and useful for clinicians. To this end we have provided tables, charts, and case study examples to help guide readers through the development of difficult concepts. We have demonstrated use of the tables and have furnished opportunities for practicing some essential skills.

Administering the WISC-III may be a necessary but only a first step in beginning to understand a child's functioning. Indeed, clinicians must ask themselves, What is the purpose of assessment? Diagnosis or explanation of cognitive strengths and weaknesses should not be an end unto itself. The goal of such assessment must be intervention and planning. We do not discount the value of obtaining information from ability measures such as the WISC-III. Indeed, we find them very beneficial when placed in the appropriate context. Nevertheless, until some measure of achievement is included, no evaluation is complete. In other chapters in this volume, the authors make use of measures of achievement in obtaining complete information about a child. However, little attention has been given to the issues specifically involved in using achievement measures with the WISC-III.

Traditionally, in discussions of assessment, achievement has received a short shrift. In fact, Kamphaus, Slotkin, and DeVincentis (1990) stated that, "one striking aspect of clinical measures of achievement is the lack of attention they receive from researchers" (p. 552). Indeed, in studying a number of texts (e.g., Kaufman, 1994) used to provide guidance to students and clinicians, although integration of achievement testing is understood through the use of case studies, guidance in the use of such measures is seldom provided. Many authors (e.g., Kamphaus, 1993; Kaufman, 1994) have concentrated complete volumes on ability testing. Much of the discussion in these volumes centers around profile analysis of the measures themselves. The usefulness of such profile analysis using only ability measures has been questioned (McDermott, Fantuzzo, & Glutting, 1990, 1992), yet we continue to be devoted to it. Although we do not discount the value of using ability measures to understand cognitive strengths and weaknesses, the bottom line is in translating these results into educational planning. This translation must include determination of present levels of academic performance. This means achievement testing in some form. There are some who question whether ability and achievement measures really provide different kinds of information at all. It may be argued that the tasks included on both kinds of tests are very similar. However, in our opinion there is enough of a distinction to warrant the use of both kinds of measures and comparisons to be made between them. It seems to us that ability measures, although influenced by learning, are less influenced by specific instruction in certain subject areas. For example, it might be useful to think of an ability measure such as the WISC-III as giving us some sort of probability statement about how well a student might succeed (Jeff Braden, personal correspondence, August 1996). The achievement measure then reflects how that probability has been operationalized. To illustrate, a student with a WISC-III Full Scale IQ (FSIQ) of 100 would be expected to be about as successful in learning to read as a majority of his or her peers. If reading achievement is considerably lower than that, we start to look for explanations for why the student has not been "successful." Certainly there may be any number of explanations, ranging from not having appropriate opportunities to learn to processing and intellective factors to personality variables. These variables are difficult to tease out one from the other; however, it is our responsibility as psychologists to formulate and test hypotheses about which variables influence achievement outcomes in each instance.

In practice, achievement measures are given for any number of reasons. Although overachievement is mentioned and studied by researchers (e.g., Glutting, McDermott, Prifitera, & McGrath, 1994; Rutter & Yule, 1975), most clinicians are primarily involved with evaluating children who do not succeed for any number of different reasons. Again, we are not discounting the concepts of over- and under-achievement, just the practical use of such terms. By studying overachievement, we may better learn which variables are important. In the case of overachievement, our goal is to provide adequate experiences to help a child reach his or her potential.

The usefulness of individually standardized achievement measures can be debated. For the most part they are very reliable. However, some have questioned their validity. It is also abundantly clear that alternative types of tests do not fare well when compared psychometrically with well-known achievement batteries. Standardized achievement tests remain mainstays in batteries administered to students for the purpose of eligibility determination under categories defined by the *Diagnostic and Statistical Manual of Mental Disorders* (APA, 1994) (*DSM-IV*) and Individuals with Disabilities Act (IDEA). In fact, most state education agencies require use of standard scores from achievement tests for determining eligibility for receiving services for nearly every handicapping condition addressed under the law. This is illustrated very well for the category of learning disabilities (LDs) (Frankenberger & Fronzaglio, 1991; Mercer, King-Sears, & Mercer, 1990). Lyon (1996) related that under IDEA the number of children identified as LD has been increasing steadily since 1972 and that approximately half of all students receiving special education services nationally, or about 5% of the total public school population, are identified as having LDs. Consequently, school psychologists report spending a large portion of their time in diagnosing such children. Indeed, Ross (1995) fond that over half the national sample of school psychologists she surveyed reported spending more than 40% of their time devoted to activities connected with the identification of students with LDs.

There still continues to be no universally accepted definition of LDs. However, consistent with the federal definition, the one "driving clinical force" in diagnosis has been that an LD involves some discrepancy between potential and achievement (Lyon, 1996). In conjunction with this definition, a growing number of states have included an ability–achievement discrepancy as the defining factor. Frankenberger and Fronzaglio (1991) and Mercer, et al. (1990) in surveying state education departments concluded that nearly every state required, either in their laws or accompanying regulations, documentation of a severe discrepancy and that standard scores were required in a majority of those states. Ross (1995), in her follow-up study of practitioners, found that such quantification was happening in actual practice. Therefore, discussion of the use of standardized achievement measures from which standard scores may be obtained is essential to any chapter on the subject.

Many have argued against using discrepancy criteria to identify children with LDs (e.g., Fletcher, Espy, Francis, Davidson, Rourke, & Shawitz, 1989; Lyon, 1996). The literature seems clear that, at best, ability predicts no more than about 50% of the variance in achievement, leaving an additional 50% or greater to be explained by other factors. Additionally, researchers are more and more in agreement that reading disorders are primarily caused by deficiencies in phonological and/or orthographic processing with or without significant discrepancies between actual and predicted achievement based on ability (Stanovich, 1993).

However, the fact remains that many clinicians are obligated by laws and regulations to determine such discrepancies on a daily basis. In order to be competent clinicians we must have a good foundation in understanding the ramifications and issues involved with using measures of achievement. This means turning our discussion to the measurement of achievement and its relationship to ability measures such as the WISC-III.

According to Kamphaus (1993), the most popular IQ tests have been those in the Wechsler series. While he also points out that the WISC-III is substantially different from its predecessor the WISC-R, he also asserts that there is no reason to assume that the WISC-III will be less popular. Therefore, the WISC-III can be predicted to be used extensively in practice. Again, although the WISC-III is similar to the WISC-R, it is most assuredly a different instrument. Therefore, extrapolation of findings from studies of the WISC-R to the WISC-III can be misleading. This is particularly true of relationships of the WISC-III with achievement tests.

BACKGROUND LITERATURE

The information that follows was compiled from an exhaustive (and sometimes exhausting) review of test manuals, published journals, and unpublished documents. Every effort was made to include all known studies linking the WISC-III to achievement testing. In spite of this, our search revealed very few published or unpublished sources of information.

The first logical source of information about the relationship between the WISC-III and standardized achievement tests seemed to be manuals for the tests themselves. Three studies between the WISC-III and achievement are reported in the WISC-III manual. Correlations between the WISC-III FSIQ, Verbal IQ (VIQ), Performance IQ (PIQ), and Freedom from Distractibility (FD), Verbal Comprehension (VC), Perceptual Organization (PO), and Processing Speed (PS) Index scores, and the Wide Range Achievement Test—Revised (WRAT-R; Jastak & Wilkinson, 1984) were reported for 23 children, 13 of whom had been diagnosed as having an LD and 10 with Attention Deficit Hyperactivity Disorder (ADHD). These correlations, corrected for variability, ranged from .09 to .73. The WRAT-R has been criticized for its lack of psychometric soundness as well as its brevity and has been superseded by the WRAT—Third Edition (WRAT-3; Wilkinson, 1993).

WISC-III scores were also correlated with group-administered achievement tests and school grades. Citing a study with the WISC-R (Figueroa & Sassenrath, 1989), Kamphaus (1993) stated that, "an important finding from concurrent and predictive validity studies is that the Verbal Scale of the WISC-R and the WISC-III is more highly correlated with school achievement than is the Performance scale"

(p. 131). This may be somewhat overstated for the WISC-III, because the relationship depends on which measure of achievement is used. For example, scores from five different achievement tests for 358 children aged 6–16 years were collectively correlated with various WISC-III scores. Correlations ranged from .37–.74. The FSIQ and VIQ were somewhat more highly related ($r = .57$ to .74) to group achievement tests than were the PIQ and POI ($r = .42$ to .58). Grades in mathematics, English, reading, and spelling as well as grade-point average (GPA) correlated from .28 to .48 with the WISC-III for 617 children ages 6–16 years. Differences among the various WISC-III scores and their relationships with school grades were slight. These results suggest that although the FSIQ score may be preferred because of its global nature and reliability, the choice of a preference for other of the available scores may not be as straightforward as we might have thought.

In examining manuals for popularly used achievement tests, only the Wechsler Individual Achievement Test (WIAT; 1992) and the WRAT-3, which were published subsequent to the WISC-III, reported correlations with the WISC-III. The WRAT-3 manual included results from one study that used 100 students ages 6–16 (Mean = 10.9, SD = 3.1), but no other data about the sample were given. Correlations between factor, index, and subtest scores from the WISC-III and subtests of the WRAT-3 ranged from .28 to .70. The WIAT manual gives extensive tables of correlations between the various available scores from the WISC-III and the WIAT for a "linking" sample of over 1,000 children on whom the tests were conormed. The correlations ranged from .17 to .95, with the majority of those with FSIQ falling between .30 and .70. Correlations between the WIAT and a number of other achievement tests are given in the WIAT manual and may provide some comparison of the achievement tests. Statistics for a variety of special populations are also given in the WIAT manual. Unfortunately, although WISC-III scores were used to verify various definitions, no correlations between the WISC-III and the WIAT for these subgroups were included.

It is not surprising, given the fact that the two tests were conormed on the same standardization sample, that some researchers have chosen to study the WISC-III and the WIAT. Using correlations between the WISC-III and the WIAT found in the WIAT manual, Flanagan and Alfonso (1993a, 1993b) developed tables of predicted achievement and significant difference values using VIQ and PIQ scores. These tables were designed to help clinicians who decided that comparisons made with either VIQ or PIQ scores were more defensible than using the FSIQ score.

Slate (1994) studied the relationship between the WISC-III and the WIAT for a sample of students who had been referred for difficulties. Of these, 202 had been diagnosed as having specific LDs, 115 with mental retardation (MR), and 159 who did not meet eligibility criteria for special education services. Corrected correlations were highest for the MR group and lowest for the group that did not qualify for services. Highest correlations with the FSIQ were for Math Reasoning, Reading Comprehension, Numerical Operations, and Listening Comprehension (ranging from .70 .81). Lowest with FSIQ were .36 and .45 for Written Expression and Oral Expression, respectively. VIQ was more highly related than PIQ to the WIAT scores for these groups, with one exception for the noneligible students where Numerical Operations had a higher correlation with PIQ ($r = .64$) than VIQ ($r = .55$). Correlations with Index scores were more varied than those found for the IQ scores.

Correlations between the WISC-III and the WRAT-3 were delineated by Hishinuma and Yamakawa (1993), Smith, Smith, and Smithson (1995), Vance, Mayes, Fuller, and Abdullah (1994), and Vance and Fuller (1995a,b). Smith et al. (1995) reported correlations between the FSIQ, VIQ, and PIQ of the WISC-III and both blue and tan forms of the WRAT-3 for 37 children from rural Arkansas who had been referred for evaluation because of academic difficulties. Correlations were consistent with those found in the study reported in the WRAT-3 manual, although the authors noted that they were somewhat lower due to possible range restriction. The Vance et al. (1994) and Vance and Fuller (1995a,b) articles appear to report the same correlation matrix for the same sample, with coefficients for FSIQ, VIQ, and PIQ with the various subtests ranging from .58–.79. Their sample consisted of 60 youngsters referred for evaluation for special education services. Hishinuma and Yamakawa reported selected correlations between the WISC-III and the WIAT-3 for their sample of 78 students, which included gifted, gifted LD, LD, and "other." It is somewhat unfortunate that the one single test for which we found a number of studies was the WRAT-3. It is brief, easy to administer, and score. However the skills tapped do not cover all areas of achievement as specified by IDEA. At best it is a brief screen and should be used only as such.

Slate, Jones, Graham, and Bower (1994) investigated the relationships between the WISC-III, the WRAT-R, the Key Math-R, and the Peabody Picture Vocabulary Test—Revised (PPVT-R). For their 64 subjects from northeast Arkansas they found little correlation of the WISC-III with the WRAT-R and moderate correlations with the Key Math-R (.50–.66) and the PPVT-R (.49–.59).

We located two sources for correlations between the WISC-III and the Kaufman Test of Educational Achievement (K-TEA). In the single published study, Lavin (1996) calculated correlations for 72 children referred for placement for emotional and learning handicaps. For these children who scored in the low average category, coefficients ranged from .05 to .67, with the highest being with the verbal scale. Significant relationships for the performance scale were found only for the Math subtests and the Composite Score. We were able to locate one other unpublished study by McCloskey et al. (1992), which is available from American Guidance Service. Means, standard deviations, and correlations across four age groupings are reproduced by permission in Table A1 in the Appendix of this chapter. Their matrix is based on 134 children between the ages of 6-0 and 16-11-30 from eight geographically diverse areas. Subjects were selected from the general population to reflect the national census as closely as possible. Thirty-six percent were female and 64% were male. Approximately 18% of the sample were students enrolled in special education programs during the 1991–1992 school year. The sample included 10% Black, 5% Hispanic, 81% White, and 4% with no ethnic information provided.

Weiss, Prifitera, and Roid (1993) reported correlation coefficients for White, Black, and Hispanic groups as well as males and females between WISC-III full-scale scores and group achievement measures. These coefficients were generally moderate. Most coefficients were very similar across groups, supporting the use of the WISC-III predicting fairly across various groups.

Teeter and Smith (1993) used the WISC-III with the Woodcock Johnson Psychoeducational Battery for 60 males between the ages of 11 and 16, 30 of whom had severe emotional disturbance and 30 without academic or emotional problems. No correlation matrix between the WISC-III scores and the achievement portion of the test was reported.

It is unfortunate that there are so few studies available that examine the relationship between the WISC-III and the great number of remaining individually administered standardized achievement measures. For example, in her April 1996 article, Claire Lavin stated, "There are no published studies on the relationships between the K-TEA and WISC-III" (p. 120). This lack of information is particularly disturbing in light of the fact that many achievement tests other than the WIAT and WRAT-3 seem to be preferred by practicing school psychologists (Woodin, Peterson, Croombs, & Wasielewski, 1996).

Currently, the K-TEA and the Peabody Individual Achievement Test—Revised (PIAT-R) are being renormed. We talked with a spokesperson from American Guidance Services (AGS) who assured us that in conjunction with the renorming of the K-TEA, Key Math, Woodcock Reading Mastery Test, and linking studies with the WISC-III were being conducted. Correlations between the WISC-R and various achievement tests are available either in the manuals or from the literature. However, care must be taken not to be too ready to extrapolate these results to relationships with the WISC-III.

ISSUES IN USING ABILITY
AND ACHIEVEMENT MEASURES

Since 1980 the largest growing category of students identified under special education laws is those with LDs. There is no current universally accepted test, test battery, or standard used to identify children with LDs (Lyon, 1996). There has been and continues to be much debate about the definition of and identification of children with LDs. However, regardless of such academic conversations, the defining feature of such disabilities continues to be some notion of underachievement as related to potential. In fact, the federal definition of LDs in IDEA stipulates that a discrepancy between IQ and achievement is to be documented. However, the federal law does not include guidelines for how such a discrepancy is derived and quantified. It seems clear that for a majority of states (see Frankenberger & Fronzaglio, 1991; Mercer et al., 1990; Ross, 1995) such criteria remain the *sine qua non* of determining eligibility for placement in programs for people with LDs. However, it is equally clear from these surveys that a great deal of variability in such determinations is present on a state-by-state basis. In 1990, Frankenberger and Fronzaglio found that 88% of the states that they surveyed had discrepancy criteria listed in their definition or in the criteria. By 1995, Ross found that practitioners reported the same trend. However, this discrepancy may be operationalized in a number of ways.

Regardless of how it is quantified, the determination of ability–achievement difference seems to be a fact of life for clinicians involved with students with LDs. Therefore, it is necessary for clinicians to make decisions based on the best information available. It also seems clear from the literature that despite the shortcomings of different methods used to operationalize ability/achievement discrepancies, that clinicians with adequate information make decisions that are more accurate and have greater interrater reliability than those for whom such information is not available (Ross, 1992). Therefore one of our goals has been to provide clinicians with useful and practical information presented in such a way as to be easy to use and interpret.

Comparison between ability and achievement tests seems to be a fundamental activity of psychologists and other professionals dealing with children. For nearly every category of exceptionality listed under IDEA, a multifactored achievement test is to be included as part of the evaluation. Indeed, eligibility criteria focus on impaired educational performance. The essential word here seems to be "educational." If the "disability" does not interfere with education then students are not served under IDEA. Clinicians must also often make comparisons of ability and achievement for other children as well. For instance, although gifted students are not served under IDEA, measures of achievement are important for determining whether they might be underachieving or learning impaired or for continued placement and programming.

SELECTING ACHIEVEMENT TESTS

There are a number of factors to be considered in selecting achievement tests. Generally, omnibus achievement tests are designed to assess the extent to which students have profited from schooling and other experiences when compared to others of the same age or grade (Salvia & Ysseldyke, 1991). In making comparisons such as those that follow, the user must keep in mind that the value of such comparisons is only as good as the tests used to make them. Selection of the criterion (measure of achievement) should receive as much attention as selection of the predictor (ability measure). In selecting or evaluating a multiskill achievement test, we suggest that clinicians ask the following questions:

1. Does the test measure important concepts and skills that are part of the curriculum?
2. Is the content suitable? Does it match the instruction provided?
3. What is the nature of the standardization sample? How well does it match your population?

4. Does the achievement measure have adequate evidence of reliability and validity?

5. Are floor and ceiling effects apt to influence scores? Especially at the bottom of age and ability spectra, is the item gradient adequate? In other words, how many raw score points are needed for substantial increases in standard scores? Is it possible for a person to score much higher by successfully completing one more item?

6. Are correlations available between this test and other measures (such as the WISC-III) for which comparisons are to be made?

ABILITY–ACHIEVEMENT COMPARISONS

The issues surrounding the use of ability–achievement comparisons are dealt with in depth elsewhere (Berk, 1984; Cone & Wilson, 1981; Reynolds, 1984, 1990; Shepard, 1980). The value of such comparisons is that the ability measure gives a standard against which to judge actual performance. Perhaps the correct terminology for such comparisons should be "predicted" versus obtained achievement comparisons. Indeed, the use of the ability measures allows one to make predictions about what might be expected from groups of youngsters on achievement tests given their ability levels. The use of such terminology may help to reframe the use of formulas and the like to a much more descriptive way of looking at these youngsters. We do not really compare ability and achievement, but expected achievement versus obtained achievement. This allows us to rethink the meaning of such discrepancies. It is our job as good detectives to try to discover the influencing factors that make for "under-" or "over-" achievement. Indeed, with this refocusing may come a more positive view of the value of intervention and other situational variables, which in turn puts less emphasis on indigenous characteristics that may seem immutable. Our search must include alternative explanations that account for variability in achievement. This attitude may help us to intervene to "kill" the prediction in a positive fashion.

Conversely, learning affects performance on IQ tests. The same processing difficulties that work to lower scores on achievement measures may be present in ability testing as well. Some have even suggested that ability and achievement measures are so much alike as to be virtually the same thing. However, we see value in making such comparisons in an intelligent manner (à la Kaufman, 1994). Many critics of the practice focus specifically on using ability–achievement discrepancies for identification of children with LDs. Again, this literature is extensive, and readers are urged to turn to more complete treatments of the subject (e.g., Keogh, 1993; Lyon, 1996; Stanovich, 1993). However, regardless of its critics, some sort of ability achievement discrepancy is the most prevalent method of identifying children with LD in the United States (Ross, 1995). If this practice is widespread then practitioners should be as well informed as possible about the process. We also urge that the most scientifically sound methods available be used.

The achievement versus ability discrepancy has most often been conceptualized in one of four ways: deviation from grade level, expectancy formulas based on grade level scores, simple difference methods, and predicted-achievement methods using regression formulas (Evans, 1990; Heath & Kush, 1991; Reynolds, 1984, 1990). A very limited number of states continue to use a deviation from grade level or grade-based expectancy method. However, because of the many psychometric failings of such methods, the present authors cannot in good conscience support their use. Readers can find complete discussions of these methods elsewhere (e.g., Berk, 1984; Heath & Kush, 1991; Reynolds, 1984, 1990). Therefore, two more psychometrically sound methods, simple difference scores and regression discrepancy scores, will be discussed and demonstrated here. A number of different formulas for standard errors and the like appear in various sources. We have chosen to use those suggested by Reynolds (1984). Some authors (Glutting et al., 1994) have advocated a more multivariate approach to discrepancy analysis. Although this method has not received much attention from practitioners, it will also be explored.

BEST PRACTICES IN THE USE
OF DISCREPANCY SCORES

The most error-free method of computing discrepancy scores is through use of software such as the *Scoring Assistant for the Wechsler Scales* (SAWS; Psychological Corporation, 1995) or in setting up various tables, and so on, on a spreadsheet program. However, those without access to such programs, or where these programs are not available for certain pairs of tests, can calculate all of the needed information using a hand-held calculator. In using any discrepancy-based procedure, the reader is urged to consider the following (Berk, 1984; Reynolds, 1990; Shepard, 1980):

1. Both ability and achievement test scores should be individually administered. Age-based standard scores are preferred in most cases over grade-based standard scores.

2. The tests should satisfy standard criteria for technical adequacy. Measures should have a high degree of reliability and evidence of validity.

3. The tests should be conormed; that is, their standardization samples should consist of the same children. If this is not possible then tests with comparable samples (e.g., same demographic characteristics, same time period, etc.) should be used.

4. Use FSIQ scores wherever possible to determine expected achievement levels. The FS is the most reliable score and if it adequately captures the individual's abilities should be used as the basis for further comparisons. VIQ and PIQ scores should be used for comparisons only when FSIQ is not reflective of a child's abilities. We would suggest using Kaufman's (1994) overview (pp. 134–135) as a guide in making this determination. The difference between VIQ and PIQ must

be both statistically significant and diagnostically meaningful in most cases. Index scores should be used advisedly for such comparisons, and we would suggest that only the VC and PO indices even be considered. Clinicians, however, should also be able to use their own judgments based on behavioral observations and test behaviors to determine which score is most representative of the child's abilities.

5. Multiple scores such as FSIQ and PIQ should never be used. Once a determination of which ability score has been made, all subsequent comparisons should be based on this one standard. The availability of computer programs such as SAWS (Psychological Corporation, 1995) makes it possible for multiple comparisons to be made. This does not mean that it is legitimate to do so, and intelligent interpreters will use such information advisedly. Such fishing expeditions in the data guarantee inflated error rates. McDermott et al. (1994) have suggested that if both VIQ and PIQ scores are used to make comparisons with the composite scores of the WIAT, the overall error rate will exceed .20. One would hope that such practices would not occur.

6. Discrepancy procedures should take into account the correlation between ability and achievement scores by using appropriate standard errors for determining whether real differences occur. Discrepancy (or difference) scores are less reliable than either of the tests from which they are calculated. The higher the correlation between the two tests, the less reliable the discrepancy score. Correlations between achievement and ability measures should be based on an appropriate sample.

7. The determination of a "severe" discrepancy should be made based on statistically significant and diagnostically meaningful difference criteria.

a. Clinicians should allow for multiple comparisons by use of "conservative" values. In most cases we suggest using .05 as the minimum alpha level. Reynolds (1984) cogently argued for use of a one-tailed statistical test. However, we have seldom seen other than two-tailed tests used in practice. For example, the WIAT manual provides formulae only for two-tailed tests. Tables for simple and predicted differences between FSIQ and WIAT subtests and composites needed at various levels of statistical significance are given in the WIAT manual in Table D.6 (pp. 366–376). Tables of differences using the regression discrepancy model for the linking sample of WISC-III and WIAT for VIQ and PIQ are given in Flanagan and Alfonso (1993a). Tables A6 and A7 in the Appendix provide values of both simple and predicted differences needed for significance for the WISC-III FSIQ, VIQ, and PIQ with the subtests of the K-TEA.

b. Use prevalence estimates as well as statistical significance to guide decision making. This allows for use of diagnostically meaningful comparisons (Kaufman, 1993) as well as for statistical significance. Prevalence rates for the population are given for comparisons of the WIAT and FSIQ in Tables C.5 (p. 353) and C.9 (p. 356) in the WIAT Manual. Tables of prevalence rates for VIQ and PIQ based on the WISC-III/WIAT linking sample are given in Tables A2–A5 in Appendix A of this chapter. All of these values for FSIQ, VIQ, and PIQ for both simple difference and regression methods and for various alpha levels are available in the computer scoring for the WISC-III and WIAT (SAWS). Spadafore (1993) has provided an outline for using the SAWS program in LD determination. Readers are urged to turn to his description for more specific information. However, the reader is also cautioned that he uses a single discrepancy criterion of 15 points that is not necessarily supported on the basis of standard errors.

8. Remember that determination of a significant and diagnostically meaningful discrepancy does not in itself constitute an LD. What it does mean is that a youngster does or does not meet specific criteria that may be as much politically and socially motivated as scientifically specific. There are a number of exclusionary factors that also must be taken into account. Nonetheless, the absence of such a discrepancy does not guarantee that no processing problem exists and that a youngster may not have significant school-related problems.

SIMPLE DIFFERENCES SCORES

Although we recommend the regression discrepancy model, given evidence that it is the most psychometrically sound procedure (Reynolds, 1984) and does not systematically eliminate certain segments of the population (Braden, 1987), it is clear that more states continue to use simple difference scores than any other method for eligibility determination (Ross, 1995). In defense of this procedure, it does provide an improvement over the use of grade-equivalent methods in that standard scores are used. In correct use of the procedure, standard errors of the difference scores are also accounted for. Nevertheless, before we begin our discussion, a few of the shortcomings of use of this method must be mentioned. Because they fail to take into account the phenomenon of regression toward the mean (Thorndike, 1963), simple difference score methods have been shown (Braden, 1987; McKleskey & Waldron, 1991) to produce disproportionate racial representation in LD classes (i.e., African-American students are underrepresented).

Maybe more problematic is that many states mandate use of a single discrepancy criterion (e.g., 15 points) regardless of the pair of tests being compared. In fact, in the newest version (1.0) of SAWS for Windows, a minimum number of score points must be designated before simple difference scores can be calculated. Such use ignores the differences in standard errors based on different reliabilities of tests and the correlations between them. By forcing users to make a designation, results printed by the computer program may be misleading in some ways. As we will discuss later, sometimes appropriate standard errors are greater than 15 points. More commonly, for WISC-III–WIAT comparisons, significant and meaningful differences are often less than 15 points. In order to guard against such use, it is urged that the method outlined below, including computation of standard errors, be used.

For comparisons between the WISC-III and WIAT, tables of simple difference values required for significance and prevalence values for FSIQs are provided in the WIAT Manual. These differences and the significance of such differences can also be easily obtained from the scoring software SAWS. Prevalence rates for simple difference scores for the WISC-III–WIAT linking sample for VIQs and PIQs are provided in Tables A2 and A3. Simple difference criteria based on McCloskey et al. (1993) are provided for the WISC-III and K-TEA in Table A6. Examples and comparisons of different discrepancy formulas using various sources of information are given as they refer to the case studies presented at the end of the chapter.

PROCEDURE FOR CALCULATING
SIMPLE DIFFERENCE SCORES

1. Obtain scores on ability and achievement measures.
2. Convert the scores to a common metric. For example, both scores could be converted (if necessary) to the IQ scale used for the WISC-III (mean = 100, SD = 15). Indeed, these scores are commonly available for the most popular achievement tests.
3. Subtract the achievement test score from the IQ score:

$$d = \text{IQ} - \text{Achievement}$$

4. Compute d' needed for statistical significance, where:

$$d' = 1.96 \ SD \ \sqrt{2 - r_{xx} - r_{yy}} \quad p < .05 \ (\text{two-tailed})$$
$$d' = 2.58 \ SD \ \sqrt{2 - r_{xx} - r_{yy}} \quad p < .01 \ (\text{two-tailed}),$$

where d' = difference needed for significance at given probability level; r_{xx} = reliability of the ability (IQ) measure; and r_{yy} = reliability of achievement measure.
5. If $d \geq d'$, the difference is significant. We can reject the hypothesis that the difference is due to chance.
6. Compare d with prevalence rates if available to see what proportion of the "normal" population have differences at least this large.

REGRESSION DISCREPANCY SCORES

It seems clear from the literature (e.g., Braden, 1987; Reynolds, 1984) that the most scientifically defensible procedure is one that accounts for regression toward the mean and standard errors of differences between test scores. For comparisons between the WISC-III and WIAT, tables of predicted difference values required for statistical significance are provided in the WIAT manual. These differences and the significance of such differences can also be easily obtained from the scoring software SAWS. Prevalence rates for the WISC-III–WIAT linking sample for VIQs and PIQs are provided in Table A4 and A5. Predicted achievement versus obtained achievement differences for the WISC-III and K-TEA are found in Table A7. These calculations were based on the McCloskey et al. (1993) correlations provided earlier. Examples and comparisons of different discrepancy formulas using various sources of information are given as they refer to case studies below.

PROCEDURE FOR CALCULATING PREDICTED–
OBTAINED ACHIEVEMENT DISCREPANCIES

1. Using ability and achievement scores that have been converted to the same scale, calculate predicted achievement.[1]

$$\hat{Y} = 100 + r_{xy} (X - 100),$$

When both ability and achievement tests have Means = 100 and SDs = 15, $\hat{Y}$ = predicted achievement, r_{xy} = correlation between ability and achievement, X = ability score.

2. Find the difference between predicted and actual achievement

$$\hat{Y} - Y = d,$$

where Y = Actual achievement score and d = discrepancy score.

3. Determine the magnitude of difference (discrepancy) required at the designated level of significance.

$$\Delta = 1.96 \ SD \ \sqrt{1 - r_{xy}^2} - 1.65 \ SE_{resid} \qquad p < .05 \ \text{(two-tailed)}$$

$$\Delta = 2.58 \ SD \ \sqrt{1 - r_{xy}^2} - 2.33 \ SE_{resid} \qquad p < .01 \ \text{(two-tailed)}$$

where Δ = Minimum value needed for statistical significance; r_{xy}^2 = squared correlation between ability and achievement; SE_{resid} = Standard error of the residual, defined below:

$$SE_{resid} = SD \ \sqrt{1 - r_{xy}^2} \ \sqrt{1 - r_{resid}} \ ,$$

where SE_{resid} = standard error of the residual and r_{resid} = reliability of the residual score, defined below:

$$r_{resid} = \frac{r_{yy} + r_{xx} r_{xy}^2 - 2r_{xy}^2}{1 - r_{xy}^2},$$

where r_{yy} = internal consistency reliability of the achievement test and r_{xx} = internal consistency reliability of the ability test.

4. Compare difference obtained in Step 2 with prevalence rates from a "normal" population. Examples of use of regression discrepancies are given in the case studies.

---

[1] Values for predicted achievement based on various correlations between scores has been provided in Table A8 in the Appendix. Intermediate values of correlations can be interpolated. However, using .05 increments provides for a good approximation of the predicted value. Berk (1984) suggested that if the correlation between achievement and ability is not known then .65 makes an adequate approximation. However, it must be stressed that this gives an approximation and interpretations should account for this.

MULTIVARIATE COMPARISONS

Some attention has been given to using multiple comparison techniques. For example, Glutting et al. (1994) outlined procedures based on cluster analyses of the factor indexes from the WISC-III and the composite scores of the WIAT. These analyses were restricted to those ranges (8 years, 9 months through 16 years, 11 months) for which all subtests of the WIAT are administered. No multivariate procedures seem to have been explored for other combinations of achievement tests with the WISC-III.

Glutting et al. (1994) support use of multivariate comparisons over what they designate as univariate regression procedures because of limitations in the latter. For example, they state that the consistency of regression methods is limited by instrument unreliability, the choice of IQ and achievement instruments, and the choice of cutoff scores. Their multivariate method really does not address these issues either. They do use the WISC-III and the WIAT, which have been normed together. However, many regression comparisons are available for this pair of tests (e.g., WIAT Manual, SAWS software, Flanagan & Alfonso, 1993a, b).

The same authors seem to focus on the ability to use multivariate comparisons to be able to look at multiple abilities simultaneously. For example, they ask the reader to consider the possibility that the processing problems that make children perform poorly on achievement tests also affect ability measures, therefore making discrepancy methods questionable. If achievement and ability scores are both affected by a processing problem, comparing the two does not result in substantial differences such as those required. They further aver that in order to compensate for this difficulty, clinicians commonly compare multiple IQs from the WISC-III one at a time to achievement scores. Such practice results in inflated error rates. For instance, when FSIQ, VIQ, and PIQ all are compared to a single achievement score at the .05 level, the resulting p value is really $p < .10$, and if the four-factor index scores are compared to a single achievement test, then the true error rate is $< .20$. This sounds alarming, and we certainly would not advocate such practice. When ability achievement comparisons are called for we urge the clinician to follow Kaufman's (1994) guidelines for "intelligent" interpretation. If the FSIQ "captures" the child's abilities then that should be used. If for some reason (a number of which are outlined in Kaufman, 1994) the FSIQ is not the appropriate indicator, then an alternate choice can be made. This choice should not be made inadvisably. We suggest that differences be evaluated not only for statistical significance but for diagnostic meaningfulness. Notice that we say *an* alternate choice. It is not good practice to make all possible comparisons. This will produce false positive errors and overidentify youngsters for whom programming is appropriate. Glutting et al. (1994) also advise that because joint prevalence rates are not available for those students evidencing multiple deficits, even the use of prevalence rates does not improve use of discrepancy criteria.

Their cluster analysis resulted in six core profile types against which comparisons can be made. They outline this procedure in their article. However, a serious user of the procedure may wish to also consult the Errata pages provided in a later issue of the same journal (*School Psychology Review,* 1995, vol. 24). Essentially, their step-by-step procedure compares a student's scores against the three subtype scores that are closest to the student's scores. Using the D^2 values from the population, they propose using a D^2 cutoff that identifies approximately 5.8% of the population. However, for the interested reader they also give values corresponding to other percentages as well.

Basically, their procedure works like this:

1. Start with the table of values for the six core subtypes. A worksheet with these values has been provided in Table 1.

2. Select the subtype most like the student of interest by choosing the FSIQ closest to the child's FSIQ.

3. Write the child's scores under the scores from the closest subtype.

4. Subtract the child's scores from those for the subtype.

5. Square the differences obtained in step 5.

6. Sum the squares of the differences.

7. Repeat the procedures with the second and third closest FSIQ scores.

8. Compare the sums of the squared differences to 1,295 (the critical value of D^2 needed to identify 5.8% of the population.

9. If all three sums are individually $\geq$ 1,295 then the profile is considered to be "uncommon."

10. If the profile is unusual (from step 9) then determine if it shows under- or overachievement. Subtract the highest WIAT Composite from the highest WISC-III factor score. A positive difference suggests a multivariate achievement versus IQ deficit (overachievement); a negative difference indicates a multivariate achievement versus IQ advantage (overachievement).

A worksheet is provided in Table 12.1 to help in calculations. However, we simplified the procedure and obtained more accurate results using a spreadsheet program. Glutting et al. (1994) refer to a computer program they developed that runs within SPSS and reads WISC-III Index and WIAT Composite scores from a data file. Children are matched to core types, and D^2 values are printed. It will also identify the best "match" of core subtype and prints means and standard deviations for that type. For a number of reasons it would be helpful to include the possibility for such typology analysis within the existing SAWS software. First is data entry. Scores that have already been entered into the SAWS program are not able to be exported as a text file necessitating duplication of data entry. Anytime data entry is involved there is an increased chance in introducing error. Additionally, many clinicians do not have access to SPSS software, which is fairly expensive to purchase.

Unless the procedure is included in the scoring software, it may not be worth the time it takes to use it. Additionally, we believe the concern here would be in false negative errors (not identifying a child who is truly in need of services). However, multivariate methods are another useful tool for researchers and may provide insights not available through the "univariate" techniques mentioned previously.

TABLE 12.1 Worksheet for Glutting et al. (1994) Comparisons[a]

FSIQ	VCI	POI	FDI	PSI	ReadC	MathC	LangC	WriteC	Sum $\sum(A-B)^2$
A. Type 1 FSIQ = 118	118	114	117	111	117	118	113	114	
B. Student's scores									
A–B									
$(A-B)^2$									
A. Type 2 FSIQ = 110	105	114	105	116	105	107	103	110	
B. Student's scores									
A–3									
$(A-B)^2$									
A. Type 3 FSIQ = 100	100	105	96	93	98	100	102	91	
B. Student's scores									
A–B									
$(A-B)^2$									
A. Type 4 FSIQ = 99	99	92	104	104	105	104	101	108	
B. Student's scores									
A–B									
$(A-B)^2$									
A. Type 5 FSIQ = 85	86	89	88	95	90	88	92	92	
B. Student's scores									
A–B									
$(A-B)^2$									
A. Type 6 FSIQ = 75	72	81	80	85	74	76	81	76	
B Student's scores									
A–B									
$(A-B)^2$									

[a]FSIQ, Full-Scale IQ; VCI, Verbal Comprehension Index; POI, Perceptual Organization Index; FDI, Freedom from Distractibility Index; PSI, Processing Speed Index.

TABLE 12.2 Multivariate Comparisons of Slate's Learning-Disabled Group with Cluster for WISC-III and WIAT[a]

FSIQ	VCI	POI	FDI	PSI	ReadC	MathC	LangC	WriteC	Sum $\Sigma(A-B)^2$
A. Type 4 FSIQ = 99	99	92	104	104	105	104	101	108	
B. Student's scores 84.6	83.7	89.9	84.7	95	86	82	81	74	
A–B	15.3	2.1	19.3	9	19	22	20	34	
$(A–B)^2$	234	4.41	372.49	81	361	484	400	1156	3094.99
A. Type 5 FSIQ = 86	86	89	88	95	90	88	92	92	
B. Student's scores 84.6	83.7	89.9	84.7	95	86	82	86	74	
A–B	2.3	–0.9	3.3	0	4	6	6	18	
$(A–B)^2$	5.29	0.81	10.89	0	16	36	36	324	430.99
A. Type 6 FSIQ = 75	73	81	80	86	74	76	81	76	
B. Student's scores 84.6	83.7	89.9	84.7	95	86	82	86	74	
A–B	–11	–8.9	–4.7	–9	–12	–6	–5	2	
$(A–B)^2$	114	79.21	22.09	81	144	36	25	4	507.79

[a]FSIQ, Full-Scale IQ; VCI, Verbal Comprehension Index; POI, Perceptual Organization Index; FDI, Freedom from Distractibility Index; PSI, Processing Speed Index.

Clinicians are urged not to accept the premises of this procedure without further experimentation and use in their own practices with real cases. The clinical utility of the procedure has not been verified. It must be noted that cluster analysis is a descriptive procedure. For example, different clusters may emerge using different methods such as those used by Roid (1994). Indeed, using correlation coefficients rather than distance criteria may give more substantively meaningful clusters.

Information obtained from clustering best applies to groups of individuals, and we were interested in comparing known groups with the clusters. However, when we compared the mean scores from Slate's (1994) LD group of 202 students with LDs, we failed to identify any multivariate differences. This comparison is provided in Table 2. It is not clear what conclusions can be drawn. However, using group means and standard deviations has a tendency to obscure individual differences such as those that are important for clinical evaluations of youngsters. It might be argued that existing methods for identifying LD students are inadequate and therefore that Slate's group may not be a "pure" LD group. Nevertheless, the Glutting et al. cluster analysis would have been much more meaningful had well-defined "clinical" groups such as those used for the Personality Inventory for Children (PIC; Wirt, Lachar, Klinedinst, & Seat, 1977) been included. If these well-defined clinical groups could be used for comparisons, then the procedure seems much more promising. We provide one more example of completed calculations for the multivariate procedure in the second case study.

CASE STUDIES

The two case studies provided in Tables 12.3, 12.4, and 12.5 are actual cases that were seen through a university-based clinic.

CASE STUDY #1: JON BIRD

Case Study #1, Jon Bird, was chosen because his assessment results allow us to illustrate a number of the concepts discussed in the chapter. Jon was referred to determine why he was having a difficult time in school. Jon had been retained in kindergarten and was having significant difficulties in learning in the first grade. His parents, who referred him, wondered also about memory problems. Jon didn't seem to be able to follow directions or to remember information presented orally. The scores obtained from the WISC-III, WIAT, and K-TEA are presented below. Regression-based differences needed for statistically significant differences with the various K-TEA and WIAT scores are also provided. Differences for the K-TEA were obtained from Table A7 in the Appendix and for the WIAT from Flanagan and Alfonso (1993a). Frequency values based on the linking sample for WISC-III and WIAT comparisons based on PIQ were obtained from Table A5 in the Appendix.

There is a statistically significant ($p < .01$) and diagnostically meaningful difference (i.e., less than 10% of the population had differences this large) of 22 points

TABLE 12.3   Case Study #1, Jon Bird, Age 7 years, 5 months, Grade 1,
Referral Question: LD?, Memory Problems

WISC-III Profile

IQs		Factor indexes	
Full Scale	93	Verbal Comprehension	84
Verbal	83	Perceptual Organization	106
Performance[a]	106	Freedom from Distractibility	78
		Processing Speed	106

Verbal	Scaled score	Performance	Scaled score
Information	7	Picture Completion	12
Similarities	9	(Coding)	(12)
Arithmetic	7	Picture Arrangement	12
Vocabulary	7	Block Design	9
Comprehension	5	Object Assembly	11
(Digit Span)	(5)	Symbol Search	10
		(Mazes)	(11)

Kaufman Test of Educational Achievement (K-TEA) Comprehensive Form

	SS	Predicted[b]	d	Δ[c]	Sign.
Reading composite	80	103	−23	21.93	*
Reading Decoding	81	102	−21	20.65	*
Reading Comprehension	81	103	−22	18.85	*
Mathematic composite	89	104	−15	16.51	ns
Mathematics Computation	91	103	−12	17.05	ns
Mathematics Application	90	104	−14	15.26	ns
Spelling	76	103	−27	18.68	*

Wechsler Individual Achievement Test (WIAT)

	SS	Predicted[d]	d	Δ[e]	Sign.	Freq.[f]
Reading Composite	76	103	−27	18.97	*	2%
Basic Reading	80	103	−23	19.50	*	2%
Reading Comprehension	82	103	−21	16.95	*	4%
Mathematics Composite	90	103	−13	16.95	ns	15%
Mathematics Reasoning	92	103	−11	16.71	ns	15%
Numerical Operations	91	103	−12	15.11	ns	15%
Language Composite	79	103	−24	16.34	*	2%
Listening Comprehension	76	103	−27	13.64	*	2%
Oral Expression	93	102	−9	18.89	ns	>25%
Spelling	72	102	−30	18.42	*	<1%

Wide Range Assessment of Memory and Learning (WRAML)

General Index	79				
Verbal Memory Index	65	Visual Memory Index	88	Learning Index	98
Story Memory	4	Picture Memory	8	Verbal Learning	11
Sentence Memory	6	Design Memory	9	Visual Learning	10
Number-letter Memory	4	Finger Windows	8	Sound Symbol	8

[a]Calculated using Symbol Search instead of coding.

[b]From Table A8 using correlations between WISC-III and K-TEA subtests from Table A1 in Appendix.

[c]At $p < .05$ (two-tailed) from Table A7 in the Appendix.

[d]From Table A8 in Appendix using the correlation with PIQ from WIAT manual.

[e]At $p < .05$ (two-tailed) from Table 2, page 129, Flanagan and Alfonso (1993a).

[f]From Table A5 in the Appendix.

TABLE 12.4   Case Study #2, Steve Michaels, Age 10 years, 4 months, Reason for Referral:
School Problems, Inconsistency in Mathematics

WISC-III Profile

IQs		Factor indexes	
Full Scale IQ	105	Verbal Comprehension	98
Verbal IQ[a]	97	Perceptual Organization	114
Performance IQ[a]	114	Freedom from Distractibility	96
		Processing Speed	99

Verbal	Scaled score	Performance	Scaled score
Information	8	Picture Completion	12
Similarities	13	Coding	(8)
Arithmetic	9	Picture Arrangement	12
Vocabulary	9	Block Design	14
Comprehension	8	Object Assembly	11
Digit Span	(9)	Symbol Search	11
		Mazes	(11)

WIAT

Composite or subtest	Scaled score	Composite or subtest	Scaled score
Reading Composite	92	Mathematics Composite	83
Basic Reading	95	Mathematics Reasoning	89
Reading Comprehension	90	Numerical Operations	81
Language Composite	125	Writing Composite	78
Listening Comprehension	106	Spelling	84
Oral Expression	130	Written Expression	77

[a]Calculated using Symbol Search instead of coding.

(Kaufman, 1994, p. 101) between Jon's VIQ and PIQ scores. No statistically significant difference between index scores was determined, nor was unusual scatter present. Because the FSIQ does not adequately reflect Jon's abilities, the VIQ and the PIQ should be interpreted separately. Jon evidenced a distinct preference for hands-on manipulative activities over abstract and verbal activities. Therefore, subsequent discrepancy calculations were based on PIQ. Although we would suggest using a regression discrepancy procedure, an example of calculation of a simple difference based on PIQ and the Reading Composite for the K-TEA is given below. The correlation coefficient between the two tests was obtained from Table A1 in the Appendix. The reliability coefficients were obtained from the WISC-III and K-TEA manuals.

Calculation of Simple Difference Based on PIQ and Reading Composite Score from the K-TEA

1. Obtain scores on ability and achievement measures. Because Jon had a significant and meaningful difference between his VIQ and PIQ, it was decided that the FSIQ was not an adequate representation of his ability. The PIQ was used for all subsequent comparisons. It should be noted that although several comparisons are made here, in practice one would choose a single method.

2. Convert the scores to a common metric. For example, both scores could be converted (if necessary) to the IQ scale used for the WISC-III

TABLE 12.5 Additional Information for Steve Michaels, Case #2

Kaufman Test of Educational Achievement (K-TEA) Comprehensive Form

	Scaled score		Scaled score
Reading Composite	95	Mathematics Composite	106
Reading Decoding	93	Mathematics Application	107
Reading Comprehension	94	Mathematics Computation	104
Spelling	85	Battery Composite	95

Behavior Assessment System for Children (BASC)—Teacher Report
All scales within normal limits

Behavioral Assessment System for Children–Parent Report
(All validity scales within normal limits)[a]

	Mother	Father		Mother	Father
Behavioral symptoms index	86*	77*	Internalizing problems	76*	72*
Externalizing problems	72*	67^	Anxiety	67^	67^
Hyperactivity	76*	73*	Depression	91*	69^
Aggression	82*	64^	Somatization	53	65^
Conduct problems	49	56	Adaptive skills	42	46
Atypicality	76*	76*	Adaptibility	47	50
Withdrawal	38	57	Social skills	44	45
Attention problems	58	66^	Leadership	39	44

Child Behavior Checklist (CBCL)
Clinical elevations for

Total composite	70
Internalizing	72
Somatic complaints	72
Anxious/Depressed	72
Attention problems	75

Personality Inventory for Youth (PIY)
Clinical elevations for
Depression
Isolation
Social skills deficits

Conners Continuous Performance Test
Overall index = 6.16 (+ suggests an attention problem)

Home Situations Questionnaire—Revised
(Mean = 5.15, Standard deviation = 4.64)
Number of problem settings = 9
(Mean = 3.17, Standard deviation = 1.84)
Severity = 4.67

School Situations Questionnaire—Revised
(Mean = 2.98, Standard deviation = 3.08)
Number of problem settings = 3
(Mean = 3.56, Standard deviation = 1.68)
Severity = 2

Children's Self Report Project Inventory

Children's Depression Inventory

[a]* Clinically significant; ^ At risk.

(Mean = 100, SD = 15). Indeed, these scores are commonly available for the most popular achievement tests. In our case, scores with a mean of 100 and SD of 15 are readily available in the respective manuals.

3. Subtract the achievement test score from the PIQ score:

$$d = 104 - 80 = 24$$

4. Compute d' needed for significance:

$$d' = 1.96\ 15\ \sqrt{2 - .92 - .98} = 10.18 \quad p < .05 \text{ (two-tailed)},$$

where d' = difference needed for significance at given probability level; r_{xx} = .92 for PIQ, Table 5.1, p. 166, WISC-III manual; and r_{yy} = .98 for Reading Composite – average of the reliabilities for ages 6 and 7, Table 6.2, p. 187 K-TEA manual.

Or look up difference needed from an appropriate table, such as Table A6 in the Appendix.

5. If $d \geq d'$, the difference is significant. Our obtained difference of 24 points is larger than our 10.18; we can reject the hypothesis that the difference is due to chance.

6. Compare d with prevalence rates if available to see what proportion of the "normal" population have differences this large. Unfortunately, we don't have this information.

Using this same pair of tests, an example of a regression difference calculation is given next. Again, we based our calculations on the correlation coefficients in Table A1 in the Appendix.

Procedure for Calculating Predicted versus Obtained Achievement Discrepancies

1. Using ability and achievement scores that have been converted to the same scale, calculate predicted achievement:

$$\hat{Y} = 100 + .43 \, (104 - 100) = 102,$$

when both ability and achievement tests have Means = 100 and SDs = 15, where $\hat{Y}$ = predicted achievement and r_{xy} = .43 obtained from Table A1 in Appendix A for ages 6–7.

Or look up predicted achievement in Table A8 based on a correlation of .43.

2. Find the difference between predicted and actual achievement

$$102 - 80 = 24,$$

where 102 = predicted achievement; 80 = actual achievement; and 24 = discrepancy score.

3. Determine the magnitude of difference (discrepancy) required at the designated level of significance.

a. Compute r_{resid}:

$$r_{resid} = \frac{.98 = .92(.43)^2 - 2(.43)^2}{1 - (.43)^2} = .9573157$$

b. Compute SE_{resid}:

$$SE_{resid} = 15 \sqrt{1 - (.43)^2} \sqrt{1 - .9573157} = 2.7978921$$

c. Compute Δ:

$$\Delta = 1.96(15)\sqrt{1 - (.43)^2} - 1.65(2.7978921 = 21.93 \quad p < .05 \text{ (two-tailed)}$$

Or get value from Table A7 in the Appendix.
4. Compare difference obtained in 2 with prevalence rates from a "normal" population. No prevalence rates are available for the K-TEA.

Examples of results from the SAWS program for Jon are provided in Table 12.6 and 12.7. Both simple difference and regression difference data have been provided for comparison. However, either one or the other should be chosen, not both. For comparison, discrepancies for the WIAT based on FSIQ are also given in Tables 12.8 and 12.9 generated from the SAWS program. A general pattern of difficulties in reading, spelling, and listening comprehension would have been identified using FSIQ. However, individual differences for basic reading and listening comprehension would not have been statistically significant using a regression procedure. Additionally, in states where a single discrepancy standard such as 15 points is used, although the simple differences are statistically significant, it may be difficult to make a case for adequate provision of services for this child because differences are not greater than 15 points. It appears clear from these data that Jon has statistically and diagnostically meaningful discrepancies in the area of reading, listening expression, and spelling. Testing from both the WIAT and the K-TEA are similar. However, it is not clear what the sources of these difficulties are. Subsequent investigation of background information, teacher reports, testing, and classroom observation led to the conclusion that Jon had adequate opportunities to learn and that other environmental factors could not adequately account for his learning problems. In order to follow up to help determine the sources of Jon's

TABLE 12.6   Output from SAWS Program for Simple Differences Based on Performance IQ for Jon Bird[a]

	PIQ score	WIAT score	Difference[b]	Significance	Frequency
WIAT subtests					
Basic Reading	106	80	−26*	.01	5%
Mathematics Reasoning	106	92	−14	.05	15%
Spelling	106	72	−34*	.01	3%
Reading Comprehension	106	82	−24*	.01	10%
Numerical Operations	106	91	−15*	.05	15%
Listening Comprehension	106	76	−30*	.01	3%
Oral Expression	106	93	−13	.05	25%
Composites					
Reading	106	76	−30*	.01	3%
Mathematics	106	90	−16*	.01	15%
Language	106	79	−27*	.01	5%

[a]Ability–achievement discrepancy analysis: Date of ability testing: 11/10/95; Ability score type: PIQ; Ability score: 106. Copyrighted © 1995 The Psychological Corporation.
[b]* greater than or equal to critical difference of 15 points.

TABLE 12.7   Output from SAWS Program for Predicted–Achievement Method Based on Performance IQ for Jon Bird[a]

	Predicted score	Actual score	Difference	Significance[b]	Frequency
Subtests					
Basic Reading	103	80	−23	.05*	2%
Mathematics Reasoning	103	92	−11	ns	15%
Spelling	102	72	−30	.01*	<1%
Reading Comprehension	103	82	−21	.05*	4%
Numerical Operations	103	91	−12	ns	15%
Listening Comprehension	103	76	−27	.01*	2%
Oral Expression	102	93	−9	ns	>25%
Composites					
Reading	103	76	−27	.01*	2%
Mathematics	103	90	−13	ns	15%
Language	103	79	−24	.01*	3%

[a]Ability–achievement discrepancy analysis: Date of ability testing: 11/10/95; Ability score type: PIQ; Ability score: 106. Copyrighted © 1995 The Psychological Corporation.
[b]* significant at the .05 level.

TABLE 12.8   Output from SAWS Program for Simple Differences Based on FSIQ for Jon Bird[a]

	FSIQ score	WIAT score	Difference[b]	Significance	Frequency
WIAT subtests					
Basic Reading	93	80	**−13**	**.01**	15%
Mathematics Reasoning	93	92	−1	ns	>25%
Spelling	93	72	−21*	.01	5%
Reading Comprehension	93	82	**−11**	**.05**	15%
Numerical Operations	93	91	−2	ns	>25%
Listening Comprehension	93	76	−17*	.05	10%
Oral Expression	93	93	0	ns	>25%
Composites					
Reading	93	76	−17*	.01	10%
Mathematics	93	90	−3	ns	>25%
Language	93	79	**−14**	**.05**	15%

[a]Ability–achievement discrepancy analysis: Date of ability testing: 10/04/95; Ability score type: FSIQ; Ability score: 93.
[b]* greater than or equal to critical difference of 15 points.

difficulties, the Conners Continuous Performance Test (CPT; Conners, 1994), the Auditory Continuous Performance Test (ADCPT: Keith, 1994), the Wide Range Assessment of Memory and Language (WRAML; Sheslow & Adams, 1990), and the Behavior Assessment System for Children (BASC; Reynolds & Kamphaus, 1992) were also administered.

TABLE 12.9   Output from SAWS Program for Predicted-Achievement Method Based
on FSIQ for Jon Bird[a]

	Predicted score	Actual score	Difference	Significance[b]	Frequency
Subtests					
Basic Reading	96	80	**-16**	**ns**	**5%**
Mathematics Reasoning	95	92	-3	ns	>25%
Spelling	96	72	-24	.01*	2%
Reading Comprehension	95	82	**-13**	**ns**	10%
Numerical Operations	96	91	-5	ns	>25%
Listening Comprehension	96	76	-20	.01*	>3%
Oral Expression	97	93	-4	ns	>25%
Composites					
Reading	95	76	-19	**.05***	**3%**
Mathematics	95	90	-5	ns	>25%
Language	96	79	-17	.01*	10%

[a]Ability–achievement discrepancy analysis: Date of ability testing: 10/04/95; Ability score type:
FSIQ; Ability score: 93.

[b]* significant at the .05 level.

No significant difficulties were noted on either continuous performance test.
On the BASC, scores for the Attention Problems Scale were in the "at-risk" range.
Accompanied by the results of the WRAML, it was concluded that Jon is experiencing difficulties primarily with verbal and auditory memory. The subsequent
case conference determined Jon to be eligible for services as a student with LDs.
Multivariate comparisons could not be made for this 7-year old because the cluster analysis did not include students under 8 where writing composite scores are
not obtained.

CASE STUDY #2: STEVE MICHAELS

For our second case study, see Tables 12.4 and 12.5. We chose Steve Michaels
to illustrate a very different outcome as a result of discrepancy analysis. Steve is a
10-year-old male referred by his parents, who reported Steve's difficulty in completing schoolwork and inconsistencies in performance, especially in mathematics. Steve was seen by his teacher as compliant but somewhat withdrawn without
many friends. She noted inconsistencies in performance and difficulty in completing assignments. She also expressed concern about fine motor skills and slow processing speed.

There is a statistically significant difference between VIQ and PIQ, but the difference is not diagnostically meaningful. Therefore, the FSIQ was used to make
subsequent comparisons. In comparing FSIQ with the WIAT scores, there are statistically significant differences between expected and obtained achievement (see
Table 12.10) for mathematics reasoning and numerical operations and written and
oral expression. Interestingly, there is an advantage for oral expression. The ex-

TABLE 12.10   Output from SAWS Program for Predicted-Achievement Method Based on FSIQ for Steve Michaels[a]

	Predicted score	Actual score	Difference	Significance[b]	Frequency
Subtests					
Basic Reading	103	95	−8	ns	20%
Mathematics Reasoning	104	89	−15	.01*	5%
Spelling	103	84	−19	.05*	4%
Reading Comprehension	103	90	−13	ns	10%
Numerical Operations	103	81	−22	.01*	2%
Listening Comprehension	103	106	3	ns	>25%
Oral Expression	102	130	28	.01*	2%
Written Expression	102	77	−25	.01*	3%
Composites					
Reading	103	92	−11	ns	15%
Mathematics	104	83	−21	.01*	2%
Language	103	125	22	.05*	2%
Writing	103	78	−25	.01*	2%

[a]Ability–achievement discrepancy analysis: Date of ability testing: 12/10/96; Ability score type: FSIQ; Ability score: 105. Copyright © 1995 The Psychological Corporation.
[b]* significant at the .05 level.

aminer noted problems in the mathematics subtests in paying attention to signs and other evidence of "carelessness" and/or inattention. When presented arithmetic problems orally both on the WISC-III and WIAT, Steve often asked for repetition of questions and was seen to calculate using his fingers. Therefore, a second achievement test was given to verify the results of the WIAT. Those results are given in Table 12.5.

On this second measure of mathematics achievement, Steve's performance was much better even though the tasks were similar. Although a severe discrepancy was documented for mathematics on the WIAT, on the K-TEA no such discrepancy was documented. Therefore, alternative hypotheses to a LD were explored. Several hypotheses were developed through personality and other testing, the results of which are presented in Table 12.5.

Personality and behavioral assessment from individually administered parent reports noted similar clinically significant areas of concern. Throughout the assessment process, various personality and behavioral measures were elicited from Steve. On such measures he consistently endorsed items suggesting feelings of anger and depression. He also expressed some feelings of isolation and alienation and remarked about conflict he perceived within his family. He communicated a desire for greater social interaction, but indicated that he thought he had deficient social skills. The possibility of ADD or an LD in written expression cannot be ruled out, but determination must be made in light of the social and emotional problems. Many of the difficulties seem to be centered around home situations rather than at school. It was recommended that Steve and his parents be seen by a

TABLE 12.11 Multivariate Comparisons for Steve Michaels for WISC-III and WAIT[a]

FSIQ	VCI	POI	FDI	PSI	ReadC	MathC	LangC	WriteC	Sum $\sum(A-B)^2$
A. Type 2 FSIQ = 110	105	114	105	116	105	107	103	110	
B. Student's scores 103	98	114	96	99	92	79	125	78	
A–B	7	0	9	17	13	28	–22	32	
(A–B)²	49	0	81	289	169	784	484	1024	2882
A. Type 3 FSIQ = 100	100	105	96	93	98	100	102	91	
B. Student's scores 103	98	114	96	99	92	79	125	78	
A–B	2	–9	0	–6	6	21	–23	13	
(A–B)²	4	81	0	36	36	441	529	169	1298
A. Type 4 FSIQ = 99	99	92	104	104	105	104	101	108	
B. Student's scores 103	98	114	96	99	92	79	125	78	
A–B	1	–22	8	5	13	25	–24	30	
(A–B)²	1	484	64	25	169	625	576	900	2846

[a] FSIQ, Full-Scale IQ; VCI, Verbal Comprehension Index; POI, Perceptual Organization Index; FOI, Freedom from Distractibility Index; PDI, Perceptual Organization Index; FDI, Freedom from Distractibility Index; PSI, Processing Speed Index.

TABLE 12.12   Output from SAWS Program for Simple Differences Based on FSIQ for Steve Michaels[a]

	FSIQ score	WIAT score	Difference[b]	Significance	Frequency
WIAT subtests					
Basic Reading	105	95	−10	.05	20%
Mathematics Reasoning	105	89	−16*	.01	10%
Spelling	105	84	−21*	.01	5%
Reading Comprehension	105	90	−15*	.01	10%
Numerical Operations	105	81	−24*	.01	3%
Listening Comprehension	105	106	1	ns	>25%
Oral Expression	105	130	25*	.01	10%
Written Expression	105	77	−28*	.01	4%
Composites					
Reading	105	92	−13	.01	10%
Mathematics	105	83	−22*	.01	3%
Language	105	125	20*	.01	10%
Writing	105	78	−27*	.01	3%

[a]Ability–achievement discrepancy analysis: Date of ability testing: 12/10/96; Ability score type: FSIQ; Ability score: 105. Copyright © 1995 The Psychological Corporation.

[b]* Critical difference ≥ 15 points.

therapist in order to deal with his concerns. It was also recommended that the parents consult a physician for evaluation for possible pharmacological intervention for depression. Educational intervention was aimed at increasing his ability to get his thoughts down on paper and included use of a tape recorder for composing, with subsequent computer and spell-checker.

We also completed a multivariate analysis of Steve's profile using the Glutting et al. (1994) method. These results are presented in Table 11. Steve's profile differs from the three comparison groups (all d's are ≥ 1295). However, if the final step of the procedure is followed—that is, subtracting the *highest* WIAT composite score, Oral expression, 130, from the *highest* factor index from the WISC, in this case POI of 114, we would have a negative difference. The WIAT score is higher than the WISC score. Therefore, we conclude that Steve is an "overachiever." It would be difficult to make a case for such a conclusion based on present evaluation data and class performance. This case illustrates the difficulty of applying group results to individual cases and the difficulty in "real world" situations in blindly applying mathematical calculation. This case also illustrates the powerful influence of nonintellective factors on test scores.

If we look at Table 12.12, which gives the simple difference calculations for WISC–WIAT comparisons, we also see an illustration of the tendency for students who score higher than 100 to be overidentified using simple difference scores. In this case, almost every score on the WIAT is indicated to be significantly discrepant from the obtained FSIQ score. The results in Table 12.11 from a regression discrepancy analysis give us a much more realistic view of Steve's difficulties.

These two case studies illustrate the complicated process of clinical evaluation, but also highlight the importance of including achievement information within such evaluations. It has also become clear through our discussion that many factors are involved in using achievement tests with the WISC-III. These issues stem from the instruments themselves and also their use in combinations

SUMMARY

Any psychoeducational assessment of a child is incomplete without the inclusion of some measure of achievement. There are many issues surrounding use of achievement measures with the WISC-III. As yet, there is a paucity of research linking the WISC-III to a majority of available standardized achievement measures. Regardless of problems inherent in its use, a severe discrepancy between actual achievement and that predicted by ability remains ubiquitous in defining LDs. Given that clinicians use and sometimes misuse this procedure, guidance in making informed choices about which procedures to use as well as practice with various methods have been provided in this chapter. Case studies illustrating many of the issues surrounding use of achievement measures with the WISC-III have been provided. However, these same cases illustrate the limitations of mathematical techniques. Readers are cautioned to combine all available information with test scores in forming hypotheses and in guiding educational decision making.

APPENDIX

TABLE A1 Correlations between the K-TEA Comprehensive Form and the WISC-III[a]

	WISC-III		Correlation with K-TEA Comprehensive Form subtest or composite						
WISC-III Scale	Mean	SD	Reading decoding	Reading comprehension	Reading composite	Math applications	Math computation	Math composite	Spelling
Ages 6–7									
Verbal	100.1	11.9	.53	.52	.55	.63	.55	.65	.51
Performance	100.1	13.1	.43	.50	.46	.57	.45	.58	.44
Full Scale	99.9	11.8	.57	.60	.60	.71	.58	.72	.56
(n = 32) K-TEA Mean			94.5	93.2	93.6	97.8	91.6	94.8	92.8
SD			19.7	14.1	17.5	13.4	14.7	13.7	14.3
Ages 3–10									
Verbal	97.2	16.3	.77	.81	.82	.80	.70	.78	.76
Performance	96.5	15.8	.59	.69	.65	.64	.62	.65	.59
Full Scale	96.5	16.4	.73	.80	.79	.77	.70	.77	.73
(n = 44) K-TEA Mean			94.0	94.5	94.2	97.8	95.8	96.7	92.6
SD			15.9	15.8	16.5	18.2	15.7	17.7	14.9
Ages 11–13									
Verbal	94.5	16.8	.72	.85	.83	.86	.68	.84	.61
Performance	99.2	17.0	.58	.71	.69	.68	.70	.73	.57
Full Scale	96.4	17.1	.70	.84	.82	.83	.74	.84	.64
(n = 29) K-TEA Mean			94.5	97.2	96.2	98.0	94.2	95.8	89.4
SD			12.9	16.4	15.4	17.4	14.7	16.4	12.3
Ages 14–16									
Verbal	87.7	17.4	.78	.81	.84	.84	.73	.80	.68
Performance	89.5	17.3	.67	.73	.75	.69	.67	.69	.59
Full Scale	87.5	18.2	.75	.80	.83	.79	.73	.78	.66
(n = 29) K-TEA Mean			85.6	87.4	85.3	86.7	82.3	84.2	85.1
SD			16.9	18.1	18.2	18.3	16.9	17.7	17.8

[a]Table of correlations reported in Research Report KT-2 used with permission. Prepared by George McCloskey, Kaufman Test of Educational Achievement (K-TEA) by Alan and Nadeen Kaufman © 1985. Both available from American Guidance Service, Inc., 4201 Woodland Road, Circle Pines, MN 55014-1796.

TABLE A2   Ability–Achievement Discrepancies: Simple Differences between Ability and Achievement Scores Obtained by Various Percentages of Children Ages 6:00 to 16:11 in the Standardization Linking Sample for the WISC-III and the WIAT Using the Verbal IQ Score

WIAT subtests and composites	Percentages								
	25	20	15	10	5	4	3	2	1
Subtests									
Basic Reading	5	7	9	12	17	18	22	25	27
Mathematical Reasoning	4	6	9	11	16	17	18	21	24
Spelling	6	9	11	15	20	21	23	26	31
Reading Comprehension	5	7	9	12	16	17	19	21	24
Numerical Operations	7	8	11	14	19	21	23	25	28
Listening Comprehension	6	8	10	14	18	21	23	25	28
Oral Expression	9	12	15	19	26	28	29	31	36
Written Expression	11	13	16	20	26	28	29	31	36
Composites									
Reading	5	7	9	11	16	18	19	21	25
Mathematics	5	7	9	12	16	17	18	20	23
Language	7	10	12	16	21	22	23	25	29
Writing[a]	8	11	12	15	19	22	23	26	31

[a]Written Expression and Writing Composite values are based on scores obtained by children ages 8:0–19:11.

TABLE A3   Ability–Achievement Discrepancies: Simple Differences between Ability and Achievement Scores Obtained by Various Percentages of Children Ages 6:00 to 16:11 in the Standardization Linking Sample for the WISC-III and the WIAT Using the Performance IQ

WIAT subtests and composites	Percentages								
	25	20	15	10	5	4	3	2	1
Subtests									
Basic Reading	10	12	15	19	25	26	29	31	36
Mathematical Reasoning	9	11	14	17	23	25	26	30	32
Spelling	11	13	16	20	27	29	32	35	38
Reading Comprehension	10	13	16	19	24	25	27	30	33
Numerical Operations	10	12	15	19	26	18	30	33	37
Listening Comprehension	11	13	16	19	25	27	30	32	37
Oral Expression	13	15	18	23	29	32	34	37	40
Written Expression	13	16	19	23	30	32	33	35	39
Composites									
Reading	10	13	15	19	25	26	27	32	34
Mathematics	9	11	14	18	25	26	28	31	34
Language	12	15	17	21	26	28	29	31	35
Writing[a]	11	14	18	22	28	30	32	36	40

[a]Written Expression and Writing Composite values are based on scores obtained by children ages 8:0–19:11.

TABLE A4   Ability–Achievement Discrepancies: Differences between Predicted and Actual Standard Scores Obtained by Various Percentages of Children Ages 6:00 to 16:11 in the Standardization Linking Sample for the WISC-III and the WIAT Using the Verbal Score

WIAT subtests and composites	Percentages								
	25	20	15	10	5	4	3	2	1
Subtests									
Basic Reading	4	6	8	10	15	16	17	19	21
Mathematical Reasoning	4	5	7	10	13	14	15	17	19
Spelling	6	8	10	12	16	17	19	20	23
Reading Comprehension	4	7	9	11	14	15	16	17	19
Numerical Operations	5	7	9	12	17	18	19	20	24
Listening Comprehension	6	7	9	11	16	18	19	21	25
Oral Expression	8	10	13	17	20	21	23	24	29
Written Expression	10	12	14	17	22	23	25	26	30
Composites									
Reading	5	7	9	11	15	16	17	18	22
Mathematics	5	7	8	12	14	15	17	19	21
Language	7	9	12	14	17	18	19	22	24
Writing[a]	7	9	11	14	18	20	21	23	25

[a]Written Expression and Writing Composite values are based on scores obtained by children ages 8:0–19:11.

TABLE A5   Ability–Achievement Discrepancies: Differences between Predicted and Actual Standard Scores Obtained by Various Percentages of Children Ages 6:00 to 16:11 in the Standardization Linking Sample for the WISC-III and the WIAT Using the Performance IQ Score

WIAT subtests and composites	Percentages								
	25	20	15	10	5	4	3	2	1
Subtests									
Basic Reading	7	9	11	14	18	20	21	23	25
Mathematical Reasoning	7	9	11	14	19	20	21	22	26
Spelling	8	9	12	15	20	21	22	25	27
Reading Comprehension	8	10	12	15	19	20	22	24	25
Numerical Operations	7	9	12	16	20	22	24	26	28
Listening Comprehension	8	10	13	16	20	21	23	25	28
Oral Expression	9	12	14	18	22	23	25	27	31
Written Expression	11	13	16	19	24	25	26	28	30
Composites									
Reading	8	10	13	16	20	22	24	26	29
Mathematics	8	10	12	16	20	21	23	25	28
Language	9	11	14	17	21	22	23	24	28
Writing[a]	9	11	14	17	22	23	25	28	31

[a]Written Expression and Writing Composite values are based on scores obtained by children ages 8:0–19:11.

TABLE A6 Simple Difference Discrepancies Required for Significance between WISC-III and K-TEA Scores

Ages WISC-III scale	p	K-TEA subtests and composites						
		Reading decoding	Reading comprehension	Reading composite	Math application	Math computation	Math composite	Spelling
Ages 6–7								
Verbal	.05	9.75	10.18	8.82	12.12	12.82	10.60	11.39
	.01	12.84	13.41	11.61	15.96	16.87	13.95	14.99
Performance	.05	10.60	11.00	9.30	12.82	13.47	11.39	12.12
	.01	13.95	14.48	12.24	16.87	17.73	14.99	15.96
Full Scale	.05	8.82	9.30	7.78	11.39	12.12	9.75	10.60
	.01	11.61	11.61	10.24	14.99	15.96	12.84	13.95
Ages 8–10								
Verbal	.05	8.82	9.75	8.32	11.00	10.60	9.30	9.30
	.01	11.61	12.84	10.95	14.48	13.95	12.24	12.24
Performance	.05	10.60	11.39	10.18	12.47	12.12	11.00	11.00
	.01	13.37	14.99	13.41	16.42	15.96	14.48	14.48
Full Scale	.05	8.32	9.30	7.78	10.60	10.18	8.82	8.82
	.01	10.79	12.24	10.24	13.95	13.41	11.61	11.61
Ages 11–13								
Verbal	.05	8.82	10.81	8.32	10.18	10.60	8.82	9.75
	.01	11.61	13.41	10.96	13.41	13.95	11.61	12.84
Performance	.05	11.00	12.12	10.60	12.12	12.47	11.00	11.76
	.01	14.48	15.96	13.95	15.96	16.42	14.48	15.48
Full Scale	.05	8.82	10.18	8.32	10.18	10.60	8.87	9.75
	.01	11.61	13.41	10.95	13.41	13.95	11.61	12.00
Ages 14–16								
Verbal	.05	9.30	10.60	9.30	10.60	10.60	9.30	9.75
	.01	12.24	13.95	12.24	13.95	13.95	12.24	12.84
Performance	.05	10.60	11.76	10.60	11.76	11.76	10.60	11.00
	.01	13.95	15.48	13.95	15.48	15.48	13.95	14.48
Full Scale	.05	8.82	10.18	8.82	10.18	10.18	8.82	7.30
	.01	11.61	13.41	11.61	13.41	13.41	11.61	12.24

TABLE A7 Regression Discrepancies Required for Significance between WISC-III and K-TEA Scores

Ages WISC-III scale	p	K-TEA subtests and composites						
		Reading decoding	Reading comprehension	Reading composite	Math application	Math computation	Math composite	Spelling
Ages 6–7								
Verbal	.05	13.89	18.61	19.53	13.98	15.25	14.93	17.53
	.01	23.51	23.88	25.23	17.56	19.19	18.95	22.34
Performance	.05	20.65	18.80	21.93	15.26	17.05	16.51	18.68
	.01	26.62	24.10	28.42	19.23	21.57	21.02	23.84
Full Scale	.05	26.62	17.07	18.70	11.95	14.79	13.15	16.70
	.01	18.29	21.85	24.15	14.89	18.60	16.61	21.25
Ages 8–10								
Verbal	.05	12.23	9.70	10.58	9.00	13.00	11.38	12.16
	.01	15.47	12.05	13.34	11.01	16.34	14.31	15.34
Performance	.05	17.13	13.34	15.89	13.77	14.69	15.00	18.80
	.01	21.91	16.80	20.29	17.79	18.53	19.04	24.10
Full Scale	.05	13.96	10.40	12.22	10.41	13.18	12.04	13.48
	.01	17.80	12.99	15.53	12.91	16.61	15.20	17.12
Ages 11–13								
Verbal	.05	14.38	7.42	10.12	6.91	13.61	9.16	16.36
	.01	18.33	9.00	12.71	8.33	17.15	11.41	20.87
Performance	.05	16.97	12.12	14.38	13.12	12.11	12.90	16.63
	.01	21.61	15.12	18.27	16.46	15.08	16.27	21.17
Full Scale	.05	14.71	7.92	10.58	8.40	11.65	9.16	15.57
	.01	18.76	9.66	13.34	10.29	14.58	11.41	19.82
Ages 14–16								
Verbal	.05	11.38	8.93	8.72	7.55	12.01	10.55	14.42
	.01	14.31	10.96	10.79	9.13	15.04	13.21	18.30
Performance	.05	14.51	11.43	11.82	12.77	13.40	13.93	16.40
	.01	18.49	14.21	14.83	16.00	16.83	17.64	20.89
Full Scale	.05	12.78	9.60	9.51	12.55	12.22	11.65	15.20
	.01	16.17	11.86	11.85	15.76	15.32	14.69	19.35

TABLE A8   Predicted Achievement Based on IQ Score Using the Regression Formula

	Correlation between ability and achievement										
IQ score	0.35	0.4	0.45	0.5	0.55	0.6	0.65	0.7	0.75	0.8	0.85
	Predicted Achievement Calculated using = 100 + rxy (X-100)										
70	90	88	87	85	84	82	81	79	78	76	75
71	90	88	87	86	84	83	81	80	78	77	75
72	91	89	87	86	85	83	82	80	79	78	76
73	91	89	88	87	85	84	82	81	80	78	77
74	91	90	88	87	86	84	83	82	81	79	78
75	91	90	89	88	86	85	84	83	81	80	79
76	92	90	89	88	87	86	84	83	82	81	80
77	92	91	90	89	87	86	85	84	83	82	80
78	92	91	90	89	88	87	86	85	84	82	81
79	93	92	91	90	88	87	86	85	84	83	82
80	93	92	91	90	89	88	87	86	85	84	83
81	93	92	91	91	90	89	88	87	86	85	84
82	94	93	92	91	90	89	88	87	87	86	85
83	94	93	92	92	91	90	89	88	87	86	86
84	94	94	93	92	91	90	90	89	88	87	86
85	95	94	93	93	92	91	90	90	89	88	87
86	95	94	94	93	92	92	91	90	90	89	88
87	95	95	94	94	93	92	92	91	90	90	89
88	96	95	95	94	93	93	92	92	91	90	90
89	96	96	95	95	94	93	93	92	92	91	91
90	97	96	96	95	95	94	94	93	93	92	92
91	97	96	96	96	95	95	94	94	93	93	92
92	97	97	96	96	96	95	95	94	94	94	93
93	98	97	97	97	96	96	95	95	95	94	94
94	98	98	97	97	97	96	96	96	96	95	95
95	98	98	98	98	97	97	97	97	96	96	96
96	99	98	98	98	98	98	97	97	97	97	97
97	99	99	99	99	98	98	98	98	98	98	97
98	99	99	99	99	99	99	99	99	99	98	98
99	100	100	100	100	99	99	99	99	99	99	99
100	100	100	100	100	100	100	100	100	100	100	100
101	100	100	100	101	101	101	101	101	101	101	101
102	101	101	101	101	101	101	101	101	102	102	102
103	101	101	101	102	102	102	102	102	102	102	103
104	101	102	102	102	102	102	103	103	103	103	103
105	102	102	102	103	103	103	103	104	104	104	104
106	102	102	103	103	103	104	104	104	105	105	105
107	102	103	103	104	104	104	105	105	105	106	106
108	103	103	104	104	104	105	105	106	106	106	107
109	103	104	104	105	105	105	106	106	107	107	108
110	104	104	105	105	106	106	107	107	108	108	109
111	104	104	105	105	106	106	107	107	108	108	109
112	104	105	105	106	107	107	108	108	109	110	110
113	105	105	106	107	107	108	108	109	110	110	111
114	105	106	106	107	108	108	109	110	111	111	112

(continues)

TABLE A8   *(continued)*

	Correlation between ability and achievement									
IQ score	0.35	0.4	0.45	0.5	0.55	0.6	0.65	0.7	0.75	0.8	0.85
	Predicted Achievement Calculated using = 100 + rxy (X-100)									
115	105	106	107	108	108	109	110	111	111	112	113
116	106	106	107	108	109	110	110	111	112	113	114
117	106	107	108	109	109	110	111	112	113	114	114
118	106	107	108	109	110	111	112	113	114	114	115
119	107	108	109	110	110	111	112	113	114	115	116
120	107	108	109	110	111	112	113	114	115	116	117
121	107	108	109	111	112	113	114	115	116	117	118
122	108	109	110	111	112	113	114	115	117	118	119
123	108	109	110	112	113	114	115	116	117	118	120
124	108	110	111	112	113	114	116	117	118	119	120
125	109	110	111	113	114	115	116	118	119	120	121
126	109	110	112	113	114	116	117	118	119	120	121
127	109	111	112	114	115	116	118	119	120	122	123
128	110	111	113	114	115	117	118	120	121	122	124
129	110	112	113	115	116	117	119	120	122	123	125
130	111	112	114	115	117	118	120	121	123	124	126
131	111	112	114	116	117	119	120	122	123	125	126
132	111	113	114	116	118	119	121	122	124	126	127
133	112	113	115	117	118	120	121	123	125	126	128
134	112	114	115	117	119	120	122	124	126	127	129
135	112	114	116	118	119	121	123	125	126	128	130
136	113	114	116	118	120	122	123	125	127	129	131
137	113	115	117	119	120	122	124	126	128	130	131
138	113	115	117	119	121	123	125	127	129	130	132
139	114	116	118	120	121	123	125	127	129	131	133
140	114	116	118	120	122	124	126	128	130	132	134
141	114	116	118	121	123	125	127	129	131	133	135
142	115	117	119	121	123	125	127	129	132	134	136
143	115	117	119	122	124	126	128	130	132	134	137
144	115	118	120	122	124	126	129	131	133	135	137
145	116	118	120	123	125	127	129	132	134	136	138
146	116	118	121	123	125	128	130	132	135	137	139
147	116	119	121	124	126	128	131	133	135	138	140

REFERENCES

American Psychiatric Association (1994). *Diagnostic and statistical manual of mental disorders* (4th ed.) Washington, DC: Author.

Berk, R. A. (1984). *Screening and diagnosis of children with learning disabilities.* Springfield, IL: Charles Thomas.

Braden, J. P. (1987). A comparison of regression and standard score discrepancy methods for learning disabilities identification: Effect on racial representation. *Journal of School Psychology, 25,* 23–29.

Cone, T. E., & Wilson, L. R. (1981). Quantifying a severe discrepancy: A critical analysis. *Learning Disability Quarterly, 4,* 359–371.

Conners, C. K., (1994). *Conners' Continuous Performance Test (CPT)*. North Tonawanda, NY: Multi-Health Systems.

Crocker, L. & Algina, J. (1985). *Introduction to classical and modern test theory*. Chicago: Holt, Rinehart & Winston.

Evans, L. D. (1990). A conceptual overview of the regression discrepancy model for determining severe discrepancy between IQ and achievement scores. *Journal of Learning Disabilities, 23*, 406–412.

Figueroa, R. A., & Sassenrath, J. M. (1989). A longitudinal study of the predictive validity of the System of Multicultural Pluralistic Assessment (SOMPA). *Psychology in the Schools, 26*, 1–19.

Flanagan, D. P., & Alfonso, V. C. (1993a). Differences required for significance between Wechsler verbal and performance IQS and the WIAT subtests and composites: The predicted-achievement method. *Psychology in the Schools, 30*, 125–132.

Flanagan, D. P., & Alfonso, V. C. (1993b). WIAT subtest and composite predicted-achievement values based on WISC-III verbal and performance IQS. *Psychology in the Schools, 30*, 310–320.

Fletcher, J. M., Espy, K. A., Francis, D. J., Davidson, K. C., Rourke, B. P., & Shaywitz, S. E. (1989). Comparisons of cutoff and regression-based definitions of reading disabilities. *Journal of Learning Disabilities, 22*, 334–338, 355.

Frankenberger, W., & Fronzaglio, K. (1991). A review of states' criteria and procedures for identifying children with disabilities, *Journal of Learning Disabilities, 24*, 495–500.

Glutting, J. J., McDermott, P. A., Prifitera, A., & McGrath, E. A. (1994). Core profile types for the WISC-III and WIAT: Their development and application in identifying multivariate IQ-achievement discrepancies. *School Psychology Review, 23*(4), 619–639.

Hishinuma, E. S., & Yamakawa, R. (1993). Construct and criterion related validity of the WISC-III for exceptional students and those who are at risk. *Journal of Psychoeducational Assessment: WISC-III Monograph*, 94–104. Cordova, TN: Psychoeducational Corporation.

Jastak, S., & Wilkinson, G. S. (1984). *Wide Range Achievement Test—Revised*. Wilmington, DE; Jastak and Associates.

Kamphaus, R. W. (1993). *Clinical assessment of children's intelligence: A handbook for professional practice*. Boston: Allyn and Bacon.

Kamphaus, R. W., Slotkin, J., & DeVincentis, C. (1990). Clinical assessment of children's achievement. In C. R. Reynolds & R. W. Kamphaus, *Handbook of psychological & educational assessment of children: Intelligence and achievement* (pp. 552–569). New York: Guilford.

Kaufman, A. S. (1994). *Intelligent testing with the WISC-III*. New York: John Wiley & Sons.

Keith, R. W. (1994). *Auditory Continuous Performance Test (ACPT)*. San Antonio, TX: The Psychological Corporation.

Keogh, B. K. (1993). Linking purpose and practice: Social-political and developmental perspectives on classification. In G. R. Lyon, J. F. Kavanagh, & N. A. Krasnegor (Eds.), *Better understanding learning disabilities: New views on research and their implications for education and public policies* (pp. 273–307). Baltimore: Paul H. Brooks.

Lavin, C. (1996). The relationship between the Wechsler Intelligence Scale for Children—Third Edition and the Kaufman Test of Educational Achievement. *Psychology in the Schools, 13*, 119–123.

Lyon, G. R. (1996). Learning disabilities. *The Future of Children: Special Education for Students with Disabilities, 6*(1), 54–76.

McCloskey, G., Brown, R., Carson, S., Chen, T-H., Erickson, S, Hanson, S, & Perro, B. (1992). *Correlations between the KTEA Comprehensive Form and the WISC-III*. (Research Report No KT-2). Available from American Guidance Services, 4201 Woodland Rd., Circle Pines, MN 55014-1796.

McDermott, P. A., Fantuzzo, J. W., & Glutting, J. J. (1990). Just say not to subtest analysis: A critique of Wechsler theory and practice. *Journal of Psychoeducational Assessment, 8*, 290–302.

McDermott, P. A. Fantuzzo, J. W., & Glutting, J. J. (1992). Illusions of meaning in the ipsative assessment of children's abilities. *Journal of Special Education, 25*, 504–526.

McKleskey, J., & Waldron, N. (1991). Identifying students with learning disabilities: The effect of implementing statewide guidelines. *Journal of Learning Disabilities, 24*, 501–506.

Mercer, C. D., King-Sears, P., & Mercer, A. R. (1990). Learning disability definitions and criteria used by state education departments. *Learning Disabilities quarterly, 13*, 141–152.

Psychological Corporation (1995). *Scoring assistant for the Wechsler scales.* San Antonio: author.

Reynolds, C. (1984). Critical measurement issues in learning disabilities. *Journal of Special Education, 18,* 451–475.

Reynolds, C. R. (1990). Conceptual and technical problems in learning disability diagnosis. In C. R. Reynolds & R. W. Kamphaus (Eds.), *Handbook of psychological and educational assessment of children: Intelligence and achievement* (pp. 571–592). New York: Guilford.

Reynolds, C. R., & Kamphaus, R. W. (1992). *BASC: Behavior Assessment System for Children.* Circle Pines, MN: American Guidance Service.

Roid, G. H. (1994). Patterns of writing skills derived from cluster analysis of direct-writing assessments, *Applied Measurement in Education, 7(2),* 159–170.

Ross, R. P. (1992). Aptitude-achievement discrepancy scores: Accuracy in analysis ignored. *School Psychology Review, 21(3),* 509–514.

Ross, R. P. (1995). Impact on psychologists of state guidelines for evaluating under achievement. *Learning Disabilities Quarterly, 18(1),* 43–56.

Rutter, M., & Yule, W. (1975). The concept of specific reading retardation. *Journal of Child Psychology and Psychiatry, 16,* 181–197.

Salvia, J., & Ysseldyke, J. E. (1991). *Assessment (5th ed.)* Boston: Houghton Mifflin.

Shepard, L. (1980). An evaluation of the regression discrepancy method for identifying children with learning disabilities. *Journal of Special Education, 14,* 79–91.

Sheslow, D., & Adams, W. (1990). *Wide Range Assessment of Memory and Learning (WRAM-L).* Wilmington, DE: Jastak.

Slate, J. R. (1994). WISC-III correlations with the WIAT. *Psychology in the Schools, 31,* 278–285.

Slate, J. R., Jones, C. H., Graham, L. S., & Bower, J. (1994). Correlations of WISC-III, WRAT-R, KM-R, and PPVT-R scores in students with specific learning disabilities. *Learning Disabilities Research & Practice, 9* (2), 104–107.

Smith, T. D., Smith, B. L., & Smithson, M. M. (1995). The relationship between the WISC-III and the WRAT3 in a sample of rural referred children, *Psychology in the Schools, 32,* 291–295.

Spadafore, G. J. (1993). The WISC and WIAT: A good marriage for determining LD discrepancy. *The Psychologist, 16,(3).*

Stanovich, K. E. (1993). The construct validity of discrepancy definitions of reading disability. In G. R. Lyon, J. F. Kavanagh, & N. A. Krasnegor (Eds.), *Better understanding learning disabilities: New views on research and their implications for education and public policies* (pp. 273–307). Baltimore: Paul H. Brooks.

Teeter, P. A., & Smith, P. L. (1993). WISC-III and WJ-R: Predictive and discriminant validity for students with severe emotional disturbance. In B. Bracken & R. S. McCallum (Eds.), *Journal of Psychoeducational Assessment, Advances in psychoeducational assessment, WISC-III* (pp. 114–124). Memphis, TN: Psychoeducational Publishing Co.

Thorndike, R. L. (1963). *The concepts of over- and under-achievement.* Bureau of Publications, Teachers College, Columbia University, New York.

Vance, B., & Fuller, G. B. (1995a). Relation of scores on WISC-III and WRAT-3 for a sample of referred children and youth. *Psychological reports, 76,* 371–374.

Vance, B., & Fuller, G. (1995b). Relationship of scores on the WISC-III and the WRAT3 for a sample of referred children and youths, *Psychological Reports, 76,* 371–374.

Vance, B., Mayes, L., Fuller, G. B., Abdullah, A. A. (1994). A preliminary study of the relationship of the WISC-III and WRAT-3 with a sample of exceptional students, *Diagnostique, 19* (4), 15–21.

Wechsler, D. (1991). *Manual for the Wechsler Intelligence Scale for Children—Third Edition (WISC-III).* San Antonio, TX: Psychological Corporation.

Wechsler Individual Achievement Test (WIAT) (1992). San Antonio: The Psychological Corporation.

Weiss, L. G., Prifitera, A., & Roid, G. (1993). the WISC-III and fairness of predicting achievement across ethnic and gender groups. In B. Bracken & R. S. McCallum (Eds.), *Journal of Psychoeducational Assessment: Advances in psychoeducational assessment, WISC-III* (pp. 35–42). Memphis, TN. Psychoeducational Publishing Co.

Wilkinson, G. S. (1993). *Manual for the Wide Range Achievement Test (3rd ed.).* Wilmington, DE: Wide Range.

Wirt, R. D., Lachar, D., Klinedinst, J. K., & Seat, P. D. (1977). *Multidimensional description of child personality: A manual for the Personality Inventory for Children. Los* Angeles: Western Psychological Services.

Woodin, M. F., Peterson, K., Croombs, Y., & Wasielweski, S. (1996). *Achievement test preferences among Indiana school psychologists.* Available from senior author.

13

ASSESSMENT
OF TEST BEHAVIORS WITH
THE WISC-III

THOMAS OAKLAND

Department of Foundations of Education
University of Florida
Gainesville, Florida

JOSEPH GLUTTING

College of Education
University of Delaware
Newark, Delaware

THE TESTING PROCESS

Psychoeducational testing is a process in which skilled examiners carefully observe the actual performance of persons under standardized conditions.[1] The process incorporates elements of both science and art and draws upon informal and formal assessment methods. From science we obtain rules that govern the collection, recording, and interpretation of data so as to establish standardized methods that guide the use of a test in every setting in which it is applied. Alternatively, examiners' artistic qualities come from their extended experience in administering tests and working in other ways with children, youth, and adults. This artistic and/or clinical aspect of assessment is especially important when working with individuals whose dispositions make them difficult to test. No set of rules can govern the manner in which a test always is administered. As every clinician knows,

---

[1] As a matter of convenience, the terms *children* and *child* will be used in this chapter to refer to all age ranges covered by the WISC-III.

WISC-III Clinical Use and Interpretation:
Scientist–Practitioner Perspectives

children differ in their personal needs and test-related qualities. In addition, test-ing conditions vary from setting to setting.

Two examples are provided. Christine willingly comes with the examiner. They develop rapport easily. She is eager to help the examiner set up the testing room, listens attentively to directions, endeavors to do her best, and sustains a high level of interest and motivation throughout the examination. In contrast, David accom-panies the examiner to the testing room only after considerable encouragement, seems distracted and inattentive, is uncooperative, and displays low levels of in-terest and motivation. The needs and test-related behaviors of Christine and David differ considerably. Keen observation skills are needed to assist in guiding the test's administration, in interpreting results from cognitive (i.e., intelligence and achievement) measures, and in deciding whether the test results are valid.

The two examples illustrate the importance of observing behaviors peripheral to scorable test responses. Examiners traditionally have relied on informal meth-ods (e.g., observations, interviews) almost exclusively to better understand condi-tions that impact the test's administration and children's test behaviors. However, their use of formal observational methods, including instruments designed specif-ically for this purpose, is increasing.

In this chapter, we review qualities that may impact a child's test's performance and discuss in detail those qualities found through research to have a measurable influence on the performance. Discussion focuses on individually administered measures of cognitive abilities. Possible benefits in using test-behavior informa-tion are identified. Several measures currently used to record children's test per-formance also are discussed. The most widely used standardized measure of test performance, the *Guide to the Assessment of Test Session Behavior* (GATSB; Glutting & Oakland, 1993), is described in some detail.

EXAMINER'S OBSERVATIONS
ARE CRITICAL TO TEST USE

An examiner's observations are critical to all features of test use. Their obser-vations enable them to accurately record children's responses to test items. More-over, information obtained through observations enables examiners to better understand the manner in which children arrive at their answers, and to identify cognitive and other personal strengths and weaknesses, thus facilitating test inter-pretations. Their observations also enable examiners to describe children's spon-taneous behaviors while being tested, including their interpersonal and learning styles and other qualities that may directly or indirectly impact test performance. This information enables examiners to make needed modifications in the manner in which the test session is orchestrated, to construct systematic records of chil-dren's behaviors, to compare their observations with reports from others who know the child, to assist in interpreting the test results, and to draw comparisons between the child being tested and others who are similar in terms of salient qualities. Thus, the employment of observational methods is critical to the assessment process (Sattler, 1988).

EIGHT IMPORTANT QUALITIES
THAT MAY IMPACT TEST PERFORMANCE

Professionals prepared to systematically observe behavior are keenly alert to various qualities important to the assessment process. Children's responses to a test's questions constitute the most central and important behaviors to which examiners should attend. For example, when administering the WISC-III (Wechsler, 1991), examiners diligently observe and record a child's responses to each test item.

In addition, examiners observe various other qualities that fall just beyond this central focus, ones that may facilitate or adversely impact children's test behaviors and thus their ability to demonstrate their best performance. The following eight qualities fall within this second important focus: conditions within the testing room, language qualities, physical and motor qualities, rapport, personal readiness, motivation, and temperament. In addition, some test behaviors are associated with specific handicapping conditions. An examiner's knowledge of these qualities can greatly enhance the evaluation process.

Until recently, these eight qualities were assessed informally by the examiner, keeping a watchful eye out for conditions that may impede test performance or jeopardize test validity. The somewhat recent development of standardized measures to assist in the assessment of test behaviors has aided the examiner, especially in the assessment of qualities related to rapport, personal readiness, motivation, temperament, and special conditions associated with some handicapping conditions. As will be noted, measures of test-taking behavior are intended to utilize and supplant and not substitute for well-honed observations skills.

Testing Room Conditions

Examiners are responsible for ensuring the testing room provides a comfortable and distraction-free testing environment. Furniture should be of appropriate height and comfortable to the children. Their attention and concentration should not be attenuated by auditory and visual distractions. Young children, children with moderate to severe handicapping conditions, and those for whom testing is a new experience often need additional time to become oriented to the testing room. Examiners must remain alert to signs that children are uncomfortable or distracted and, when present, work to alleviate problems. Examiners must ensure the physical conditions enhance the assessment process by creating conditions that are relatively standard from test to test, ones that enable the examinee to feel comfortable and relaxed, encourage suitable test-taking behaviors, and promote valid testing.

Language Qualities

Language qualities also figure importantly. Most measures of cognitive abilities rely on language to form a bridge between the examiner and examinee, enabling them to communicate. Although the WISC-III is not intended to assess language directly, the quality and nature of children's language can facilitate or impede test use. Language qualities include both receptive (i.e., listening comprehension and reading) and expressive (oral expression and writing) skills and abilities together with pragmatic (i.e., functional) language features. Language also may reflect dialect differences, including the use of nonstandard English. In addition, some children have little to no knowledge of English.

Examiners typically rely on informal observations and information from interviews together with prior test data in forming judgments of children's language abilities. More formal assessment of language is warranted when language deficits and differences are apparent. In addition, modifications in test use may be needed when using them with children who exhibit deficits or differences in one or more of these language areas. Modifications will be needed when using tests with children not fluent in English. The examiner's keen attention to children's language-related test behaviors together with information provided by other sources enable them to conduct their work in a more effective and efficient fashion.

Physical-Motor Qualities

Children's physical and motor qualities also may impact test performance. Information on general health conditions (e.g., respiratory problems, cardiovascular conditions, chronic or acute diseases and illnesses) and muscle control should be acquired from a parent or other informed adult. Gross muscle control can impact the assessment of adaptive behaviors. Find muscle control is important to writing and other physical manipulations important to finger dexterity. Control of muscles in the oral cavity is prerequisite to comprehensible speech. Examiners must remain alert to physical and motor qualities that may adversely impact children's test performance.

Rapport

Rapport refers to the nature of the interpersonal relationships between the child and examiner. Good rapport is characterized by harmony, conformity, and cooperation. The child should feel comfortable with the examiner and the examination process. The examiner's behaviors are intended to promote trust and faith, qualities that are enhanced by taking time to talk with the child before beginning the test, encouraging the child to be of assistance (thereby promoting cooperation), smiling frequently, using the child's name liberally, and reinforcing the child's efforts (e.g., "I really like the way you are working hard").

The manner in which the test is introduced also is intended to facilitate rapport. The following introduction may be used to introduce the WISC-III and other measures of cognitive abilities: "I will be giving you a test that most people enjoy. Some of the questions will be easy and others will be hard. I do not expect you to answer every question. However, I do want you to do your very best. Do you have any questions before we begin?"

Readiness

Personal readiness refers to physical and psychological qualities prerequisite to valid testing. Children must have the physical stamina needed to complete the examination. In addition, alertness, attention, and concentration also are prerequisite to valid testing. Various psychological qualities also contribute to readiness: self-confidence, willingness to leave one's teacher or mother with an examiner who often is unknown to the child, and lack of shyness. Nutritional and sleep conditions also contribute to readiness. Information as to whether the child has had adequate food, drink, and sleep should be acquired prior to the test.

Motivation

Motivation refers to a child's willingness to engage in the testing activity and to sustain such engagement over a period of time. Motivation often is enhanced by providing suitable physical conditions for test taking, building and maintaining rapport, and ensuring personal readiness. In addition, motivation is enhanced when activities are thought to be neither too easy nor too hard yet somewhat challenging. Motivation also is enhanced by novelty, changing the nature of the tasks (as occurs when administering different WISC III subtests), and by taking periodic breaks.

Temperament

Children's temperament also may impact their test performance. Children who display strong preferences for extroversion or introversion styles, practical or imaginative styles, thinking or feeling styles, and organized or flexible styles (Oakland, Glutting, & Horton, 1996) are likely to display different behaviors while taking tests. Some examples follow.

Children who are strongly extroverted generally prefer to express their ideas verbally. Moreover, their ideas often becomes coalesced and better known to them after they hear themselves express their initial thoughts. In contrast, those who are strongly introverted generally prefer to express their ideas in writing and after they have time to reflect on the question.

Children who express strong practical preferences often are very attentive to details and can memorize well. In contrast, those who express strong preferences for imaginative styles are less attentive to detail, more interested in theories, and are more inclined to have problems memorizing specific facts and figures.

Children who are inclined toward thinking preferences generally enjoy competitive activities and displaying their knowledge. In contrast, those who express strong preferences for feeling are most inclined to disdain competition and favor cooperation and rely on personalized standards when evaluating others.

Children who prefer organized styles like their lives to be well organized, problems resolved, and things settled as quickly as possible. In contrast, those with flexible styles are more inclined to postpone decisions, generally prefer fewer rules and regulations, and enjoy situations that are not highly organized.

Examiners often observe these and other temperament-related behaviors while testing children and youths. These qualities may impact children's test performance styles. Examiners are encouraged to administer a measure of temperament to children and youths (e.g., Oakland et al., 1996) so as to better understand their preferred styles and the impact these styles may have on their test and school performance.

Moderate to Severe Handicapping Conditions

Various alterations often are needed when testing children who evidence moderate to severe handicapping conditions (e.g., children with visual or auditory handicaps, mental retardation, cerebral palsy, autism, emotional difficulties). The nature of the alterations that may be needed when testing them will depend on the age of the child, the nature and severity of their handicapping condition, and prior testing experiences.

Popular textbooks on intelligence testing discuss these issues in considerable detail (Gregory, 1992; Kamphaus, 1993; Kaufman, 1994; Palmer, 1983; Sattler, 1988). Thus, with the exception of referencing research on test-taking behaviors of children with attention deficit disorders (ADDs), test-taking behaviors associated with each handicapping condition are not discussed here. Nevertheless, examiners must remain attentive to the special needs of children with handicapping conditions and strive to make modifications in the testing process while maintaining standardized methods. Considerable ingenuity and experience may be required when testing children with severe and multiple disorders.

BACKGROUND INFORMATION AND PERSONAL QUALITIES

Some qualities identified above (e.g., medical, motor, food, sleep, acuity, and language status) can be considered as background variables (Bracken, 1991). Information on them should be acquired before tests are administered. This information may assist the examiner in planning for the evaluation, in preventing the occurrence of problems, and addressing them should they occur.

Other qualities consist of ethnographically relevant expressions of personal qualities that can be observed only during testing. These include rapport and children's readiness for testing, their temperament, and motivation. Whereas scales designed to assess test-taking qualities may include some emphasis on background variables, they always should focus on ethnographically relevant personal qualities.

INFORMAL METHODS TO COLLECT AND EVALUATE TEST BEHAVIORS

Some examiners may allege the primary advantage of using informal processes over standardized and structured measures to evaluate test-taking behavior lies in their flexibility, enabling examiners to tailor their observations in light of each child's qualities. For example, the test-taking behaviors most likely to impact the performance of children who are visually impaired will differ somewhat from those who are autistic. However, flexibility is applicable to both informal and formal (i.e., standardized) evaluation procedures.

DISTINGUISH BETWEEN COLLECTING AND EVALUATING TEST BEHAVIOR

Distinctions should be drawn between the process of collecting test-behavior information and evaluating this information. In collecting this information, examiners focus on qualities thought to facilitate and impede the administration of standardized tests. Examiners using informal or formal methods to collect test-behavior data enjoy similar degrees of flexibility when selecting the behaviors on which they focus. However, those using formal measures must include within their focus those qualities the test identifies as being important. Those using informal methods are neither guided by this knowledge nor governed by this constraint.

THREE STANDARDS FOR EVALUATING INFORMATION

In evaluating this information, examiners must decide the standard to use in judging whether the test-taking behaviors are suitable. Three standards may be used. Examiners may evaluate a child's test-taking behaviors in reference to their notions of perfection, potential, or from normative standards.

Perfection

Perfection refers to whether the child's test behaviors were impeccable and unblemished, a condition that rarely occurs. In addition, few examiners would agree as to the exact qualities that constitute a perfect administration or be able to judge them reliably.

Potential

Potential refers to whether the test behaviors were as good as can be expected, given the conditions found among the eight previously described qualities that may impact test performance. This standard also is difficult to form and thus to use knowledgeably and reliably.

Par or Normative Standards

Normative standards are derived from data acquired from nationally standardized and well-validated measures designed specifically to assess test-taking behaviors. The use of this standard does not preclude consideration of the other two.

Examiners who rely only on informal evaluation methods also must rely on standards of perfection and potential. Those who use formal (i.e., structured) evaluation methods have the added advantage of using normative standard when age-appropriate norms are available for the structured rating scale they are using.

All examiners do and should use observational methods to describe the eight previously identified test-related behaviors. Differences exist in how they use this observational information in an evaluative format to form judgments about the suitability of a child's test-taking behaviors and the resulting validity of the test data.

SOME BENEFITS
TO USING INFORMAL PROCESSES

Some benefits may occur from using informal processes to evaluate test behaviors. Some examiners have years of experiences in testing children with specific types of disabilities (e.g., autism, visual handicaps) and thus are able to judge whether a child's behaviors are similar to those who also have the disability. Nationally standardized scales designed to assist in evaluating test-taking behaviors do not provide norms for the various handicapping conditions. In addition, some examiners dislike the need to purchase test-taking scales and the structure they provide. Moreover, examiners often resist change and tend to follow traditions. They often continue to use a battery of measures they were taught in graduate school. Standardized measures of test-taking behaviors are relatively new. Thus, many examiners were not introduced to them during their graduate training. Their widespread use will require both time and knowledge as to their benefits.

SOME DISADVANTAGES
TO USING INFORMAL PROCESSES

Informal methods to evaluate test behaviors have a number of disadvantages. Eight are identified below.

QUALITIES OBSERVED MAY BE IRRELEVANT

Examiners differ in the test-taking qualities they believe are most important. Their clinical preparation on this topic often is very uneven. Some receive excellent coursework and supervision, whereas others labor under inadequate instructional systems that reflect diminished resources for expensive clinical graduate programs. As can be expected, examiners differ in their knowledge as to what test behaviors are most important to record and how to evaluate this information. Items on standardized measures help overcome some of these differences in preparation by enabling examiners to focus on important test-taking behaviors.

QUALITIES ARE UNSUPPORTED BY RESEARCH

Examiner's information about test behaviors rarely is based on solid research. Information on informal methods generally is embedded within extensive discussions of test-taking behaviors (cf. Bracken, 1991; Culbertson & Willis, 1993;

Gregory, 1992; Kamphaus & Reynolds, 1990a,b). Despite the volumes written on this topic (Culbertson & Willis, 1993; Epps, 1988; Gregory, 1992; Jensen, 1980; Kamphaus & Reynolds, 1987; Kaufman, 1990; Kaufman, 1994; Palmer, 1983; Reynolds & Kamphaus, 1990; Salvia & Ysseldyke, 1988; Sattler, 1988; Simeonsson, 1996), the amount of research in well-respected publications on test-taking behaviors is meager and can be carried easily by a 3-year-old child. Thus, our scientific knowledge as to the qualities that constitute test-taking behaviors is inadequate. In addition, reliance on informal methods to evaluate test behaviors has contributed to this deficit. The availability of standardized measures of test-taking abilities is likely to lead to more research on this important topic and thus improved literature on this important component of assessment.

QUALITIES EMANATE FROM FOLKLORE

Related to the first two points, informal methods are difficult to replicate and often breed folklore (i.e., opinions that over time take the form of widely held established fact.) The use of informal methods to clinically assess test-taking skills has contributed to folklore about various test-related issues. For example, examiners often believe that behaviors persons evidence while taking a test (e.g., shyness) express personal traits the persons are likely to display in their everyday life. As we will see later, there is little evidence for this widely held belief. The continued overreliance on informal methods prevents the validation of this and other clinical folklore.

OBSERVATIONS ARE UNSTRUCTURED

Informal methods lack standardized methodology to record and score important test-taking behaviors. Methods to record and evaluate test behaviors differ from examiner to examiner as well as within an examiner. These conditions jeopardize the reliable and valid collection of information and thus attenuate their use.

EXAMINERS ARE LESS CREDIBLE

Examiners are less able to justify their conclusions. They increasingly are being called on to justify their finding to colleagues while testifying, and in other legal settings. They are likely to be asked to justify the validity of their test results and often face challenging questions as to the nature of the test conditions and the examinee's behaviors. Failure to record these qualities at the time of test administration jeopardizes their ability to successfully face cross-examination. Reliance on informal methods also may further jeopardize their testimony.

AGE-RELATED DIFFERENCES MAY BE OVERLOOKED

Examiners may be insensitive to important age-related differences. Children display different test behaviors at different ages (Glutting & Oakland, 1993). In general, the test behaviors improve with age. Examiners who rely on informal methods to evaluate test-taking behaviors may be unaware of subtle but important age-related differences.

NORMS ARE LACKING

Clearly, the greatest limitation in using informal measures lies in their lack of a normative basis for comparisons. The availability of current and properly stratified norms is consistent with commonly accepted standards (i.e., *Standards for Educational and Psychological Testing,* American Psychological Association, 1985) for test use as well as the expectations of those who receive clinical services. Thus, all attempts to evaluate best behaviors without the use of norms invite error.

FAILURE TO CO-NORM OBSERVATION SYSTEM WITH STANDARDIZED TESTS

The co-norming of two or more tests is becoming more common. This process enables examiners to better utilize information from the tests through their knowledge of relationships between them. The process also enables testing companies to economize when standardizing tests. One measure of test-taking ability, the *Guide to the Assessment of Test Session Behavior* (GATSB; Glutting & Oakland, 1993) has been co-normed with both the WISC-III and the Wechsler Individual Achievement Test (WIAT, Wechsler, 1992), thus providing direct normative linkages with two widely used measures. Before discussing the GATSB, other formal measures designed to asses test-taking qualities will be identified.

PREVIOUS ATTEMPTS TO DEVELOP FORMAL MEASURES OF TEST-TAKING BEHAVIOR

Many clinicians were introduced to the importance of test behaviors through a chapter by Caldwell (Caldwell, 1951), which provides an integrated view of test session behavior. This chapter also introduced the *Test Behavior Observation Guide* (TBOG) (Caldwell, 1951). The TBOG was the first formal (i.e., structured) measure of test-related qualities. It contains 19 items that identify preexisting background characteristics as well as 15 items that focus on observable test behaviors.

Some standardized measures of intelligence include a structured test-behavior scale. For example, the *Stanford-Binet Observation Schedule* (SBOS; Terman & Merrill, 1960; Thorndike, Hagen, & Sattler, 1986) appeared as part of the test's record booklet beginning with the 1960 edition and continuing through to its most recent version. Rational analysis was used in selecting the items that assess five domains: Attention, Reaction during Test Performance, Emotional Independence, Problem-Solving Behavior, and Independence of Examiner Support. Despite its availability and widespread visibility, evidence as to the scale's reliability and validity may be found in one study (Glutting & McDermott, 1988).

Three measures have been published more recently. The *Test Behavior Checklist* (Aylward & MacGruder, 1986) contains 18 items, three of which focus on preexisting conditions and 15 on test-related behaviors. The *Behavior and Attitude Checklist* (Sattler, 1988) contains 28 items covering 10 domains. Eight items assess speech-language and motor coordination qualities. The remaining 20 items are used to evaluate children's test-related attitudes and behaviors. Finally, the *Kaufman Integrated Interpretive System Checklist for Behaviors Observed During Administration of WISC-III Subtests* (Kaufman, Kaufman, Dougherty, & Tuttle, 1994) is an inventory that was developed to measure behaviors specific to individual subtests from the WISC-III. Example items include "has difficulty understanding the long verbal directions to nonverbal tasks such as Picture Arrangement and Coding" and "was distracted when trying to repeat digits forwards and backwards or solve oral arithmetic items."

DEFICIENCIES IN THESE FORMAL SCALES

The structured nature of each of the foregoing scales makes them somewhat valuable in codifying children's test behaviors. Nevertheless, a number of qualities limit their utility. Threats to the interpretability of these and other tests occur as a result of construct irrelevant variance (i.e., domains that are not relevant to the purpose of the test) and construct underrepresentation (i.e., relevant domains that are not included on the test). The tests cited above do not meet these standards.

Sound observation covers all relevant and verifiable aspects of child functioning, including normal development (Glutting, 1986; McDermott, 1986; McDermott & Watkins, 1985). Most items on the above structured test-behavior scales overlook normal and healthy adjustment (Glutting & Oakland, 1993). Instead, they are largely limited to evaluating pathological symptoms and negative behaviors.

A potentially more serious problem relates to the identification of integral dimensions (i.e., scales) underlying item sets. The majority of structured, test-behavior instruments are composed of undifferentiated lists of symptoms, or rationally derived symptom "domains." These test-behavior measures do not present empirical evidence in support of either a single unifying construct or for their separate domains.

Perhaps their greatest deficiency is the absence norms, information needed when evaluating how one child's behaviors compare to those of others. As a result, examiners are left to their own resources in determining when a given child's test behavior is normal or exceptional.

EMPIRICAL RESEARCH ON CHILDREN'S TEST BEHAVIORS

Until the last decade, little was known about the validity of test observations because test observations rarely were formally studied. Conditions changed during the 1980s as researchers began to initiate a series of investigations designed to better understand the construct and criterion-related validity of test observations.

CONSTRUCT VALIDITY

A synthesis of research on test-behavior studies completed over the last decade was conducted recently (Glutting, Youngstrom, Oakland, & Watkins, 1996). Only two studies were located that examined the construct validity of children's test behaviors (Glutting & McDermott, 1988; Glutting, Oakland, & McDermott, 1989). Each study reported the results of factor-analyzed data from existing, formal scale of children's test behavior in order to determine the psychometric properties of these instruments and simultaneously to identify the number and nature of integral domains (i.e., scales) underlying children's test behaviors.

Our initial investigation (Glutting & McDermott, 1988) examined the SBOS (Terman & Merrill, 1960; Thorndike et al., 1986). The sample comprised 155 kindergartners. A factor analysis of the SBOS yielded two dimensions that accounted for 54% of the variance. The larger of the two factors was identified as Avoidance and the smaller domain was identified as Inattentiveness.

The factor structure and reliability of TBOG-related test observation data obtained from children between the ages of 7 and 14 (Glutting et al., 1989) yielded a three-factor model that explained 58% of the total item variance. Respectively, the names and ordering of the factors were as follows: Inattentiveness, Avoidance, and Uncooperative Mood. Internal consistency estimates, based on Cronbach's (1951) formula for coefficient alpha, were .88, .77, and .72, respectively.

Results across these two factor-analytic studies showed that empirically derived domains of children's test behavior possessed only modest relationships with rationally derived domains (Glutting & McDermott, 1988; Glutting et al., 1989). More importantly, empirically derived domains were fewer in number and had demonstrated reliability. Thus, the findings served to demonstrate that structured symptom lists and scales developed through the rational analysis of children's test behaviors are likely to be unproductive for the bulk of referrals examiners encounter and generally should not be used for these purposes.

CRITERION-RELATED VALIDITY

The concept of criterion-related validity, when applied to test observations, concentrates on relationships between children's test-session behavior and their scores on formal tests (e.g., cognitive abilities) or behaviors observed in other contexts. Intrasession validity, a term we coined, refers to the strength of association between measures of test-session behaviors and the formal test scores they accompany (cf. Glutting & McDermott, 1988; Glutting et al., 1989). Thus, intrasession validity examines the potential impact of test behaviors on children's formal scores on the WISC-III and WIAT as well as other individually administered measures of cognitive abilities and indicates the extent to which scores from these measures can be considered to be accurate.

The construct of ecological validity draws attention to the importance of examining the generalizability of test behaviors to diverse settings (cf. Neisser, 1991). We developed the term *exosession validity*, similar in meaning to the constructs of external validity or generalizability, to describe the degree of accuracy of conclusions about relationships between children's behaviors as measured in the context of a particular test session and their behavior and conduct in other situations (Glutting et al., 1989).

Our synthesis of previous test-behavior research (Glutting et al., 1996) found six studies on the topic of intrasession validity. The sources yielded a total of 33 correlation coefficients. An averaged coefficient was calculated according to the meta-analysis procedures recommended by Hunter, Schmidt, and Jackson (1982) and Rosenthal (1991). The overall relationship was $-.34$ between children's test behaviors and IQs obtained during the same test session.

Our literature search identified four sources (Glutting et al., 1996) that discussed exosession validity. These studies produced 26 correlations. The average correlation was .18 between children's test behaviors and their conduct in other contexts (e.g., their classroom or community).

The pattern of the two averaged coefficients shows modest but meaningful levels of intrasession validity (average $r = -.34$). Moreover, the magnitude of intrasession validity is higher than that found for exosession validity (average $r = .18$). The findings of high intrasession validity provide important evidence that clinicians are able to utilize test observations to form judgments of children's test behaviors that are both reliable and valid, These findings also provide a foundation for establishing a formal measure of test-taking behaviors that, following norming, would enable examiners to more accurately acquire and interpret test observations. When used jointly with measures of cognitive abilities, information from a measure of test-taking behaviors then could be used to help validate scores obtained from measures of cognitive abilities and to form inferences regarding children's test-taking qualities.

The evidence of limited exosession validity was not surprising. Behaviors that occur in natural settings are best understood by acquiring information from multiple sources and using multiple assessments methods. Examiners should not expect to be able to describe complex peripheral behaviors only while observing persons in controlled testing situations. Evidence of limited exosession validity does not diminish the value of test observations. Instead, this knowledge simply encourages clinicians to refrain from drawing conclusions as to the generalizability of test observations to conditions outside of the immediate test situation. This inference is consistent with other information regarding the situational specificity of children's behavior. A meta-analysis of behavioral data (Achenback, McConaughty, & Howell, 1987) demonstrated that much of the behavior observed by parents at home and teachers in school is contextually dependent and specific to the situation in which it occurs.

GUIDE TO THE ASSESSMENT
OF TEST SESSION BEHAVIOR
FOR THE WISC-III AND WIAT

The GATSB (Glutting & Oakland, 1993) was constructed to overcome the shortcomings of other measures of children's test behaviors. The GATSB is a structured 29-item behavior-rating instrument designed to quickly and reliably evaluate the test-session behavior of children when administering measures of cognitive abilities. The instrument is brief and requires less than 5 min to complete. Examiners rate GATSB items immediately after testing. As a result, the process of rating does not interfere with the recording of children's performance on the standardized test that is being administered, and the behavioral picture is recorded while still easily recalled.

Childrens' behaviors are rated using a three-point scale (i.e., 2, 1, or 0) in reference to "usually applies," "somewhat applies," and "doesn't apply." Higher raw scores denote inappropriate behavior. Raw scores are summed and converted to standard T scores ($M = 50$, $SD = 10$) according to three-factor based scales (Avoidance, Uncooperative Mood, Inattentiveness). In addition, a Total Score is obtained. The Total Score is a combination of scores from the GATSB's three other scales and also is expressed as a standard T score.

ITEMS

Example items are presented from the three-factor-based scales. The examples make clear that the GATSB does not overlook normal and healthy adjustment; its items depict appropriate as well as inappropriate behavior.

Avoidance
  "Shows marked interest in test activities"
  "Hesitates when giving answers"
Uncooperative Mood
  "Performance deteriorates towards end of testing"
  "Asks how soon testing will finish"
Inattentiveness
  "Listens attentively to directions and test items"
  "Attempts to answer before questions are completed"

NORMS

The GATSB was designed for use with children aged 6 years 0 months, to 16 years 11 months. It was co-normed with both the WISC-III and the WIAT. Thus, unlike all previous measures for evaluating children's test behaviors, the GATSB alone provides norms. As previously noted, norms are essential in determining when children's test behaviors are sufficiently aberrant, compared to others of similar age and experience, to affect the validity of test scores.

Each of the GATSB's two standardization samples (one each for the WISC-III and for the WIAT) included 640 children. The samples were stratified on the basis of the 1988 U.S. census data according to age, race-ethnicity, gender, and parent education. Furthermore, the samples were selected to ensure that children's overall intellectual abilities (*M* WISC-III FSIQ $\cong$ 100, *SD* $\cong$ 15) and their achievement levels (*M* WIAT Total Battery Composite $\cong$ 100, *SD* $\cong$ 15) matched those of the general population. Otherwise, ratings on the GATSB would be atypical of the common distributional mean, standard deviation, kurtosis, and skewness of children's ability and achievement levels.

AGE-BASED STANDARD SCORES

An analysis of variance (ANOVA) was conducted using the factor-based raw scores from the two standardization samples in order to determine whether norms could be collapsed over years or should be provided for each year for which the GATSB was designed. Results showed some age differences in test-related qualities, warranting the need for separate norms for three age groups: 6–8 years, 9–12 years, and 13–16 years. Consequently, norms of the GATSB respect age-related differences that occur in children's test behaviors.

RELIABILITY

Internal consistency reliability estimates for the GATSB are high. Alpha coefficients were calculated separately for the three age groups from the WISC-III standardization sample. Results showed an averaged coefficient of .92 for the Total score and coefficients between .84 to .88 for the three-factor based scales. Stability estimates (*M* interval $\cong$ 1 day) also are high. Results across the three age levels show an averaged .87 for the Total Score and .71 to .77 for the three-factor based scales.

CONSTRUCT VALIDITY

The GATSB was not developed using rational analysis. Instead, its scales were assembled according to the substantive or construct approach to test development (cf. Cronback & Meehl, 1955). Thus, both theoretical and empirical issues were considered. Factor analytic findings from our earlier studies indicated that test behavior is not a unitary construct and instead is governed by as many as three underlying dimensions (Glutting & McDermott, 1988; Glutting et al., 1989). These findings served as the theoretical underpinning of the GATSB.

Both item and factor analyses were used with the WISC-III–GATSB standardization data (*N* = 640) to develop a final scale composed of 29 items. Initial items in the pool (*n* = 102) were deleted when they showed no appreciable loading on the three hypothesized factors and when an item loaded appreciably on a factor contrary to theory. Thus, retained items were required to show structural relationships (i.e., factor loadings) paralleling theoretical relationships postulated for children's test behaviors; in turn, this methodology increased the probability that GATSB items would become manifestations of important underlying behavioral constructs evident during testing.

Principle components analysis and principle axis factor analysis (using both orthogonal and oblique rotations) yielded three dimensions for the standardization sample: Avoidance, Uncooperative Mood, and Inattentiveness. These dimensions are theoretically congruent, align with findings from previous studies of children's test behaviors, and are similar to established dimensions for evaluating children's adjustment and well-being in other contexts (cf. Achenbach & Edlebrock, 1983; Quay, 1986).

THREE SECONDARY FACTORS

Avoidance

The first pattern found for the GATSB is directly related to task aversion and fearfulness. Therefore, it is considered to be a dimension of Avoidance. Strong conceptual links exist between this factor and a major constellation of behaviors children display both in home and school environments. The factor is similar to one labeled Anxiety Withdrawal by Quay (1986) and Internalizing by Achenbach and Edlebrock (1983). On the GATSB, 11 items load on the Avoidance domain. This factor captures the lion's share of the total variance (49%) and suggests that children's task engagement and/or avoidance is likely to have the largest impact on their obtained intelligence and achievement test scores.

Uncooperative Mood

The second GATSB factor, Uncooperative Mood, consists of eight items. It accounts for 11% of the total item variance on the GATSB and reflects children's improper initial adjustment, lack of cooperation, and/or need for praise and encouragement during the examination session. Thus, the second factor appears to measure behaviors more specific to test sessions than the first factor.

Inattentiveness

The third and smallest factor, Inattentiveness, consists of 10 items and accounts for about 8% of the total variance. This factor is characterized by inadequate impulse control and attending behaviors. It, like the Avoidance factor, is associated with other overarching dimensions of child behavior. In the contexts of home and school, this factor is similar to one labeled Conduct Disorder by Quay (1986) and Externalizing by Achenbach and Edelbrock (1983).

CRITERION-RELATED VALIDITY

A substantial number of criterion-related validity studies are presented in the GATSB manual, including bivariate correlation analyses, canonical correlation analyses, and discriminant function analyses. However, other studies were needed. Since its publication, researchers have used the GATSB to investigate whether children's test behaviors are affected by criterion-related bias (Glutting, Oakland, & Konold, 1994), item bias (Nandakumar, Glutting, & Oakland, 1993), and factor bias (Konold, Glutting, Oakland, & O'Donnell, 1995). The criterion-related validity of the GATSB also has been examined for children with attention deficit/hyperactivity disorders (Glutting, Robins, & de Lanecy, in press), and for samples of both normal and referred children (Glutting et al., 1996).

Findings from the investigations cited above all strongly attest to the GATSB's validity for use with children who differ by age, gender, race, and ethnicity. Perhaps the most interesting finding from these studies is that children with inappropriate test behaviors, as measured by the GATSB, were found to obtain WISC-III Full Scale IQs (FSIQ) anywhere from 7 to 10 points lower than children with more suitable test behaviors. Effect sizes this large (more than one-half of a standard deviation) represent a substantial difference in IQs and testifies to the importance of observing peripheral test behaviors as a means of validating the integrity of formal scores obtained on standardized tests of intelligence and achievement.

POSSIBLE USES OF TEST BEHAVIOR INFORMATION

Accomplished examiners typically rely heavily on their observations to assist them in various components of the assessment process. As previously noted, this information assists them in understanding the processes used by children in arriving at their responses, in screening important qualities not measured directly by the test, in discussing the child's qualities intelligibly in conferences with parents and teachers, and in making needed modifications in how the test is administered. Knowledge of test behaviors also enables examiners to decide whether the test results accurately reflect the child's cognitive abilities.

TWO TEST PERFORMANCE STANDARDS

One of two standards typically is used when evaluating whether the test data are considered to be valid: optimal and typical performance. Examiners often differ in their views as to which should be used. Each is described below.

Optimal Performance

Examiners favoring optimal performance strive to create conditions that facilitate the examinee's highest (for tests of ability) or most representative (for tests of personality and social skills) performance as the standard for test performance. They view inappropriate test behaviors as negatively influencing test performance and attenuating or in other ways distorting scores. Those who employ optimal performance standards generally believe test scores from examinees who display unmotivated, uncooperative, and inattentive test behaviors are invalid and thus should be discarded.

Typical Performance

Examiners favoring typical performance standards also are likely to interpret these test behaviors as being inappropriate and negatively influencing test performance. However, unlike those with optimal performance standards, those with typical performance standards are likely to interpret these behaviors as correctly reflecting personal traits and accept the test results as being valid, given their belief that the deleterious traits observed during the test also are likely to negatively influence the examinee's general behaviors. Thus, the results from cognitive tests are thought to reflect real-life conditions and thus are valid.

TWO CASE STUDIES

The actual case studies described next, taken from the GATSB manual, demonstrate how the GATSB data may be used to facilitate the assessment of cognitive abilities.

CASE ONE

Lee, an 8-year-old, was evaluated at the request of his mother. She was seeking more detailed information about his achievement and abilities in order to determine whether he qualifies for a program for academically gifted students. His dress was very causal: his cotton slacks were dirty and too large, his T-shirt ripped at the sleeves, his loafers too large and worn without socks, and his hair unkempt. His mother was somewhat apologetic about his dress but indicated it was typical of him.

Lee's height and weight are normal, as are his fine- and gross-motor skills and linguistic proficiency (i.e., fluency and articulation). School records reflect visual and auditory acuity within normal limits. Attendance is generally good; however, there is some tendency for him to miss school on Mondays. When asked about this tendency, his mother reported that Lee has been diagnosed as having ADD. Moreover, although Lee's pediatrician recommended medication to improve his behavior, his mother has refused, believing it will adversely affect his development. Except for his ADD, Lee is described as being in good health but does complain of stomach aches and other vaguely defined ailments, mainly on Monday mornings. Although she generally encourages him to attend school on these occasions, Lee's mother sometimes gives in to his desire and allows him to stay home from school.

Lee's scores on the GATSB were obtained after WIAT testing, and the results follow.

Scale	T scores	Confidence interval magnitude (68% level)	Cumulative percentile rank
Total Score	79	±2.65	97.8
Avoidance	62	±4.24	89.4
Inattentiveness	84	±4.00	98.7
Uncooperative Mood	61	±3.46	88.7

Lee's Total Score T score of 79 reflects an atypical pattern of test-session behavior. This atypical pattern is most strongly reflected in his highly elevated score on the Inattentiveness scale. Lee often did not respond when queried, had difficulty following directions, did not willingly accept help from the examiner, and repeatedly expressed concern about his performance. These behaviors are consistent with those associated with attention and concentration problems.

Lee's scores on the Avoidance and Uncooperative Mood scales did not indicate inappropriate test-taking behaviors. In subsequent examinations the examiner should be alert to Lee's tendency to display some uncooperativeness, as exemplified by his resistance to limits imposed by the examiner, his attempts to distract the examiner, and his tendency to blame teachers for his failure to answer items correctly.

Because Lee's inattentiveness is transituational and because the examiner conducting the evaluation used *typical* performance as a standard, the examiner concludes the results from the WIAT are accurate. The inattentive behaviors Lee displayed while taking the WIAT also are clearly present at home, and they are likely to be evident in class. Thus, the WIAT scores are believed to be accurate reflections of his current levels of achievement. The examiner recommends, however, that the WIAT be readministered when Lee's attentiveness and concentration improve significantly.

CASE TWO

Anne, a 13-year-old middle-school student, was seen for testing and a clinical interview on one occasion, from 8:30 A.M. to 11:45 A.M. She was suitably dressed and groomed, wearing tennis shoes, modest jewelry, and a matching skirt and blouse. Her short hair was clean and informally styled. Anne is of average height and somewhat overweight. School records indicate normal visual and auditory acuity, and her primary and only language is English. School attendance is regular. Anne indicated an absence of medical problems; moreover, no problems were apparent in her fine- and gross-motor coordination skills and in her linguistic proficiency. Anne had been informed about and was fully oriented to the testing; however, she expressed concern about being tested. As indicated in the following GATSB results, her test-taking behaviors, assessed after administration of the WISC-III, were problematic.

Scale	T scores	Confidence interval magnitude (68% level)	Cumulative percentile rank
Total Score	74	±2.83	96.8
Avoidance	76	±3.74	97.4
Inattentiveness	84	±4.80	98.7
Uncooperative Mood	59	±3.46	85.8

Anne's Total Score T score of 74 reflects an atypical pattern of test-session behavior. This atypical pattern is also reflected in the highly elevated scores on the Avoidance (T score = 76) and Inattentiveness (T score = 84) scales. The highly elevated Avoidance score reflects Anne's inability to remember test directions, her lack of eye contact with the examiner, her frequent requests to take a break, and a deterioration in performance during the last three WISC-III subtests that was a result of her withdrawal.

Anne's highly elevated score on the Inattentiveness scale reflects her difficulty in completing work within time limits and her failure to attend to test directions. It also reflects her increasing restlessness during the test session and the deterioration in her efforts toward the end of the session.

Discussions with Anne's English teacher and counselor after the testing confirmed the presence of the inappropriate behaviors in class. Thus, there is some indication that the behaviors observed during the WISC-III administration are transituational. The examiner conducting this evaluation uses *optimal* performance as a standard. Consequently, Anne's WISC-III results are not reported. The examiner will confer with Anne's parents and Anne to discuss the extent to which these and similar behaviors may be displayed at home. After these conferences the examiner will work with Anne to minimize any adverse effects avoidance and inattentive behaviors have on a second administration of the WISC-III.

CONCLUSIONS

Progress is being made in the ability to carefully observe and understand the relevance of test-taking behaviors of children and youth. Research during the last decade has helped define the nature of important test-taking behaviors, to measure them reliably, and to understand their important impact on measures of cognitive abilities. Continued progress in improving the use of these observational abilities requires added emphasis in two areas: instruction and research.

In reference to instruction, most clinicians have little formal study on issues important to observing, recording, and interpreting test-taking behaviors. As a result, clinicians generally rely on time-honored but untested informal methods when recording and interpreting test-taking behaviors. Researchers now have available a new and growing body of information that leads to the conclusion that the use of standardized and norm-referenced measures of test-taking behaviors can significantly enhance assessment. Professors teaching assessment courses should include this content when preparing student clinicians. Established professionals should become acquainted with this content in other ways.

Research on test-taking behaviors began about 10 years ago and thus is in its infancy. Additional research is needed to help verify the full range of behaviors that may characterize test-taking behaviors, to fully define this construct, and to continue investigations as to possible demographic differences in these qualities. Relationships between measures of test-taking behaviors (e.g., the GATSB) and performance on measures other than the WISC-III and WIAT are greatly needed. We concur with the Kaufmans (Kaufman & Kaufman 1995) that information from the GATSB may be relevant to the understanding of a wide range of measures.

These may include the Clinical Assessment of Language Functions, Differential Abilities Scale, Kaufman Assessment Battery for Children, Stanford-Binet Intelligence Scale, Woodcock-Johnson Psycho-educational Battery, and various other individually administered measures. In addition, the assets and limitations of test behaviors to our understanding of noncogntive qualities (e.g., personality and temperament) deserves further study.

REFERENCES

Achenback, T. M. & Edelbrock, C. (1983). *Manual for the Child Behavior Profile.* Burlington, CT: University of Vermont, Department of Psychiatry.

Achenbach, T. M., McConaughty, S. H , & Howell, C. T. (1987). Child/adolescent behavioral and emotional problems: Implications of cross-informant correlations for situational specificity. *Psychological Bulletin, 101,* 213–232.

American Psychological Association. (1991). *PsychoINFO psychological abstracts information services users reference manual.* Washington, DC: Author.

American Psychological Association. (1985). *Standards for education and psychological testing.* Washington, DC: Author.

Aylward, G. P., & MacGruder, R. W. (1986). *Test Behavior Checklist.* Brandon, CT: Clinical Psychology Publishing.

Bracken, B. A. (1991). The clinical observation of preschool assessment behavior. In B. A. Bracken (Ed.), *The psychoeducational assessment of preschool children* (2nd ed.) (pp. 40–52). Boston: Allyn and Bacon.

Caldwell, B. M. (1951). Test Behavior Observation Guide. In R. Watson (Ed.), *The clinical method in psychology* (pp. 67–71). New York: Harper & Brothers.

Cronbach, L. J. (1951). Coefficient alpha and the internal structure of tests. *Psychometricka, 16,* 297–334.

Cronbach, L. J., & Meehl, P. E. (1955). Construct validity in psychological tests. *Psychological Bulletin, 52,* 281–302.

Culbertson, J., & Willis, D. (Eds.). *Testing young children.* Austin, TX: Pro-ed.

Epps, S. (1988). *Best practices in behavioral observations.* In A. Thomas & J. Grimes (Eds.), *National Association of School Psychologists* (pp. 95–112).

Glutting, J. J. (1986). The McDermott Multidimensional Assessment of Children: Applications to the classification of childhood exceptionality. *Journal of Learning Disabilities, 19,* 331–335.

Glutting, J. J., & McDermott, P. A. (1988). Generality of test session observations to kindergartners' classroom behavior. *Journal of Abnormal Child Psychology, 16,* 527–537.

Glutting, J. J., & Oakland, T. (1993). *GATSB: Guide to the Assessment of Test Session Behavior for the WISC-III and WIAT.* San Antonio, TX: The Psychological Corporation.

Glutting, J. J., Oakland, T., & Konold, T. R. (1994). Criterion-related bias with the Guide to the Assessment of Test-Session Behavior for the WISC-III and WIAT: Possible race, gender, and SES effects. *Journal of School Psychology, 32,* 355–369.

Glutting, J. J., Oakland, T., & McDermott, P. A. (1989). Observing child behavior during testing: Constructs, validity, and situational generality. *Journal of School Psychology, 27,* 155–164.

Glutting, J. J., Robins, P. M., & de Lancey, E. (in press). Validity of test observations for children with attention-deficit/hyperactivity disorder. *Journal of School Psychology.*

Glutting, J. J., Youngstrom, E. A., Oakland, T., & Watkins, M. W. (1996). Situational specificity of generality of test behaviors for samples of normal and referred children. *School Psychology Review, 25,* 64–107.

Gregory, R. (1992). *Psychological testing.* Boston: Allyn and Bacon.

Hunter, J. E., Schmidt, F. L., & Jackson, G. B. (1982). *Meta-analysis: Cumulating research findings across studies.* Beverly Hills: CA: Sage.

Jensen, R. (1980). *Bias in mental testing.* New York: The Free Press.

Kamphaus, R. W. (1993). *Clinical assessment of children's intelligence.* Boston: Allyn and Bacon.

Kaufman, A. A. (1990). *Assessing adolescent and adult intelligence.* Boston: Allyn and Bacon.

Kaufman, A. S. (1994). *Intelligent testing with the WISC-III.* New York: Wiley.

Kaufman, A. S., Kaufman, N. L., Dougherty, E. H., & Tuttle, K. S. C. (1994). *Kaufman Integrated Interpretive System Checklist for Behaviors Observed During Administration of WISC-III Subtests.* Odessa, FL: Psychological Assessment Resources.

Kaufman, N., & Kaufman, A. (1995). Test review of GATSB. *Journal of Psychoeducational Assessment, 13,* 318–325.

Konold, T. R., Glutting, J. J., Oakland, T., & O'Donnell, L. (1995). Congruence of test-behavior dimensions among child groups varying in gender, race-ethnicity, and SES. *Journal of Psychoeducational Assessment, 13,* 111–119.

McDermott, P. A. (1986). The observation and classification of exceptional child behavior. In R. T. Brown & C. R. Reynolds (Eds.), *Psychological perspectives on childhood exceptionality: A handbook* (pp. 136–180). New York: Wiley Interscience.

McDermott, P. A., & Watkins, M. A. (1985). *Microcomputer systems manual for McDermott Multidimensional Assessment of Children.* New York: The Psychological Corporation.

Nandakumar, R., Glutting, J. J., & Oakland, T. (1993). Mantel-Haenszel methodology for detecting item bias: An introduction and example using the Guide to the Assessment of Test Session Behavior. *Journal of Psychoeducational Assessment, 11,* 108–119.

Neisser, U. (1991). A case for misplaced nostalgia. *American Psychologist, 46,* 34–36.

Oakland, T., Glutting, J. J., & Horton, C. B. (1996). *Student Styles Questionnaire: Star qualities in learning, relating, and working.* The Psychological Corporation: San Antonio, TX.

Palmer, J. (1983). *The psychological assessment of children.* New York: Wiley.

Quay, H. C. (1986). Classification. In H. C. Quay & J. S. Werry (Eds.), *Psychopathological disorders of childhood* (3rd ed., pp. 1–34). New York: Wiley.

Reynolds, C. R., & Kamphaus, R. (Eds.). (1990). *Handbook of psychological and educational assessment of children: Personality, behavior, and context.* New York: Guilford Press.

Rosenthal, R. (1991). *Meta-analytic procedures for social research.* Newbury Park, CA: Sage.

Salvia, J., & Ysseldyke, J. (1988). *Assessment.* Boston: Houghton Mifflin Company.

Sattler, J. M. (1988). *Assessment of children* (3rd ed.). San Diego, CA: Author.

Simeonsson, R. (1996). *Psychological and developmental assessment of children.* Newton, MA: Allyn and Bacon.

Terman, L. M., & Merrill, M. A. (1960). *Stanford-Binet Intelligence Scale: Manual for the third revision. Form L-M.* Boston: Houghton Mifflin.

Thorndike, R. L., Hagen, E. P., & Sattler, J. J. (1986). *Stanford-Binet Intelligence Scale.* Chicago: Riverside.

Wechsler, D. (1991). *Wechsler Intelligence Scale for Children: Third edition.* San Antonio, TX: The Psychological Corporation.

Wechsler, D. (1992). *Wechsler Individual Achievement Test.* San Antonio, TX: The Psychological Corporation.

Author Index

References in *italics* denote main citation(s).

SUBJECT INDEX